IMPERSONAL INFLUENCE
How Perceptions of Mass Collectives Affect Political Attitudes

People's perceptions of the attitudes and experiences of mass collectives are an increasingly important force in contemporary political life. In *Impersonal Influence*, Mutz goes beyond simply providing examples of how impersonal influence matters in the political process to provide a micro-level understanding of why information about distant and impersonal others often influences people's political attitudes and behaviors.

Impersonal influence is worthy of attention both from the standpoint of its impact on contemporary politics, and because of its potential to expand the boundaries of our understanding of social influence processes, and media's relations to them. The book's conclusions do not exonerate media from the effects of inaccurate portrayals of collective experience or opinion, but they suggest that the ways in which people are influenced by these perceptions are in themselves not so much deleterious to democracy as absolutely necessary to promoting accountability in a large-scale society.

Diana C. Mutz is Associate Professor of Political Science at the University of Wisconsin–Madison.

Cambridge Studies in Political Psychology and
Public Opinion

General Editors

James H. Kuklinski and Dennis Chong
University of Illinois, Urbana-Champaign and
Northwestern University

Editorial Board

This series has been established in recognition of the growing sophistication in the resurgence of interest in political psychology and the study of public opinion. Its focus ranges from the kinds of mental processes that people employ when they think about democratic processes and make political choices to the nature and consequences of macro-level public opinion.

Some of the works draw on developments in cognitive and social psychology, and relevant areas of philosophy. Appropriate subjects include the use of heuristics, the roles of core values and moral principles in political reasoning, the effects of expertise and sophistication, the roles of affect and emotion, and the nature of cognition and information processing. The emphasis is on systematic and rigorous empirical analysis, and a wide range of methodologies are appropriate: traditional surveys, experimental surveys, laboratory experiments, focus groups, in-depth interviews, as well as others. These empirically oriented studies also consider normative implications for democratic politics generally.

Politics, not psychology, is the primary focus, and it is expected that most works will deal with mass publics and democratic politics, although work on nondemocratic publics is not excluded. Other works will examine traditional topics in public opinion research, as well as contribute to the growing literature on aggregate opinion and its role in democratic societies.

Other books in the series

Asher Arian, *Security Threatened: Surveying Israeli Opinion on Peace and War,* 0 521 48314 X, 0 521 49925 9

Other books in the series *(continued)*

James DeNardo, *The Amateur Strategist: Intuitive Deterrence Theories and the Politics of the Nuclear Arms Race*, 0 521 48121 X, 0 521 48446 4

John Hibbing and Elizabeth Theiss-Morse, *Congress as Public Enemy: Public Attitudes Toward American Political Institutions*, 0 521 48299 2, 0 521 48336 0

Robert Huckfeldt and John Sprague, *Citizens, Politics, and Social Communication*, 0 521 45298 8

George E. Marcus, John L. Sullivan, Elizabeth Theiss-Morse, and Sandra L. Wood, *Experimenting with Violence* 0 521 43396 7, 0 521 43997 3

Paul M. Sniderman, Richard A. Brody, and Philip E. Tetlock, *Reasoning and Choice: Explorations in Political Psychology*, 0 521 40255 7, 0 521 40770 2

John Zaller, *The Nature and Origins of Mass Opinion*, 0 521 40449 5, 0 521 40786 9

IMPERSONAL INFLUENCE

How Perceptions of Mass Collectives Affect
Political Attitudes

DIANA C. MUTZ

CAMBRIDGE
UNIVERSITY PRESS

PUBLISHED BY THE PRESS SYNDICATE OF THE UNIVERSITY OF CAMBRIDGE
The Pitt Building, Trumpington Street, Cambridge CB2 1RP, United Kingdom

CAMBRIDGE UNIVERSITY PRESS
The Edinburgh Building, Cambridge CB2 2RU, UK   http://www.cup.cam.ac.uk
40 West 20th Street, New York, NY 10011–4211, USA   http://www.cup.org
10 Stamford Road, Oakleigh, Melbourne 3166, Australia

First published 1998

Printed in the United States of America

Typeset in Sabon 10/12 pt, in Quark XPress™ [RF]

A catalog record for this book is available from
the British Library.

Library of Congress Cataloging-in-Publication data is available.

ISBN 0 521 63132 7 hardback
ISBN 0 521 63726 0 paperback

to Robin

Contents

ix

Contents

Part IV: Conclusion

Figures

Figures

Tables

Tables

Preface

When I first began studying what I later dubbed "impersonal influence," I approached it from the perspective of someone attempting to shed light on a pernicious phenomenon. As a graduate student interested in media's impact on the political process, media's role in portraying the opinions of large collectives seemed obviously detrimental to the democratic system. I sympathized with those who sought to curtail the publication of poll results and those who wanted to abandon the sequential primary system because of its dynamic component. Surely these practices detracted from the independence and rationality of people's political decisions. The emergence of the sociotropic voting studies only confirmed my concerns, in this case about media portrayals of mass collectives. If people ignored their own personal experiences and instead voted on the basis of media-derived perceptions of collective experience, surely the accountability of public officials was suffering as a consequence.

It was not until I decided to combine my various studies into a book and sat down to write the conclusion chapter that I realized just how far my thinking had evolved. In fact, close readers may notice that although I draw on some data from my previously published studies, in many cases the conclusions I draw here are quite different from the conclusions that I drew in my journal articles on these same topics. There is a very simple explanation for these discrepancies: I changed my mind. The more studies I did, the more difficult I found it was to stay with my initial conclusions.

I was extremely reluctant to drop the ominous tone inherent in my earlier conclusions. There is a certain respectability in suggesting that media are menacing agents of false consciousness that perpetuate inaccurate perceptions of collective experience and opinion, thus threatening democratic accountability. Moreover, such an argument tends to meet with little opposition because, deservedly or not, media are everyone's favorite whipping boy.

Preface

The conclusions I arrived at in this book do not exonerate media from the effects of inaccurate portrayals of collective experience or opinion, but they suggest that the ways in which people are influenced by these perceptions are, in themselves, not so much deleterious to democracy as absolutely necessary to promoting accountability in a large-scale society. In chapters 4 and 5 I lay out the argument as to why this is so in the context of perceptions of collective experience, and in chapters 6, 7, and 8, in the context of collective opinion. Chapter 9 elaborates on both of these contentions and their broader relationship to democratic accountability.

My book's title is derived from the groundbreaking work of Elihu Katz and Paul Lazarsfeld entitled *Personal Influence: The Part Played by People in the Flow of Mass Communications*. Both of these books deal with the relationship between mass media and social influence. Nonetheless, readers should be forewarned that this is not a book about the power of personal influence on political attitudes or a comparison of the relative impact of mass and interpersonal communication. My major reason for making an implicit reference to Katz and Lazarsfeld is to point out what differentiates personal and impersonal influence.

Katz and Lazarsfeld were particularly impressed by the extent to which information obtained through interpersonal relations had an obvious advantage over information gleaned from media. As they put it, "People can induce each other to a variety of activities as a result of their interpersonal relations, and thus their influence goes far beyond the content of their communications . . . persons have two major avenues of influence while formal mass media, like radio and print, have only one." In other words, people obviously care what other people think of them and their opinions; moreover, they have reasons to trust many of their personal acquaintances. Information from media cannot bring to bear the power of normative social influence the way that interpersonal communication can.

Instead, the persuasive power of impersonal influence is rooted in the nature of its content. What media, and national media in particular, do best is to supply us with information about those beyond our personal experiences and contacts, in other words, with impressions of the state of mass collectives. Although people can certainly develop such impressions based on their own personal experiences and contacts, the consistent divergence between people's perceptions of their immediate lives and communities and their perceptions of the nation as a whole suggests that they tend, quite logically, to rely on media expertise when judging the world beyond their own field of vision.

What makes an influence impersonal is that it results from people's perceptions of the experiences or opinions of a mass collective. As Katz and Lazarfeld's "two-step flow" suggested, such information could be obtained from media and then relayed interpersonally as well. Whereas these authors were explicitly concerned with communication channels, I focus on the impersonal nature of a message's content and the unique power it holds to influence political attitudes. Although channel and content are conceptually independent dimensions, in practice media convey more information about large-scale collectives, and interpersonal communication about individuals.

In addition to the implicit contrast with the kind of social influence process exercised best by interpersonal channels, a secondary reason for choosing *Impersonal Influence* as my title was a thinly veiled desire to get cited as often as Katz and Lazarsfeld. One of the early reviewers of this manuscript suggested that by virtue of the book's title it "commanded a space on the shelf next to *Personal Influence*." I had not thought of it quite that way before, but I liked the sound of it. Thus, with apologies to Katz and Lazarsfeld, I climb onto the shoulders of giants to offer my own view of a very different kind of social influence process.

Acknowledgments

The idea for this study took shape very slowly; thus I am indebted to a great number of people and institutions that have supported me personally, intellectually, and financially over the years as bits and pieces of this research were done. For both the time and financial support necessary for this research, I am particularly grateful to the National Science Foundation, the Freedom Forum Media Studies Center, and the Graduate School of the University of Wisconsin–Madison. In particular, Everette Dennis was instrumental in encouraging me to turn my ideas into a book-length project.

Several people reviewed this manuscript in its entirety and provided invaluable suggestions for its improvement. These included Jim Kuklinski, Michael MacKuen, Bob Huckfeldt, Dick Merelman, Darrell West, and Susan Herbst. I am also indebted for commentary on specific chapters to Jim Baughman, Jeff Mondak, Al Gunther, Laurie Mason, and Dennis Chong. The enthusiasm and attention of Alex Holzman, my editor at Cambridge University Press, has benefited the manuscript and buoyed me along in the process as well.

My colleagues at the Department of Political Science and in the School of Journalism and Mass Communication at the University of Wisconsin have improved this manuscript through their interest and encouragement and through seemingly endless recommendations on additional sources of material that have broadened and enriched my perspective. Through these departments I have also had the good fortune to work with a number of diligent graduate students, including Paul Martin, Joe Soss, and Mira Sotirovic. Special thanks are due to Paul, who had the misfortune of serving as my assistant when I worked on the references.

I owe a special debt of gratitude to Paul Sniderman for pioneering the innovative use of experiments embedded within national surveys and for bringing the potential contributions of this approach to my attention. This method, which is used in most of the studies in Chapter 8, con-

Acknowledgments

tributed immensely to my understanding of impersonal influence processes. In this same vein, I am extremely fortunate to have had the pleasure of working with Bob Lee of the University of Wisconsin Survey Center. When other survey directors would have balked at the idea of administering experimental designs that involved sometimes well over thirty versions of a survey, Bob was always ready to give it a try.

I also want to thank the *American Journal of Political Science*, the *Journal of Politics*, *Public Opinion Quarterly*, the *Journal of Communication*, *Political Behavior*, JAI Press, and Westview Press for permission to use portions of material I have published elsewhere. My book was also enriched through the use of data from the American National Election Studies and from the South Bend study originally collected by Bob Huckfeldt and John Sprague.

Three of the studies discussed in this book involved co-authors; thus I thank Kevin Barnhurst, Jeff Mondak, and Joe Soss for their willingness to have their work appear in my book. They do not necessarily endorse the overall views I espouse in my book, and I value their friendship all the more for that. Of course, none of these people are responsible for the errors or excesses contained within these pages. Instead, all errors ultimately should be blamed on Dan Lewis of Northwestern University for first suggesting that I go to graduate school. Were it not for him I obviously would never have had the opportunity to commit such grievous errors, at least not publicly.

I also want to express thanks to my friends and colleagues at Stanford University, including Steven Chaffee, Cliff Nass, Dick Brody, Byron Reeves, Don Roberts, and Jeremy Cohen. They taught me that the best social science research always begins in hot tubs, a lesson that has not been forgotten. The pure enjoyment of research that they conveyed was contagious and helps to make it fun even a decade later.

I thank my son, Walden Pemantle, for giving me a terrific excuse to delay writing this book, and my daughter, Maria Mutz, who, while in utero, provided the good swift kicks that were needed to compel me to finish this manuscript shortly before her birth. I am also grateful to Colleen McMullin for her very important role in giving me the time I needed to finish this manuscript.

Finally, as a man of many talents, my husband Robin Pemantle contributed positively in ways that ranged from arguing with me about key points to editing references to entertaining the kids. Most of all I am grateful to him for his unwavering confidence in me whenever my own flagged.

PART I

THEORY AND HISTORICAL CONTEXT

I

The Generalized Other:

SOCIAL INFLUENCE IN CONTEMPORARY AMERICAN POLITICS

Reality . . . has anyway long ceased to be what it was for my grand-mother, who lived in a Moravian village and still knew everything through her own experience: how bread is baked, how a house is built, how a pig is slaughtered and the meat is smoked, what quilts are made of, what the priests and the schoolteacher think about the world; she met the whole village every day and knew how many murders were committed in the country over the last ten years; she had, so to speak, personal control over reality, and nobody could fool her by maintain-ing that Moravian agriculture was thriving when people at home had nothing to eat. My Paris neighbor spends his time in an office, where he sits for eight hours facing an office colleague, then he sits in his car and drives home, turns on the TV, and when the announcer informs him that in the latest public opinion poll the majority of Frenchmen voted their country the safest in Europe (I recently read such a report), he is overjoyed and opens a bottle of champagne without ever learning that three thefts and two murders were committed on his street that very day. . . . [S]ince for contemporary man reality is a continent visited less and less often and, besides, justifiably disliked, the findings of polls have become a kind of higher reality, or to put it differently: they have become the truth.

> Milan Kundera, *Immortality* (New York: HarperPerennial, 1991), p. 115

The kind of world inhabited by Kundera's grandmother has ceased to exist for most citizens of advanced industrialized democracies. For better or worse, much of what people know about the world no longer comes to them through personal experience. Mass feedback mechanisms such as public opinion polls are just one of many factors that have accelerated this trend. This book is about the changes that have led to this state of affairs and the implications that they have for social influences on po-litical attitudes and behaviors.

3

The basic premise of the book is that an increasingly important force in contemporary political life involves what may be termed "impersonal influence"; that is, influence that derives from people's perceptions of others' attitudes, beliefs, or experiences. "Others" in this case refers not to the close friends and acquaintances that concerned the authors of classics such as *The People's Choice* and *Personal Influence*, but rather to the anonymous "others" outside an individual's realm of personal contacts. For example, impersonal influence takes place when the outcomes of early primaries or caucuses affect attitudes toward candidates in later primaries as they did for Gary Hart in 1984 (Bartels 1988; Brady and Johnston 1987). Likewise, when people vote on the basis of their perceptions of how the nation as a whole is faring economically rather than on their own pocketbooks, they are also being influenced by perceptions of impersonal others (Kinder and Kiewiet 1981).[1] And when people demand that greater public resources be directed at a problem like violent crime based on their perceptions that others are increasingly victimized even though they themselves are not, impersonal influence also may be said to occur.

Impersonal influence is worthy of attention both from the standpoint of its impact on contemporary American politics and because of its potential to expand the boundaries of our understanding of social influence processes and media's relation to them. This type of influence is deemed "impersonal" because it is brought about by information about the attitudes, beliefs or experiences of collectives outside of an individual's personal life space. In other words, impersonal influence is not about the direct persuasive influence of media messages that attempt to promote one viewpoint over another; it is strictly concerned with the capacity for presentations of collective opinion or experience to trigger social influence processes. The perceptions of mass collectives that initiate this type of influence tend to originate with media, though this need not necessarily be the case.[2] But media content is particularly well suited to serving as a credible channel of information about large-scale collec-

1 "Impersonal" is not meant to connote others who are cold or aloof, but rather collective others with whom one has no personal association.
2 The channel through which information reaches a person (interpersonal communication versus mass media) is obviously distinguishable from the kind of information transmitted (about individuals or collectives). As noted, my focus is on information about the state of mass collectives, regardless of whether that information reaches a person directly, via secondary transmission of mediated information, or in some other fashion. Nonetheless, media tend to be the most important conduit for information about mass collectives, while interpersonal communication conveys the bulk of information that is exchanged about individuals. As discussed in Chapter 2, contemporary media tend to report much less news about personally identified individuals, except when they serve as exemplars of some larger social problem.

tives. Although mediated channels lack the trustworthiness that would make them valued sources of opinions on many matters, they possess a degree of expertise in matters beyond the realm of people's personal experiences that makes them seem far more reliable as sources of information about the larger world in which we live.

Mass media undoubtedly facilitate the influence of anonymous others by devoting considerable time and attention to portraying trends in, and states of, mass opinion and experience. But the concern with social influence has been investigated most thoroughly at the level of personal acquaintances and group influence. The legacy handed down by *Personal Influence* and related work was that interpersonal information sources carried tremendous credibility as trustworthy sources of political opinion (Katz and Lazarsfeld 1955). People's perceptions of the attitudes of more distant, impersonal others were therefore of little theoretical or practical interest. It was assumed that what was most important in explaining Americans' political attitudes could be found close to home in their immediate social environments.

Today there are numerous reasons to reconsider the relevance of the impersonal to American politics. A wide variety of historical changes have focused Americans' attention on the world outside of their immediate life space. Moreover, the literature on American political behavior is replete with examples of situations in which people's political behaviors are influenced by their perceptions of the attitudes or experiences of mass collectives, collectives that exist well beyond the boundaries of communities they know through personal experience.

At the same time that concern about situations facilitating impersonal influence has increased, research on the effects of mass media increasingly suggests that its primary impact is on social-level perceptions rather than on personal attitudes or beliefs. In other words, media are far more likely to convince people that public attitudes toward abortion have become increasingly favorable than they are to alter people's personal attitudes toward this issue. To extend Cohen's (1963) well-worn maxim, one might say that mass media may not be particularly influential in telling people what to think, or perhaps even what to think about, but media are tremendously influential in telling people what *others* are thinking about and experiencing. These perceptions, in turn, have important consequences for the political behavior of mass publics and political elites as well.

A few concrete examples should serve to illustrate this phenomenon. One of the most widely known current illustrations of impersonal influence occurs in the contemporary furor surrounding violent crime. In the American political culture of the 1990s, we speak about crime as if it were a peculiarly modern problem, with presumably modern causes

(*Economist* 1994). For example, President Clinton's crime bill was said to be offered in response to a "wave of crime and violence." According to public opinion polls, the American public is also convinced that crime has risen over the past two decades (Jencks 1991: 98). Crime rates in the United States have always been high relative to other affluent countries, but for most people the point of reference is not so much other nations as America's own past. And here there is clearly a pervasive sense that America is increasingly violent.

Nonetheless, public records show that rates of both violent and non-violent crimes are no higher now than in the seventies, thus providing little evidence of an overtime increase. In fact, the most reliable measures suggest precisely the opposite (Warr 1994).[3] Most people also believe that crime has increased more in poor black areas than in white areas of America. Although blacks continue to be more likely to die violently, a black man's or woman's chances of being murdered were about the same in 1985 as they were in 1950 (Jencks 1991). Through its portrayals of others' experiences, media coverage has at times created "crime waves" without any concrete evidence of actual increases in crime (Scheingold 1991).

In these examples as in many others, people are responding to a media-constructed pseudoenvironment rather than their immediate personal experiences or those of friends and acquaintances. Journalists are highly selective in their attention to crime statistics. They may be most likely to report precisely those crimes that are least likely to occur (Warr 1994). In addition, they often report increases in the number of crimes without converting the figures to rates and/or without reporting simultaneous changes in population size (Warr 1994; Biderman et al. 1967).[4] Moreover, as Jencks (1991: 99) has noted, "When crime declines, as it did in the early eighties, editors assume the decline is only temporary and give it very little air time. When crime increases as it did in the late eighties, both journalists and editors see it as a portent of things to come and give it a lot of play."

---

3 Media frequently rely on highly unreliable FBI data without telling readers about the well-known problems with those data (see Warr 1994). While FBI figures show a 66% rise in total crime between 1973 and 1992, the National Crime Victimization Surveys show a 6% decline. Violent crime rose by 24% over the period, but if population growth is taken into account, the rate of violent crime fell slightly (see Jencks 1991).

4 For example, in 1990 the Senate Judiciary Committee released a report that received front-page news coverage all across the country because it predicted that the number of murders would reach an all-time high in 1990. What journalists neglected to note in the alarmist headlines spawned by this report was that the population would also reach an all-time high by 1990, so that the projected murder rate in 1990 would be the same as it was in the 1970s (Jencks 1991: 99–100).

All of this is not meant to suggest that some pockets of the country may not be experiencing increases in crime. Some American cities are in fact more dangerous than they once were. And since many journalists are based in Washington, D.C., and New York, it is hardly surprising that their reporting in the national media reflects a far grimmer picture than what most Americans are personally experiencing. The more general point is that mass media play an indispensable role in the construction of social problems in the public mind. Their role in helping to create an impersonal social reality is most clear when there is evidence that public reality is operating independently of the aggregate of private realities.

Public attitudes toward health care provide yet another current example of a disjuncture of this kind. It is tempting to think that all the recent attention this issue has received is a result of Americans' mounting discontent with the health care available to them. But data from the past three decades suggest that there have been few significant changes in public opinion toward personal health care (Jacobs and Shapiro 1994). If the situation is critical, it has probably been so for over thirty years. Even more surprising, survey data suggest that people with access to health care have given consistently high marks to their doctors and are generally satisfied with their care. Survey data typically underrepresent the most impoverished segment of society; still the consistency of responses over time among those who are accessible to survey researchers belies the conventional wisdom.

As Jacobs and Shapiro (1994) report, over the past thirty years, between 70 percent and 95 percent of Americans report being personally satisfied with the treatment provided by their doctors and hospitals as well as with the general quality and accessibility of their health care. More than 80 percent reported being satisfied with the care they and their families received as well as with the time and explanations provided by their doctors.

In the face of all this contentment, one has to wonder where the tremendous amount of support for health care reform comes from. Counter to what one might think, it does not appear to come from the many Americans who are not adequately covered by health insurance. Those who had had difficulty covering their medical expenses were no more likely to support universal health care than those who had never encountered such problems (Mutz and Chan 1995). Here, once again, the disjuncture between the personal and impersonal social worlds becomes important in explaining this puzzle.

While a relatively small percentage of Americans have been, and continue to be, unhappy with their personal health care coverage, perceptions of the collective well-being of Americans with regard to health care have been overwhelmingly negative (Jacobs and Shapiro 1994). This same gap is evident in support for health care reform. Twice as many people thought reforms would help improve the quality of health care for *other* Americans relative to the number who thought it would improve the quality of their own personal health care (Jacobs and Shapiro 1994). Of course, these data do not address the issue of who would actually benefit a great deal from reforms. But they do indicate that for most people reforms were perceived to be something that would largely help impersonal others, and not necessarily one's self, one's immediate family, or one's community.

Examples such as these would be entertaining, yet largely unimportant, were it not for the fact that collective public definitions of problems typically have a greater influence on American politics than aggregated individual ones. Just as people are more likely to hold government accountable for collective as opposed to personal economic problems (Kiewiet 1983), so too their general policy attitudes are more easily driven by perceptions of collectively defined social problems.

Despite many journalistic accounts to the contrary, the mass public's opinions toward health care reform were not driven primarily by negative personal experiences with the health care system. Instead, public support for reform was driven by perceptions of the experiences of impersonal others. Regardless of one's stance on this particular issue, there is an obvious danger inherent in policy attitudes that stem from perceptions of events that are beyond the realm of what one can personally know or experience. Since the "conventional wisdom" also provides a set of assumptions that guide the deliberations of elected officials and policy experts (Jacobs and Shapiro 1994: 212), policy makers may operate on the basis of inaccurate depictions of social problems or mistaken perceptions of mass concern.

Even more likely, policy makers may seize upon the manipulability of perceptions of mass collectives to further their own goals. These goals may or may not be consistent with the aggregate of individual opinions, but the impression of mass support can provide a powerful ally in itself. President Reagan's first term in office provides an interesting case in point. The press consistently exaggerated Reagan's popularity with the mass public, "in part because of an ardent, if cynical, belief among Washington insiders that anyone who looked and sounded as good on television as Reagan did *must* be popular" (King and Schudson 1995:17). According to presidential approval ratings, the standardized method for assessing presidential popularity, the "Great Communicator" was actually the least popular president in the post-World War II period. Nonetheless, Reagan's cultivation of the *im-*

pression of mass popularity contributed greatly to his tremendous success in getting Congress to support his legislation (Jones 1988; Kernell 1986).

These examples are just a few of a growing number of situations in which perceptions of collective opinions, beliefs, or experiences have important political consequences. In addition to providing empirical evidence on how such perceptions affect political behavior, a primary goal of this book is to explain how developments in this century have contributed to this form of social influence. Toward that end, I first sketch the larger social transformations that have facilitated the increasing importance of impersonal influence. Impersonal influence requires both mediated associations with others and the communication of social information across traditional boundaries of social interaction; two parallel social trends – changes in the nature of social interaction and the compartmentalization of personal and collective judgments – have contributed greatly toward these two requirements.

CHANGES IN THE NATURE OF SOCIAL INTERACTION

Impersonal influence is possible only when political communication is mediated, and thus indirect. One distinctive characteristic of contemporary society is the proliferation of indirect associations (Bender 1978; Coleman 1980). In fact, most theorists of nineteenth-century social transformations mention a shift away from communal, person-to-person relationships toward indirect associations with others (Beniger 1987). Indirect associations involve the mediation of communication technologies, markets, or other complex organizations, as opposed to direct relationships that require face-to-face interpersonal communication. Whereas political and economic affairs used to be organized on the basis of local community and face-to-face economic exchange, direct interpersonal relationships now organize less of American public life (Calhoun 1991). One need not meet face-to-face with a local seamstress in order to obtain a new shirt; it is far more efficient to order it from a catalog and have it delivered to one's home. Likewise, one need not show up for a Thursday night meeting in the church basement in order to promote environmental issues; one can send a donation to the Sierra Club and quickly become apprised of which products and companies to boycott as environmentally unfriendly.

As people increasingly interact with others through mediated systems, their need for information about remote and anonymous others also

increases.⁵ Thus there is an even greater need for media content that
provides information about the beliefs, attitudes, and experiences of people outside the realm of personal contacts. The development of communication technologies has both facilitated the proliferation of indirect
associations and provided a natural source of information about impersonal others.

Media and markets are among the most prominent systems of indirect
associations. Moreover, the decision-making practices of citizens part-
icipating in politics through a mediated system are similar to those
confronting traders conducting economic exchange through a market
system; "The right price, after all, depends primarily on what other people, not just you yourself, think that price should be." (Heilbroner 1991:
70). Early in this century, John Maynard Keynes (1936: 156) described
successful trading as primarily a matter of gauging the opinions of anonymous others:

Professional investment may be likened to those newspaper competitions in
which the competitors have to pick out the six prettiest faces from a hundred
photographs, the prize being awarded to the competitor whose choice most
nearly corresponds to the average preferences of the competitors as a whole; so
that each competitor has to pick, not those faces which he himself finds prettiest,
but those which he thinks likeliest to catch the fancy of the other competitors,
all of whom are looking at the problem from the same point of view.

The problem Keynes describes is similar to the situation confronting the
contemporary voter in a three-way race or presidential primary; a person
who bases his or her selection on strategic considerations will try to
assess likely winners and losers by gauging the opinions of others in
order to make a vote decision (Abramowitz and Stone 1984).

It is no mere coincidence that many examples of impersonal influence
flow from the economic realm; media and market systems have a lot in
common as impersonal means of communicating. Buyers and sellers of
goods now communicate with one another through indirect rather than
face-to-face relationships; people promoting candidates and causes also
are more likely to communicate through impersonal means than they
were a century ago. And economic signals representing the collective
behavior of others communicate information in markets, just as impersonal influence suggests that the political views expressed by others communicate information to those who observe them. Just as some traders
may "free ride" on better-informed traders by watching stock prices,

5 Coleman (1980) suggests that the need for this type of information spawned the
development of the Columbia school of sociology with its emphasis on characterizing large populations. As the distance between consumer and producer increased, producers could no longer assess their markets informally, and thus
market research was invented to fill this gap.

some citizens may free ride on those more politically informed by relying on the collective opinions and experiences of others. When collective public definitions of a situation directly affect subsequent developments, it is a peculiarly human phenomenon. As Merton (1968: 477) notes, this phenomenon "is not found in the world of nature, untouched by human hands. Predictions of the return of Halley's comet do not influence its orbit."

COMPARTMENTALIZATION OF PERSONAL AND COLLECTIVE JUDGMENTS

The proliferation of indirect associations has not necessarily meant a decline in direct relationships. Clearly, people still have meaningful interpersonal relationships.[6] However, as indirect associations have increased in number and importance, the gap between the worlds of direct and indirect experience has widened. Distinctions between "everyday life" and "the big picture" used in common parlance are indicative of "divergent ways of trying to understand the social world" and "an experiential and intellectual split": "We contrast the quotidian no longer with the extraordinary days of feasts and festivals so much as with the systematically remote, with that which 'counts' on a large scale" (Calhoun 1991: 96). The impersonal has not replaced the personal as *gesellschaft* is often claimed to have replaced *gemeinschaft* (Tonnies 1940), but an increase in the number of indirect associations has made the worlds of direct and indirect relationships more compartmentalized. Social theorists generally concur that a primary feature of modern social life is an increased split between the world of direct interpersonal relationships and large-scale social systems, or what Habermas refers to as "the system and the lifeworld" (Bender 1978; Habermas 1984). Most importantly, they acknowledge the increased compartmentalization of what we know through lived experiences and face-to-face interactions with those who are known to us, as opposed to through sources that are mediated by those beyond our experience or acquaintance.

A recurrent finding in contemporary social science research is that Americans often have perceptions of the larger social world that are quite distinct from perceptions of their own immediate life situations. This persistent gap between individuals' personal and collective-level judgments is an important consequence of mass-mediated society. Mass

6 Some versions of this argument clearly do suggest that interpersonal relationships have declined in number and importance as impersonal ones have increased (see Beniger 1987); however, this is not necessary for the argument I make here (see Chapter 9).

media play a crucial role in constructing people's images of the larger social world outside the realm of personal experiences and contacts. Although this idea is not new, its importance in the political realm has not been fully acknowledged. The tendency for people to "morselize" personal experiences (Lane 1962), failing to see them as parts of broader trends or larger phenomena, has now been amply documented across a wide range of issues. Perceptions of collective experience, on the other hand, are more readily linked to the political world. Thus it is precisely the type of (collective) judgment subject to influence from mass media that is also most politically relevant (Kinder and Kiewiet 1981; Kiewiet 1983).

In studies of public opinion, this split is probably observed most often in perceptions of the economy. In 1988, the *Christian Science Monitor* captured this phenomenon in a headline that read, "I'm doing better than we are." The article discussed the fact that according to the latest polls, the American public perceived the nation's economy to be in poor shape and getting worse. But this same poll showed that most Americans felt that their own personal economic situations were in good condition and likely to improve (Ladd 1988). Again, as coverage of the economy surged in late 1991, most Americans pronounced the nation's economy lousy and their own economic positions satisfactory (*Public Perspective* 1992). In 1993, a study of eight leading industrial nations concluded that "in every country, people are more sanguine about things close to home that they can know about from personal experience than about things remote and abstract that they can know about only by reading or watching television" (*Public Perspective* 1993: 92). In short, they seemed to be of two minds, with a split between the worlds of direct and indirect experience.

This pattern is not limited to the economic realm. A Carnegie Foundation study of college seniors' views of the future demonstrated a similar finding: When asked about prospects for the state of the nation five years hence, most felt the prospects were pretty bleak; the ozone layer was being destroyed, nuclear war was going to break out, and so forth. When these same students were asked about the prognosis for their own futures, the results were quite different; they were going to obtain good educations, prestigious jobs, make a lot of money, and live well – never mind the ozone layer or the pesky nuclear war (Levine 1980).

Enthusiasts of experiential learning see splits between personal- and societal-level thinking as the result of different means of knowing the personal and collective worlds; while one comes to us primarily through personal experience, the other usually reaches us by means of abstracted discussions conveyed through impersonal channels. As Palmer (1987: 22) notes: "They [students] have always been taught about a world out there somewhere apart from them, divorced from their personal lives; they never have been invited to intersect their autobiographies with the life story of the world. And so they can report on a world that is not the one in which they live."

In political science, the largest body of empirical evidence bearing directly on the gap between personal and social levels of judgment comes from research on the political impact of personal experiences. A large accumulation of evidence shows that personal experiences are rarely connected to political judgments (Sears and Funk 1990). Whether the issue is busing, the Vietnam War, or any of a host of public policy issues, personal experiences – even those indicating an obvious self-interest – typically play little or no role in determining policy preferences. Surprisingly, even people's personal financial experiences and perceptions of national economic conditions are maintained largely independent of one another (Kinder and Kiewiet 1981).

While personal experiences tend to be disconnected from the political world, people's perceptions of collective conditions reliably influence their political attitudes (Kiewiet 1983). Candidates of the incumbent party do worse when the economy is declining, but the people whose personal financial situations are worsening tend not to be those voting against the incumbents. Instead it is people's perceptions of the nation's economic condition that is most likely to influence vote choice (Kiewiet and Rivers 1985).[7]

By providing a technological means by which indirect associations can be established, mass media may contribute to widening the gap between personal and social levels of judgment. Some corroborating evidence for mass media's role in encouraging this split comes from examining similar relationships in countries without well-developed national media systems, where researchers have found more of a link between people's personal sense of well-being and attitudes toward government (Hayward 1979). At the same time, the sociotropic pattern – whereby personal experience and perceptions of collective experience are maintained independent of one another – is common to many Western democracies with well-developed national media systems (Eulau and Lewis-Beck 1985).

Although evidence is limited, to the extent that the development of a sophisticated national communications network broadens the gap between the personal and political worlds, the sheer existence of mass me-

---

7 This is not to suggest that personal experience *never* plays an important role in political attitudes or that personal experience *never* enters into political judgments indirectly, by influencing perceptions of collective conditions. While there are undoubtedly some exceptions (see, e.g., Markus 1988), this general conclusion has withstood extensive examination.

dia on a national scale may contribute to turning politics into somewhat of a spectator sport – something that goes on "out there" but does not have much to do with individuals' daily lives. Since it is easier for people to connect their perceptions of collective experience to political judgments, mass media take on an even more important role politically when this gulf widens.

It is important to differentiate the argument I am making here from the usual claims about the extent to which mass media, and particularly television, have contributed to turning politics into a spectator sport. Liberals and conservatives alike have blamed media for a host of political ills including decreased turnout and general political apathy (Bloom 1987; Lasch 1988). Although impersonal influence may well encourage political voyeurism, I do not mean to suggest a normative comparison to political participation and decision making that was necessarily of a higher quality in the past. Most such comparisons consist primarily of a romanticization of the past and very thin empirical evidence (Schudson 1992; Converse 1962). Instead my point is that large-scale media systems have influenced the *nature* of political decision making by making it possible to formulate independent perceptions of the personal and political worlds. As discussed in the chapters that follow, political judgments that include impersonal components are not necessarily inferior to decisions made on the basis of information in a person's immediate lifespace and they do not necessarily demonstrate altruistic tendencies. Nonetheless, they may be biased in systematic directions that have important implications for mass political behavior.

Media content has been largely irrelevant to the changes discussed thus far; media influence social behavior "by changing the 'situational geography' of social life," rather than through their content (Meyrowitz 1985: 6). In this sense, the argument I have made thus far is reminiscent of technological determinists such as Harold Innis and Marshall McLuhan, who argued that the medium itself was what was of real importance. But media content plays an important role in facilitating impersonal influence as well. By providing information about distant and impersonal collectives that is often at odds with people's personal experiences, media content contributes to widening the gap between personal and social levels of judgment.

Media alone probably would not alter perceptions of the social environment unless its content included fairly large quantities of nonlocal social information. Thus change in the structure, as well as the type of social relationships, is central to creating the potential for impersonal influence. Indirect associations are different from direct ones not just in the sense that they are mediated; they also transcend locality in a way that is typically not possible with direct interpersonal relationships.

INTELLECTUAL FORERUNNERS

Current social and political conditions clearly have increased the importance of impersonal influence. Nonetheless, its implications have yet to be analyzed in relation to contemporary politics except in the context of relatively narrow empirical questions. One can find, for example, literatures on the impact of exit poll results on voting behavior or on the impact of collective economic conditions on political behavior. But these studies are usually not considered to be related in any meaningful way. In making a case for impersonal influence, I draw on a tremendous amount of research done by others in addition to my own original contributions. My point is not so much to indulge in extensive literature review as it is to demonstrate that this broad collection of theories and evidence, heretofore seen as unconnected, is actually working within a single research tradition – that of impersonal influence.

In addition to being manifestations of a more general phenomena, they also share a common theoretical lineage. Impersonal influence is at root an old idea. Although many mass feedback technologies are relatively recent phenomena, this is clearly not the first time concerns have been raised about social influences that occur outside of primary groups or face-to-face interaction. In fact, concern with the influence of larger society on the individual was an important part of late nineteenth- and early twentieth-century political and social thought. In Europe, French sociologist Gabriel Tarde sought evidence of suggestibility or imitation in large masses. His suggestion that publicized suicides might lead to imitation on the part of others led Émile Durkheim to his classic empirical study of this topic.

Although Durkheim found no such evidence, his development of the concept of "collective representations" pointed to forms of social influence that might exist outside the bounds of traditional interpersonal relations.[8] These "social facts," or "states of the social mind," were said to represent a "special mechanism of collective thought" (Durkheim 1903: 45). Collective representations were said to represent entities which are "not ourselves but society alive and active within us" (Durkheim 1893: 99), and they were "endowed with a power of coercion over

---

8 Durkheim used the term quite broadly to refer to a range of forms that included science, religion, and myth – or any belief – that could be considered part of a "common reality."

individual behavior." They allow us to say that "the aggregate in its totality . . . thinks, feels, wills, though it could not will, feel, or act save by the intermediation of particular minds" (Durkheim 1898: 295).

Impersonal influence fits the Durkheimian notion of a "collective representation" in the sense that it refers to the impact or consequences of a collective belief or common reality. But an even more precise conceptual predecessor can be found in George Herbert Mead's description of the "generalized other." According to Mead, the way anonymous collectives exercise control over individual behavior is by entering into a person's thought processes. In his words, "The individual transcends what is given to him alone when through communication he finds that his experience is shared by others. . . . The individual has, as it were, gotten outside of his limited world by taking the roles of others. It is against this common world that the individual distinguishes his own private experience" (Mead 1934: xxiv).

Mead used the analogy of a baseball game to describe the situation in which each person's own actions are determined by his or her assumptions about the actions of others who are simultaneously playing the same game: "We get then an 'other' which is an organization of the attitudes of those involved in the same process," and it is that organization "which controls the response of the individual." The attitude of the generalized other is the attitude of the whole community and the individual is said to engage in an "internalized conversation" with this collective other, not unlike the external conversations carried on with others in interpersonal contexts (Mead 1934: 154).

Mead has been credited with extending reference group theory to the demands of modern mass societies by replacing the notion of social relationships built exclusively on interpersonal ties with a "social community of the mind":

It is in the form of the generalized other that the social process influences the behavior of the individuals involved in it and carrying it on, i.e., that the community exercises control over the conduct of its individual members; for it is in this form that the social process or community enters as a determining factor into the individual's thinking. In abstract thought, the individual takes the attitude of the generalized other toward himself, without reference to its expression in any particular other individuals (Mead 1934: 155).

Impersonal influence encompasses precisely the forms of social influence Mead had in mind. At the same time, impersonal influence processes are quite different from the usual types of social influence that are studied in political psychology because they are not based on group identification or pressures to conform in order to obtain the approval of others.[9]

9 When identification takes place, the attractiveness (or repulsion) of the group identity is the source of power enabling a group to influence an individual (Kel-

Impersonal influence incorporates a wide range of reactions that individuals may have to their perceptions of the attitudes, beliefs, or experiences of diffuse others who are not known to them personally; in this one sense it is the antithesis of personal influence, which derives its power from the trustworthiness of interpersonal relations that bring firsthand knowledge of others' experiences. As elaborated in Chapter 7, group identification and normative conformity are undoubtedly important to understanding mass political attitudes, but they are often ill suited to explaining influence that flows from perceptions of amorphous and impersonal others.[10]

The seeds of interest in impersonal influence processes were planted

---

man 1961). In contrast, when influence is truly impersonal in nature, the power of influence does not derive from the attractiveness of the collective's identity so much as its sheer existence as a large-scale collective.

10 I have chosen not to incorporate influence processes such as group identification under the umbrella term of impersonal influence. At an operational level, this distinction is sometimes difficult to discern. For example, one could argue that even representations of diffuse opinion at the level of "all Americans" trigger group identification processes. To the extent that Americans respond to these opinion cues strictly because they derive satisfaction from defining themselves as Americans, identification is the mechanism through which representations of national opinion are influencing subsequent attitudes. But to the extent that people react for reasons *other than* their identification with the collective, the influence can be deemed truly impersonal in nature.

Likewise, if perceptions of the larger opinion environment alter people's expectations regarding their interpersonal contacts and that expectation, in turn, leads them to alter their behavior in some way, I do not consider that kind of effect an impersonal one. In other words, I consider impersonal influence to be occurring strictly when the motive is something other than the maintenance of personal relationships or the desire to avoid social disapproval. It is in this sense that impersonal influence contrasts with personal influence. I leave it to subsequent chapters (see especially Chapter 7) to describe the precise nature of the alternative processes that account for impersonal forms of social influence.

In circumscribing the type of phenomena to which impersonal influence will refer, this distinction points out that it is the nature of the influence process evoked, rather than the nature or size of a collective, that is the defining characteristic of impersonal influence. A process of influence is impersonal if it is not brought about by the personal relationship an individual has with the collective or by personal characteristics such as the likability of the group or other affective ties. Thus, in Chapter 4, for example, even perceptions of groups such as the "middle class" can evoke impersonal influence when the influence occurs even among those who have no affective tie to this group label. Instead of deriving power to influence from the trustworthiness of interpersonal sources of political opinion or the attractiveness of group identities, impersonal influence derives its power of influence from numbers. This is not to say that attractiveness does not matter to other forms of social influence – a lengthy research literature obviously suggests otherwise. But if a person is influenced by news that one American thinks Saddam Hussein should be driven out of Iraq, impersonal influence suggests that he or she should be influenced far *more* by news that thousands of equally attractive persons are of this mind.

by social theorists early in this century, but only recently have social scientists begun to investigate to what extent thoughts about collective others can serve as potent social environments. For example, the contemporary work of Moscovici (1981) proposes a theory of "social representations," suggesting that people's inner representations of collective phenomena can change attitudes. Moscovici argues that these representations are created through communication and that they constitute an important social environment; they are a substitute for things we cannot directly observe, socially constructed realities that nonetheless influence our attitudes and behaviors. Like Mead, Moscovici sees the need for such a concept as an outgrowth of contemporary mass mediated society:

In fact, for our "man in the street" (now threatened with extinction, along with strolls in the street, and soon to be replaced by the man in front of the TV set), most of the opinions derived from science, art and economics which relate to reified universes differ, in many ways, from the familiar, handy opinions he has constructed out of bits and pieces of scientific, artistic and economic traditions and from personal experience and hearsay (Moscovici 1984: 25).

Benedict Anderson (1983) coined the term "imagined communities"[11] to refer to the same kind of large, reified collective that concerns Moscovici. Collective entities that people recognize, but for which they have no knowledge of the other members as concrete individuals, are said to result in a new form of social relationship: "Thus we develop categorical identities like those of nations or within them those we ascribe to or claim as members of different ethnic groups, religions, classes or even genders. Some of the time, at least, we imagine these categorical identities on analogy to the local communities in which we live" (Calhoun 1991:107).

Long before terms such as "imagined community" had been coined in response to advances in communication technology, early twentieth-century social theorists such as Charles Horton Cooley, John Dewey, and Robert Park had very similar concepts in mind. Cooley, for example, argued that advances in mass communication had made possible a "great community" since what speech insured for the primary group, mass communication made possible for the whole of society. Likewise, Dewey (1927:211) argued that "The Great Community, in the sense of free and full intercommunication, is conceivable."

11 Anderson (1983) uses this term in describing the spread of nationalism because nations are imagined communities in the sense that their members will never know most of their fellow members even though there is a shared identity. The cognitive awareness of "nation-ness" is similar to the reification of large-scale collectives necessary for impersonal influence processes. However, Anderson also emphasizes the deep emotional attachments that people feel toward nations, whereas impersonal influence assumes no particular affective ties to these amorphous group labels.

So while imagined communities have long existed to some extent, advances in communication technology have contributed to making them more imaginable. In particular, Anderson focuses on the effects of the development of printing as a means of transmitting information over long distances. Whereas location and physical presence once formed the boundaries of social relationships, printing extended these boundaries. Electronic media have accelerated further the building of imagined communities (Calhoun 1991). Since electronic media can transcend both time and space, the physical structures that once divided and defined social contexts are no longer determinative: "Where one is has less and less to do with what one knows and experiences" (Meyrowitz 1985: viii).

Media have abetted this trend to an even greater degree since people exposed to information from newspapers and television are aware that others are simultaneously consuming it. What Tocqueville (1835: 520) noted about the newspaper is doubly true of broadcast media with its vast audiences: "It speaks to each of its readers in the name of all the rest." According to Anderson (1983), it is this pattern of thinking and awareness of simultaneous consumption that makes entities such as nations imaginable.

Imagined communities facilitate impersonal influence because people can easily conceive of large-scale social entities as communities; they have been reified to the point where their existence is seldom questioned. Since journalists can also conceive of them, they can write about them, report poll results on them, and otherwise perpetuate their existence as if they were true communities.

Despite these similarities, there are important differences between social groups formed out of direct relationships among members and social categories defined exclusively by external attributes. The give and take of interpersonal communication is difficult, if not impossible, for members of imagined communities. The degree of trust and intimacy cultivated by interpersonal relations is usually missing as well. So too, theories of social influence grounded in the world of direct interpersonal contact often adapt poorly to impersonal contexts (Price and Allen 1990). Although small group studies of majority influence have been used as post hoc explanations for the influence of representations of mass collectives, most of the key factors influencing the extent of conformity in small group environments are missing from situations in which impersonal influence occurs (Mutz 1992a). For example, the "group" in this case is not particularly attractive, cohesive, or interdependent, as is typically necessary for normative social pressures to operate. While normative social pressures dominate in interpersonal settings where people interact in face-to-face contexts, the mechanisms underlying social influence from anonymous and impersonal collectives are less straightforward.

We now live in a society where it makes a certain amount of sense to speak of aggregates of persons as social entities (Tilly 1983). In fact, the ubiquitousness of indirect associations makes it quite difficult not to. Reification of the systemworld is a nearly inescapable form of false consciousness, an "almost unavoidable condition of practical thought in the modern world" (Calhoun 1988: 233).

Moreover, as I argue throughout the book, this tendency has important political consequences for political elites and the mass public. For a long time, the received view has been that people are only susceptible to the influence of media in areas where they lack personal experiences (Zucker 1978; Ball-Rokeach and DeFleur 1976). Perhaps foreign policy attitudes were at risk of being misled by media misrepresentations of distant social realities, but surely with issues such as inflation or crime, people's perceptions of collective reality were firmly anchored in their own personal experiences and those of their friends and neighbors. In a large-scale society such as ours, even this reasoning becomes fallacious:

In understanding the world about us, we human beings are increasingly drawn into beliefs about that which we cannot experience or personally recognize. We have beliefs about "society" that are public in the sense both of being shared and of being about an aggregate of events which we do not and cannot experience personally. A great many people in the United States have had direct and personal experience with automobile crashes and collisions. These are personal facts. The total number of automobile fatalities is not. It is a public fact. No one observes all the automobile crashes. . . . What is "true" about society is more than a reflection of individual experiences; it is also a set of beliefs about the aggregated experiences of others (Gusfield 1981: 51-2).

While it may have been possible to retain personal control over reality in the type of small, preindustrialized society Kundera described, it is clearly not possible in today's large, mass-mediated and industrialized societies. The kind of "social facts" that concerned Durkheim are readily available and widely distributed via the mass media. They are also a mainstay of political dialogue, for both elites and the mass public. Moreover, many contemporary representations of the state of mass collectives are based on compilations of statistical information that lend them a ring of legitimacy and authority. In short, they are ideally positioned to play an important role in influencing American political behavior.

On first consideration, those familiar with the social psychology literature documenting the general neglect of base rate information may doubt the relevance of people's perceptions of mass collectives to their political attitudes. After all, a sizable number of studies have shown that even when making judgments or attributions for which information about the size of the larger population is obviously relevant, people tend to ignore or underweight evidence of this kind (Kahneman, Slovic, and Tversky 1982; Nisbett and Borgida 1975). However, upon closer examination this well-known evidence is not at odds with any of the premises of impersonal influence because it focuses on when base rates matter in predictions about individuals or populations within that collective. For example, the general neglect of base rate information suggests that people who hear about rising unemployment in some city will be unlikely to use that information properly in deciding how likely a target person in the city is to lose his job.[12] Instead, their judgments will be inordinately affected by the specifics that they know about the individual's personal characteristics, employment history, and so forth. This kind of base rate neglect is not the same thing as suggesting that perceptions of rising unemployment will have no influence on attitudes toward political candidates or parties. The dependent variables in this case are not individual parts of the aggregate that comprises the base rate observation. Impersonal influence focuses specifically on whether base rate information informs people's political opinions. As discussed at greater length in Chapter 4, attitudes toward political issues and actors are precisely the type of judgment most likely to respond to information about mass collectives.[13]

ORGANIZATION OF THE BOOK

It is commonly argued that there is an inherent tension between being "scientific," particularly in the tradition of quantitative social science, and being historically relevant (Delia 1987). My goal in the chapters that follow is to do both: I first examine impersonal influence processes from a broad historical perspective and then provide concrete empirical examples of the operation of impersonal influence that are very much in the tradition of quantitative social science. Moreover, I attempt to go beyond simply providing examples of how impersonal influence matters

12 It is also worth noting that the literature on whether people use base rate information in making attributions is answering a fundamentally different question from the studies addressing the use of base rate information in social judgment (Kassin 1979b). The attribution studies use the null hypothesis as their basis for comparison by asking whether consensus information is utilized or ignored. The social judgment studies instead make comparisons with a formal probability model to examine whether respondents make appropriate use of base rate information.

13 In addition, the relative weighting of base rate information and evidence drawn from individual cases is relevant to how people integrate information from media and personal experiences in forming perceptions of collective-level phenomena (see discussion in Chapters 3 and 4).

to provide a microlevel understanding of *why* information about distant and impersonal others often influences people's political attitudes and behaviors.

Toward these multiple goals, the book is organized into four parts. In the remainder of Part I, I outline the major historical changes that have contributed to the increased relevance of impersonal influence in understanding contemporary political phenomena. I describe the rise of impersonal associations and their increasing importance in American political life, with particular emphasis on media's contribution. Over the past century, major changes have transpired in the nature of social relationships, the nature of media content, and the complexity of political decision making, all contributing to an increased potential for impersonal influence. In Chapter 3, this section concludes with empirical evidence bearing on media's unique capacity to influence perceptions of collective opinion and experience.

The two sections that follow explore in turn the political consequences of perceptions of collective experience and opinion. Impersonal influence is not a unitary theory so much as a collection of closely related phenomena that I have united under this umbrella term. Although these phenomena are similar and it is useful to consider their implications collectively, the theories that account for them differ substantially based on whether people are responding to perceptions of collective *experience* or perceptions of collective *opinion*. Both forms of impersonal influence can alter political attitudes, but people respond to perceptions of collective opinion and experience differently and for different reasons, thus they require separate examinations.

In Part II, I examine the role of perceptions of mass experience in influencing political attitudes. How, for example, do people's perceptions of crime or unemployment as collective-level problems influence their political attitudes? Consistent with previous research, I find that perceptions of collective-level experience matter more to political attitudes than people's personal experiences. This finding persists even beyond the well-documented economic realm. Do mass media either facilitate or inhibit the politicization of personal experiences? My findings suggest that media have the capacity to do either, depending upon the predominant view of collective experience that media portray. Individuals either learn that their experiences are shared with many others, and thus are easily attributed to government leaders and policies, or that their experiences are unique, which discourages them from holding national leaders accountable. The outcome of this thought process is far from predetermined. Thus sources of systematic bias in personal- and collective-level judgments have important implications for the extent to

which impersonal influence encourages or discourages political accountability.

In Part III, I explore the effects of perceptions of collective opinion on
individual political attitudes and behaviors. How is it that people are
influenced by their perceptions of the attitudes of even diffuse and anonymous others? In this section, I delve into the social-psychological rationale for these phenomena and outline a general framework for
understanding the psychological mechanisms underlying impersonal influence. Although the potential for impersonal influence is not limited to
one particular sector of the population, the mechanism driving it is likely
to be different for citizens with differing levels of information and involvement in political decision making. Using empirical findings from a
series of experiments embedded in national surveys, combined with studies incorporating measures of political behavior as well as opinion, I go
beyond the social determinism of most bandwagon theories and test a
model in which different segments of the citizenry are influenced by fundamentally different processes of social influence. As with perceptions
of collective experience, people engage in internalized conversations with
perceptions of collective opinion. When they learn that a particular candidate or issue is popular or unpopular, their implicit interactions with
these generalized others prompt them to alter or refine their own political
views.

An underlying concern throughout Parts II and III is the extent to
which impersonal influence flowing from perceptions of collective experience and opinion serves to facilitate or hinder the extent to which
the public holds political leaders accountable for the effects of their policies. Both forms of impersonal influence are generally assumed to detract from this end. In the realm of collective experience, the potential
for distorted perceptions of collective experience suggests a lack of accountability that personal experience-based politics appears to insure. In
the case of collective opinion, people whose opinions are shaped by perceptions of collective others' views are assumed to be unduly conformist,
and thus their opinions are presumed to be of a lesser quality than opinions formed independently of such influence. In Chapter 9, I discuss why
these conclusions are overly simplistic characterizations of the implications of impersonal influence for democratic accountability. I come to
the conclusion that we would not, as a polity, be better off attempting
to eliminate social influence of this kind.

To be sure, both impersonal influence from perceptions of mass experience and impersonal influence flowing from perceptions of mass
opinion pose potential problems for democratic accountability. In the
former case, the danger is that people will respond to perceptions of a

false social environment; in the latter, that independence of judgment will be compromised through social pressures emanating from mediated representations of others' views. But in order to evaluate these risks properly, it is important to consider the alternative mechanisms that might lead to greater accountability than would a system depending upon media.

With respect to the prospects for holding leaders accountable for the effects their policies have on citizens' collective experience, two specific possibilities are considered at length in Chapter 9: a politics rooted in the politicization of personal experience and communitarian approaches that emphasize renewing local community politics and institutions. Ultimately, I conclude that neither of these commonly offered alternatives provides a solution to the accountability risks posed by large-scale society or to the problematic psychological disjuncture that large-scale societies erect between people and their government. A system relying on people's perceptions of collectives beyond their immediate experiences undoubtedly has its risks, but it is preferable to the likely alternatives.

The dangers posed by mediated representations of collective opinion are real, but this type of impersonal influence also has the potential to encourage greater individual reflection and a higher-quality public opinion. Trends toward more homogeneous communities and the demographic balkanization of American citizens have made mass media an increasingly important source of information about people different from oneself. Although mass media clearly present a restricted range of viewpoints, people's interpersonal contacts are likely to be even more parochial. As a result of media portrayals of others' views, people are exposed to a broader range of political ideas. This exposure does not automatically compel them to change their views. But when multiple others endorse a particular view, it is more likely to prompt a reassessment of their own positions in light of this new information. Thus, contrary to the conventional wisdom, impersonal influence need not be synonymous with empty-headed, sheeplike behavior or mass susceptibility to media influence. A balanced assessment of impersonal influence must also recognize the positive contributions it makes to a democratic system. In a large-scale society such as the United States, impersonal influence represents the potential for greater political accountability and a more reflective public opinion.

In the concluding chapter of the book, I use mass society theory as a framework for explicating precisely what impersonal influence suggests about the nature of social influences on political attitudes and behaviors in twentieth- and perhaps twenty-first-century America. The historical transitions described in this book fit quite comfortably within the traditional framework of mass society theory. This extremely influential social theory incorporated some of the very same trends that are central to the rising potential for impersonal influence: revolutions in transportation and communication, the emergence of a nationalized communications network, and the rise of impersonal associations – all contributing to an increasingly centralized society, with important implications for mass political behavior. But mass society theory suggested further that modern life had destroyed important social bonds and produced alienated, atomized individuals who were at the mercy of centralized agents of mass persuasion. Although the potential for impersonal influence depends on many of the same trends characterizing the mass society tradition, in Chapter 9, I come to decidedly different conclusions than mass society theorists did concerning the role of mass media and the prospects for accountability in a large-scale society.

It is often a tremendous leap between grand historical theories and concrete data; they never correspond precisely, and narrow empirical studies often seem a weak sister, paling in comparison with the richness of the theories they are designed to examine. A table of statistics from any given study seldom does justice to the theory that spawned it. This book attempts to combine the discussion of specific empirical studies with much broader assertions about one important dimension of historical change and its consequences for the quality of political reasoning. This hybrid approach is essential because it is impossible to comprehend the macrolevel consequences of impersonal influence without first understanding the microlevel processes underlying the effects of perceptions of mass collectives. By combining multiple methods across multiple political contexts, my hope in the pages that follow is to paint as broad a portrait as possible of how impersonal forms of social influence have altered the political landscape.

2

Beyond Personal Influence

THE RISE OF IMPERSONAL ASSOCIATIONS

In outlining the increased importance of impersonal forms of social influence in contemporary American society, I have focused thus far on changes in the nature of mass communication that have transpired over the last century. But to look at changes in mass communication alone would miss the tremendous significance of parallel changes in interpersonal social relationships. Moreover, to locate the roots of this trend exclusively in the present century would be to overlook important relationships between impersonal influence and large-scale economic and social changes that date back to the founding of the country. Although the impact of changes in mass communication has undoubtedly been enormous, I begin this chapter by sketching the backdrop against which these changes occurred. Major transformations in the nature of social relationships paved the way for the four major trends in the structure and content of media that have facilitated impersonal influence: the nationalization of mass media, rising media attention to portrayals of collective experience, the decline of event-centered news coverage, and widespread belief in the power of media in the political process.

TRANSFORMATION OF AMERICAN
SOCIAL RELATIONSHIPS

Historian Gordon Wood has argued that although the American Revolution was very conservative by such standards as the number of fatalities or the amount of economic deprivation that transpired, "if we measure the radicalism by the amount of social change that actually took place – by transformations in the relationships that bound people to each other – then the American Revolution was not conservative at all; on the contrary: it was as radical and as revolutionary as any in history" (Wood 1991: 5).

The key transformation was from a society that was based almost exclusively on interpersonal relationships to one that involved a consciousness of, and interaction with, impersonal entities as well. Wood (1991: 11) describes colonial life as one where "all aspects of life were intertwined. The household, the society, and the state – private and public spheres – scarcely seemed separable." Before the Revolution, the American colonies comprised a small-scale society, dependent almost exclusively on face-to-face relationships. The provincial governments were not yet impersonal bureaucracies, and public business was just an extension of private social relationships (Warner 1968). People exchanged goods exclusively with those they knew and trusted, thus placing a premium on personal ties. In this era of information scarcity, political information was of necessity relayed through face-to-face exchanges with well-known personal contacts. As Brown (1989: 278) suggests, "Sometimes consciously, though often not, people acted with the understanding that information moved from person to person and so, if it was important, they ought to pass it along to others who would not only expect them to do so, but who had done the same for them in the past as they would also in the future."

The way people were connected to one another had changed quite radically by the beginning of the 1800s. Many of these changes were economic in origin. In the mid-eighteenth century, the colonies had no large trading companies or banks, no stock exchange, and no readily available currency. Economic exchanges thus had to be between people who knew one another and could trade in a face-to-face context. As Wood (1991: 66–7) explains, "Colonial economic life remained remarkably simple and personal, and few colonists other than overseas merchants knew anything of the large impersonal institutions and public worlds that were transforming the consciousness of Englishmen at home. This backwardness, this primitiveness, of colonial society put a premium on patronage and individual relationships." Although credit sometimes took the place of barter in economic transactions, early forms of credit were considered a form of charity and were themselves based on the trust that developed through personal relationships. By the turn of the century, the introduction and widespread availability of specie and paper money dramatically changed American economic life. Paper money made it possible for people to participate more impersonally in the economy – something that was scarcely possible in the personal patron–client relationships that characterized pre-Revolutionary America (Wood 1991).

During the nineteenth century, a variety of other changes also shifted the structure of social interaction away from an emphasis on the local and personal toward national and impersonal interactions. In the late nineteenth century, the development of a transnational railroad network made it possible for the manufacturing of many goods to move from a local to a national basis (Coleman 1980). Had the railroads been built to connect large cities as they were in many other countries, it is doubtful that rural America could easily have been incorporated into national markets. However, American railroads often connected "Nowhere-in-particular to Nowhere-at-all": The railroad was built "in the hope that it would call into being the population it would serve" (Boorstin 1974: 119).

The more recent development of retail credit further "disrupted the social as well as the economic arrangements between individuals and their local suppliers of food, clothing, furniture and services" (Arena 1995: 1). Although retail credit was not a significant part of the American economy until the early twentieth century, it began to spread at the end of the 1800s. As transportation improved, more and more economic exchanges took place between distant strangers. Once credit records were amassed, they "produced a parallel, transportable self that could be known and acted upon when the 'real' self was distant in time and space" (Arena 1995: 2–3). Retail credit reorganized social relations by placing individuals within a national economy where they could interact with distant and impersonal others. In 1927, John Dewey pronounced "the invasion of the community by the new and relatively impersonal and mechanical modes of combined human behavior" as "the outstanding fact of modern life" (p. 98).

By the early twentieth century, the manufacturing of many goods had moved from a local to a national basis (Coleman 1980). The rise of national markets was important in two ways. First, it created a need for national advertising, which subsidized the growth of national magazines and newspapers. But the rise of national markets might not, in itself, have contributed to the potential for impersonal influence, were it not for its indirect effects. After all, catalogues carried little straightforward information about social and political conditions that might shape people's political behavior. But national markets also meant that it now made sense for the city dailies to reach rural audiences with news and advertising from more distant locales. The rise of national markets created "consumption communities" comprised of consumers who would never meet, but who shared an awareness of one another through newspapers: "The old world, where so much of 'news' concerned people one knew, the world of the neighborhood community, was slipping away. In its place there was forming a world where more of the communities to which a man belonged were communities of the unseen"(Boorstin 1974: 136).

The community metaphor was particularly fitting from the perspective of national merchants who worked very hard to cultivate the kind of trust that was needed in order to get people to buy something sight unseen from a merchant they had never met. For example, even when they had hundreds of thousands of customers, Montgomery Ward "took pains to reassure each of them that the company was his friend" (Boorstin 1974: 123). Early catalogues carried pictures of the founders, and the buyers for various departments personally signed catalogue guarantees. The correspondence Mr. Ward received suggests that he was largely successful in cultivating the impression of a small community. People wrote him as if he were a personal friend, asking him for advice on lawyers, and where to find summer boarders and a baby to adopt. Ward also received hundreds of letters a year from men seeking wives. In response to all of these letters, customers received personalized and sympathetic replies. And as in a face-to-face economy, many asked if they could pay for goods in livestock, produce, or secondhand furniture instead of cash. Some even felt obliged to explain why they had not written for a while:

I suppose you wonder why we haven't ordered anything from you since the fall. Well, the cow kicked my arm and broke it and besides my wife was sick, and there was the doctor bill. But now, thank God, that is paid, and we are all well again, and we have a fine new baby boy, and please send plush bonnet number 29d8077 (Boorstin 1974: 124).

Ward's efforts have obvious modern day counterparts in the computerized personalization of direct mail appeals, laser-printed "hand written" mass mailings, and even prerecorded telephone messages from the president of the United States (Beniger 1987). As interactions have become increasingly impersonal, people have taken even greater pains to cultivate impressions of a highly personal community.

Despite herculean efforts to foster the impression of personal relationships and small-scale community, national markets inevitably resulted in even more impersonal relationships between buyers and sellers: "Producers no longer had direct and informal contact with their customers; they were too far removed. The structural distance between producer and consumer had begun to transcend the ability of producers to assess their market informally, assimilate information about it, and plan on the basis of that" (Coleman 1980: 335). The local seller received direct and immediate feedback from customers. But in a national marketplace, the need for information about distant customers – now conceived of as collective markets – led to the development of large-scale market research, the goal of which was to characterize the attitudes and behaviors of large collectives. By midcentury, the increased availability of highly abstract, aggregated information about collectives without names or faces inevitably made its own contribution to the potential for impersonal influence. Thus the rise of national markets also facilitated impersonal influence by creating a need for market research that, in turn, further encouraged the reification of collectives linked by complex organizations, markets, and communication.

Although findings from market research were probably of interest strictly to those who owned or worked for companies with large-scale markets, the desire for information about people and events outside of one's personal experience also was increasing among the public at large. During World War II, the wartime economy encouraged migration away from rural areas into the cities, often moving individuals away from their places of birth (Coleman 1980). This demographic shift gave people an increased interest in events that were not proximate and local.

Changes in the nature of the federal government further contributed to less parochial interests during the course of the twentieth century. As Schudson (1978: 148–9) notes, "Until World War I, and to some extent until World War II, it was possible for Americans to think of their affairs as distinct from European and world politics, and it was even possible for Americans to be relatively uninterested in national politics, for the federal government had only remote connections to the daily lives of most citizens." As a result of depression and New Deal policies, more attention became focused on national policy makers. Between the 1930s and the 1960s in particular, the federal government grew tremendously in size and complexity.

As a result of the increased amount of federal government activity, more problems came to be seen as "national problems" rather than local or personal ones, and national as well as local leaders were expected to address them. As social problems became divorced from people's day-to-day experience, citizens became increasingly dependent upon mediated information. "National conditions" now garnered a great deal of attention. This same shift was reflected in people's individual psychology as well; people came "increasingly to conceive of themselves as members of very large collectivities linked primarily by common identities but minimally by networks of directly interpersonal relations" (Calhoun 1991: 95–6). In short, the nation as community was now easily imaginable.

FOUR TRENDS IN MASS COMMUNICATION

The impact of these social and political changes over the course of three centuries was great; yet in many ways they pale in comparison to the contribution that new communication technologies made to the potential for impersonal influence. Four major trends in the structure and content of mass media have contributed to the potential for people to be influenced by those beyond their personal life spaces. First, I explore the well-

The Rise of Impersonal Associations

documented contributions involving the nationalization of mass media and the increased coverage of collective experience and opinion. Next I provide original evidence from a study bearing on the often asserted, but less well documented, claim that news has become progressively less event centered and more focused on portrayals of large-scale, collective phenomena. Finally, I document the significance of the widespread belief in the power of mass media in elevating the importance of impersonal forms of social influence.

The Nationalization of Mass Media

Although we often think of the nationalization and internationalization of communication as a relatively recent phenomenon, this trend dates back to the very early history of the United States. Before television, radio, or telephones, the national postal service was the first medium of communication that could reach national audiences. Tocqueville's survey of America in 1831 made special note of the impressive amount of nonlocal information that reached Americans through the postal service. At this time, the United States had roughly seventy-four post offices for every hundred thousand inhabitants, compared with only seventeen for Great Britain and four in France (John 1995). Most localities had a post office by then, but as late as 1890, under 40 percent of Americans had mail delivered to their doors, and these people were primarily in cities. By the first decade of the twentieth century, postal service was extended to virtually all Americans. Once the national postal system was in place, parcel post and the rise of mail-order merchandising followed less than ten years later. Rural free delivery was an especially noteworthy change for the rural dweller: "Now he was lifted out of the narrow community of those he saw and knew, and put into continual touch with a larger world of persons; events and things read about but unheard and unseen" (Boorstin 1974: 133).

These dramatic changes were not without controversy. As newspapers and magazines sought to reach larger and more distant audiences by mail, conflict emerged over what the postal policy should be with respect to the delivery of periodicals. As Kielbowicz (1989) explains, this was a debate between those who wanted to promote a national culture and those who wanted to preserve local affiliations and a "quiet, stable, localized, face-to-face society" (Kelley 1979: 160). The former wanted to promote widespread circulation by making it easy and inexpensive to send information across large distances, with low rates and few zones that differentiated price according to distance. The latter championed policies that protected local interests and discouraged supralocal communication.

In 1845, Congress established free local circulation of newspapers within a thirty-mile radius of a newspaper's office. Only two years later, this policy was discontinued. In 1852, Congress established postal rates for newspapers that were virtually uniform: Delivery was free within a county, and they could be sent across the country for a very small amount. Although it was in some ways a compromise between advocates of local and national interests, the net result was to encourage the circulation of information across larger distances and thus to link people to national associations and larger geopolitical units (Kielbowicz 1989).

Although early American newspapers were typically geared to local interests, with time their content has become progressively more regional, national, and international in scope. In the mid-1800s, the first wire service contributed to this trend by making it possible to transmit national news quickly over long distances (Shaw 1968). Today, traditional wire services such as the Associated Press and United Press International have been augmented by newspaper news services that also provide more detailed and analytic news of national interest. Despite the early capacity for transmitting news on a national basis, producing and distributing a daily newspaper on a truly national scale remained difficult even as late as the early 1970s. By the 1990s, satellite communication and computerized printing systems had made regional and national newspapers feasible (Abramson, Arterton, and Owen 1988; Schudson 1995).

Television and radio are generally blamed or praised most for creating a national communication network, despite the fact that the trend toward nationalization clearly predates the emergence of broadcast communication. Nonetheless, the development of electronic media has led the nation to communicate on an even more national, mass basis by eliminating the need to physically transport information, thus making it easier to reach populations distant from the original news source. Radio had become a part of everyday life in America by the 1930s, thus providing an ongoing link between the world "out there" and the private sphere. Although radio networks originally had agreed to refrain from news gathering and to stick to simply reporting news from the wire services, they soon were in the news-gathering business as well. With tremendous support from national advertisers, radio grew to the point that by 1939, most Americans claimed that radio was their major source of news (Czitrom 1982). Compared to newspaper reports, radio news had a greater sense of drama, immediacy, and urgency; announcers sought to make their listeners part of the audience to events even though they were not physically present. Radio commentators provided background and analysis for major news events in far-off places, thus providing information well beyond people's personal life experiences. By

32

combining visual and verbal stimuli, television further extended people's social environments. Mediated communication increasingly resembled live, face-to-face interaction by making people audiences to events happening elsewhere and by showing its viewers how other people thought, felt, and behaved (Stott 1973).

Across both print and broadcast media, a combination of market forces, technological advances, and the changing professional norms of journalists have contributed to more homogeneity in the picture of the world that most Americans receive through mainstream news media. Control of news organizations is now more concentrated than ever before. For example, in 1900 there were over 2,000 owners of daily newspapers. In 1980, this number had declined to around 760. If one takes into account the increased size of the population, the concentration is even more pronounced, moving from one newspaper per 38,000 citizens in 1900 to one in 300,000 in 1980 (Bagdikian 1984). Radio, magazines and television are characterized by even smaller numbers of owners. Due to a wave of mergers in the eighties, twenty-six corporations controlled half or more of the media business by 1987, compared to twenty-nine in 1986 and fifty in 1982 (Bagdikian 1987). Although it remains unclear what the consequences of the telecommunications legislation passed by Congress in 1996 will be, it has already prompted even more mergers and joint alliances.

As locally based media organizations have become giant corporations and conglomerates, the audiences to whom they direct their information have become increasingly national in scope.[1] The centralization of ownership has contributed to a shift in the conceptualization of news from one that was heterogeneous and locally dominated to one that is national and international in scope. Chain ownership did not necessarily mark the end of local autonomy among newspapers, but it has made it more difficult for local newspapers to maintain their ties to the community. A genuine community newspaper supposedly "forms a link in the local chain of gossip and discussion, as its staff members participate in face-to-face relations with their readers" (Kornhauser 1959: 95). However, as more and more chain-owned newspapers are rapidly bought and sold to other chains, reporters and editors are less likely to be long-term members of the local community. In addition, many chains are acquiring groups of nearby papers in order to benefit from economies of scale (Glaberson 1996). These papers can share articles and rely on a single reporter to cover a given beat such as news from the statehouse. As local

---

[1] Although the rise of narrowcasting and highly specialized publications may seem at odds with this trend, it is important to note that these types of media are also directed at national and international audiences, though ones with specific shared interests.

papers become commodities traded among outsiders, organizational and market considerations at the national level substitute for local idiosyncrasies in coverage.

The rise of a dominant national journalistic culture has accompanied the nationalization of news institutions (Schudson 1995). Concentration of ownership and the decline of competitive newspaper markets have provided further incentives toward a more uniform, politically bland product. In a town with competing partisan newspapers, journalists had incentives to differentiate their reporting from the competition. Today, two-newspaper towns are rare, and objectivity is well accepted as a desirable, if unattainable, professional norm; thus there are few incentives toward heterogeneous coverage (Abramson et al. 1988). The shift toward a more objective style of reporting has facilitated impersonal influence by encouraging greater homogeneity of media messages (Roshco 1975). Across media, most studies find high levels of homogeneity in the presentation of news (Patterson 1980; 1989, Graber 1980b). Even local newspapers do not vary substantially in content from other media including television news, radio, news magazines, and national newspapers (Neuman, Just, and Crigler 1992; Mondak 1995). Ultimately, there is relatively little variation in journalistic discretion in deciding what is news.

Traditionally, the division of people into different experiential worlds helped to foster varied world views (Meyrowitz 1985); now, regardless of people's physical locations, they receive similar impressions about the state of the larger "community" in which they live. Although one can certainly find different issue opinions in various news sources, there is less disagreement with respect to news agendas and what *others* are said to be thinking or experiencing. More often than not, these impressions are reinforced across different media and across varied sources within a given medium. The end result is a reified world, an imagined community that people know a lot about, but that is not the one in which they live on a day-to-day basis.

Media Portrayals of Collective Experience and Opinion

The current emphasis on nonpartisan, professionalized news is also highly congenial to presentations of the collective experiences and opinions of others. In the case of collective *opinion*, coverage of this kind distances the reporter from the opinions expressed because they are not the reporter's opinions or those of some particular individual, but rather those of some objectively defined collective. Likewise, in the case of portraying collective *experience*, it is easier to provide a neutral description of unemployment rates than it is to discuss the validity of various proposals for alleviating joblessness. Nonetheless, the underlying causes of trends toward portrayals of collective opinion and portrayals of collective experience are somewhat different and thus are worth examining separately.

Portraying Collective Experience. The use of aggregated statistical information to describe large-scale collectives was part of a much broader trend toward quantification of social and political phenomena. Although the earliest attempts to gather census information were in Europe, the United States was the first country to initiate a systematic periodic census, largely because of the need to assess population size for purposes of allocating districts for the House of Representatives (Porter 1986). It was not until the mid-1800s that the census included detailed information about the population. Moreover, early census information was not widely publicized and so had little influence on people's perceptions of their larger environments. In 1878, the first *Statistical Abstract of the United States* was published, initiating a tradition of self-examination that has expanded and accelerated since then.

Although censuses were sometimes done at the local level, statistics was the science of the "statist" (Porter 1994), and the concept of society to which it contributed was a large-scale one, one that could not be known on the basis of personal experience. By the nineteenth century, the Belgian astronomer/mathematician Quetelet developed what he called "social physics" and "moral statistics," which involved the quantification of psychological facts and customs to predict social behavior. His theory of the *homme moyen* (average man) laid the groundwork for social comparisons outside the realm of interpersonal contact. Quetelet went so far as to analogize that the average man was the "true type of the human species," and deviations from it were simply a matter of error; the consistencies in aggregate statistics on phenomena such as crime and suicide rates were evidence of the reality of society and its power over individuals. According to Quetelet's statistical determinism, free will "produces nothing more than trifling accidental deviations" (Porter 1994: 1,346–7).

As the social sciences began to take root in the United States in mid-twentieth century, many American students went to Europe to receive training in quantitative approaches to social science. About the same time, the development of sample surveys made it feasible to collect statistical data without the time and expense of a full census (Converse 1987). In the 1960s, researchers in the "social indicators movement" began advocating the systematic collection of statistical data on all aspects of social life, beyond the already widely known economic series (Bauer 1966). This movement actively promoted examination of the country as a collective entity and the development of techniques to document important aspects of social change.

Although social indicators proponents readily confessed to not having explored the second-order consequences of widespread awareness of seemingly objective, incontrovertible information of this kind, they saw their efforts as a "major contribution to man's efforts to find out where he has been, where he is, and where he is going" (Bauer 1966: ix, xvii). Today the availability of social indicators and their frequent inclusion in news reports has created an important feedback loop that provides citizens with ongoing information about the state of large-scale imagined communities. These statistical "facts" are readily incorporated into news reports, usually without any means of independent confirmation (Maier 1995; Crossen 1994).

Portraying Collective Opinion. The quantification of collective opinion lagged considerably behind efforts to quantify collective experience. The earliest systematic opinion polls did not appear until the 1930s, but they formed an immediate alliance with mass media (Weaver and McCombs 1980). Today, perhaps the most conspicuous factor contributing to impersonal influence is mass media's ongoing preoccupation with portrayals of public opinion. Poll results on controversial issues ranging from whether the public supports a capital gains tax to whether O. J. Simpson is innocent, to whether children still believe in Santa Claus, are all part of ongoing coverage of mass opinion. But this emphasis is clearly most pronounced in election coverage. The extent of so-called horse race coverage now goes without question. There is widespread agreement that mass media coverage of elections is dominated by information about popular opinion including who is ahead, who is gaining ground, and predictions about who ultimately will win (Patterson and McClure 1976; Robinson and Sheehan 1983).

News concerning mass opinion is so extensive and prominent that the public is well aware of the opinions of others as they are being portrayed by the latest polling data. For example, a month before the 1988 election, 71 percent of Americans reported that they were aware of opinion polls predicting the likely winner, and 95 percent could name Bush as the leader. Although the public claims to dislike horse race coverage, that clearly does not prevent them from paying attention to it. Robinson and Clancey (1985: 62) suggest that there is a psychological preference given to this type of information such that "winners and losers stick better in the national memory than other day-to-day news events" (see also Brady and Johnston 1987; Nadeau, Niemi, and Amato 1994).

The development of public opinion polling has contributed to this emphasis. While coverage of collective opinion is by no means limited to poll-based coverage, polls provide a news peg for a good number of stories of this type. For example, in the 1980 primary season the three networks broadcast 290 stories based on polls before the party conventions (Broh 1983). General election coverage is also saturated with information about mass opinion. In 1984, over half of the stories about the election that ran in the *New York Times* during the last month of the campaign made some mention of poll findings (Patterson and Davis 1985; Keenan 1986). During this same time period in 1988, the *Washington Post* ran poll-based stories on its front page in over two thirds of its issues (Ratzan 1989).

Syndicated polls have been around since the thirties and forties, but in the 1970s many media organizations began their own polling operations. By 1986, a majority of papers with circulations of fifty thousand or more used polling. In 1989, 40 percent of daily newspapers were directly involved in polling by either conducting or contracting for poll data (Holley 1991). Since in-house polling represents a large financial investment for most media organizations, it produces an incentive to devote even greater proportions of the news hole to portrayals of public attitudes and beliefs (Crespi 1980).

The extent and memorability of coverage of this kind means that portrayals of mass opinion undoubtedly reach large audiences. Yet the question remains as to whether coverage of mass opinion truly has increased. After all, media have always demonstrated a strong interest in portraying public opinion (Herbst 1993), even when their evidence consisted of only informal straw polls, editorials in the local paper, crowd assessments, or other forms of unsystematic evidence (Geer 1991).

Although historical data over sufficient time periods are scant, available evidence suggests that while little about election coverage has changed since the nineteenth century, horse race coverage may be the exception. In their study of election coverage between 1888 and 1988, Sigelman and Bullock (1991) found that newspaper coverage of this kind skyrocketed, particularly in the late twentieth century. Interestingly, they found that horse race coverage was also very prominent in the late 1800s, indicating that it is a time-honored form of political coverage. But the more recent upsurge in this century has surpassed even this earlier emphasis.

Whether or not there has been a proliferation in the number of polls in recent years is a subject of considerable debate.[2] Even if the number of media polls has not increased of late, there is some justification for

---

2 Judgments depend on whether people are referring to the actual number of polls being conducted, the number of media as opposed to privately sponsored or syndicated polls, or the amount of media attention given to polls once conducted (e.g., Broh 1983; Traugott and Rusch 1989; Keenan 1986).

widespread public perceptions that polls have proliferated. The number of references to polls in the national print media has increased, and the prominence of references to polls has increased in both print and broadcast media (Traugott 1991).

The Decline of Event-Centered Reporting

A subtle, but more pervasive, shift contributing to the potential for impersonal influence has been spawned by a change in the nature of media content. Many observers of contemporary journalism have noted shifts in reporting style away from reporting single events, toward creating news roundups and analyses that characterize collective phenomena. Closely related terms describe the news as having shifted from descriptive to analytic coverage, from event-centered to interpretive reporting, or from episodic to thematic coverage. In what Barnhurst (1991: 110) has termed the "new long journalism," "[i]ndividual lives . . . came to be treated as examples of larger problems, and the newspaper became distanced from the individual citizen. . . . In the long journalism, the house across town didn't burn, instead society confronted a chronic wiring problem in its aging stock of housing."

In his history of major Chicago newspapers, Nord (1985: 426) describes similar changes in the style of late nineteenth-century publications. At midcentury, the news pages "conducted a marketplace of information with something for everyone – a spectacular bazaar that reflected more than interpreted the complexity and diversity, the individualism and privatism of the modern metropolitan city." This "smorgasbord model of something for everyone" reflected a conception of the city as "simply the aggregation of private lives, and the task of the newspaper was to serve these private interests, diverse, discrete, and individual" (p. 435). Column after column of "never-ending miscellany" reflected "the strange randomness of news" attempting to serve the individual tastes of individual readers (pp. 433, 421).

In contrast, by the end of the century, the *Chicago Daily News* had established the form of the modern urban newspaper, a condensed, compact version of the news, "edited so that a majority of the content would appeal to a majority of the readers" (p. 428). According to Nord (1985), whereas the diverse, fragmented, and disorganized pages of newspapers at midcentury aptly reflected the complex and bewildering modern city, the style of the *Daily News* reflected an attempt to reestablish order amidst this chaos by locating common interests within a large urban community.

Whatever the precise nature or timing of this shift toward a new reporting style, to the extent that media content now seeks to portray issues and events as collective, societal phenomena rather than as individual problems and events, media's influence on perceptions of collective social reality should increase. Unfortunately, most evidence pertaining to such a shift has been isolated or anecdotal. Some indirect evidence substantiating this trend comes from the examination of patterns in newspaper design. The penny press of the previous century popularized the idea that news consisted of the local happenings of the police, crimes, fires, and so forth; news was "geared to the interests of the 'nearby and everyday' " (Abramson, Arterton, and Owen 1988). Thus the front page of 1885 was "a dense jungle of news items . . . [that] gave an impression of diversity, randomness, and complexity, leaving it to the reader to make sense – or draw a map – of the world" (Barnhurst and Nerone 1991: 14). The random appearance of the nineteenth-century newspaper "in effect said to the reader, 'These items are gleanings from a world too big and noisy for us to make sense of; you make sense of it yourself' " (Barnhurst and Nerone 1991: 14). The design of contemporary newspapers, on the other hand, illustrates newspapers' desire to map the world for their readers; as journalism has become more professionalized, journalists have taken it upon themselves to digest and organize the news for readers by grouping individual events into general, societal-level trends or themes.

Shifts in newspaper design confirm that there has been a trend away from the compendium of individual events toward a spatial map of issues (Nerone and Barnhurst 1995), but we know little about how such a trend may be manifested in changes in newspaper content. To the extent that journalists present news events as part of large-scale collective phenomena, they contribute further to facilitating impersonal social influence.

To find out to what extent systematic evidence drawn from the content of newspapers would support this assertion, Kevin Barnhurst[3] and I initiated a content analysis designed to examine changes in reporting style across a full century. Since a relatively small proportion of American newspapers have been continuously publishing over a hundred-year period, a random sample of newspapers was not possible. Instead, we purposely selected three papers with differing circulations and that served cities of varying sizes. These included the Portland *Oregonian*, the *Chicago Tribune*, and the *New York Times*.

Our total sample of news stories was comprised of six independent random samples drawn at twenty-year intervals beginning in 1894 and ending in 1994. For each of these years we wanted to obtain a reason-

3 Kevin Barnhurst is Associate Professor, Department of Communications, University of Illinois at Chicago.

able number of stories on a variety of different topics. To cover such a broad historical period, these topics needed to be very general and not time bound, yet adequately well defined to produce reliable coding of stories. For these purposes, we chose accidents, crime, and jobs. Using this strategy we sampled a total of 240 stories per topic per newspaper, or 2,160 stories in total.

We used this sample to look at specific changes in reporting style that could facilitate media's influence on perceptions of large-scale, collective reality. It seemed to us that any of several aspects of the traditional five-W's of newswriting could enhance the potential for impersonal influence. In particular, *where* might incorporate a broader context or range of locales; *when* could show greater emphasis on times other than the present; *what* would include a larger number of events in single stories; and *who* might de-emphasize individuals, so that people become identified less often by name and more often by demography or group affiliation. In general, we also anticipated greater emphasis on news analysis and the *why* part of the traditional five-W's formula.[4]

4 For each story, coders answered a variety of questions about individual actors or groups in the text, the number of events reported, when these events transpired, and how the locations of events were described. They also identified (a) whether the story reported any information about background context, implications, interpretations, or recommendations; and (b) whether the story reported any causes, general problems, or collective social issues or themes. On a scale from 1 to 10, they rated the extent to which the story emphasized highly specific event-centered coverage (1) or very general news analysis (10). Finally, they also rated the length of each article from 1 (very brief) to 5 (very long).

For each location reported in an article, coders identified the smallest site named (e.g., street or address, city or town, state, region, U.S. national, international, or outside United States). By weighting these indicators according to their progressively broader definitions of location and then dividing by the total number of events, we created an index of the extent to which events were defined in a highly localized versus geographically broad fashion. The formula used to construct this index was as follows, the entity in parentheses being the number of locations of a particular kind identified in a given story:

$$y = \frac{1 \text{ (street)} + 2 \text{ (city or town)} + 3 \text{ (state)} + 4 \text{ (regional)} + 5 \text{ (national)} + 6 \text{ (international)}}{\text{sum (street, city, state, regional, national, international)}}$$

After an initial coder had progressed through a small sample of stories, we had an identically trained second coder go through the same procedures for locating and coding stories. Given the general complexity of the coding scheme, the reliability of coding was surprisingly high. Reliabilities ranged from .92 to .67, with an average coefficient of .80 across all of the measures reported in this study. For the indicators of how specific individuals in the story were identified, the average reliability of items used in these analyses ranged from correlations of .76 to .91, with an average correlation of .84. For groups, the reliabilities ranged from .72 to .86, with an average of .80. The coders' indicators of how many single events were reported in a given article produced a correlation coefficient of .79. Coding of the specific times reported in the articles produced reliabilities averaging

Figures 2.1 through 2.7 summarize these results. Because our hypotheses were specifically about historical change, we analyzed these data with an eye toward significant over-time trends that transcended individual topics or newspapers.[5] The major findings were remarkably consistent across news topics as well as across newspapers. First, do contemporary news stories incorporate a broader range of locales? Using an index constructed to represent the range from narrowly to broadly defined locations in the story, Figure 2.1 illustrates the specificity of locations over the past century. The trend line shows the overall extent to which locations were defined in terms of highly specific as opposed to very broad locales. This index indicates that there has been a significant increasing linear trend toward more broadly defined locations ($p < .05$); whereas coverage used to emphasize highly specific locations such as street addresses, more recent coverage situates these same topics more expansively in regional, national, or international contexts. The bar graphs illustrate what has happened to the two diametrically opposed components of the index. The number of locations described at the most specific level of street addresses has significantly decreased with time ($p < .01$), while there has been a significant increase in events situated in locations that are international in context ($p < .001$).

This shift is best illustrated by two crime stories. The first, from 1894, envisions a robbery by focusing tightly on a highly specific location: "The Post Office is in a small building a short distance from the Long Island Railroad station. There is a very little room outside of the parti-

.72. Despite changes in fonts and formats over these historical periods, rating an article's length on a five-point scale also proved to be highly reliable, the coders correlating at .92. Two potentially unreliable measures in the coding scheme required coders to assess whether the articles reported (a) context, implications, interpretations, or recommendations; and (b) causes, problems, or collective social issues or themes. Spearman's coefficients indicated that in both cases, coders were fairly successful in doing this reliably, with coefficients of .77 in both cases. The location index produced by the two coders resulted in a correlation coefficient of .83. Finally, the most subjective coding characteristic of all simply asked coders to assess on a ten-point scale the extent to which the article emphasized event-specific coverage or news analysis. Despite the difficulties inherent in making a summary judgment of this kind, the two coders' scores produced a correlation coefficient of .72, roughly on par with the reliabilities of other indicators. In short, our coding procedures produced reasonably to highly reliable indicators of some very subjective characteristics of news coverage from the past as well as the present.

5 We tested our hypotheses initially by looking for significant linear trends holding across the entire pooled data set and then subsequently analyzed coverage within the smaller data sets for individual newspapers and for specific topics. For continuous variables, we used analyses of variance with linear trend tests; for dichotomous variables, we employed logistic regression to test for the impact of year, after controlling for issue and newspaper.

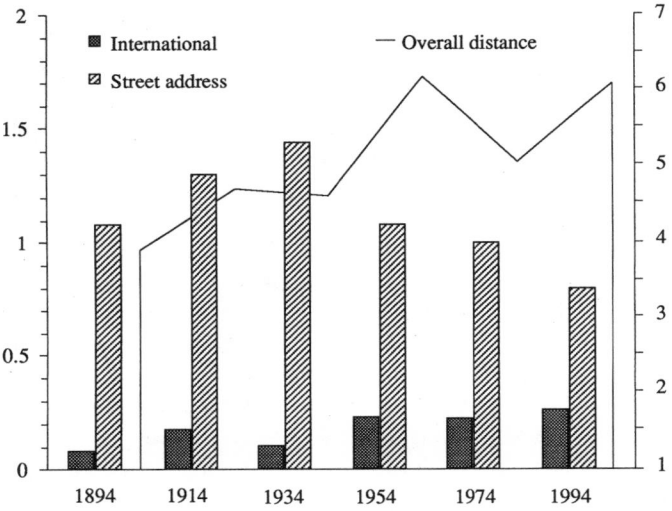

Figure 2.1. Distance and location.
Mean number of references to closest and most distant locations (left scale), and the mean distance of coverage, indexed on a scale (right) with low scores for events at street addresses, followed by towns and cities, states, regions, nations, and so forth.

tion. In one end of the latter is a door, and inside, near the door, stands a small safe" (*New York Times*, April 21, 1894, p. 1). The second, from 1994, reports a murder quite differently. Two maps accompanying the article show the Caribbean and the island of St. Thomas, with the caption, "The slaying of a tourist in Charlotte Amalie has become a symbol of crime in the Virgin Islands." It begins with the following paragraph: "According to the license plates on the cars and buses that hail tourists around this bustling port, the Virgin Islands are still an 'American Paradise.' But a surge in violent crime over the last year, including the slaying of a San Diego swimming instructor this week, has put that in jeopardy" (*New York Times*, April 19, 1994, p. A17).

The story runs twenty-six paragraphs, the full news hole on its page. It takes the entire island as its location. The event is provided with historical development by linking all homicides related to the place. Government officials describe social problems, blaming the influence of television. A subhead provides the theme based on national origin: "Island officials say mainland values are leading the young astray."

The new long journalism could also facilitate impersonal influence by de-emphasizing individuals and increasing attention to groups, particularly as they represent larger categories of actors. Figure 2.2 shows the

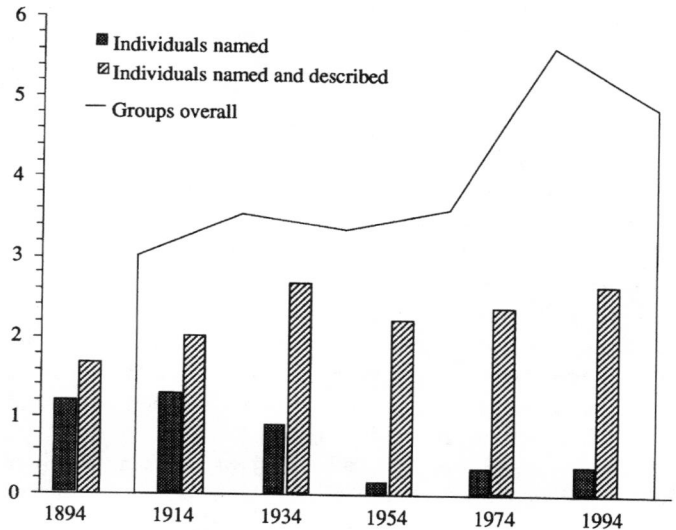

Figure 2.2. Who gets covered?

Mean number of references to groups and mean number of references to individuals by name and by name and description (e.g., by gender, race, age) per article.

major historical trends for the number of individual and group actors. First, the number of individuals identified by name only has experienced a significant decline ($p < .001$). This trend is extremely consistent: It is significant for coverage of each of the individual issues (for accidents and crime, $p < .001$, and for jobs, $p < .01$) and for coverage of each individual newspaper as well (for the *Times*, $p < .05$, *Oregonian*, $p < .01$, and *Tribune*, $p < .001$). In contrast, named individuals are increasingly identified by some kind of demographic information ($p < .001$). For example, in 1894, a *New York Times* report of a railroad accident in Hazelton, Penn., listed every casualty by name, occupation, and medical condition in a format that emphasized individuals:

The man killed was DAILEY, PATRICK, of Milton, Penn. He was riding on the freight train. The injured are:
ARTHUR – Sunbury, Penn., conductor of freight train; back injured.
BIDDLE – brakeman of express train; body bruised and back wounded (April 16, 1894, p. 1).

Likewise, an 1894 *Chicago Tribune* story about an accident at a school listed each injured child's home address, age, and medical condition in a separate paragraph (April 10, pp. 1, 7). In 1914, individuals' names were still in the lead paragraph in an article describing an accident: "Four men were seriously injured when their automobile rolled down an embankment near Gary, Ind., today. One of the injured men is F. W. Kurtz of Chicago. The others are Fred Hass, Thomas Murrey, and Frank Whitson of Knox., Ind." (*Chicago Daily Tribune*, April 20, 1914, p. 11). In stark contrast to the earlier examples of accident coverage, a jetliner crash in 1994 focused only on the national origins of those involved and listed no names of casualties (*New York Times*, September 28, p. A9). In other words, individuals are less important in stories as individuals per se, but they are increasingly important as exemplars of particular categories or types of people.

Also evident in Figure 2.2 is the increase in the number of groups identified in news stories. Again, this trend was significant not only in the sample as a whole ($p < .001$), but also within each of the individual subsamples when broken down by newspaper (*Times*, $p < .001$, *Oregonian*, $p < .001$, and *Tribune*, $p < .05$) or by issue (accidents and crime both, $p < .001$ and jobs, $p = .10$). The trend is straightforward in that far more groups of all kinds appear in news articles, either identified by name or by description.

Are news stories also less centered in the present, thus emphasizing broader, collective phenomena such as over-time trends? As an initial test of this hypothesis, we looked at the number of references to different time points – past, present and future – within each article. As Figure 2.3 indicates, some issues have always included more temporal references than others do. Coverage of jobs, in particular, incorporated far more references to multiple time points, and coverage of accidents involved far fewer. Still, the most conspicuous pattern was the very consistent growth in time references per article. This trend was significant for coverage of each individual issue ($p < .001$ for all three) as well as for each individual newspaper (for the *Times* and *Oregonian*, $p < .001$, and for the *Tribune*, $p < .05$). Moreover, the timing of the trend was virtually identical for each issue and for each newspaper. There was a small dip between 1894 and 1914, followed by a slow, but steady increase continuing through 1994.

In order to understand the specific changes underlying this general pattern, we also looked at the extent to which articles made explicit references to change over time and to time points that were either in the past, present, or future. Almost without exception, stories dealt with the present, and this was as true in 1994 as in 1894. The lack of variance in this measure made it clear that there had been no fundamental change in this regard. However, as shown in Figure 2.4, journalists also are no more prone toward speculation about the future than they have been

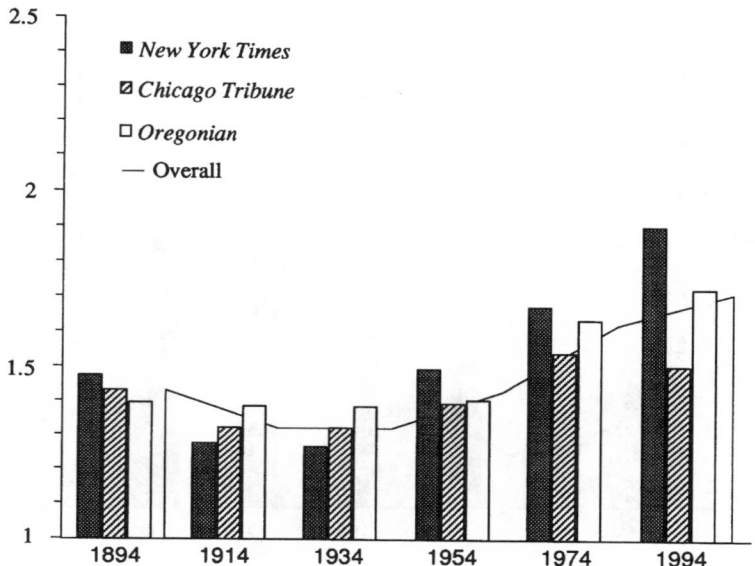

Figure 2.3. Points in time.
Mean number of references per article to different time periods by newspaper and issue.

historically (none of the topics shows evidence of a significant trend). What drove up the number of temporal points within news articles was a significant increase in references to the *past* ($b = .25$, $p < .001$). In fact, as the bar graph in Figure 2.4 shows, more than twice as many articles in 1994 include references to the past compared with a century ago. Likewise, the trend line in Figure 2.4 shows that the number of articles referring to change over time has increased significantly ($b = .41$, $p < .001$). In 1894, less than 2 percent of articles incorporated the notion of change over time. By 1994, more than 7 percent of articles did so. This was down a bit from the peak in 1974, yet still considerably higher than newspapers at the turn of the century.

Consistent with observations of election coverage, analysis and contextualization of stories also has increased over the past century. The trend line in Figure 2.5 demonstrates that most stories were still judged to be more event-centered than analytic; nonetheless, the overall trend toward more analytic coverage was statistically significant ($p < .001$), as were the linear trends within each of the three separate issue samples ($p < .001$ in all three cases).

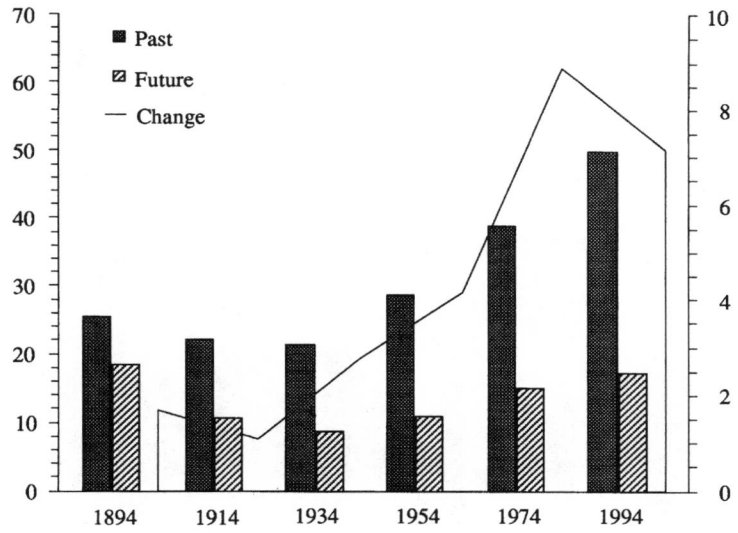

Figure 2.4. References to change over time.
Percentage of articles referring to past and future time periods (left axis) and
percentage of stories including some reference to change over time (right axis).

The bar graphs in Figure 2.5 also show the percentage of stories that
included references to "how," that is, any information about background
context, implications, interpretations or recommendations, or
references to "why," that is, any causes, general problems, or collective
social issues or themes. Using logistic regression, we analyzed these dichotomous dependent measures controlling for issue and newspaper and
confirmed a positive trend through time toward greater emphasis on
both how and why (coefficients for year were .20, $p < .001$, and .21, $p
< .001$, respectively).[6]

There were tremendous differences between topics in the extent to
which context, implications, and interpretations were offered. For example, consistent with other research (Iyengar 1991), coverage of jobs
emphasized context much more than did coverage of crime or accidents.
Nonetheless, the historical trend toward greater emphasis on context
also was significant in three separate tests for each of the individual
issues. For measures of how, these same trends were statistically signif-

6 In a logistic regression, the effects of year on the probability that an article will
include information on how or why are nonlinear, but they are monotonic, thus
allowing us to safely conclude that there has been a positive trend over time.

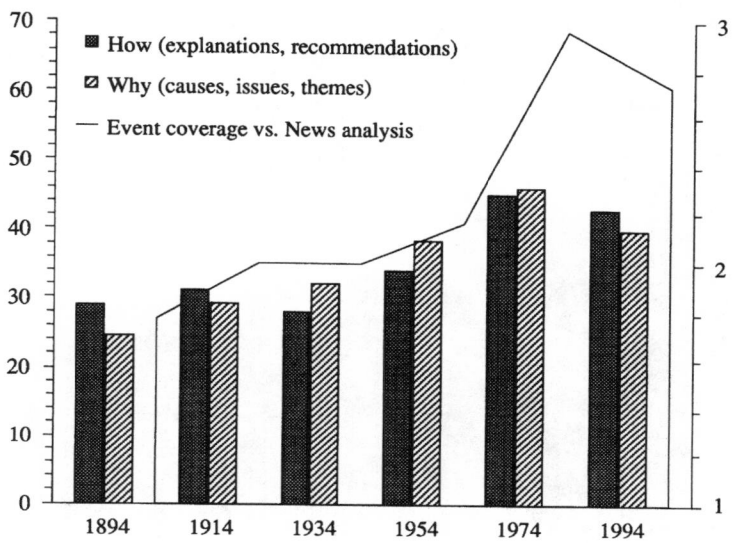

Figure 2.5. Events versus analysis.

Percentage of articles explaining the how and why of events (left scale), compared with the mean content of articles rated on a scale (right) from 1 (the most specific event-centered coverage) to 10 (the most general news analysis).

icant across individual tests of each newspaper as well. For why, the measures increased significantly with time for the *New York Times* and the *Oregonian*, but the differences did not meet standards of statistical significance for the *Chicago Tribune*.

To this point we had assumed that the new long journalism was largely a function of incorporating a greater number of events per story: News reported today is simply grouped differently so that each article reports more events than a century ago. However, as Figure 2.6 shows, the pattern did not meet these expectations at all. In fact, the number of events per article declined significantly over time ($p < .001$). Regardless of which newspaper we looked at, the trend toward fewer events per article proved significant (for the *Times* and *Tribune* each, $p < .001$ and for the *Oregonian* $p < .05$). Likewise for coverage of accidents and jobs, the number of events decreased significantly with time ($p < .01$, $p < .001$, respectively). The sole exception was crime, which basically reported the same number of events in each article throughout the period. No topic went against the trend, and the general consistency of the pattern for newspapers and topics is indicative of a fundamental redefinition

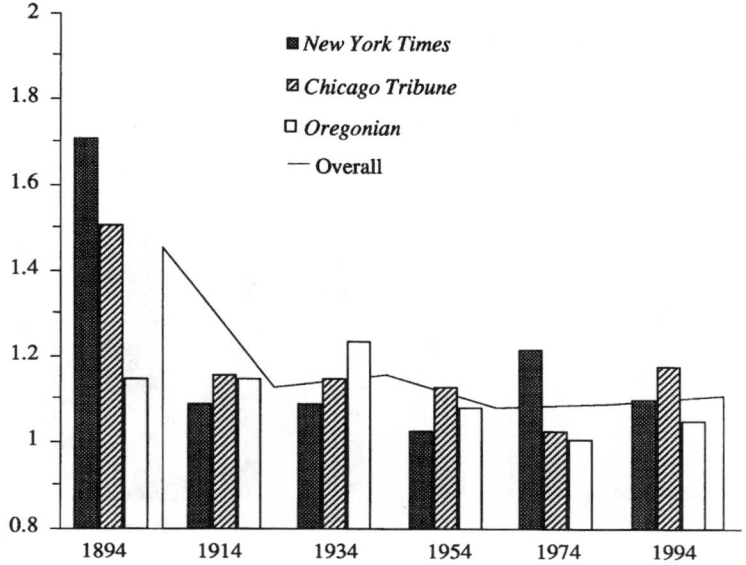

Figure 2.6. Number of events.
Mean number of different events reported per article by newspaper and issue.

in reporting, not a simple change in the way reporters group the events they cover.

Although it may not report on a larger number of events, today's journalism is truly longer. Figure 2.7 illustrates the mean length scores for articles by year for each of the three topics and for each of the three newspapers. In addition to a positive and statistically significant overall trend ($p < .001$), the length of articles increased clearly and consistently within each of the three topic areas, and across all three newspapers. In short, the new journalism is at least aptly named.[7]

Journalism for all three topics in all three newspapers has gotten

---

7 The new long journalism clearly incorporates many changes in the content of news stories as well as in their length; the content of contemporary newspapers is not simply more of the same old content. But to what extent do these changes in content result from the increased length of stories?

To answer this question we reanalyzed our findings, controlling for the increased length of stories over time. In the summary analyses incorporating data from all newspapers and issues, we found that only two of the previously reported findings diminished to statistical insignificance. The increased number of references to how and why no longer constituted significant increasing linear trends

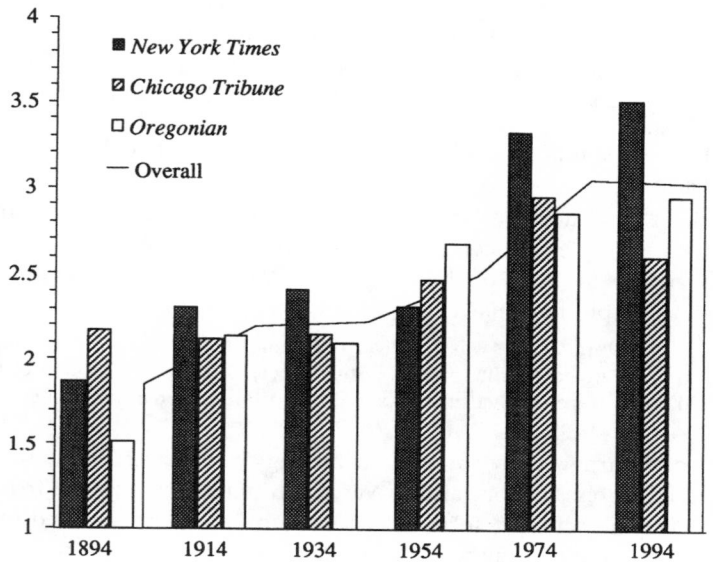

Figure 2.7. Article length.
Mean length of articles by newspaper and issue, rated on a scale of 1–5.

longer. Coverage has also become more oriented toward analysis – answering questions such as how and why. The share of stories reporting interpretations is substantially higher now than in 1894 as is the share of stories describing causes, problems, and social issues or themes. Compared to a one-paragraph story on a factory adding jobs in 1894, a 1994 story on the revival of a port on Staten Island runs twenty-seven paragraphs. It analyzes the return of jobs as part of an effort by New York City to regain "world class" status lost in the 1960s (*New York Times,* September 27, p. B1).

The same stenographic style is evident in early reporting on crime and

after controlling for length. But surprisingly, all of the other original findings persisted, including the trend toward less event-centered coverage and more news analysis. The increased length of news stories undoubtedly allows for more in-depth analysis. One might also expect that news content would have grown proportionately as newspapers grew thicker. But it did not. The increased size of pictures, headlines, and text typography and the greater share of the news page devoted to graphics, indexes, self-promotional items, and advertising have all conspired to minimize growth in the amount of actual news that newspapers accommodate (Barnhurst 1994). While news stories and newspapers are indeed longer, the changes we have documented represent a significant departure from previous styles of reporting.

accidents. In 1894, an incident of assault was summarized without fanfare in a single paragraph in the *Chicago Tribune*:

James McCune of 319 South Green street, a packer, is at the County hospital with a fractured skull. He was knocked down by William Warrington of 528 South Halstead street, a teamster. The men quarreled at West Congress and South Halstead streets. The police held Warrington without booking him (April 15, 1894, p. 10).

After the 1960s, accident stories showed a steep increase in interpretation. Two examples of accident stories illustrate how analysis increased. Shortly before the turn of the century, the *New York Times* contained a two-paragraph item that began as follows:

Four-year-old Dora Cohen was run over before her father's eyes by a horse and wagon in front of her home, at 87 Hester Street, at 7:30 o'clock last evening. The child's ribs were crushed in and she died an hour later in her father's arms (April 17, 1897, p. 8).

The second paragraph reported a chronology of the accident, describing the street, express wagon, and driver. Such items disappeared from the *Times* over the century, so that by 1994 any accident reported had to have much broader significance. For example, a report on flooding in Fort Fairfield, Maine, included information on state emergency measures and past events, as well as the causes and consequences of the accident (April 19, p. A12).

Although the specific histories of the *New York Times*, the Portland *Oregonian*, or the *Chicago Tribune* could account for the observed changes, the fact that our findings replicated nearly identically in three newspapers and in three different areas of coverage enhances confidence in the general trend. The greater length of articles, the greater emphasis on connecting events to one another, and the general increase in contextualization of events all lend support to the claim that contemporary news coverage de-emphasizes individual events and pays increasing attention to portraying large-scale social phenomena. The emphasis on collectives, rather than on individuals, and on events that are linked to other similar events across times and places, means that media are situated to play an increasingly important role in constructing people's perceptions of large-scale, collective phenomena. Many overlapping historical trends are likely to have contributed to this shift, as fully discussed by Barnhurst and Mutz (1998), but whatever its origins, this shift represents a significant modification in the conception of news, one that furthers the potential for news media to shape perceptions of collective opinion and experience.

The trend toward greater interpretation and less event-centered coverage has been asserted largely in terms of newspaper coverage. Contemporary comparisons across media suggest, not surprisingly, that magazines provide even more thematic coverage than newspapers, and television far less (Baughman 1987; Neuman, Just, and Crigler 1992; Wills 1983). Although evidence of historical trends pertaining to other media is generally lacking, some analyses suggest that television coverage is also shifting toward more thematic and less event-centered coverage. In his study of television news coverage from 1960 through 1988, Hallin (1994) documents a fundamental change in the structure of the TV news story in which "rather than simply being reproduced and transmitted to the audience," the words of the newsmaker "are treated as raw material to be taken apart, combined with other sounds and images, and integrated into a new narrative" (Hallin 1994: 7, 8). By drawing on more outside material and material from a variety of different settings, the TV journalist now packages stories by imposing "the unity of a clear story line" in a way that did not characterize earlier stories. Although Hallin proposes that technological advances in television reporting account for some of the change, he too sees this shift toward more mediated stories as part of a more general changing conception of news.

Widespread Belief in the Power of Media

One final factor contributing to the potential for impersonal influence is the belief in a powerful media. While the power social scientists attribute to media has waxed and waned, there is unquestionably a strong and indefatigable belief in the United States concerning the importance of media in politics. This belief would not, in itself, increase the potential for impersonal influence were it not for the fact that in the political world, perceptions often matter much more than reality. Belief in the power of media influences people's perceptions of what others think; thus its consequences are real even if the media's persuasiveness has been overrated.

This tendency can be seen most clearly with respect to policy makers. Media have an important influence on the perceptual environment in which American policy making takes place. Thus policy makers often feel compelled to shift their attention from pressing problems in order to respond to issues being covered by the media (Cohen 1963). Policy makers react to media coverage in this fashion because they think that the issues receiving media attention are "those that constituents [will] soon be posing as concerns to their elected representatives" (Tipton 1992: 131).[8] Policy making takes place in the future perfect tense, that

---

8 As Tipton (1992) has noted, policy makers' beliefs in the effects of media on the public was the basis for Cohen's (1963) formulation of the well-known agenda-setting hypothesis.

is, on the basis of what one expects will have been the case (Pritchard 1992), and media coverage serves as a predictor of public opinion.

Anecdotal evidence of this phenomenon is common. In one case, policy makers in Minnesota were prompted to take action based on the mere threat of having media attention directed toward a controversial corporate takeover attempt. Lobbyists showed advertisements directly to legislators "to provoke visions of panicked constituents ringing their phones off the hook" (Fiedler 1987: 59). Although the ads were never actually run for the general public, the lobbyists were successful in changing legislative opinion. In another example, claims carried by the media about the popularity of the "Contract with America" were reported to be successful in convincing many members of Congress that the contract's proposals were favored by the American public. Although these "poll results" were later exposed to be bogus, they temporarily created a false impression that was said to have influenced votes (Greve 1995).

Policy makers find media content useful "because they often have no better indicator of public opinion" (Pritchard 1992: 111). In the absence of polls, "the views expressed in the media are equated with public opinion" (Cohen 1986: 59). But beyond anecdotes (Dunn 1969; Peters 1980), there has been some limited empirical evidence of policy makers' use of media as a surrogate for public opinion. Studies linking news coverage with subsequent legislative action have provided some basis for inferences about policymakers' use of news coverage to infer public opinion. For example, attention to crime in metropolitan newspapers predicts legislative activity with respect to crime (Heinz 1985), and press attention to crime is related to legislative outcomes as well (Hagan 1980). Prosecutorial decision making is also affected by news coverage, independent of factors relating to the seriousness of the crime (Pritchard 1986; Pritchard, Dilts, and Berkowitz 1987; Pritchard and Berkowitz 1989); in other words, prosecutors appear to use media coverage as a cue indicating likely public concern. In addition, in a series of studies on the impact of investigative reports, Protess and colleagues (1991) found evidence that policy makers anticipated change in public opinion even before media reports had been published or aired and then acted to bring about policy change based on those anticipated reactions.

In each of these cases, the mechanism assumed to underlie these relationships is a process whereby policy makers attend to media coverage because of a need to monitor and anticipate public reaction; their actions are then based on assumptions about the power of media to garner public attention and alter public opinion. Perceived opinion is the actual causal agent, and media coverage simply serves as a convenient, if imperfect, way for policy makers to assess the views of large publics. If these perceptions were consistently accurate, one might argue that media were simply facilitating an important linkage function between public and policy. But even at the level of federal policy making where poll-based measures of opinions are more widely available, a variety of factors contribute to inaccuracies in elite perceptions of constituent opinion (Pritchard and Berkowitz 1989). For example, in Miller and Stokes's (1963) study of determinants of U.S. representatives' votes, the most important predictor was the individual representative's *perception* of constituent opinion, rather than actual constituent opinion.

Policy makers are not the only people who believe in a powerful media. Members of the general public also regularly assume that media content has a substantial effect on others' views.[9] This hypothesis is consistent with a large literature on the "third person effect," which suggests that people systematically infer greater media influence on others than on themselves (Davison 1983; Perloff 1993). In other words, their perceptions of the tone of media coverage form the basis for expectations about the state of collective opinion. Moreover, Gunther (1998) has reported both experimental and survey evidence consistent with a "persuasive press inference," that is, a tendency for people whose views are personally unaffected by media coverage to infer that other readers or viewers have been influenced by the tone or perceived slant in a story.

There is convincing evidence that belief in the power of media alters perceptions of collective opinion among both policy makers and the public. From a historical perspective, however, the important question is to what extent the image of a powerful media has been amplified and extended over time. The introduction of television appears to have intensified and accelerated these assumptions in the latter half of this century. Popular imagery suggests that television in particular is a key factor, if not *the* major influence on American public opinion (Lasorsa 1992). As Hess (1988: 67–8) notes, "One of the best college textbooks on government warns that the 'impact of television on American politics since 1952 should not be underestimated.' Judging from the literature, this has never been a problem." In a recent article in *U.S. News and World*

---

9 This appears to be an extremely robust finding: People consistently perceive mass media to have a tremendous impact on others' attitudes and behaviors. The few studies that have compared perceived to actual influence have found that people both overestimate the amount of influence news reports have on others' attitudes (Cohen et al. 1988) and underestimate the influence it has on themselves (Perloff 1993).

Report (1987) entitled "Television's Blinding Power: How It Shapes Our Views," television is credited with changing public opinion toward the Vietnam War, Kennedy's victory over Nixon, and attitudes toward the Nicaraguan Contras (cf. Hallin 1984; Kraus 1996). Media have also been blamed for a host of political ills including increased political apathy and decreased voter turnout. In 1980, the *New Yorker* concluded that the United States was "a nation whose politics (so virtually everyone agrees) have been taken over, veritably subsumed, by television" (p. 172).

This notion of powerful impact now dominates the way politics is perceived. Reporters themselves have perpetuated perceptions of powerful media through preoccupation with their own role in the process. Greenfield (1982: 13) cites 1980 as the year in which "the media itself began to look at television and the press almost as intensely as they looked at the candidates and the election. Never before, it seemed, had so many reporters, correspondents, editors, executives, candidates, consultants, and just plain citizens been so conscious of the power of the press." Although it is doubtful that this phenomena emerged full blown in 1980, it is likely to have contributed further to public perceptions of a powerful media. Media's coverage of its own role in the political process promotes mass society imagery replete with references to the helpless and malleable public. In a postmodern twist, campaign "metacoverage," or coverage of the coverage, invites viewers to be "cognoscenti of their own bamboozlement" (Gitlin 1990: 19). It allows citizens to feel clever by telling them more about "how politics works rather than what politics does" (Hart 1994: 88).

Media professionals have become fascinated with themselves as a political force (Greenfield 1982: 15; Kerbel 1994). Thus in 1988, Dukakis's loss was attributed to his failure to "package" himself successfully for the demands of media politics, and Bush's success was attributed to his superior media consultants (Popkin 1991). According to many journalists, the story of the campaign now consists of analyzing the candidates' use of media to manipulate the public into voting for them.

The questionable underlying premise of all this activity is that media, more than any other factors, determine the outcome of elections. Despite an impressive and continually accumulating body of research documenting certain types of media power in politics, there is little evidence to this effect (Baughman 1992: xv). Popkin (1991: 20) concurs: "The claim of political savants and insiders that the right commercials and the right consultants can win any election . . . is fed by the self-serving myth that certain 'magic moments' on television have turned elections around." Even the most ardent advocates of massive media impact point out that stable, competing flows of political information often cancel one another out, leaving a negligible net impact (Zaller 1996). This is not to say that media cannot have substantial, measurable net impacts under the right conditions; these conditions just appear to be the exception rather than the rule. Contemporary media coverage, on the other hand, suggests that these conditions are ubiquitous and that evidence of media power is all around us. The tendency to blame media for undesirable election outcomes is a pastime for liberals and conservatives alike: "What better excuse than that the game was rigged, the press bought, the television networks intimidated, . . . and the voters led like lambs to the polling booths?" (O'Sullivan 1988: 52).

Survey questions on public perceptions of media power generally echo this assessment. For example, almost three-quarters of the American public think that the media are an important influence in determining national policies.[10] When relying on poll responses, it is difficult to assess the meaning of these percentages without some basis for comparison. But at the very least, the American public is more convinced of media's importance than are the citizens of other Western democracies. Figure 2.8 shows the results of a five-country comparison of perceptions of media power. According to surveys of citizens in Great Britain, France, West Germany, Spain, and the United States, Americans perceive their media to be a more potent force in influencing public opinion as well as all three branches of government. The United States leads in all categories, with as high as 88 percent perceiving media's influence on public opinion to be "very large" or "somewhat large." Interestingly, the largest discrepancies between the United States and other countries pertain to the perceived influence of media on the institutions of government. Unlike the citizens of these other nations, Americans see media as an active player not just with regard to shaping public opinion, but within the major branches of government as well.

Of the five countries studied, people in the United States also were most likely to believe that their media have too much power (Parisot 1988). This finding has been replicated in many studies of the American public; in fact, a consistent majority thinks the media have too much power in general,[11] and over 80 percent think the media have too much

---

10 "Do you think television and the media are very important, fairly important, not too important, or not at all important in determining national policies?" (Gallup/ *Newsweek* poll, May 17, 1987).

11 "In general, do you feel that the media has too much power in the United States, or does not have too much power in the United States?" Has too much: 51%; Does not have too much: 37% (Yankelovich, Skelly, and White for *Time*, November 5, 1985). "Generally speaking, do you think the news media have too much influence over what happens today, too little influence over what happens or do the news media have just the right amount of influence over what happens

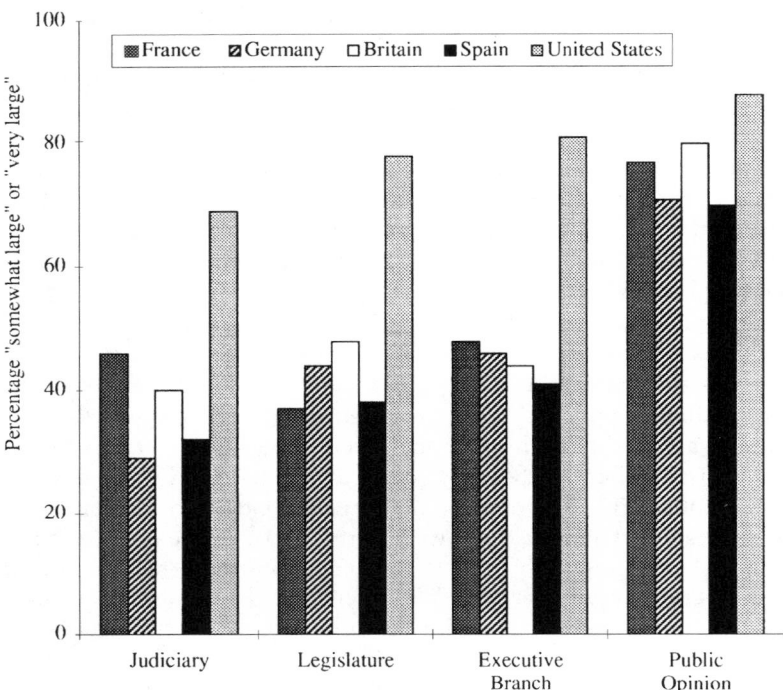

Figure 2.8. Perceived influence of media across five nations.

Source: Parisot (1988). "Would you say that the influence exerted by the media on (name institution) is very large, somewhat large, not very large, or not large at all?" *France*: Survey by Louis Harris France, April 9–13, 1987; *Germany*: Emnid Institute GMBH and Co., April 1–13, 1987; *Great Britain*: The Harris Research Centre, April 3–5, 1987; *Spain*: SOFEMASA, April 4–9, 1987. *United States*: Louis Harris and Associates, April 10–15, 1987.

influence on government.[12] Even in the aftermath of widely glorified Watergate journalism, most felt the media had more impact than they should.[13] More to the point, a majority of Americans thinks journalists

today?" Too much: 59%; Too little: 5%; Right amount: 32% (*Los Angeles Times* Poll, March 17, 1993).

12 "Which of these groups do you think have too much influence in government and which have too little. . . ." Too much: 83%; Too little: 13% (Yankelovich Partners, Inc. for *Time*, Cable News Network, September 1, 1994). "And now a question about the power of different groups in influencing government policy, politicians, and policy makers in Washington. Do you think the news media have too much or too little influence on Washington?" Too much: 79%; Too little: 13%; About right: 4% (Louis Harris and Associates, November 17, 1994).

13 On a scale of 1 to 10, the American public thought the news media should have

are more interested in wielding power than in what is good for the country.[14]

Although the evidence is generally convincing as to the strong perceived impact of mass media and the extent to which people perceive it to be excessive, it does not bear on the issue of whether perceptions of media power have increased. After all, popular assumptions about the importance of media in winning elections were also high in the 1940s. According to popular legend, Roosevelt's victories were attributed to his "superb radio voice," which enabled him to exploit the medium better than Landon or Willkie (Lazarsfeld, Berelson, and Gaudet 1944: 129). Although some survey questions on media impact have been asked more than once, none has been repeated over a sufficient period of time to make historical comparisons possible.

Perhaps more importantly, people perceive the impact of the news media on public opinion to have increased over the years.[15] Over 60 percent perceive news organizations to be growing in influence.[16] Politicians are also convinced of the media's power, typically awarding its importance a "10" on a ten-point scale (Arterton 1984; Popkin 1991). Interestingly, these popular perceptions have thrived even as academic researchers have struggled to find convincing evidence of media's persuasive impact.

If not from concrete evidence, then where did such perceptions originate? How did the belief in powerful media become such an important

an influence of around 5.4, but perceived it to have an influence of 8 (ABC News/ *Washington Post* poll, May 18, 1981). The 1992 presidential nomination race produced similar reactions: A consistent majority of people thought news organizations were having too much influence on which candidate became their party's nominee (*Times Mirror*, February 20, 1992, and January 3, 1992). In the late 1980s, a full 86% perceived their own newspaper and television stations to have some or a great deal of influence on the opinions of people in their communities. They also felt that news organizations generally had too much influence on which candidates became their party's presidential nominees (*Times Mirror* poll, October 25, 1987).

14 "Do you agree or disagree with the following statements? Journalists are more interested in wielding power than in what is good for the country." Strongly/ somewhat agree: 52%; Disagree somewhat/strongly: 38% (The Freedom Forum First Amendment Center, Vanderbilt University, November 1993).

15 "In recent years, would you say the news media have had more and more influence over the opinions of people living in your community, or about the same amount, or have they had less influence?" (*Los Angeles Times* poll, February 23, 1985).

16 Gallup poll for *Times Mirror* study of "The People and The Press," June 22, 1985. "I'm going to read you some pairs of opposite phrases. After I read each pair, tell me which one phrase you feel better describes news organizations generally. If you think neither phrase applies, please say so." Growing in influence: 63%; Declining in influence: 17; Neither: 7%.

part of American political culture? Contrary to popular assumptions, these beliefs took root long before the emergence of television. In fact, there were active efforts to promote perceptions of large-scale media power early in the twentieth century. Shortly after the turn of the century, propaganda analysis emerged as a reformist movement whose progressive mission was "to help an essentially competent public against the new co-option of communication channels by powerful institutions" (Sproule 1989: 225). As techniques from wartime propaganda were adopted by large corporations, propaganda analysis was used as a "device to alert the public to the dangers of manipulation that lurked behind the marriage of powerful social organizations to the new agencies of communication" (Sproule 1989: 229). Case studies emphasizing the threat of mass manipulation were written up and distributed as widely as possible with the aim not so much of documenting propaganda's actual influence as preventing people from being manipulated by presenting purposely extreme examples of propaganda's potential effects. Like many other consumer education movements, the Institute for Propaganda Analysis targeted children, over one million of whom received yearly instruction from the Institute (Fine 1941).

Despite the noble aims of this mission, some critics were concerned about its unintended consequences. For example, they worried that the movement's emphasis on the aims and tricks of propagandists, which was designed to produce vigilance and resistance to manipulation, actually produced a "destructive cynicism in students" (Smith 1941: 241). This concern is strikingly similar to those voiced today by Patterson (1993), Hart (1994), and others with respect to contemporary media's emphasis on exposing the strategy and tactics behind political persuasion: that in an attempt to prevent the public from being "had," media encourage an unhealthy cynicism toward politics. Another unintended consequence was that Americans were encouraged to think of mass media as extremely powerful institutions of mass persuasion. By playing up the media's *potential* power, propaganda analysts sought to reduce it. Ironically, all of this attention may have inadvertently elevated media's status in the political process.

In addition to the efforts of the Institute for Propaganda Analysis, an influx of European scholars from the Frankfurt Institute for Social Research in the 1930s brought with it immensely influential theories about how modern media served to extend political and economic domination. The Frankfurt scholars had an important impact on academic thinking about media in the United States. They lacked the progressive outlook of the propaganda analysts, but their perspective also emphasized a powerful media, in this case coupled with an atomized audience, devoid of important social bonds, that would almost inevitably succumb to agents of mass persuasion.

Even taken together, the influence of propaganda analysis and the Frankfurt émigrés provide an incomplete explanation for the prevalence of beliefs in all-powerful media. Although organizations such as the Institute for Propaganda Analysis still exist, they are no longer engaged in educational missions of this scale. Moreover, the preponderance of evidence from academic election studies by midcentury seemed to contradict the assumptions of mass society theory. Perhaps this notion has been perpetuated by the sheer amount of time people spend with media and television in particular. This belief also may persist as an outgrowth of some of the same impulses that drove the progressive mission of propaganda analysis. The current "discourse of savviness," as Gitlin has termed it, refers to an effort by media professionals and by the general public to put themselves above manipulation. Emphasis by reporters on strategy and tactics is termed "handicapping coverage," a defensive maneuver designed to show that they are immune from the influence to which others fall prey (Gitlin 1990: 19).

Not surprisingly, the public has picked up on the discourse of savviness. They see politics as mainly a matter of image construction and thus exhibit a postmodern fascination with the behind-the-scenes, inside dopester perspective (Hart 1994). The popularity of movies such as "The Candidate" and, more recently, "The War Room" and "Wag the Dog" provide further testimony to the appeal of the insider's perspective on politics. In short, whether they themselves are influenced or not, media coverage of politics makes viewers feel sophisticated because they are now privy to how so many others are manipulated (Hart 1994).[17]

Although perceptions of massive media power clearly predate television, the vividness of this medium has probably further contributed to this widespread belief. Despite dozens of studies and widespread assumptions to the contrary, psychologists have found little evidence that vivid messages actually are more persuasive than pallid ones. People perceive vivid messages to be more generally persuasive of others, though not themselves. This illusion seems to be based on the fact that people infer persuasive power from the levels of interest and attention that information draws (Collins et al. 1988). As an extremely vivid medium,

17 The "ad-watch," or "truth-box," genre of campaign journalism exemplifies this approach (Cappella and Jamieson 1994). By critically analyzing candidates' advertising, journalists hope to assert their independence from manipulation by candidates and to prevent voters from being duped by deceptive ads. Nonetheless, some research suggests that these efforts backfire, creating additional support for the candidates whose ads are being examined, and decreasing intentions to vote among nonpartisans (Ansolabehere and Iyengar 1995).

television draws interest and attention that probably lead to greater attributions of persuasive power as well.

Whether people's own opinions are actually influenced a lot or very little by various forms of media, their perceptions of massive influence alter their impressions of their social environment. If crime is receiving a lot of coverage, people reason that others must be experiencing it and think it is an important social problem even if they themselves are not experiencing it. And if media coverage of a presidential candidate seems increasingly complimentary, they reason as a result that public opinion is surely shifting in his direction.

Unfortunately these perceptions are not harmless. In Thomas's oft-quoted words, "If men define situations as real, they are real in their consequences" (Merton 1968: 475). The consequences of media power in politics are real because politicians, journalists, and the American public have few doubts about media's importance. Whether true or mythical, the American belief in a powerful media encourages politicians and the mass public to use media coverage as a surrogate for public opinion, simply assuming a transference that may or may not have a basis in political reality. In this fashion, media influence people's perceptions of collective opinion even when media content does not specifically address this topic.

Several major historical trends have contributed to creating the potential for impersonal forms of social influence. The rise of complex organizations and the nationalization of mass media have promoted a proliferation of indirect associations and thus created important alternative avenues for social influence. Interestingly, unlike the days of controversy over postal rates for newspapers, few today question the goal of promoting national and international dissemination of news. Without risking criticism, President Clinton himself regularly touts the "information superhighway" and its eradication of not just local, but also national, borders as a welcome addition.

Changes in the content of mass communication also have facilitated impersonal influence through their increased emphasis on abstract portrayals of collective opinion and experience and through greater emphasis on reporting that links individual events to larger, nonlocal contexts. Furthermore, through coverage that emphasizes its own importance in the political process, mass media play an influential role in shaping people's perceptions of the mass public. It would be overly simplistic to suggest that media alone have driven this phenomenon. Indeed, many of these changes in media are interdependent with changes in the larger social, economic, and political environment. Nonetheless, in combination, these changes have altered the political landscape by creating new forms of social influence on political attitudes. In short, they have helped to "establish in the imagination of a people a psychologically potent entity – a 'community' – that can be located nowhere on the ground" (Schudson 1995: 15).

3

The Origins of Perceptions of Mass Collectives

MASS MEDIA'S ROLE

Notwithstanding all the potential created by the historical trends discussed in Chapter 2, how much empirical evidence is there that mass media play an important role in shaping ordinary citizens' perceptions of opinion and experience beyond their immediate life space? This chapter examines both theory and evidence pertaining to this question.

At one level, this hypothesis seems so obvious that it is hardly worth pursuing; how else can people acquire information about collectives beyond their immediate life space and experience? But subtractive logic is a weak foundation on which to build a theory. In fact, many prominent theories of media influence caution against such an assumption, as does a large body of evidence from social psychology. The evidence drawn together in this chapter suggests that the primary reason for confusion is the lack of attention to the multiple levels of judgment on which effects may be assessed. When somewhat subtle differences in the nature of dependent variables are taken into account, findings are surprisingly, if not astonishingly, consistent in supporting media's role in shaping perceptions of collective experience and opinion. Before assessing the case bearing directly on mass media's influence, I consider evidence pertaining to three other possible sources of information on collective experience and opinion: rationalization based on partisan predispositions, personal experience, and interpersonal communication. Finally, I present a general model of the origins of perceptions of collectives and then test the model using two empirical studies, one focusing on media's impact on perceptions of collective opinion and the other, on perceptions of collective experience.

Origins of Perceptions of Mass Collectives

RATIONALIZATION OF COLLECTIVE EXPERIENCE AND OPINION

Rationalizing Collective Experience

Probably the least theoretically interesting possibility is that perceptions of collective experience are mere rationalizations of people's underlying partisan or ideological predispositions. If the president is not of our party, we tend to perceive the collective state of affairs as in decline, and vice versa if the president is one of our own. Although partisan rationalization certainly takes place, available evidence suggests that it is far from the whole story. For example, in forming retrospective assessments about the state of inflation and unemployment, the effects of partisan attitudes play a very modest role in biasing retrospective accounts (Mutz 1992b; Conover, Feldman, and Knight 1986), though partisan preconceptions appear to play more of a role when people formulate prospective economic forecasts (Conover, Feldman, and Knight 1987).

The origins of collective-level perceptions are far more complex than partisan rationalization alone can explain. The most widely studied collective perceptions are of economic issues, and here there is a tremendous amount of individual-level variation in perceptions of mass experience that remains to be accounted for. Some have argued that these individual differences represent simple error variance from survey data since, after all, the economy can only be either improving or declining at any given point in time (Kramer 1983). But individual-level variation in economic assessments is, in fact, meaningful. It is more than simple error variance; it plays an important role in evaluations of presidential and congressional performance and in influencing vote choice (Kiewiet 1983). Likewise, variations in people's perceptions of collective experience of all kinds – whether it be crime rates, unemployment, or the incidence of out-of-wedlock births – are important because they influence where people think the resources of government should be directed.

Rationalizing Collective Opinion

In the realm of perceptions of mass opinion, the analogous process is for people to project their own personal views onto collective others. The "looking glass" or "false consensus" effect refers to the well-documented tendency for people to see others as more like themselves in their opinions and behaviors than they actually are (Wallen 1943; Ross, Green, and House 1977). In other words, a person holding a particular opinion will estimate that a larger proportion of others share that opinion than would a person holding an alternative viewpoint.

Casual evidence of the false consensus phenomenon has been around as far back as the Roosevelt versus Hoover contest (Hayes 1936) and also was documented in *The People's Choice* (Lazarsfeld, Berelson, and Gaudet 1944), where people generally expected their own candidate to win. But surely such distortion would be lessened in today's campaign environment with the proliferation of polls and ongoing assessments of the state of the horse race.

In a review of over one hundred recent studies examining the false consensus phenomenon, Mullen and colleagues (1985) found consistent and robust evidence of projection. However, in most of these studies, the subjects were college students, and the reference population was other college students or peers, not the loosely defined, amorphous group of others suggested by impersonal influence. The few studies that have involved the attitudes of highly general groups such as other adults in the country have generated similarly supportive findings (Brown 1982; Judd and Johnson 1981; Van der Pligt, Ester, and van der Linden 1983).

In studies of projection and *political* attitudes, the purpose generally has been to see whether people project their own views onto *candidates* rather than onto mass collectives (Granberg and Brent 1980). As Krosnick (1990: 161) explains, "The projection hypothesis does not argue that people simply assume that all others share their own attitudes. Rather, liking of the target person regulates the impact that one's own attitude has on expectancies regarding others, instigating either positive projection or negative projection." In this respect, it is unclear what the projection hypothesis should predict about collectivities without clear identities that do not elicit strong affective responses.

But available evidence suggests that false consensus operates even when people are assessing the political views of mass, impersonal collectives rather than a small number of carefully specified others. For example, a survey of Detroit area respondents found across several issues that the vast majority of people believed other people in their neighborhood and in the Detroit area agreed with their views (Fields and Schuman 1976). Likewise, in presidential elections from 1952 to 1980, people expected their preferred candidate to win by a ratio of 4:1 (Granberg and Brent 1983). Fabrigar and Krosnick (1995) also found consistent evidence of false consensus effects across a wide range of political issues when students were asked to estimate the percentage of all Americans holding similar and dissimilar views.

Reality apparently does impose some constraints; the more people are exposed to accurate information on others' views, the less distortion toward consensus will occur (Mullen et al. 1985; Granberg and Brent 1983). For example, in election years in which polling has made the outcome of the presidential race relatively unambiguous, the false consensus effect has been diminished, but it has remained a significant influence on people's perceptions. Education also decreases, but does not eliminate, projection effects, as do smaller, less-diffuse collective entities such as states relative to nations (Granberg and Brent 1983). However, the effect apparently persists despite even direct efforts at educating people about the false consensus bias (Krueger and Clement 1994). Even when people are given readily available statistical information on others' views, they continue to show the false consensus bias. In short, the effect can be moderated, but it is seldom erased entirely.

Despite robust and proliferating findings, there is no general agreement as to why false consensus effects occur (Marks and Miller 1987). The most obvious explanations have not fared well upon further study. For example, it does not appear to be related to egocentrism (Yinon, Mayraz, and Fox 1994) or to perceptual biases resulting from the relative salience of personal attitudes compared to others' views (Tversky and Kahneman 1974). Since people tend to associate with those similar to themselves, it could result from biased sampling of the social environment. However, selective affiliation and most of the other explanations for false consensus suggest that there should be stronger effects for issues people consider personally important, and this has not been borne out. Attitude importance does not affect the extent of false consensus, thus results are largely inconsistent with the assumption that it is a result of attitudes directly or indirectly influencing perceptions of others (Fabrigar and Krosnick 1995).

It is important to note that most false consensus evidence is correlational in nature; that is, it has tacitly assumed that people's endorsements of various positions or candidates causes high or low consensus estimates and not vice versa. Thus one recent review suggests that we "might as well entertain the possibility that making high consensus estimates causes people to agree with items and making low consensus estimates causes them to disagree" (Krueger and Clement 1994). In other words, the design of most false consensus studies makes it impossible to distinguish false consensus from evidence that people's views are being influenced by perceptions of impersonal others. This is not to suggest that false consensus effects do not occur; indeed, both kinds of processes are likely to be taking place simultaneously. Nonetheless, this acknowledgement illuminates the methodological difficulties involved in establishing clear evidence of either of these phenomena individually.

GENERALIZATION FROM PERSONAL EXPERIENCE

The most obvious and most accessible sources of information about collective-level reality come from people's own day-to-day life experiences and observations. For example, one can observe long lines at the unemployment office and experience things such as inflation or crime in the course of everyday life. If perceptions of social problems originate in individual problems, then the answer to the question of where perceptions of collective reality come from is fairly simple and straightforward. People extrapolate from their personal experiences, observe and interact with others, and collectively come to define a social problem. Aggregated personal problems translate into social problems, and mass media merely reflect the aggregate of individual experiences.

But as the constructionist literature warns, social problems seldom emerge from objective conditions. It is generally a mistake to assume that any harmful condition will become recognized as a social problem once it affects a large enough number of individuals. In fact, some problems – high school dropouts, for example – become recognized as problems only when the incidence of personal experience drops *below* a certain level.[1]

Despite the accessibility and obvious salience of personal experiences, they very seldom have a large or significant effect on judgments about collective-level reality. For example, studies of the effects of crime victimization show that personal experience with crime influences people's personal fear of victimization (DuBow et al. 1978; Skogan and Maxfield 1981; Tyler 1980), but it has no effect on people's beliefs about the seriousness of crime at a collective level (Tyler 1980; Furstenberg 1971). Similar separations of personal and social-level judgments have been amply documented in the psychological literature on risk perception (Tyler and Lavrakas 1985) and base rates (Borgida and Brekke 1981).

More importantly, since personal experience and perceptions of collective social problems remain relatively independent of one another, there is an ongoing gap between personal and social levels of judgment about many contemporary issues. As noted in Chapter 1, and discussed more extensively in Chapter 4, this is often seen in the economic realm, but it is not limited to this arena; in fact, one finds the same gap with respect to health care, crime, and many other social issues, as discussed by Perloff and Fetzer (1986). Individual-level measures of personal experience and perceived collective experience are sometimes significantly correlated, but typically only weakly so (Kinder 1981).

In short, there is little evidence that perceptions of collective problems are formed as generalizations or extensions of people's personal life experiences. Although these findings may initially seem counterintuitive given the immediacy of personal experience and the tendency for people

---

1 I owe this particular example to Steve Chaffee.

to project their own *opinions* onto others, one might consider this a quite rational distinction for people to make: Since one's own experiences are highly unlikely to be representative of the larger society, they usually are discounted when forming impressions of large-scale collectives.

CONTRIBUTIONS OF INTERPERSONAL
COMMUNICATION

Mass media are obviously not the only sources of information about the world beyond one's immediate personal experiences: People also learn about the experiences of others through informal social communication. Those concerned with "contextual" effects are essentially hypothesizing that influential information reaches people through interpersonal communication. As Weatherford (1983b: 870) noted in his study of the origins and consequences of economic judgments, "the evaluation of economic conditions is a natural situation for contextual effects to operate through interpersonal contact; individuals are readily aware of coworkers and acquaintances who are unemployed, and shoppers in markets as diverse as food and real estate commonly compare their experiences with inflation." In other words, interpersonally transmitted information may have independent effects beyond those of personal experience (Conover 1985; Kinder, Rosenstone, and Hansen 1983).

Like personal experience, interpersonal communication appears to alter personal-level judgments. For example, talking to others who have been victimized by crime increases personal fear of crime *and* people's assessments of the risks they face personally (Skogan and Maxfield 1981; Tyler 1978, 1980). It also encourages people to engage in a greater number of self-protective behaviors. Communication from friends and neighbors also has been found to alter personal health-related attitudes and behaviors such as seatbelt and contraceptive use (Antonovsky and Anson 1976; Kunreuther 1978).

A strong effect on personal-level judgments and behaviors is obviously quite useful for many preventive purposes; it would be highly dysfunctional if people had to personally experience heart attacks before they took any actions to prevent them. But for purposes of understanding impersonal influence, interpersonal communication is important primarily if it can influence people's *social*-level judgments. Some very limited evidence suggests that interpersonal communication may influence social levels of judgment as well, but findings in this realm are inconsistent (Mazur and Hall 1990; Tyler and Lavrakas 1985). Thus hearing about other people's problems may make people more worried about their own personal situations, but it may also make them more aware that the problem is shared by others and thus that it is an important social problem.

In examining the origins of perceptions of collective opinion as opposed to collective experience, the effects of interpersonal communication are even less well documented.[2] Nonetheless, it is generally assumed that interpersonal communication contributes to patterns of false consensus in perceptions of mass opinion by influencing the availability of viewpoints in a person's environment. Since people tend to live and work among those who are similar to themselves, their interactions may result in de facto selective exposure to those with similar views. The nonrandom sample of views obtained through interpersonal communication would logically influence perceptions of the larger opinion climate in the direction of greater consensus. Interpersonal communication also could influence perceptions of mass opinion by making some views more "top of mind" than others in terms of their cognitive availability (Kennamer 1990).

EFFECTS OF MASS MEDIA

By and large, political scientists have attributed the origins of collective-level economic perceptions to mass media (Weatherford 1983a; MacKuen, Erikson, and Stimson 1992). Nonetheless, these have been strictly assumptions in many cases, and not rigorous empirical tests. Moreover, many theories of media effects would caution against this assumption. Two characteristics of this hypothesis prompt hesitation. For one, the effect would have to be a directional effect of positive and negative news presentations; for example, good news about the economy would be expected to make perceptions of economic trends more positive, and bad news should make them more negative. Although this sounds eminently plausible, perhaps owing to early disappointments with research on mass media's effects on political attitudes, there has been little research on effects that result from directional aspects of media content. Studies differentiating positive from negative news generally have been interested in attitudinal, rather than cognitive, effects of mass media coverage (Brody and Page 1975; Fan 1988; Page, Shapiro, and Dempsey 1987). In other words, they have tried to document media's role in directly altering people's political opinions rather than media's role in altering

---

2 Some studies come close to accomplishing this, but most focus on other aspects of immediate networks. For example, although Huckfeldt and colleagues (1995) examine the extent to which the macroenvironment influences perceptions of the political views of people's immediate networks, they do not assess the extent to which those immediate networks may bias perceptions of opinions within the larger environment.

potentially politically relevant beliefs about the state of mass opinion or experience. In addition, the spate of research calling for reconsideration of the limited-effects model of media influence has been based primarily on effects resulting from the mere presence or absence of coverage rather than the direction or bias in its content (e.g., Iyengar and Kinder 1987).

In addition to the scarcity of evidence on directional effects, a second factor cautioning against the assumption that media are the source of collective perceptions is that many political issues – the economy, health care, and crime, to name just a few – have "real world" consequences whose immediacy and accessibility have long been assumed to override potential media effects (Erbring, Goldenberg, and Miller 1980; Graber 1984; Weaver et al. 1981). Typically, media "dependency" theories downplay the potential for media effects in situations where alternative information sources are available (Ball-Rokeach and DeFleur 1976; Zucker 1978); under these conditions, people should have little reason to be dependent upon media. The literature suggests weak, if any, media effects on people's perceptions when there are highly credible, more easily accessible sources of information available in the form of people's own personal experiences.[3] Personal experiences in particular have long been considered "superior" information sources that will override any communication influence: "Personal experience is a more powerful teacher . . . than are the mass media, at least with regard to those issues that have a direct impact on the daily lives of voters" (Weaver et al. 1981: 156).[4]

When considering judgments specific to large-scale collectives, these generalizations do not hold up well. Personal experiences are clearly not as influential in altering social-level judgments as they are personal-level ones (Tyler and Lavrakas 1985). Moreover, the disappointing studies that led researchers to shy away from studies of directional aspects of media content were looking for *persuasive* effects on individual opinions rather than effects on individual cognitions. In the sections that follow, I reassess five areas of research on the cognitive effects of mass media –

---

3 For example, when issues used in agenda-setting studies do not generate strong effects on public opinion, the explanations for these differences are often based on a characteristic of issues known as "obtrusiveness" (e.g., McCombs and Shaw, 1972; Zucker, 1978). Foreign affairs, by contrast, are considered unobtrusive issues since they do not intrude into peoples' personal life space.

4 Steering clear of issues or situations in which people can have available direct experiences with reality is not specific to research on mass communication: "Sherif, for example, studied social influence in . . . a situation in which direct experience with reality was ambiguous, and Festinger explicitly directed the study of social comparison processes away from situations in which direct experience with physical reality was available" (Tyler 1980: 14).

agenda setting, priming, risk perception, cultivation, and political learning – with specific attention to what their findings suggest about media's capacity to alter perceptions of collective reality. My purpose in doing so is to point out that even without counting a few recent innovative studies that address this question directly in these terms, there is already a large body of evidence consistent with this hypothesis.

Agenda Setting

Agenda setting is a prime example of the type of media effect assumed to be caused by the mere presence or absence of coverage without regard to directional thrust; it suggests that the sheer amount of media coverage alters the salience people attach to issues, regardless of the valence of that coverage (McCombs and Shaw 1972). Nonetheless, evidence of agenda-setting impact by the media pertains to the potential for media to influence perceptions of mass collectives in two ways. First, agenda-setting findings illustrate how dependency theory supports, rather than contradicts, assumptions about the constrained power of personal experience relative to mass media. Secondly, this field of research has inadvertently produced evidence of media's directional impact on social judgment.

Studies of agenda setting can be differentiated based on whether personal- or social-level definitions of audience agendas have been used; that is, whether the dependent variable was assessed in terms of what the most important issues facing the *country* were perceived to be, as opposed to the issues that most concerned the respondent *personally*. Mass media are typically found to have a greater impact on people's perceptions of the collective salience of issues than on the salience of the issues to individuals themselves (McLeod, Becker, and Byrnes 1974; Becker, McCombs, and McLeod 1975). In other words, a person may not perceive some problem as more important to him or her personally just because he or she has seen news concerning it, but that person will be very likely to think that it is an important issue to other people and, thus, an important social problem. This pattern of findings meshes well with dependency theory. When agenda setting focuses on personal salience, personal experiences are relevant and override potential media influence. But when making judgments about collective others, personal experience is of limited relevance, so people depend upon mass media for information about what concerns the larger society.

In addition to providing evidence of media's impersonal impact on issue salience, agenda-setting research unintentionally also has provided empirical evidence of media's influence on perceptions of collective experience. In theory, agenda-setting studies seek to equate amounts of media coverage, regardless of direction, with the salience of particular political issues. However, in practice, operational measures of both the dependent and independent variables in this theory often have incorporated directional effects with implications for impersonal influence. For example, in assessing issue salience, many researchers have asked respondents to volunteer their perceptions of the most important "problems" facing the country. In this case, salience is confounded with direction; if crime is cited by more people as an important "problem," it is clearly because they perceive crime to be bad or worsening rather than good or improving.

The independent variable in agenda-setting studies also has been subject to confounding. Based on the nondirectional theoretical explanation, agenda setting should work with positive as well as negative news presentations of issues; viewing news coverage showing the economy as improving should increase the salience of the issue as much as coverage portraying the economy as in decline.[5] Many agenda-setting studies have adhered in theory, though not strictly in practice, to a nondirectional definition of the independent variable. MacKuen (MacKuen and Coombs 1981), for example, counts only *negative* news stories in the portion of an agenda setting analysis concerning economic issues. Thus his results have important implications beyond the realm of effects of coverage on issue salience. It is not simply the amount of news coverage that leads to greater salience, but rather the effects of negative economic news on perceptions of collective economic reality, which in turn heighten the salience of the issue.

For many issues, salience and direction coincide. For example, valence issues such as unemployment, inflation, crime, education, or poverty have only one side in the sense that typically no one is for crime or against education. Thus, in practice, much evidence of agenda setting turns out to be evidence that more negative news coverage leads people to think certain issues are more problematic; in other words, that media alter perceptions of collective experience just as impersonal influence suggests.

The ideal setting for "pure" tests of the agenda-setting theory is with position, rather than valence, issues; for example, a person citing abortion as a "most important problem" could mean either the lack of federal funding for it, or the lack of laws prohibiting it. In this case, studying raw amounts of coverage – regardless of direction – makes a great deal of sense for purposes of predicting issue salience. Unfortunately, agenda-setting research has involved more valence than position

---

5 This construal of agenda setting is obviously counterintuitive when measures of salience are operationalized in terms of "problems."

issues, thus making agenda-setting findings often indistinguishable from evidence that the positive or negative tone of coverage has altered perceptions of collective-level social reality. By using fuzzy or inappropriate operationalizations of the actual concepts involved in the theory of agenda setting, some studies have inadvertently produced evidence central to the premise of impersonal influence; that is, that media play a key role in influencing politically relevant perceptions of collective social reality.

Priming

In a series of innovative experiments, Iyengar and Kinder (1987) elaborated upon the basic agenda-setting idea to suggest that by paying attention to some problems and ignoring others, mass media also alter the standards people use in evaluating the performance of government and political leaders. By making some issues more accessible in people's minds than others, news priorities prime the public to attach greater weight to certain issues when they evaluate the performance of political leaders. As with agenda setting, the theoretical underpinnings of priming are said to be nondirectional; news stories manipulate the "accessibility" of issues in people's minds rather than their perceptions of whether the specific problem is improving or deteriorating.

Nonetheless, the experimental manipulations in their studies were primarily news segments presenting bad news about the issues in question; respondents were shown news about soaring unemployment rates, skyrocketing inflation, pollution, and so forth. As with agenda setting, the theoretical basis of priming suggests that television newscasts showing the economy as improving should increase the weight accorded that issue in evaluating the performance of political leaders just as bad news would. Although this idea is probably more tenable than the parallel with agenda setting, evidence in this regard is sparse. One exception is an experiment in which treatment groups included both positive and negative news about President Carter's handling of foreign affairs. Although the authors suggest this experiment as evidence that priming can result from news presentations of both achievements and failures, results did not reach conventional levels of statistical significance in the "good news" condition with any of the key dependent variables.

Some agenda-setting and priming effects probably do occur as nondirectional effects of the amount of coverage various issues receive, but evidence to date suggests that what is happening in many cases may be a directional effect instead of, or perhaps in addition to, an effect on the accessibility of certain information; respondents may perceive an issue situation as getting worse as a result of mass media coverage, and this perception of negative change may in turn heighten the salience of certain issues. In short, although agenda setting and priming are theoretically different from the proposition that media portrayals of mass experience alter perceptions of social reality, much of the evidence brought to bear on these hypotheses suggests that media are capable of altering more than simply the salience attached to a given issue or the standards people use to evaluate political leaders.

Risk Perception

Beyond research that is explicitly political in orientation, a great deal of evidence relevant to the nature of media impact can be found in studies of how communication affects people's perceptions of the risks they face from things such as diseases, accidents, or crime. Information campaigns aimed at altering individual-level risk behaviors have produced a wealth of information on when media coverage matters and when it does not. One would assume, for example, that the tremendous amount of news attention given to crime would cause viewers and readers to infer that their personal safety was often in jeopardy. But such is not the case. In fact, in study after study, this expectation has not been borne out. Mass media also have been found to have a very limited potential for altering personal attitudes and behaviors in areas such as smoking and other health-related attitudes (Mendelsohn et al. 1981), seatbelt use (Robertson 1975), and the use of contraceptives (Udry et al. 1972). Moreover, despite the large volume of coverage that crime receives, studies have shown a weak relationship or, more often, no relationship at all between exposure to crime in mass media and personal fear of victimization (Tyler 1980; Skogan and Maxfield 1981; Gordon and Heath 1981).

This accumulation of findings has led many to bemoan the relative powerlessness of information to change behaviors. Media's limited impact is problematic particularly for those who would like to encourage personal behaviors that prevent victimization. Unfortunately, even hard-boiled risk statistics tend to be interpreted as information about others that is not relevant to one's self (Tyler and Lavrakas 1985; Dunwoody and Neuwirth 1991), so media campaigns are limited in their capacity to encourage preventative behaviors.

The evidence pertaining to risk perception does not imply that mass media coverage is without any effects whatsoever; instead, media's effects are primarily on inferences about the larger, impersonal world. For example, media have a substantial impact on judgments about crime rates (Skogan and Maxfield 1981; Tyler 1980) and social-level judgments more generally (Mazur and Hall 1990). Tyler and Cook (1984) dubbed the recurrent finding of little or no media impact on personal judgments coupled with significant impact on social-level judgments the "impersonal impact" hypothesis. As in many other studies, they found that mass-mediated information influenced perceptions of the frequency or severity of a problem, but not people's judgments about the issues as personal-level problems or concerns (Tyler 1980, 1984; Pilisuk and Acredolo 1988). For example, although crime news made people more aware that crime was an important social problem, it did not make them any more cautious personally; the concern essentially did not translate to a personal level of judgment. In an interesting extension of these findings, other studies have suggested that the amount of crime presented in people's newspapers is related to their fear of encountering crime in areas outside their own neighborhoods, but not close to home. In other words, media may sometimes affect personal fears, but only highly remote ones (Heath 1984; Heath and Petraitis 1984).

To summarize, in forming judgments about personal risks, people are more influenced by personal experience and experiences conveyed through social networks than by media reports.[6] Media play an important role in spreading general information about the world, but people use information from nearby events to form impressions about their own personal lives. For designers of communication campaigns whose purpose is to change personal attitudes and behaviors, this relegates media to a less important role. However, for those interested in mass political attitudes, it promotes mass media to an even more central, more critical role because it is precisely collective-level judgments that matter most to people's political preferences. While personal-level judgments tend not to be politicized, perceptions of collective-level phenomena are easily linked to politics and politicians.

The Cultivation Hypothesis

Yet another area of research lending credibility to the idea that media shape perceptions of collective reality is the "cultivation" hypothesis, that is, the proposition that television has the capacity to cultivate erroneous perceptions of social reality in its viewers. The original cultivation studies (Gerbner and Gross 1976; Gerbner et al. 1977) used a combination of content analyses of prime-time television and survey data

---

6 Skogan and Maxfield (1981: 182) suggest that the reason for this is at least partly the way in which media cover issues. For example, in coverage of crime, the exact locations of events are often distant or left unspecified in media reports: "Most media stories about crime contain little useful information for readers which would enable them to assess their own risks."

to argue that television drama cultivates distorted perceptions of social reality. For example, distorted perceptions of the incidence of violent crime were said to result from heavy exposure to television programming that misrepresented the true incidence of these behaviors. Gerbner's "scary world hypothesis" argued that television exposure cultivated fear in the minds of its viewers, which in turn made them politically quiescent and willing to submit to political authorities for the sake of personal protection.

Gerbner's initial studies triggered a great deal of subsequent research on television's effects on perceptions of social reality that did not necessarily incorporate all of the assumptions of the original studies. More narrowly, these studies examined the idea that television entertainment content cultivated a picture of the world in the minds of its viewers that was more like the fictional world of television than the real world in which they lived.

Although there are a fair number of studies producing positive relationships between various measures of television viewing and dependent variables including beliefs about the prevalence of violence, family structures, interpersonal mistrust, fear of victimization, sex roles, family values, images of older people, attitudes toward doctors, and concern about racial problems, many of these relationships have not held up under more rigorous examination and using thorough controls for spurious associations (Hirsch 1980; Hughes 1980; Doob and MacDonald 1979). Many of the demographic correlates of heavy television watching also predict systematic differences in attitudes, thus making it difficult to make a case for television as the causal agent.

In a review of cultivation literature for the Surgeon General's Advisory Committee, Hawkins and Pingree (1982) made the important observation that the relationships that *have* held up under closer scrutiny tend to be those involving television viewing and demographic measures of social reality, or what have been dubbed "first-order" beliefs. These measures typically involve estimates of the frequency or probability of events (e.g., the crime rate), as opposed to second-order beliefs that tap personal attitudes (e.g., personal fear of crime or likelihood of victimization). If one rules out studies where the danger of spuriousness is great, there is little support for second-order effects, that is, hypotheses confirming that television exposure leads to a greater personal fear of violence, mistrust of others, or acceptance of authority (Hawkins, Pingree, and Adler 1987; Potter 1991).

In short, this research agenda also unintentionally has lent support to the idea that media's impact is primarily impersonal in nature. As with the impersonal impact of mass media on risk judgments, evidence is most supportive of television's impact on perceptions of collective, demographic characteristics of the world and less so for impact on personal-level concerns. Evidence further suggests that the perceived proximity of the judgment (local versus national) may change what kind of information people use, with television content relevant mainly to judgments of large-scale societal phenomena (Adoni and Mane 1984).

Why the differential impact on personal attitudes as opposed to judgments about the larger environment? Although there has been relatively little research directed at understanding the processes underlying cultivation effects, the most promising explanations center on the kinds of processing strategies likely to underlie set size judgments, that is, quantitative estimates of the prevalence of certain objects, people, or behaviors. The least effortful strategy for making such judgments involves heuristic processing in the form of inferring set size from the ease with which examples can be generated in mind. Several characteristics of media coverage may produce systematically more recall of certain types of events among heavy viewers. In particular, the frequency, recency, vividness, and distinctiveness of events portrayed in media coverage make them more accessible in memory and thus more likely to enter into judgments about set size (Shrum 1995).

Although many of the issues addressed in cultivation studies have obvious political implications, there has been little attention devoted to examining cultivation effects expressly in relation to political news. Television entertainment content may be responsible for long-term perceptions of the incidence of some social problems, but news programming is probably even more important, particularly in conveying information about the short-term fluctuations that are often important in elections. In the news context, people may quite rationally be persuaded politically by base rate information, but then, as is common, fail to apply it to their personal spheres.

In general, people do not consider entertainment television to depict reality accurately (Potter 1986; Shrum, Wyer, and O'Guinn 1994). Thus, when fictional accounts of events come to mind, they incorporate them into set size judgments only because they do not make an effort to remember the origins of the examples that happen to come to mind. This means that cultivation effects should be limited to low-involvement situations since two aspects of the underlying process depend upon low-involvement processing. When it comes to cultivation by news content, however, even more highly involved processing may produce such effects. Only a very few studies have examined cultivation specifically with respect to news media (e.g., Adoni, Cohen, and Mane 1983). As in studies of prime-time content, these analyses assume that the world depicted in media news diverges from the real world in important and identifiable ways.

Political Learning

When news media content accurately reflects social and political realities, people's acceptance of that information is referred to as political learning, which is probably one of the more common outcomes of exposure to mass communication (Clarke and Kline 1974). Evidence of mass media's effects on political learning has existed at least since Berelson and colleagues' classic study (Berelson, Lazarsfeld, and McPhee 1954), and more recent research has regularly corroborated political learning from mass media (Neuman, Just, and Crigler 1992; Patterson and McClure 1976). Most such studies have focused on stable items of factual knowledge, such as the ability to identify key political figures, to recognize key events and their significance, or to identify the issue positions of candidates. Although these types of knowledge are typically correlated with high levels of news media use, media's impact is often difficult to distinguish from the highly intercorrelated effects of education.

Media are ideally suited to influencing people's ongoing impressions of collective reality since regular monitoring of the news environment is the easiest way to maintain accurate impressions of conditions that are changing over time. However, since many studies of media's impact on ongoing perceptions of social reality control for objective reality, the effects of news coverage tend to be most easily observed when they relay inaccurate perceptions to the public. But if objective indicators are readily available, as they are in some areas, why should this occur? Traditional news values and practices often promote perceptions of collective reality that are at odds with objective indicators of the incidence or severity of social problems. In Chapter 4, I address the major factors influencing press portrayals of collective experience in greater detail. For purposes of establishing the more general thesis of this chapter, that media influence perceptions of collective opinion and experience, I turn next to formulating a model of the origins of collective-level perceptions and then to providing results from two empirical studies consistent with this model.

MODELING INFLUENCES ON SOCIAL PERCEPTIONS

This chapter began with the idea that mass media are the primary source of people's perceptions of collective opinion and experience. Although this still seems the most promising single answer to this question, it is ultimately too simplistic a view. The question is not whether perceptions are formed by mass media or by personal experiences or interpersonal exchanges, but rather how people integrate information that they receive from mass media, from other people, and from the experiences of their own lives. Few social scientists have studied the integration of firsthand and indirect experiences because it was considered a foregone conclusion that personal experiences would be the more important influence. Nonetheless, the validity of this conclusion clearly depends upon the type of judgment under study.

Based on the findings reviewed in this chapter, Figure 3.1 proposes two general models of how information from various sources is integrated to form the collective-level perceptions that ultimately inform political attitudes. These models are not intended as exhaustive accounts of all possible relationships among the concepts that are included in the models; instead, I focus on the key considerations strictly as they flow into perceptions of mass collectives.

The top panel of Figure 3.1 draws on Tyler's (1980) model of the origins of crime-related judgments to describe the origins of perceptions of collective experience and their influence on political judgments. It suggests that perceptions of collective experience are both personally and socially constructed, though some information sources play more important roles than others, depending upon the level of judgment being considered. First, consistent with the large body of literature reviewed in this chapter, the effects of personal experience are predominatly on personal-level judgments,[7] and mass media effects primarily on collective-level judgments.

On the basis of more limited findings, this model assigns interpersonal communication the potential to influence both personal and social perceptions. Informal social contacts reflect the aggregation of experiences across people just as media do. Nonetheless, the broken lines indicate the general thrust of previous findings: Personal experience is typically the strongest influence on perceptions of issues as personal problems, and mass media are the strongest influence on perceptions of social problems.

In addition to mass media and interpersonal communication, collective-level perceptions also may be generalized from perceptions of

---

7 The usefulness of the distinction between objective personal experience and subjective perceptions of personal experience manifests itself most clearly in studies of issues such as crime or unemployment. Individuals may personally experience victimization, for example, and then perceive themselves to be at greater personal risk as a result. But personal experience is neither a necessary nor sufficient condition for subjective perception of an issue as a personal problem.

Perceptions of collective experience

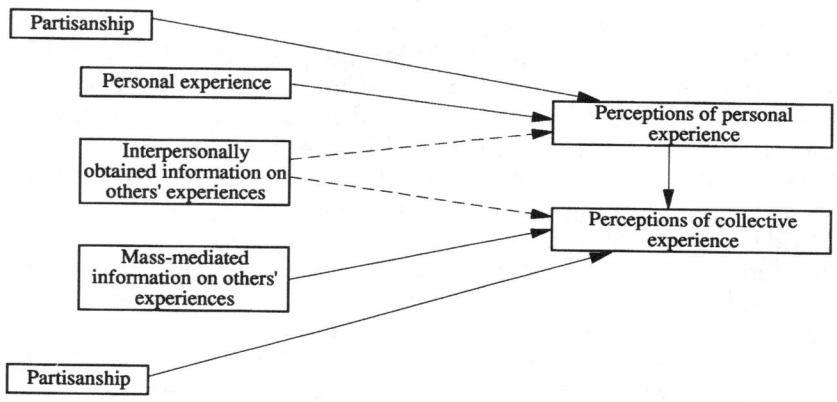

Perceptions of collective opinion

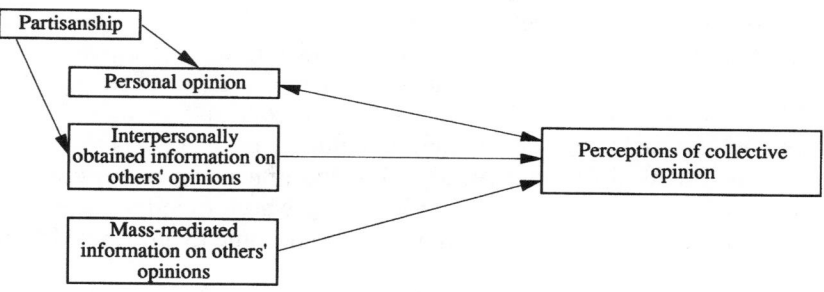

Figure 3.1. Origins of collective-level judgments.
Note: The top panel of this figure is based in part on Tyler (1980).

things that are perceived to be problems at the personal level, as the central arrow in the top panel indicates. However, previous research suggests that this link is a relatively weak one (Potter 1991); moreover, it also suggests that the reverse arrow is highly unlikely; people seldom use information about the state of collectives to draw inferences about their personal lives. Finally, partisanship has the potential to influence both personal-level concerns as well as collective-level perceptions. These arrows are consistent with evidence on the role of political predispositions in biasing perceptions of collective experience.

Some implications of this model are worth noting. First, it implies that in a society devoid of all mass media and dependent exclusively upon interpersonal communication, people's perceptions of their larger social environments would, of necessity, be extrapolations from their own personal experiences and those of their friends and acquaintances. Their own immediate problems and the issues they perceive to be problematic for the larger society would be very similar as the model essentially collapses on itself and the concepts in the center meld together.[8] Media serve as the sole means of formulating independent ideas about the world beyond people's immediate life space, thus they play a critical role in creating a divergence between personal and social levels of judgment. The model also suggests that the strength of the connection between personal and social judgments in the center of this model should vary based on the kind of collective being examined. The gap should be greatest when dealing with perceptions of national problems, and judgments should become progressively less distinct when considering state or local as opposed to national issues.[9]

The bottom panel of Figure 3.1 illustrates the origins of perceptions of collective opinion. The most obvious difference between the two models is the feedback loop between personal opinion and perceptions of collective opinion. This relationship is the greatest source of methodological difficulty in studying the origins and effects of perceptions of collective opinion. As shown in the model, people's social networks also are assumed to influence their perceptions of collective opinion. Longstanding partisan attitudes are likely to influence both personal opinions and people's social contacts, thus indirectly influencing perceptions of collective opinion. In contrast, partisanship has been found to have little effect on the type of daily news that people consume (Mutz and Martin 1997).

The top and bottom panels of Figure 3.1 show obvious differences between the origins of perceived opinion and experience, but there are also important similarities. In both cases, beliefs about the larger environment are determined through the integration of personal and socially transmitted information. In addition, in both models media coverage

8 Previous research tells us that some element of partisan rationalization also may enter into such judgments; for example, if the current leadership is not to my liking, I may project more pessimistic assessments onto national conditions as well.

9 Although perceptions of more local entities such as states draw on mediated information as well, people's willingness to generalize from personal experiences appears to be greater when the collective is closer to home (Mutz 1992b).

plays a key role in producing the kinds of short-term changes that are often important in political contexts. For collective experience, those with access to a lot of mass-mediated information will have perceptions that more closely reflect media presentations, while those relying on more parochial sources will have perceptions that reflect their immediate environments. For collective opinion, two of the three major influences are heavily structured by partisanship, and media coverage is the key factor likely to produce short-term changes in perceptions of mass opinion.

TWO EMPIRICAL EXAMPLES

I conclude this chapter with two empirical examples documenting the impersonal influence of media proposed in Figure 3.1. The first example involves a quasi-experimental investigation of media's impact on perceptions of collective opinion, and the second involves two surveys designed to assess media's impact on perceptions of collective experience.

Media Impact on Perceptions of Collective Opinion

One of the key methodological weaknesses in studies of media effects stems from our inability to predict when normally stable flows of information regarding an issue will be interrupted, thus giving us reason to expect changes in public opinion (Zaller 1996). Moreover, it is even rarer to have adequate lead time so that baseline measures of public opinion can be gathered. Post hoc statistical controls serve as the next best technique for these purposes, but because of the well-documented expectation of reciprocal relationships between opinion and perceived opinion, establishing the direction of influence can be difficult with even the best modeling techniques.[10]

This year-long, quasi-experimental study took advantage of a practice being adopted by a growing number of American newspapers in their efforts to move beyond passive response to the ongoing flow of news events and press releases that they encounter (see Mutz and Soss 1997 for full details). In recent years, a number of newspapers have adopted

---

10 A few studies have circumvented these difficulties by focusing on the impact of investigative reports for which reporters were willing to collaborate with researchers, informing them in advance about the content of the reports (Protess et al. 1991). Such studies have provided useful insights into the effects of mass media on both personal- and social-level judgments. However, the infrequent and isolated nature of investigative reports means that this form of media coverage tells us little about the usual processes of influence that occur as issue coverage accumulates over time.

the practice of editorial agenda setting, whereby the newspaper organization selects an agenda of issues to be emphasized in news coverage for the upcoming year.

In most newspapers adopting this practice, the organization's efforts do not end with simply boosting coverage of certain issues. In addition, they advocate particular solutions to the problems they target and promote specific policies that might be embraced by state and local policy makers. While some positions advocated are for less controversial issues ("eliminate street crime"), others are far more controversial ("promote industrial growth through tax policies" or "condemn hate speech policies as anti-free speech").

Although the selected agenda typically originates with the editorial staff, its impact is not limited to the content of the editorial pages. For example, in the newspaper involved in this study, efforts were made to increase both editorial and news coverage of the selected issues throughout the year. Rather than simply respond to an ongoing stream of events, journalists were encouraged to initiate stories on certain preselected topics in the news sections of the paper, while specific policy positions were advocated on the editorial pages.[11]

Since the newspaper was one of two local newspapers available in its geographic area, it provided an ideal opportunity for a field experiment comparing opinions among readers of the agenda-setting paper with those of the other daily newspaper. By collaborating with the editorial staff of the newspaper, it was possible to obtain the agenda for the upcoming year well in advance of the formal public announcement and thus to have enough advance notice to acquire a baseline measure of public opinion.

Low-income housing was selected as one of ten issues to be emphasized for the 1991 calendar year. On the first business day of the calendar year, the newspaper ran a full-page spread setting forth the agenda and elaborating on why specific issues had been chosen over others. In the case of low-income housing, the editorial board maintained two goals. First, it sought to heighten the general salience of the low-income housing issue within the community. Second, and more specifically, it sought to promote support for a rule that would require all new housing developments in the community to include some low-income housing.

The quasi-experimental design involved four successive cross-sectional surveys of respondents in the newspaper's readership area. Respondents were screened for newspaper readership habits, and the sample was

---

11 The newspaper studied in this project purposely selected issues of state and local significance. This decision reflected beliefs within the organization that its best chances for having an impact on the public and on policy makers would be at these levels.

stratified into three groups according to whether respondents regularly read the agenda-setting newspaper, the other daily newspaper, or no newspaper at all.[12] Parallel independent random samples of these three groups were collected at four time points over the period of one full year.

A baseline for attitudes toward the low-income housing issue was obtained in the late fall of 1990. Interviews were then conducted at three additional time points after the issue was announced at the beginning of the calendar year and throughout the course of 1991. The identical surveys assessed personal issue opinions[13] and personal issue salience,[14] as well as perceptions of community issue opinions[15] and perceptions of community issue salience.[16]

The three quasi-experimental groups facilitated comparisons between readers of different newspapers, as well as comparisons with nonreaders. Although readership groups obviously were not randomly assigned, the over-time collection of data made it possible to identify preexisting differences and trends among these groups. In addition, the local setting of the project made it feasible to monitor simultaneously media agendas and public agendas. A content analysis of coverage during the year of the study confirmed that the agenda-setting newspaper did, in fact, elevate its level of coverage of low-income housing beyond what outside events might dictate.[17]

12 *The Capital Times* of Madison, WI, was the newspaper carrying the specific agenda, and *The Wisconsin State Journal* did not. Citizens who read both local newspapers were excluded from the three quasi-experimental groups constituting the mass sample.
13 Personal opinion: "Would you favor or oppose a rule requiring that all new housing subdivisions in Dane County include some low-income housing? Is that strongly favor/oppose or somewhat favor/oppose?"
14 Personal salience of issue: "On a scale of 1 to 10 where 1 means not all concerned and 10 means very concerned, how personally concerned are you about – being unable to find affordable housing for you and your family?"
15 Perception of public support: "Do you think that public support for requiring all new subdivisions to include some low-income housing is gaining ground, losing ground, or staying about the same?"
16 Perceived community salience: "How about low-income housing? Leaving aside your own views, how important do you think this issue is to the people of Dane County?"
17 To confirm that the agenda-setting newspaper did, in fact, elevate its level of coverage of low-income housing beyond what outside events might have dictated, we did a content analysis of coverage in the agenda-setting newspaper and in the other daily newspaper using a computer search for key words. An analysis of coverage in the two newspapers in the four months preceding the first wave of data collection revealed that the agenda-setting paper had included slightly more coverage of this issue even before the special effort began: The agenda-setting paper included an average of 14.3 lines per day compared to 13.0 lines per day in the other daily newspaper. More importantly, our analysis of state and local

To analyze the effects of increased coverage, change over time was examined for four distinct variables including perceptions of personal and collective issue salience, personal opinions, and perceived opinion toward the issue. Impersonal influence predicts that media coverage should have little direct influence on individual attitudes toward low-income housing. At best, readers of the newspaper promoting this issue agenda should perceive the espoused position to be more popular to *others*. Likewise, media effects on the salience of low-income housing should be primarily at the level of perceived community salience rather than heightened personal concern.

These four hypotheses were tested using an analysis of variance including three main effects: (1) wave of interview – in order to control for over-time change affecting all respondents; (2) newspaper readership – to extract stable existing differences between the three quasi-experimental groups; and (3) attention to local newspaper news – in order to control for differences driven by interest and exposure to local affairs.[18] Since the main effect of wave of interview represents the over-time pattern of change in the dependent variable regardless of readership group, the effects of primary interest are represented by the interactions between wave and newspaper readership. Such an effect would indicate different patterns of over-time change for readers of different newspapers. In addition, a three-way interaction between wave of interview, newspaper readership, and attention to local news could indicate differ-

news articles during the course of the study confirmed that the total number of lines in articles dealing with low-income or affordable housing was consistently greater in the agenda-setting newspaper than in the alternative one. This pattern was true of all three time periods: Between waves 1 and 2, the agenda setting newspaper expanded coverage to devote an average of 21.8 lines per day to the issue, compared to only 14.7 in the other daily newspaper; between waves 2 and 3, this same comparison was 22.6 to 17.3; Between waves 3 and 4, the agenda-setting newspaper again topped its competitor with 17.5 lines compared to 11.1. Somewhat predictably, the difference in levels of coverage was greatest at the beginning of the year right after the announcement of the agenda when the staff of the agenda-setting paper was probably more self-consciously emphasizing agenda issues. As the year progressed and reporters became immersed in their usual routines, the difference persisted but was less pronounced.

In short, our manipulation check confirmed that during the course of the year, the agenda-setting newspaper did cover low-income housing to a greater extent than its competitor. Consistent with expectations, coverage levels were very similar before the agenda year began when both papers were simply responding to the ongoing flow of events. But shortly after one paper made an effort to cover the issue to a greater extent, the size of the gap between levels of coverage in the two papers became more than six times what it was before the study began.

18 In order to estimate the effects of these factors more efficiently, covariates also were incorporated in the model to account for the major ongoing differences among the three quasi-experimental groups.

Table 3.1. *Personal opinion toward required inclusion of low-income housing*

	Sum of squares	df	F-value
Covariates			
Republican	10.13	1	10.15**
Democrat	5.22	1	5.23*
Liberal	13.85	1	13.89***
Conservative	7.12	1	7.14**
Own Property	11.98	1	12.01**
Rural/urban	1.61	1	1.61
Race	4.54	1	4.55*
Income	21.83	1	21.89***
Education	1.37	1	1.38
Main effects			
Wave	.22	3	.07
Newspaper readership	3.32	2	1.66
Attention to news	.35	2	.17
Two-way interactions			
Wave by newspaper readership	5.24	6	.88
Wave by attention to news	10.59	6	1.77
Readership by attention	2.76	4	.69
Three-way interaction			
Wave by readership by attention	9.87	12	.83

Note: Sample n = 1,051. The dependent variable is a four-point scale ranging from "strongly oppose" (1) to "strongly favor" (4).
*$p < .05$ **$p < .01$ ***$p < .001$

ential patterns of change in the perceptions, specifically among those who are paying attention to local news.

As Table 3.1 indicates, this purposeful news agenda had little effect on individuals' issue positions concerning low-income housing. Citizen support for requiring all new subdivisions to include low-income housing did not change over the course of the year under study. More importantly, this pattern did not differ across quasi-experimental conditions: Readers of the agenda-setting newspaper were no more likely to change their personal positions on low-income housing than were readers of the alternative newspaper or nonreaders. Moreover, the three-way interaction indicates that this absence of any effects was not masked by failing to take into account differences in levels of attentiveness to local newspaper coverage. It was equally absent among citizens who paid a

Table 3.2. *Personal concern about low-income housing*

	Sum of squares	df	F-value
Covariates			
Republican	10.09	1	1.09
Democrat	3.46	1	.38
Liberal	8.37	1	.91
Conservative	.28	1	.03
Own property	1995.73	1	216.00***
Rural/urban	2.56	1	.28
Race	27.48	1	2.97
Income	118.65	1	12.84***
Education	247.35	1	26.77***
Main effects			
Wave	27.12	3	.98
Newspaper readership	179.12	2	9.69***
Attention to news	3.66	2	.20
Two-way interactions			
Wave by newspaper readership	47.21	6	.85
Wave by attention to news	66.28	6	1.20
Readership by attention	12.14	4	.33
Three-way interaction			
Wave by readership by attention	167.52	12	1.51

Note: Sample n = 1,376. The dependent variable is a ten-point scale ranging from "not at all concerned" (1) to "very concerned" (10).
***$p < .001$.

great deal of attention to newspaper coverage of state and local politics and among less attentive citizens.

In Table 3.2, the results for assessments of citizens' personal concern about the low-income housing issue indicate a similar pattern. The personal salience of low-income housing did not change significantly over the one-year period. In this regard, readers of the agenda-setting newspaper did not depart from other members of their community: The nonsignificant interaction incorporating wave and newspaper readership indicates that there were no condition-specific changes in concern for the issue over the one-year period.[19]

19 The only evidence even suggestive of an impact on personal concern appears in Table 3.2 where the three-way interaction between wave, newspaper readership and local news attention approaches statistical significance ($p < .10$). This inter-

Table 3.3. *Perceived community support for low-income housing*

	Sum of squares	df	F-value
Covariates			
Republican	.08	1	.20
Democrat	.02	1	.06
Liberal	.40	1	1.02
Conservative	.01	1	.02
Own property	.55	1	1.39
Rural/urban	.17	1	.43
Race	.76	1	1.93
Income	1.24	1	3.16
Education	.02	1	.04
Main effects			
Wave	3.62	3	3.06*
Newspaper readership	.10	2	.13
Attention to news	.67	2	.85
Two-way interactions			
Wave by newspaper readership	5.14	6	2.18*
Wave by attention to news	1.91	6	.81
Readership by attention	.26	4	.17
Three-way interaction			
Wave by readership by attention	3.60	12	.76

Note: Sample n = 1,227. The dependent variable is a three-point scale ranging from "losing ground" (1) to "gaining ground" (3). Results were confirmed using ordered logit with dummy variables representing the experimental groups. For ease of presentation, they are presented here as an analysis of variance.
*$p < .05$.

Nonetheless, the absence of effects on personal issue positions and personal issue salience does not necessarily indicate that the efforts of the agenda-setting newspaper were without consequence. In fact, results were precisely what Figure 3.1 predicted. Table 3.3 provides evidence that citizens' perceptions of popular support for low-income housing moved in a more favorable direction over the course of the year under

action results from the fact that personal concern with the low-income housing issue increases over time among readers of the agenda-setting newspaper who pay close attention to state and local news, while it decreases over time among those readers who pay little attention. Although this pattern is suggestive of an agenda-setting effect contingent upon citizen attention to local news, the overall findings are very weak.

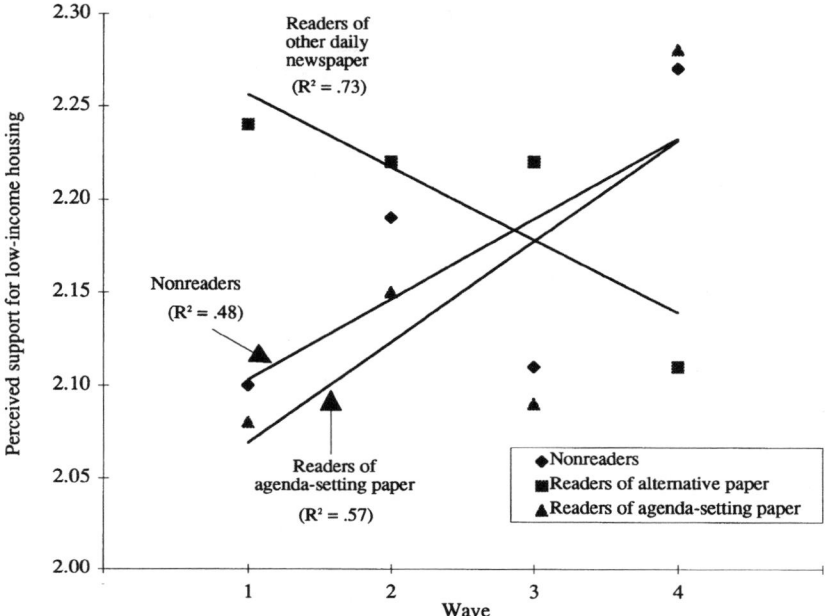

Figure 3.2. Perceived support for low-income housing by wave and newspaper readership.

Note: Lines represent best fit regression lines for the four means for each group. Both the newspaper reader group lines represent significant linear trends, while the nonreader group does not constitute a statistically significant trend. The dependent variable is a three-point scale ranging from losing ground (1) to gaining ground (3).

study. The significant interaction comprised of wave and newspaper readership indicates that changes over time in perceptions of public sentiment depended on whether one was a reader of the agenda setting newspaper, the alternative paper, or no newspaper at all.

Figure 3.2 illustrates this relationship using regression lines fitted to the four cell means. While perceived support for low-income housing went down over time among readers of the alternative paper, it went up over this same period among readers of the agenda-setting newspaper. This pattern is precisely what one would expect if purposeful news agendas move perceptions of public sentiment. While those receiving other sources of news coverage perceived public support to be on the decline, readers of the newspaper advocating support for low-income housing and emphasizing the importance of this issue more generally, perceived public support to be on the rise.

Perceived support for low-income housing among nonreaders did not produce a statistically significant trend in either direction. In contrast, the upward trend for readers of the agenda-setting newspaper and the downward trend for readers of the alternative paper were both statistically significant linear trends ($p < .05$ in both cases). The apparent stability of nonreaders' perceptions, coupled with the differential trends among readers of the two newspapers, makes perfect sense in light of the more limited access to local news among nonreaders. Thus, while readers of the agenda-setting newspaper *perceived* public support for low-income housing to be growing over this time period, evidence concerning personal issue positions indicates that, in fact, it was not.

Effects of the agenda-setting newspaper's strategy are also evident in the results presented in Table 3.4. Overall, individuals' perceptions of the importance of low-income housing to their fellow citizens did not change significantly over the course of the year. The two-way interaction between newspaper readership and wave suggests that this pattern did not differ by quasi-experimental conditions: Readers of the agenda-setting newspaper did not differ from others in their perceptions of issue salience within the community over time. However, the three-way interaction indicates that citizens who read the agenda-setting newspaper *and* paid attention to newspaper coverage of state and local politics had significantly different ideas about the perceived community importance of low-income housing ($p < .05$).

Figure 3.3 illustrates these results by plotting lines representing cell means for readers of the agenda-setting newspaper and the other daily newspaper. Over the course of the year-long news strategy, readers of the agenda-setting newspaper who paid attention to newspaper coverage increasingly perceived low-income housing to be important to others in their community.[20] In contrast, readers of the other daily newspaper who paid attention to newspaper coverage became progres-

---

20 Since these findings are based on a time series design with two varieties of no-treatment control groups, one can be fairly confident in drawing causal inferences about the effects of this newspaper's policy. One of the major strengths of this design is its ability to control for history as a threat to internal validity. By comparing the trends in other groups during the same time period, one can rule out the possibility that some change within the community at large produced the observed changes in perceptions of the political climate surrounding low-income housing. Nonetheless, the limited number of data points in this time series and the uncertainty surrounding time lags involved in producing changes in public opinion help to cloud comparisons of the quasi-experimental groups. Moreover, the interaction of increased news coverage – the quasi-experimental treatment – with characteristics of the nonequivalent groups remains a minor threat to the validity of these comparisons.

Table 3.4. *Perceived importance of low-income housing to others in the community*

	Sum of squares	df	F-value
Covariates			
Republican	1.80	1	.42
Democrat	.24	1	.06
Liberal	10.10	1	2.36
Conservative	43.96	1	10.26**
Own property	.05	1	.01
Rural/urban	3.37	1	.79
Race	.77	1	.18
Income	180.18	1	42.06***
Education	285.39	1	66.61***
Main effects			
Wave	3.09	3	.24
Newspaper readership	3.93	2	.46
Attention to news	3.04	2	.36
Two-way interactions			
Wave by newspaper readership	12.54	6	.49
Wave by attention to news	8.58	6	.33
Readership by attention	128.13	4	1.06
Three-way interaction			
Wave by readership by attention	90.36	12	1.76*

Note: Sample n = 1,418. The dependent variable is a ten-point scale ranging from "not at all important" (1) to "very important" (10).
$*p < .05$ $**p < .01$ $***p < .001$.

sively less likely to see low-income housing as important to people in their community.[21]

Consistent with the expectations of Figure 3.1, the dominant direct effects of media coverage were on collective perceptions rather than on individual opinions or salience. Although these effects were not the desired outcome from the perspective of news organizations, the ability to alter the perceptual environment in which policy changes transpire implies that news organizations may indirectly facilitate the very changes they seek. In this particular case, some policy changes did eventually transpire, but only several years later.

21 There were too few respondents who paid attention to local news, yet did not read one of the local daily newspapers, so no trend line could be estimated for the nonreader group.

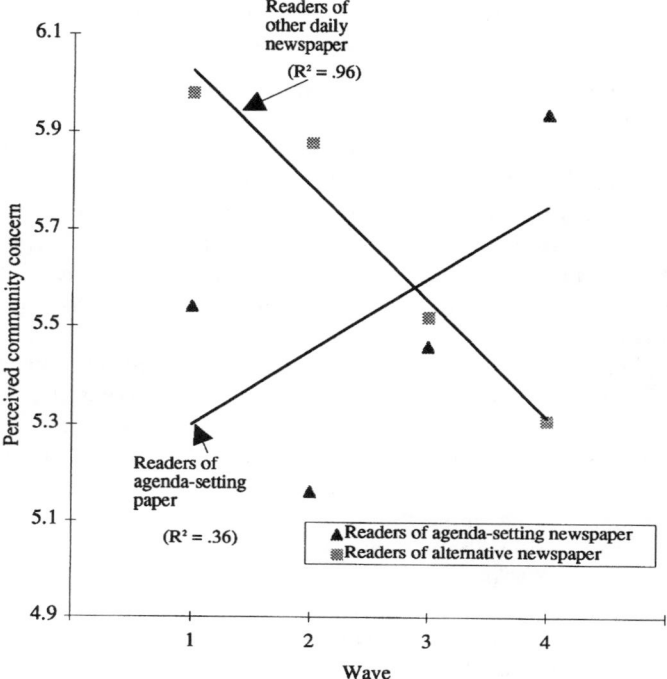

Figure 3.3. Perceived importance of low-income housing among respondents attending to local news by wave and newspaper readership.

Note: Lines represent best fit regression lines for the four means for each group. Both lines represent significant linear trends. The dependent variable is a ten-point scale ranging from not at all important (1) to very important (10).

The fact that media coverage did not directly affect individual opinions in this study is largely consistent with the relationships proposed in Figure 3.1. But upon first examination it may seem inconsistent with the idea that perceptions of mass collectives have indirect consequences for the opinions formed by individual members of the mass public. Indeed, perceptions suggesting that collective opinion supports a particular view do not automatically translate into greater acceptance of that position. Instead, the reciprocal link shown in Figure 3.1 represents a far more subtle, far more complex, and ultimately far more interesting process. I leave it to Chapters 7 and 8 to describe and document these processes of influence. The point of this example has been to illustrate the first step in what is a multistage process of influence.

MEDIA IMPACT ON PERCEPTIONS OF
COLLECTIVE EXPERIENCE

A second study, in this case oriented toward understanding the origins of perceptions of collective *experience*, made possible three independent tests of the pattern shown in the upper panel of Figure 3.1. One test involved a national-level operationalization of collective experience, while two others examined the origins of perceptions of collective experience at the state level. In all three cases, all three possible sources of information in Figure 3.1 were measured: personal experience, interpersonally obtained information, and mass-mediated information about unemployment.

Personal experience with unemployment was defined quite broadly to include any respondents reporting that they or someone else in their immediate family had been laid off or had had trouble finding a job within the past year.[22] Measures of interpersonally transmitted information inquired as to how frequently others they knew told them about having trouble finding or keeping a job.[23] And finally, mass media exposure to information about unemployment was tapped by combining survey responses on news media use with data derived from content analyses of each respondent's individual newspaper.[24]

The two surveys involved in this study tapped respondents' subjective perceptions about whether national- and state-level unemployment was getting better or worse, and whether they were more or less concerned about unemployment at the personal level.[25] To control for yet another

22 "In the past year have you or anyone in your family been laid off or had trouble finding a job?" Coded o (no) or 1 (yes).

23 "How often do other people talk to you about their employment problems, that is, having trouble finding or keeping a job? Would you say they talk to you about job security or unemployment problems everyday, three or four times a week, once or twice a week, or less often than that?" Coded on a 1 to 4 scale.

24 First respondents were asked what newspaper, if any, they read most often. Interviewers coded the name and city of publication for each paper. A systematic content analysis was done of the front pages of all mentioned newspapers for two reconstructed weeks drawn from the two months preceeding each survey. Two coders rated the directional thrust of all economic articles along a five-point, good news–bad news scale. Intracoder reliability was .95 and .87, and intercoder reliability was .76. Content measures indicating the extent of negative–positive employment news were then weighted by newspaper exposure measures: "How many days in the past week did you read the front-page news in a newspaper?" Responses were coded into nonreaders (o), seven-day a week readers (2), and occasional (one to six days a week) readers (1).

25 Unemployment at state/national levels: "Would you say that over the past year people across our state have had a harder time finding enough work, an easier time, or have things stayed about the same? Is that a little harder/easier or a lot harder/easier? And what about the United States as a whole? Would you say that

possible source of information about unemployment experience – the observation of long lines at the unemployment office, for example – analyses also included county-level unemployment statistics from each respondent's county of residence.

It is worth noting that because of the varied ways in which data on mass media exposure, interpersonally obtained information, and personal experience were collected, the measures are probably not all on equal footing with respect to the reliability of estimates. For example, interpersonal communication about unemployment was based on individual self-reports, while mediated information about unemployment was inferred on the basis of general measures of newspaper use combined with content analyses of samples of individual respondents' newspapers. Since people concerned about unemployment are probably also more likely to recall friends with employment problems, the interpersonal measures are more likely to incorporate simultaneity bias than are the media measures. In addition, the inclusion of the county unemployment measure in the model made for a quite rigorous test of the impact of media coverage. To the extent that media coverage simply mirrored local unemployment trends, the media measures would show no independent influence on collective-level economic perceptions. Media coverage would only have an independent impact on perceptions to the extent that it diverged from real-world conditions. In short, in this study the deck was stacked away from finding significant media influence on perceptions of collective experience.

The results in Table 3.5 illustrate the major predictors of retrospective perceptions of collective unemployment conditions based on data drawn from the two surveys. The findings confirm Figure 3.1 with respect to the major sources of perceptions of unemployment at the collective level. Both the tone of people's newspapers and their interpersonal contact with others influenced collective-level perceptions. These findings are consistent across two independent surveys and also true when considering both state and national levels of collective judgment. Table 3.6 shows that, again consistent with Figure 3.1, personal-level concern about unemployment is primarily a function of personal experience and secondarily of interpersonal communication.

over the past year people across the United States have had a harder time finding enough work, an easier time, or have things stayed about the same? Is that a little harder/easier or a lot harder/easier?" Personal unemployment concern: "How about you or people in your own household. Over the past year, have you been more worried about finding a job or keeping the one you have, less worried about these things, or have things stayed about the same? Is that a little more/less worried or a lot?" All three coded on five-point scales.

Table 3.5. *Influences on perceptions of unemployment at the collective level*

	State-level unemployment (Spring 1987)	State-level unemployment (Fall 1987)	National-level unemployment (Fall 1987)
Personal concern (better)	.23 (.07)***	.19 (.06)**	.13 (.06)*
Personal experience	−.25 (.15)	−.15 (.15)	.05 (.15)
Interpersonal news of unemployment	−.13 (.05)*	−.24 (.06)***	−.12 (.06)*
Exposure to newspaper coverage of employment trends	−.09 (.04)*	−.15 (.06)*	−.08 (.03)*
County unemployment rate	−.09 (.04)*	−.07 (.04)	.07 (.04)
Republican	.12 (.14)	.08 (.14)	.36 (.14)**
Democrat	−.04 (.15)	−.11 (.13)	−.16 (.13)
Age	−.01 (.04)	−.06 (.04)	−.01 (.04)
Gender	−.03 (.12)	−.28 (.11)*	−.24 (.11)*
Race	−.43 (.24)	−.40 (.25)	.01 (.25)
Income	.04 (.05)	.03 (.05)	.02 (.05)
Education	.02 (.06)	−.01 (.05)	.06 (.05)
R^2	.21	.28	.21
(n)	(257)	(264)	(241)

Note: Entries are unstandardized OLS regression coefficients with standard errors in parentheses.
*$p < .05$ **$p < .01$ ***$p < .001$.

Although they involve different dependent variables, the equations in Table 3.5 and Table 3.6 are statistically indistinguishable since they include the same variables with the positions of personal concern and collective unemployment experience simply reversed. My prediction based on previous research was that influence would flow mainly via generalization from personal to collective conditions, and not vice versa. I attempted to disentangle the potential reciprocal influence between subjective assessments of personal and collective experience using instrumental variables and two-stage least squares.

First, consistent with Figure 3.1, when collective-level employment perceptions were treated as endogenous, they had no significant effects

Table 3.6. *Influences on personal unemployment concern*

	State level (Spring 1987)	State level (Fall 1987)	National level (Fall 1987)
Collective unemployment	.19 (.06)**	.22 (.07)**	.17 (.07)*
Personal experience	−.59 (.13)***	−.72 (.16)***	−.88 (.17)***
Interpersonal news of unemployment	−.13 (.05)*	−.07 (.07)	−.08 (.07)
Exposure to newspaper coverage of employment trends	−.04 (.04)	.08 (.07)	.03 (.04)
County unemployment rate	.11 (.04)**	.03 (.04)	.00 (.05)
Republican	−.11 (.13)	.06 (.15)	.08 (.16)
Democrat	−.24 (.14)	−.09 (.14)	−.11 (.15)
Age	−.08 (.04)	.00 (.04)	−.03 (.04)
Gender	−.01 (.11)	−.03 (.12)	−.05 (.13)
Race	.04 (.22)	−.16 (.27)	−.28 (.28)
Income	.01 (.04)	.02 (.05)	.01 (.05)
Education	.08 (.05)	−.02 (.05)	−.03 (.06)
R^2	.24	.21	.22
(n)	(257)	(264)	(264)

Note: Entries are unstandardized OLS regression coefficients with standard errors in parentheses.
*$p < .05$ **$p < .01$ ***$p < .001$.

on personal-level concern in any of the three tests.[26] Second, as shown in Table 3.7, the results of this analysis partly confirmed the downward arrow in Figure 3.1; any connection between personal concern and perceptions of collective experience was found to flow in only one direction. However, the link between personal and collective perceptions existed only when considering state-level collectives. When considering perceptions of unemployment at the national level, the gap between perceptions of personal and collective experience widened to the point that there was no influence flowing in either direction.

Thus, again consistent with the model in Figure 3.1, as the collective becomes increasingly distant from an individual's immediate life space,

26 Instrumental variables included exposure to newspaper coverage of unemployment trends, the county unemployment rate, interpersonal news of unemployment, income, race, age, sex, and education.

Table 3.7. *The influence of personal-level judgments on*
collective-level perceptions

	State-level unemployment (Spring 1987)	State-level unemployment (Fall 1987)	National-level unemployment (Fall 1987)
Personal unemployment concern	.65 (.24)**	.45 (.15)**	.09 (.18)
Personal unemployment experience	−.25 (.15)	−.14 (.15)	−.18 (.14)
Interpersonal news of unemployment	−.08 (.07)	−.20 (.07)**	−.15 (.08)*
Exposure to newspaper coverage of employment trends (bad news)	−.09 (.04)*	−.14 (.06)*	−.14 (.06)*

Note: Two-stage least square results, where personal unemployment concern is endogenous. Exogenous variables included personal unemployment experience, interpersonal news of unemployment, income, race, age, sex, education, and the county unemployment rate.
*$p < .05$ **$p < .01$.

the compartmentalization of personal and collective perceptions increases. Findings also were consistent with previous research on the tendency to neglect base rate information in making judgments about one's self (e.g., Borgida and Brekke 1981): Perceptions of the incidence of unemployment at the collective level did not influence levels of personal concern.

Media's capacity to alter perceptions of collective experience and opinion is supported by previous research under a variety of labels and within a wide range of disciplines along with the new evidence presented in Chapter 3. Seemingly inconsistent evidence about the relative influence of mass media and personal experience is considerably less so when one takes into account findings pertaining to personal and collective levels of judgment.

In the sections that follow, I turn to the issue of the consequences of media's impersonal impact for political attitudes and behaviors. In other words, how does impersonal influence impact on perceptions of collective experience ultimately translate into meaningful changes in political attitudes or behaviors?

PART II

EFFECTS OF PERCEPTIONS
OF MASS EXPERIENCE

4

The Politicization of Personal and Collective Experience

Reading in a newspaper that the unemployment rate has increased by a few percentage points seems a fundamentally different experience from receiving a pink slip indicating that one has lost a job. Losing a job has an inescapable impact on an individual's everyday life; on the other hand, reading about unemployment in a newspaper appears to have greater consequences for American political life. In the economic realm, it is now a well-known finding that perceptions of collective economic experience generally play a more important role in shaping political attitudes than personal economic experiences do. A large body of findings has accumulated showing that political attitudes and behaviors are rarely affected by the economy's impact on individual lives and fortunes (Kinder and Kiewiet 1981; Eulau and Lewis-Beck 1985).[1] For example, contrary to expectations, recent personal experiences with unemployment have virtually no effect on vote choice (Schlozman and Verba 1979). Similarly, changes in family finances have little impact on voting or evaluations of incumbents (Kiewiet 1983; Kinder, Adams, and Gronke 1989). This same pattern extends to policy attitudes as well. As Kinder (1983) concluded, "Neither losing a job, nor deteriorating family financial conditions, nor pessimism about the family's economic future

1 The initial assumption in studies of the electoral impact of economic change was that this impact occurred because economically dissatisfied citizens logically voted against the incumbent party. These studies were based almost exclusively on time series data using aggregate-level indicators of objective economic conditions to predict voting or candidate popularity in presidential and congressional elections, and it was simply assumed that the aggregate relationship worked because when national economic conditions were bad, more citizens were experiencing economic problems in their own lives, and these people logically voted against the incumbent party (see, e.g., Stigler 1973; Goodman and Kramer 1975). As one study put it, voters were assumed to form political attitudes by asking of incumbents, "What have you done for me lately?" (Popkin et al. 1976). The initiation of large-scale survey research and the corresponding ability to assess pocketbook voting at the individual level called this conventional wisdom into question.

has much to do with support for policies designed to alleviate personal economic distress" (p. 403).

Despite continuously disappointing findings, self-interest rooted in personal life experience seems such a compelling basis for political behavior that this hypothesis has spawned a huge number of studies (Sears and Funk 1990). Although exceptions to this conclusion have cropped up with some measures of personal economic experience in the context of a few specific tests, the general pattern has withstood extensive repeated examination. Moreover, when statistically detectable, the effects of personal experience have tended to be small at best.[2]

The surprising lack of evidence of personal-experience-based political attitudes has led to elaborations on why the relationship fails to appear. These explanations fall roughly into two categories: one group emphasizing measurement and methodological problems,[3] and the other, theoretical explanations for the attenuated relationship between personal experiences and political judgments. Although measurement of all potentially relevant personal experiences is quite difficult and context effects in surveys may sometimes induce self-interested issue preferences (Sears and Lau 1983; Lau, Sears, and Jessor 1990), the finding of minimal impact has proved to be fairly robust even when measurement is at its best and when alternative model specifications are employed (Kinder, Adams, and Gronke 1989; Feldman and Conley 1991). This is not to say that there are no important exceptions (e.g., Green and Gerken 1989; Sears and Citrin 1982), but they are few and far between.

Substantive explanations have focused on how people understand their own personal economic problems. Sniderman and Brody (1977), for example, found that most Americans did not attribute changes in

2 With this general conclusion in mind, some exceptions should be noted. Tufte (1978) and Wides (1976), for example, did find significant relationships between personal economic experiences and presidential voting. On the whole, however, the evidence is meager even among these exceptions.

3 The strong aggregate-level findings "left people suspecting that personal self-interest at the micro-level must be operating if only we look in the right place" (Feldman 1985: 148). Rosenstone (1983), for example, suggested that the problem was caused by substantial random measurement error in the usual trichotomous measure of personal financial change. Additional evidence has demonstrated that despite the question's vague wording, it does measure concrete aspects of respondents' financial situations (Kiewiet and Rivers 1985; Rosenstone, Hansen, and Kinder 1986). Others have suggested that perhaps it is the small number of people implicated in the case of an issue like unemployment that prevents these variables from reaching statistical significance (e.g. Kiewiet 1983). Sears and Lau (1983) attacked the already thin evidence of effects of personal experiences by suggesting that the few relationships that had been documented were actually produced by artifacts of question order in the surveys. Methodological deficiencies legitimately have been blamed for both the presence and the absence of significant findings.

their personal economic situations to government. When asked to explain economic changes in their own lives, most people made reference to events in their private lives rather than to government (Brody and Sniderman 1977). This tendency to attribute economic changes to personal causes has been termed the "ethic of self-reliance" (Sniderman and Brody 1977), similar to the "sturdy individualistic strand" in American culture referred to as "The American Dream" (Schlozman and Verba 1979: 23). In both cases, a cultural emphasis on hard work and individualism is said to explain the lack of political effects from personal economic experiences.

Explanations for the lack of pocketbook voting rest at least in part on this attribution problem. When attribution of responsibility to government is taken into account in interaction with personal experiences, pocketbook voting does occur (Feldman 1982; Kinder and Mebane 1983). But since such attributions are infrequent, this relationship occurs only on occasion or within very small and select groups.[4] Thus, overall, Americans tend not to connect their personal economic experiences to larger economic problems and tend not to hold government responsible for economic events in their private lives. In other words, personal experiences and concerns do not lead to political attitudes or political actions.

Studies documenting individualistic attributions of responsibility helped a great deal in explaining why the pocketbook prediction did not work, but they did not explain the aggregate-level relationships between economic change and political behavior that were the basis of these investigations in the first place. In response to this problem, Kinder and Kiewiet (1981) proposed that the relationship between economic conditions and evaluations of incumbents stemmed not from personal economic experiences, but from collective, or "sociotropic," economic perceptions. In other words, people were evaluating incumbent politicians on the basis of retrospective perceptions of the state of the economy as a whole rather than on changes in their own personal fortunes. The question people were asking of government was not so much "What have you done for me lately?" as "What have you done for the nation as a whole lately" (Kinder and Mebane 1983: 143).

4 Sniderman and Brody (1977) found that more than 60% of respondents did not see government as a legitimate source of assistance for their personal problems (see also, Kinder and Mebane 1983). Among those who did politicize their personal problems, only 12% judged government performance sufficiently different with respect to personal and national agendas to enable drawing conclusions as to whether they were relying on personal or national referents in evaluating incumbents. Feldman (1982) also found personal economic experiences to be a significant predictor of presidential and congressional voting, but only among a very small minority (Feldman and Conley 1991).

In sharp contrast to the pocketbook findings, many subsequent studies have confirmed that economic judgments at the collective level do, in fact, have a strong impact on evaluations of incumbents at the individual level (Lau and Sears 1981; Fiorina 1981). Furthermore, these national assessments are not simply extrapolations from people's personal experiences (cf. Kinder and Mebane 1983; Fiorina 1981). "In short," Kiewiet (1983: 130) summarized, "what national assessments lack in personal relevance they make up for by being of more obvious political relevance."

Findings documenting the sociotropic nature of political judgments also are consistent with the conditions under which people have been found to use base rate information. Base rates naturally reflect external, situational causes rather than internal, individualistic factors (Kahneman and Tversky 1982). In other words, if huge numbers of people have lost their jobs, it is more likely to be because the economy is failing (external causes) than because all of those people happen to be unreliable workers (internal causes). In studies of nonpolitical judgments, whether base rates are neglected or utilized depends on whether they are attributed to external, situational factors or the peculiarities of a particular sample of people. Several studies have shown that a base rate effect can be restored by stressing the representativeness of a sample (Hansen and Donoghue 1977; Wells and Harvey 1978) or by telling subjects that the sample for which base rates were provided was large and therefore reliable (Kassin 1979a). Put differently, people's perceptions of extremely large collectives are particularly likely to influence their political views because such perceptions discourage individualistic attributions of responsibility and encourage them to blame external, governmental actors.

BEYOND ECONOMIC PERCEPTIONS

The same lack of political impact from personal experience found in the economic realm has been replicated in areas outside the context of economic change. Studies of racial attitudes, employment policies, crime, the military draft, health insurance, and support for a wide variety of other policies appear to be unaffected by retrospective or prospective personal experiences that might logically enter into these policy attitudes (Sears and Funk 1990). For example, those with children likely to be bused were no less supportive of busing to achieve racial integration (Sears, Hensler, and Speer 1979), and those vulnerable to the military draft were no more likely to oppose it (Sears et al. 1983). Likewise, those with friends and relatives in the armed services during Vietnam showed no greater opposition to the war (Lau, Brown, and Sears 1978). Across a wide variety of issues involving multiple tests of these hypotheses, indicators of personal concern have had little explanatory power.[5]

Far fewer studies have explored the sociotropic side of this relationship outside the context of economic problems. The politicization of collective economic well-being has received more attention than other potential issues partly because the economy is virtually always an issue. While other issues that help decide elections may come and go, the salience of the economy is fairly persistent and its impact on voting usually can be counted on from election to election.

Despite the general lack of attention to sociotropic influence in other issue contexts, evidence from related studies suggests a pattern quite consistent with this expectation. For example, when issues such as poverty, crime, terrorism, or racial inequality are framed as collective problems facing the nation, people are more likely to hold government responsible than when these same problems are framed as personal problems (Iyengar 1991). Unlike the usual pocketbook–sociotropic comparisons, the comparison being made in these studies is between problems framed as collective phenomena and problems framed as some *other* person's personal problem. Nonetheless, the sociotropic aspect of this pattern is consistent across a wide variety of issues: When people perceive an issue to be a large-scale social problem, and not just an individual one, they are much more likely to hold government leaders accountable for it.

The assumption that greater political consequences flow from impersonal perceptions is supported by evidence from noneconomic issues demonstrating that the effects of personal- and social-level perceptions are quite different. While personal concerns may result in changes in personal behaviors or attitudes, perceptions of collective problems are more likely to lead to social and political action. For example, when people perceive themselves as personally vulnerable to crime victimization, they will be more likely to engage in self-protective behaviors – to avoid walking alone, to choose well-lit streets, and so forth (Lavrakas 1982; Tyler 1980). But it is only when people believe that their neighborhood, city, or nation as a collective is threatened that they join anticrime groups (Dubow and Podolefsky 1982) and endorse more punitive public policies for criminals (Tyler and Weber 1982; Tyler and Lavrakas 1983). In other words, personal experiences and concerns tend to have very little political impact; instead, concern at the collective level drives the political consequences of social problems. Theoretical expla-

---

5 As Sears and Funk (1990) point out, the exceptions to this general rule are when there are clear and substantial costs and benefits. Some evidence also suggests that purposeful efforts to politicize self-interest may strengthen the effects of personal economic considerations (Lau, Sears, and Jessor 1989).

nations for the general paucity of personal experience-based political attitudes and some empirical evidence drawn from studies of attitudes toward crime both provide support for the idea that sociotropism extends beyond the realm of economic judgments.

However, very few studies have directly examined the consequences of perceptions of collective experience for political attitudes; investigations of the sociotropic pattern have been limited to the economic realm. For this reason, in the late 1980s, during the height of attention to the "drug problem," I included in a national survey parallel questions addressing personal experiences and concerns and collective-level perceptions of the drug problem. Although this issue is unlikely to have the kind of ongoing impact on judgments of presidential performance that economic perceptions do, conditions were ripe at the time for its political impact, given all of the attention it was receiving from political elites and from the press.

A question concerning retrospective perceptions of the drug problem assessed whether the state of the drug problem in the United States had gotten better, worse, or stayed the same over the past year.[6] Personal concern was assessed quite broadly to include effects that the drug problem might have had on family, friends, and acquaintances.[7] Moreover, it was phrased in terms of concern rather than actual experience, so it incorporated people's fears concerning future experiences and was not limited to the direct experiences of the relatively small population segment that has been victimized in some way by drugs, drug-related crime, and so forth.

Does the drug problem demonstrate the sociotropic finding common among economic issues? Table 4.1 shows the results of a direct analogy to pocketbook–sociotropic economic comparisons. Here, based on the results of a random national telephone sample of 1,200 people,[8] we see

6 "Would you say that over the past year the drug problem in the United States has gotten better, worse, or stayed about the same? Is that a little better/worse or a lot better/worse?"

7 "How about you and your family, friends, and acquaintances . . . over the past year have you been more worried or less worried about the drug problem affecting the people close to you, or has this stayed about the same? Is that a little more/less worried or a lot more/less worried?"

8 The University of Wisconsin Survey Center at the University of Wisconsin-Madison runs a continuous, rolling cross-sectional national telephone survey. The Survey Center's sampling procedure begins with a sample of telephone numbers representative of currently working residential phone numbers in the continental United States (including both listed and unlisted numbers) purchased from Nielsen Media Research. One person is selected at random from among the adult (age eighteen or older) members of the sample household. Interviews were conducted using a computer-assisted telephone interviewing system. Each sample number

Table 4.1. *The impact of personal- and collective-level judgments
about the drug problem on presidential performance*

	Coefficient	Standard error
Drugs as national problem	.18	(.04)***
Drugs as personal concern	.06	(.04)
Republican	.89	(.11)***
Democrat	−.75	(.11)***
Age	−.00	(.00)
Income	.07	(.02)**
Race	−.28	(.12)*
Education	−.12	(.04)**
Sex	−.19	(.09)*
R^2	.30	
(n)	(1,051)	

Note: Dependent variable is presidential performance evaluation for Ronald Reagan on a four-point scale where high is a more favorable rating. Data are from a rolling, cross-sectional national telephone sample collected in the fall of 1988.
$*p < .05$ $**p < .01$ $***p < .001$.

the effects of personal concerns and collective-level perceptions of a non-economic issue on evaluations of presidential performance.

The coefficients in Table 4.1 illustrate an extremely familiar pattern: Personal concerns appear to have a negligible impact on judgments of

was called up to ten times, using a "day of the week" calling strategy. Each day's interviews constituted a random sample of the population on that day. This requirement meant that it was necessary to deal with the problem of nonresponse in a special way, using a procedure first suggested by Kish and Hess (1959) and elaborated upon by Madow, Hyman, and Jessen (1961). The procedure depends on replacing current not-at-homes with not-at-homes saved from previous sample draws. Because the kinds of people not home on one day of the week may be different from those not at home on another, the replacement scheme is day-of-the-week specific. Some measure is added to the variability of the resulting estimates. Nonetheless, each day's interviews represent a probability sample for that particular day.

To assess the quality of the survey, the distributions of social and demographic characteristics of the Survey Center's respondents were compared with those of the American National Election Studies (ANES) and the National Survey of Families and Households (NSFH). The response rate in these surveys averages around 55% when one includes both refusals and unresolved numbers in the denominator. This is considerably lower than the ANES and the NSFH; however, comparisons suggested that distributions of respondents were quite similar with respect to major demographic variables, including household size, region, age, presidential performance, while judgments about collective experience play a significant role. Even when controlling for the effects of both party identification and demographics – a model that may well overcontrol for the potential reciprocal impact of presidential performance evaluations on judgments about the state of the drug problem nationally (see, e.g., Kiewiet 1983) – judgments about the severity of the problem to the nation as a whole have far more impact than personal fears and concerns.

The extent to which personal- or collective-level judgments enter into political assessments for any given issue will obviously be determined partly by the salience of that issue in popular political discourse at any given point in time. Although the drug problem was clearly salient enough to have some overall impact on presidential performance at the time this study was done, one would expect high levels of salience to alter the general pattern, at times producing greater or lesser effects than those seen in Table 4.1. Since these data were drawn from a rolling, cross-sectional study done over a five-month period, I compared results for those interviewed during heavier and lighter periods of media coverage of the drug issue. Calling patterns for the rolling, cross-sectional sample ensured that date of interview was a random event so that groups interviewed during periods of high and low coverage were otherwise comparable samples.[9]

As shown in Table 4.2, heavy coverage of the issue increased the extent to which collective-level perceptions entered into judgments of the president's performance. The importance of retrospective judgments

> sex, household income, marital status, religious preference, unemployment, and church attendance. Differences result from the fact that this was a telephone survey, which consequently underrepresents minorities. Educational comparisons were difficult because the Survey Center uses educational classifications based on the 1990 census concept; in general, it appears to underrepresent those with less than twelve years of education, again due to the prevalence of telephones.
>
> 9 Measures of drug coverage were obtained using a computer-assisted content analysis (see Fan 1988 for details on this kind of procedure). First, from the universe of all Associated Press wire service stories that appeared during the time frame of the survey, a random sample of 1,000 stories was downloaded from the Nexis news database. Any story qualified if it included the stem "drug." Next the sample was examined for irrelevant content and then was filtered to remove inappropriate references, primarily those stories dealing with prescription drugs, AIDS drug research, and so forth (contact author for complete list). Finally, the remaining stories were scored for the total number of paragraphs mentioning the following key words: drug, cocaine, crack, heroin, marijuana, morphine, narcotic, and snort.
>
> Coverage scores matched to respondents by their date of interview were based on a ten-day weighted average where information was assigned a half-life of one day. High and low coverage levels were designated by splitting the coverage scores at the median coverage figure.

Table 4.2. *Personal and collective judgments about the drug problem as predictors of presidential performance: Effects of media coverage*

	Low drug coverage	High drug coverage
Drugs as national problem	.10ᵃ (.07)	.22ᵃ (.05)***
Drugs as personal concern	−.02 (.07)	.11 (.05)*
Republican	.76 (.15)***	.98 (.12)***
Democrat	−.84 (.15)***	−.53 (.12)***
Age	−.00 (.00)	−.00 (.00)
Gender	−.11 (.12)	−.21 (.10)*
Race	−.55 (.16)***	−.12 (.13)
Income	.05 (.04)	.07 (.03)*
Education	−.08 (.06)	−.14 (.04)***
R^2	.31	.29
(n)	(525)	(526)

Note: Entries are unstandardized coefficients from OLS regression equations with standard errors in parentheses. Dependent variable is presidential performance evaluation for Ronald Reagan on a four-point scale where high is a more favorable rating. Data are from a rolling, cross-sectional national telephone sample collected in the fall of 1988.
ᵃIn a pooled equation, the interaction between national problem and media coverage is statistically significant (b = .15 (.07), $p < .05$), as are the main effects of drug coverage (b = −.33 (.16), $p < .05$).
*$p < .05$ **$p < .01$ ***$p < .001$.

about the drug problem was significantly greater for the group interviewed during periods of heavy coverage of this issue.[10] In contrast, high levels of coverage did not significantly increase the impact of personal concerns surrounding the drug problem. In total, the drug problem appears to demonstrate a familiar sociotropic pattern whereby perceptions of the issue's impact at the national level have a much greater influence on political judgments than the personal concerns it may generate.

As with economic issues, the political impact of the drug problem is primarily driven by perceptions of the extent to which this problem affects *others* in the nation, and not by personal concerns and experiences. Moreover, there is no reason to expect this pattern to be limited to only a few issues. To the extent that any issue has a measurable impact on

10 It should also be noted that media coverage has significant direct effects on presidential performance, in addition to the significant interaction. High levels of drug news lowered presidential approval by .33.

performance evaluations, this influence is likely to be carried not by the personal toll the issue has taken on individual members of the public, but by the larger perception of the extent to which others are influenced by the problem.

Explanations for the significant political impact of collective-level perceptions center on the same general logic as explanations for the lack of impact from personal experiences and concerns: The same attributional tendencies that make it difficult for people to link personal problems with the actions or inaction of government leaders make it far easier for citizens to hold government accountable for collective social problems. To the extent that mass media influence these collective-level perceptions, as suggested in Chapter 3, and that the public's political evaluations rest on these collective-level perceptions, the media take on an even more politically powerful role.

Although the term "sociotropic" originally was coined to denote a motivation to pay attention to others, it was not intended to signify altruism per se (Meehl 1977). Likewise, the distinction between sociotropic and personal-experience-based political attitudes generally has not been construed as motivational in origin. People are not assumed to disregard personal experience because of a tendency toward altruism; instead, sociotropic politics occurs because of variations in how different kinds of information are processed and the ease with which attributions of responsibility may be made.

Information sources continue to play a central role in theoretical explanations for this phenomenon. While personal experiences tend to be compartmentalized, information about national conditions is available from mass media in a prepackaged form that is easier to connect to judgments of national political leaders (Kinder and Kiewiet 1981). Thus, sociotropic judgments transfer quite easily to political preferences, while personal experiences do not. Weatherford (1983: 163) concurs, "Unlike the media's statistical reports on the state of the national economy, the individual's personal condition stands at some remove from the eventual economic policy judgment."

THE PROSPECTS FOR ACCOUNTABILITY

As illustrated in Chapter 3, mass media play a key role in establishing people's perceptions of collective social reality; they are an important source of "social facts" about the state of large collectives. At the same time, perceptions of mass collectives are not wholly mediated in origin; personal experiences and concerns can enter into these judgments as well. Nonetheless, media are major contributors to the *compartmentalization* of personal- and collective-level perceptions. By providing information beyond the realm of personal experience, they ensure that our perceptions of large collectives are not mere extrapolations from personal experiences.

Why does it matter whether mediated information plays a significant role in influencing judgments about impersonal others? If, as suggested by the sociotropic politics literature and the study reported above, perceptions of collective phenomena matter more to people's political attitudes than do personal problems, media acquire an indirect, yet extremely important, role by virtue of their capacity to shape judgments of collective experience. If media convey accurate representations of the state of the collective to individual members of the public, then the interests of accountability should be served.[11] But for many scholars the underlying concern is that collective-level judgments may vary independent of personal experiences (Patterson 1993; Hetherington 1996).

Indeed, the sociotropic model suggests a potential for distortion and lack of accountability that personal-experience-based politics appears to ensure. Personal concerns are anchored in real-world experience in a way that judgments of distant collectives are not. If the policies of current politicians are hurting enough people, voting on the basis of personal experience guarantees that the rascals will soon be thrown out of office. On the other hand, a citizenry forming political views on the basis of collective-level perceptions is vulnerable to manipulation. If mass media or other information sources lead people to form inaccurate perceptions, their political views cannot ensure the same level of accountability as aggregated personal experiences.

Prospective perceptions at the collective level present similar concerns. If the policies of current leaders are seen as potentially damaging to others down the road, citizens can make sure they are not reelected; but like collective-level retrospective evaluations, prospective evaluations also may lack an anchor in real-world events and experiences. No amount of media coverage will convince the unemployed person that he is doing better financially or persuade the worker who now has adequate

[11] When analyzing retrospective perceptions of economic conditions, comparisons of the sociotropic and pocketbook predictions are essentially comparisons of the predictive power of past personal economic experiences to perceptions of the economic experiences of impersonal others. For example, the personal experience of being unemployed is compared with the perception that many others have experienced undesirable joblessness in the past year. In analyses of prospective measures, these concepts become less distinct since perceptions of one's own future prospects may be based to some extent on perceptions of the future of the nation. Moreover, prospective economic perceptions at the personal level need not necessarily be anchored in real world experiences. Though measured at the personal level, they are anticipated experiences that will be based to some extent on the kind of outside information reaching a given individual.

health care coverage for the first time that she is worse off. But predicting the future is a far riskier business, especially when one is making predictions about people and events far beyond the realm of one's day-to-day knowledge and experience. Thus, political behavior that is rooted in people's personal experiences and concerns is generally deemed a preferable state of affairs to either prospective or retrospective sociotropic preferences.

This perspective generally leads to the conclusion that media-based perceptions of collective experience are a dangerously unreliable link to democratic accountability. Moreover, since candidates for office have obvious motives for trying to persuade citizens that it is "morning in America" (in the case of incumbents) or that collective affairs have gone to hell in a handbasket (in the case of challengers), perceptions of collective well-being often may be targeted for purposeful manipulation. In short, media provide a thin basis for ensuring democratic accountability, whereas personal experiences seem solidly rooted in concrete aspects of the realities we live on a day-to-day basis.

At least so the argument goes. In fact, perceptions of personal and collective experience are each biased in separate, but highly consistent, directions that have important implications for normative judgments about the desirability of the personal and sociotropic models. In the sections that follow, I first evaluate the accuracy and the sources of bias in collective-level evaluations, then those that characterize personal judgments. Finally, I discuss the political implications of the curious, but highly consistent, gap between personal- and collective-level judgments.

The Accuracy of Collective-Level Judgments

Assessing the normative implications of political behavior based on impersonal as opposed to personal judgments ultimately requires that we know something about the accuracy of these perceptions. If judgments of collectives mirror the aggregate of individual experiences, then the two models should produce roughly identical outcomes. Do people have accurate perceptions of the state of the nation, the most common referent for analyses of sociotropic judgments? Although conclusions on this front appear to be quite mixed, their implications are less so when one considers (1) the contexts in which these perceptions matter and (2) the range of perceptions that would need reliably to reflect aggregate social and political realities in order for accountability to occur across a broad range of issues.

As with studies of sociotropic politics more generally, most evidence pertaining to the accuracy of collective-level perceptions comes from the realm of economic issues. On this front, one group of studies has suggested that there is little cause for alarm. After all, what difference does it make if individuals' perceptions of their larger social world differ from their perceptions of themselves as individuals? Since the economy can only be improving or declining at any given point in time, these deviations in perceptions of collective conditions are just so much error variance that ultimately cancels itself out in the aggregate (Kramer 1983). If this were the case and errors in judging collective experience were in random directions, then there should be little reason for concern. In the aggregate, politicians could be held accountable for the results of their policies either by political views formed on the basis of personal experience or by those formed on the basis of perceptions of collective experience.

In the realm of prospective judgments,[12] MacKuen, Erikson, and Stimson (1992) have made the strongest claims about the public's ability to form rational assessments of the national economy's prospects. Although they note many individual-level studies documenting people's relative ignorance of economic statistics (Holbrook and Garand 1996; Conover, Feldman, and Knight 1986, 1987), they argue that a general sense of optimism or pessimism seeps through the public consciousness in important ways. Ultimately, they claim that expert views of the economy are accurately reflected in media coverage and that the public thereby receives accurate information on economic prospects that is used in making subsequent political evaluations:

The experts who translate the economic numbers into good times and bad times attend to more than the standard news. In the business of looking ahead, they absorb news that is critical to professional forecasting but often of little direct interest to the general public. Their translations convey their sophisticated understanding to all. Without trying, the public is exposed to the best information about the economic future that exists. Merely by noting that most forecasters say good (bad) times are ahead, the public becomes subject to the causal influence of the professional's more esoteric tools (MacKuen, Erikson, and Stimson 1992: 604).

In other words, the media act as a neutral conduit for relaying rational and highly sophisticated evaluations of economic prospects to potential voters. Leading indicators affect the judgments of economic experts who influence the content of the news, and this, in turn, influences ordinary people's judgments. Armed with this information, citizens are assumed to be able to hold leaders accountable for the nations' economic prospects. For this path to accountability to work properly, first journalists must utilize sophisticated economic information about the economy's

---

12 Since there is little agreement on whether economic evaluations matter primarily by means of retrospective judgments, prospective judgments, or both, I address the issue of accuracy from both perspectives.

likely future and relay at least the gist of these experts' expectations to the public. Second, the public must derive a sense of the economy's prospects by receiving and interpreting this information accurately so that the right people are ultimately elected or defeated at election time.

The evidence brought to bear on the media's ability to relay accurate prospective economic information is that public expectations about the economy's long-term prospects are positively correlated over time with the public's perceptions of the tone of economic news. As Clarke and Stewart (1994) have pointed out, this simply assumes, rather than tests, the premise that media portray economic affairs in accord with experts' views. An appropriate test would compare people's economic perceptions and/or media coverage to some objective economic indicator. Moreover, since MacKuen and colleagues' (1992) measure of economic news was based on survey indicators of people's *perceptions* of what they had heard and not on actual coverage, their accounts of what they heard may not reflect actual coverage. In addition, even if media relied heavily on economic experts in formulating the news, not all forecasts given to the media by experts are rational or in agreement. Some such information is biased, and reporters may purposely seek out and report on conflicting opinions for purposes of creating greater drama. Despite the proliferation of objective indicators in this arena, expert disagreement as to their interpretation is not uncommon. As David Stockman (1981) once put it, "None of us really understands what's going on with all these numbers."

Notwithstanding MacKuen and colleagues' particular study, most time series analyses of objective economic conditions and media coverage concur that there is a relationship between the "real" economy and the tone of economic coverage. For example, using data derived from media content analyses, Tims, Freeman, and Fan (1989) found that aggregated economic perceptions correlated over time with the tone of economic news in the press. In a study of the complete causal chain from expert views to news coverage to public expectations to presidential approval, Nadeau, Niemi, and Fan (1996) found that journalists did rely to some extent on elite evaluations of the current state of the economy. But what mattered in shaping the tone of news coverage was not the kind of complex, forward-looking indicators that economic experts utilized; instead, news reports were related to more straightforward economic indicators such as statistics on current unemployment and inflation. In contrast, the expectations of business elites about the future of the economy did not predict the tone of economic news. In a study relating *New York Times* coverage to levels and changes in levels of inflation, unemployment, and the domestic product, Goidel and Langley (1995) found that the total number of newspaper articles on the economy was driven by changes in objective economic conditions. However, it was mainly the number of negative stories that was driven by real world changes and not the number of positive stories. In Britain, Gavin and Sanders (1996) found a surprisingly weak set of relationships between television coverage of economic news and objective changes in macroeconomic conditions. Although coverage was related to unemployment trends over time, it did not respond to a variety of other economic indicators. Officials statistics aside, they also noted that the balance of economic coverage on television bore little relation to measures of the economy as personally experienced by individuals.

Despite evidence of ties to regularly released economic statistics, studies still lend considerable support to the idea that journalists play a significant autonomous role in determining the tone of economic coverage. For example, although Nadeau, Niemi, and Fan (1996) found that changes in objective economic statistics had a direct impact on the tone of economic news, their study also suggested that news reports contributed to mass expectations in an independent fashion, beyond the evaluations of either elites or objective conditions. Moreover, it was the tone of economic news, but not elite expectations, that contributed to mass public expectations about the economy. In other words, when economic statistics and elite views of the economy were included in the same equation as measures of media coverage, media retained a significant impact on public perceptions.

Consistent with this evidence, Blood and Phillips (1995) found that recession headlines significantly influenced consumer sentiment beyond what could be accounted for by economic statistics concerning present and future conditions. In their analyses of presidential approval, Nadeau and colleagues (1996) found that even the inclusion of straightforward, objective measures of current economic conditions did not suppress the effects that the tone of economic coverage had on public perceptions. Elite economic expectations had no direct effects at all. In other words, politically consequential expectations were rooted in media treatment of economic conditions rather than in the sophisticated views of economic experts: "Journalists manufacture politically consequential expectations, business executives do not" (p. 14). The main source of national-level economic expectations was media treatment of economic information. In a study of British media, Gavin and Sanders (1996: 9) also ruled out the possibility that "news simply and faithfully represents the lived experience of the public, and that it is this experience, rather than television representation, that informs views of government competence, and, in turn, helps drive government popularity."

To summarize, journalists appear to pay some attention to economic indicators, particularly straightforward and easily interpretable ones. The question is how much. It would indeed be quite surprising to find that journalists' reports about the economy were completely independent of the tone of readily available economic statistics. Journalists' dependence on official sources has been well established, and there is little reason to think this area should be different from others (Sigal 1973; Brody 1991). But they also exercise an independent influence on the tone that economic coverage takes. The real issue is how closely media coverage must mirror reality in order for the public to end up with unbiased perceptions of national economic well-being.

Real-world economic conditions clearly do shape economic perceptions to some extent, but is it enough to maintain the level of accountability that is needed to make sure the right candidates are elected or defeated? How many people must have inaccurate perceptions in order to alter the outcome of a presidential election? This is not a simple empirical question to answer since the salience of economic issues changes from one presidential election to the next, as does the size of the margin necessary for victory.

MacKuen and colleagues (1992) rest their case on the idea that aggregation will cancel out the well-documented errors in individual-level judgments of the economy (e.g., Conover, Feldman, and Knight 1986). But their study does not empirically demonstrate that distortions in individual judgment cancel out in the aggregate (Clarke and Stewart 1994). Since elections are cross-sectional events where the critical act occurs on one day only, these errors need to cancel one another out not just over time, but also at any one given point in time in order to ensure that election outcomes accurately hold elected officials accountable. These errors need to be both unbiased and uncorrelated, yet Haller and Norpoth (1994) find plenty of each in prospective judgments about inflation as well as in business expectations.

Hetherington's (1996) recent analyses demonstrate that the level of distortion was sufficient in 1992 to alter the election outcome. He argues that if voters had cast ballots based on actual economic statistics rather than based on their media-influenced perceptions of economic conditions, it is likely that Bush would have won. On the other hand, similar analyses of the 1988 and 1984 elections show that inaccurate economic perceptions made little difference to the outcomes of these races. Nonetheless, the potential for a breakdown in accountability clearly exists.

All in all then, there is ample evidence that media reports are influenced by certain kinds of objective economic statistics, but very little evidence that both elite and /or mass expectations are formed rationally or in a manner that is independent of autonomous media influence (Clarke and Stewart 1994; Nadeau, Niemi, and Fan 1996; Haller and Norpoth 1994; Attfield, Demery, and Duck 1991). Studies generally concur that media play an important role in altering people's perceptions of the economic well-being of the nation (MacKuen, Erickson, and Stimson 1992; Tims, Freeman, and Fan 1989).[13] Virtually all of the studies documenting a significant relationship between media and objective measures of economic change also have acknowledged media as having considerable autonomy in its tone of coverage (Goidel and Langley 1995; Van Raaij 1990; Tims, Freeman, and Fan 1989).

Evidence that the public accurately interprets coverage is sorely lacking. Particularly in the case of economic prospections, partisanship and other sources of personal bias enter into mass expectations. Because these biases tend to be stable over time, they are not important in time series analyses. However, when it comes to the bottom line – holding political leaders accountable – bias and the accuracy of economic perceptions at any given point in time are quite important. Like accuracy in other realms of political judgment, the accuracy of economic perceptions has been found to be related to socioeconomic status, race and gender (Holbrook and Garand 1996; Mutz 1992b). Citizens' views may be inaccurate in systematic, rather than random directions; thus individual differences in the extent of accuracy may introduce additional bias. This is especially worrisome because those most likely to alter election outcomes also tend to be the least informed and thus the least likely to be reached by economic information.

Although there is some support for individual links in the idealized trickle-down model where elite economic views translate to media coverage and then become public perceptions, the theory has little overall support. Certainly, it would be an overstatement to claim complete consensus on this issue. But if one examines the prospects for accountability

13 Using aggregated data, Haller and Norpoth (1995, 1996) have suggested that economic evaluations stem from real life experiences rather than news coverage. They base this judgment on evidence showing that there is a large segment of the public that is essentially without economic news and that people "without news" evaluate the state of the economy in ways similar to those with news. In this case, however, being "without news" means answering "no" to a question asking, "During the last few months, have you heard about any favorable or unfavorable changes in business conditions?" Assuming that people take this question at face value, they may have lingering impressions from previous time periods and /or they may have information about the economy that does not pertain specifically to business conditions. They are not, strictly speaking, without *any* news about the economy. Haller and Norpoth (1986: 21) suggest that this evidence "casts doubt on claims that economic opinion in the general public is largely media-inspired, while lending credence to the view that voter choices motivated by economic judgments are firmly rooted in the real world." They conclude that "ordinary citizens are capable of drawing such a picture from real-world economic cues they encounter in their everyday lives." Although the validity of their media exposure measure can certainly be debated, the considerable evidence finding minimal to limited consequences from personal economic experiences casts doubts on their overall conclusion.

under sociotropism across a broader range of issues, then this conclusion becomes even less tenable. In the realm of economic issues, reliable statistics are readily available on a periodic basis, regularly distributed to the media, and then often thematically presented in news coverage (Iyengar 1991). As a result, the trickle-down model has at least some plausibility in this issue arena. But for most issues, reporters do not have such a systematic means of monitoring change over time; thus their impressions of whether a given issue is becoming more or less problematic and whether it is improving or worsening will be based on educated guesses at best. Previous research suggests that even for issues such as crime, for which statistics are regularly available, press attention is often unrelated to the level of crime in a community (Davis 1952; Jones 1976; Antunes and Hurley 1977; Graber 1980a).[14]

Economic issues are seldom the whole story when it comes to evaluating presidential performance; incumbents are evaluated on more than economic prosperity alone. The prospects for a sociotropic model of accountability are considerably less when one considers issue areas in which national statistics are not regularly released and reported on. For example, in areas such as education, health care, illegal drug use, racial inequality, and so forth, the idea that the aggregate public listens to, and moves in accord with, an informed elite analysis becomes far less tenable. Since accountability never rests solely on one issue, we have little reassurance that sociotropic influence flowing from other issues will be based on accurate perceptions of mass experience. Thus, citizens voting on the basis of their perceptions of problems at the collective level may often make choices that do not promote democratic accountability.

Sources of Distortion in Media Presentations

A variety of factors may contribute to systematic distortions in media coverage of issues. The sources of distortion most relevant to media portrayals of collective experience include a preference for negativity, overemphasis on rare events, and a preference for stories involving change over stasis. In addition to the content conveyed in media presentations of collective experience, the specific ways they are framed may lead readers or viewers to process information in a way that encourages greater distortion.

By far the most prominent charge of late is that journalists place greater emphasis on negative news. For example, both Patterson (1993)

---

14 Moreover, police misreporting and manipulation of official crime statistics have been well documented (Seidman and Couzens 1974; Pepinsky and Jesilow 1984; Johnston 1983).

and Wattenberg (1984) have argued that the negative bias inherent in many definitions of newsworthiness has contributed to a negative slant in some types of news coverage. As the old adage suggests, "No news is good news," from which follows the logical equivalent, that good news is not news. If something is not a problem, it is unlikely to command considerable news attention. Considerable evidence from the economic realm appears to support this idea. Nadeau and colleagues (1996) found in their study of the Associated Press news wire and *Washington Post* stories that the overwhelming majority of economic stories were negative. Likewise, Haller and Norpoth (1996: 19–20) note that in the Michigan Consumer Surveys' self-reported measures of economic news, "In survey after survey, there are nearly always more respondents who report hearing bad news about the economy than do good news." In making a more general argument about the extent of press negativity toward politics and politicians, Patterson (1993: 113) also notes that during the course of the 1992 election, more than 90 percent of press references to the economy were negative compared with 75 percent in the immediately preceding period. In addition, he notes that the network's portrayal of the economy got worse as the economy was improving. Wattenberg (1984) also cites bits and pieces of evidence of a tilt toward negativity, particularly in highly interpretive economic coverage that is not based on official statistics.

Some studies suggest more complicated patterns than a straightforward bias toward negative information. In a study of television coverage of the unemployment rate, inflation rate, and growth of the real gross national product (GNP) from 1973 to 1984, Harrington (1989) found that the networks gave greater coverage to these statistics when they were declining during nonelection years, but found no such bias during election years. In nonelection years, stories about deteriorating economic statistics were 34 percent longer and twice as likely to be lead stories; in election years, increases and decreases received similar amounts of coverage. Blood and Phillips (1995) found evidence that increased presidential popularity affected the nature of economic coverage by making it more critical. Still others have suggested that there may be a cycle of economic news in which media reports tend to be more favorable to incumbents at both ends of their mandates (Brody 1991: 143; Robinson and Sheehan 1983).

Findings based on combining content analyses with survey data have suggested that negative coverage of economic perceptions results in more negative public perceptions of the state of economic conditions (Nadeau, Niemi, and Fan 1996; Blood and Phillips 1995). Although he does not combine content analyses with his survey data, Hetherington (1996) also found that higher levels of media exposure predicted more negative assessments of national economic conditions in 1992 – precisely when other content analyses were documenting overly negative coverage. The effect in 1992 was even stronger than the effects of party identification, but media consumption had no such impact in 1984 or 1988.[15]

Although self-reported information sources are notoriously unreliable, they concur with the general conclusion that negative perceptions often come from mediated portrayals. For example, when asked about the origins of negative perceptions of the crime problem, over 65 percent of the public cited mass media.[16] Likewise, when asked where they got the information that led them to their generally negative views on how much government could be trusted – personal experiences with an agency or program, what they learned from friends and family, or what they saw, heard, or read in television, newspapers, or other media – a full 72 percent reported media as the origin of their perceptions.[17]

The evidence drawn from content analyses of news coverage does not support the idea of a consistent negativity bias across all times and topics, but when such biases do exist they appear to have a substantial impact on public perceptions. Moreover, it is noteworthy that without exception, all evidence that a bias exists consistently suggests that it is in a *negative,* rather than a positive, direction.

In addition to a negative bias, rare events often capture a lot of media attention – precisely because they are rare – and this may result in an overestimation of the incidence of catastrophic risks or unusual events (Slovic, Fischoff, and Lichtenstein 1987). In other words, news values

15 Although MacKuen and colleagues (1992) find evidence of a relationship between media and public expectations, their self-report measures of exposure to economic news are likely to be unreliable indicators of actual media content (see Price and Zaller 1993). In general, the question of whether a negativity bias translates to negatively biased public perceptions of mass collectives has been difficult to evaluate because of the need for simultaneous parallel measures of objective economic conditions, perceptions of collective conditions, and media content. Instead, many studies attempting to do this compare perceptions of business conditions with measures of objective conditions or personal economic experiences that refer to general economic conditions (Haller and Norpoth 1996; MacKuen et al. 1992).

16 Based on a *Los Angeles Times* national poll of 1,516 adult respondents done the week of January 15, 1994. "Are your feelings about crime based more on what you read, see and hear in the media or more on what you, your family and your acquaintances experience personally in your community?"

17 National poll of 1,514 adult respondents done the week of November 28, 1995 by Princeton Survey Research Associates for the Kaiser Family Foundation, the Harvard School of Public Health, and the *Washington Post.* "Earlier in this interview, you said you could trust the government in Washington (just about always/most of the time/only some of the time/none of the time). Which of the following was most important in giving you the impression you have of the federal government? Was it your own personal experience with a government agency or program, what you learned from friends and family, or what you saw, heard or read in television, newspapers or other media?"

may inadvertently promote perceptions of collective experience that are skewed toward extremes rather than the median or modal experience. This practice also may contribute to media's impersonal impact; since individuals are unlikely to fit the prototype for a person at risk for a highly unusual problem, this information is likely to be processed primarily as information about *others* that is not deemed relevant to personal-level judgments.

Independent of a bias toward negativity, the trend toward greater interpretation in "long journalism" encourages journalists to proclaim and interpret trends from evidence of random fluctuation. News reports give greater attention to change than stasis; thus there is a tendency to interpret even minor changes as the development or aggravation of a trend rather than as temporary deviations from a normal situation (Van Raaij 1990). An emphasis on providing explanations and identifying causal factors may potentially lead to overreactions in either positive or negative directions (Andreassen 1987). For example, evidence of a slight and perhaps insignificant economic downturn may be made to seem more newsworthy when it is portrayed as a harbinger of things to come.

Finally, even if coverage were perfectly representative of, and proportional to, the incidence of collective phenomena of some type, the way individual readers and viewers process this information may distort the impressions they ultimately receive from viewing or reading. Most media coverage combines general statements about the range or importance of a problem, that is, base-rate information, with illustrative individual cases or exemplars. To date, evidence examining whether the vividness of exemplars produces a greater impact on people's judgments has been mixed. For example, in experimental studies of agenda setting that compared the impact of stories focusing on personalized case histories in contrast to general discussions of an issue, Iyengar and Kinder (1987) found that vivid exemplars could both strengthen and weaken perceptions of the severity of social problems. The pattern of null and mixed results may stem from experimental designs where vividness is varied in absolute terms by exposing people to messages that include *either* vivid or pallid information. Based on observing patterns in positive and negative findings with respect to the effects of vividness on judgments about social problems, Brosius and Bathelt (1994) suggest that vividness effects occur strictly when people are presented with *both* types of information and have to decide where to direct their attention. Studies combining vivid exemplars and pallid statements about general incidence, but systematically altering the distribution of exemplars, find that people's perceptions of collective opinion and experience are influenced disproportionately by the distribution of exemplars, despite the obviously greater relevance of base-rate information (Brosius and Bathelt 1994;

Zillman, Perkins, and Sundar 1991). In cases where the exemplar distribution clearly contradicted base rate information, people were guided by the exemplars. Even when exemplars were largely consistent with the base rate information (e.g., 75 percent of people are said to favor an issue, and four exemplars consistent with this opinion are presented), the exemplars led to distorted perceptions by causing people to overestimate the size of the majority endorsing this view.

This finding suggests that even if coverage of the frequency or severity of social problems is generally accurate, if news accounts are garnished with an inaccurate distribution of exemplars – perhaps individuals who remain plagued by a particular problem despite general improvement – then public perceptions of collective reality may reflect the distribution of exemplars rather than more accurate base-rate information. In other words, exemplars are yet another possible source of distortion in the extent to which media coverage contributes to accurate perceptions of mass collectives, and thus another threat to holding leaders accountable for the state of collective affairs.

COMPARTMENTALIZATION OF PERSONAL AND NATIONAL JUDGMENTS

Another more general type of evidence often martialed to support the theory of biased perceptions of collective experience involves aggregate-level comparisons of parallel personal- and national-level judgments. To the extent that perceptions of the collective are systematically different from aggregated perceptions of people's personal lives, media coverage is typically blamed for cultivating distorted perceptions of collective experience. Figures 4.1 through 4.6 provide a number of illustrations of the disjuncture between aggregated personal-level judgments and perceptions that same collective has of itself.

Although there are countless examples that might be drawn upon to illustrate this point, I have limited these selections to situations that meet fairly rigorous criteria. First, the questions about personal and societal phenomena had to have been asked using parallel question wording and identical response scales. Comparisons are often made between measures of things such as personal finances and perceptions of national business conditions, but these referents are not identical and thus rival interpretations of these disjunctures are plausible. Since very minor wording differences have been known to produce substantial differences in survey responses, solid comparisons must rest on identical referents. Second, in order to eliminate the possibility of survey house effects and changes in opinion that may have occurred within short periods of time, I further limited the comparisons to situations where the same survey organization asked pairs of questions of the same respondents at the same point in time.

Figure 4.1 presents the most common kind of example of this phenomenon. Drawing on two economic questions, one asked about the condition of the national economy and the other asked about the person's own economic situation, the mean rating on a four-point scale is significantly higher for people's assessments of their personal situations than for their assessments of the nation as a whole. How can the collective logically be faring differently from the sum of its individual experiences? Despite its implausibility, this pattern maintains across a wide range of studies with quite different purposes. Moreover, this disjuncture runs in a highly consistent direction with perceptions at the collective level persistently more negative than personal-level judgments.

Figure 4.2 demonstrates that this systematic pattern of pessimistic collective assessments coupled with positive personal assessments extends beyond the economic realm. Here, four almost identically worded questions were asked about people's own doctors and about their perceptions of other people's doctors. In the first two, positively phrased questions, people's assessments of their own doctors are systematically more positive than their assessments of other people's doctors. When questions are phrased in negative terms, as in the last two examples, the pattern of agreement reverses so that people are systematically more likely to agree with negative assessments of other people's doctors than with similar assessments of their own doctors.

In some ways, these patterns may seem reminiscent of the public's negative evaluations of Congress as a whole as opposed to generally positive evaluations of their own personal representatives (Fenno 1974). But in the case of Congress, the explanation typically offered is that people have fundamentally different expectations of their individual members (constituency service) as opposed to the body as a whole (policy making). Because Congress can make policies only as a collective unit, this separation of judgments makes some sense. Members may work well individually in providing representation and /or constituency service, yet still fail to produce the collective outcome expected of the unit as a whole (Asher and Barr 1994).

But the same logic cannot easily be applied to the example in Figure 4.2. Doctors do not work as a collective, thus there is no easy explanation for this disjuncture. Nor does it make sense that the economy could be in decline while the aggregate of people's personal economic situations is improving. Since the state of the economy is typically defined in terms of the collective well-being of the aggregate, plausible explanations are lacking.

Figure 4.3 presents additional evidence suggesting that like the soci-

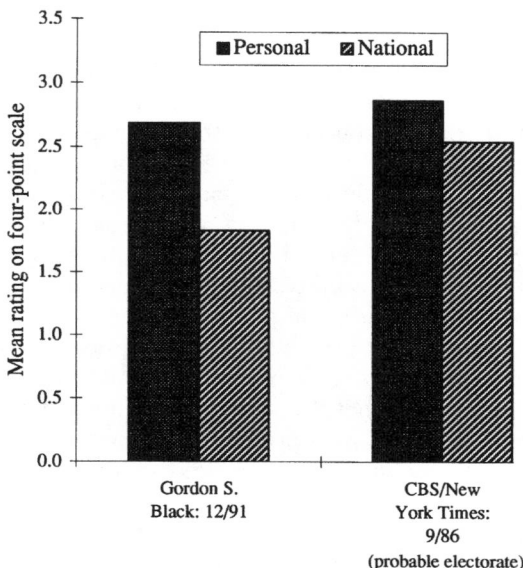

Figure 4.1. Perceptions of economic conditions at personal and national levels. *Personal*: "How would you rate your own (personal) economic situation these days? Is it very good, fairly good, fairly bad, or very bad?" *National*: "How would you rate the condition of the national economy these days? Is it very good, fairly good, fairly bad, or very bad?"

otropic pattern of economic voting, this phenomenon is not peculiarly American. When citizens of the United Kingdom were asked which adjectives described their feelings about their country's economy and which of these same terms applied to their feelings about the financial condition of their own households, a similar pattern appeared. On the left-hand side of the figure, four negative adjectives were systematically endorsed more often in the context of the national economy. The right-hand side of the figure shows that three positive adjectives were systematically endorsed more often to describe feelings surrounding people's personal financial condition.

The examples of this pattern are so numerous they need not all be recounted here. When people are asked parallel questions about their personal lives and experiences and the state of the nation as a whole, they produce consistently inconsistent findings in which the collective is perceived more negatively than the sum of its individual components. But it is natural to wonder whether this is a relatively recent phenome-

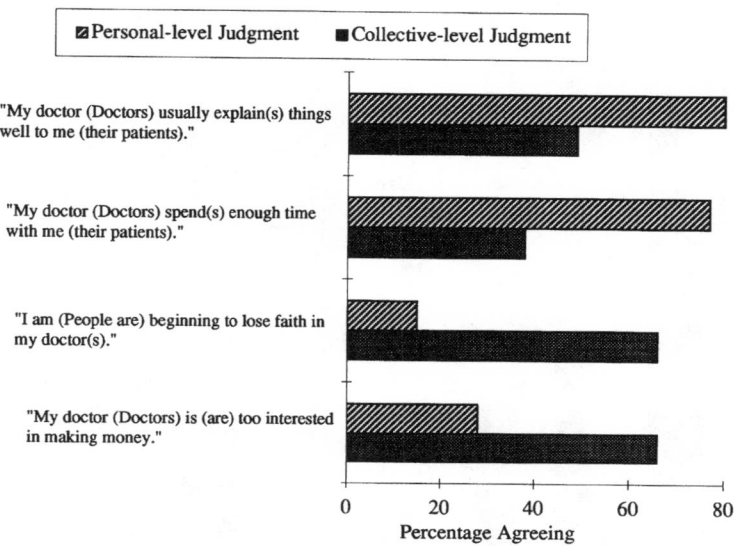

Figure 4.2. Personal- and collective-level judgments about health care.
Source: American Medical Association, "Public Opinion on Health Care Issues." Cited in Jacobs and Shapiro (1994). Words in parentheses correspond to collective-level wording of same questions.

non and/or whether there might not be an equally impressive number of counterexamples running the opposite direction if one looks back in history.

Unfortunately, there are few time series that have included parallel items asked of identical samples. There are two notable exceptions that give us some limited insight into this question using items that are similar to, though not as precisely parallel in wording as, those described in Figures 4.1, 4.2, and 4.3. One set comes from the American National Election Studies in which questions concerning personal and national prospective and retrospective economic perceptions have been asked every two years since 1980. Using a summary measure of the difference between the percentage of people saying things were getting or had gotten better minus the percentage who claimed they were getting or had gotten worse, Figures 4.4 and 4.5 confirm that, overall, perceptions of national well-being have, in fact, been consistently more pessimistic than personal evaluations.

Figure 4.4 describes prospective evaluations of one's personal economic situation and the national economy. Here we see that in seven

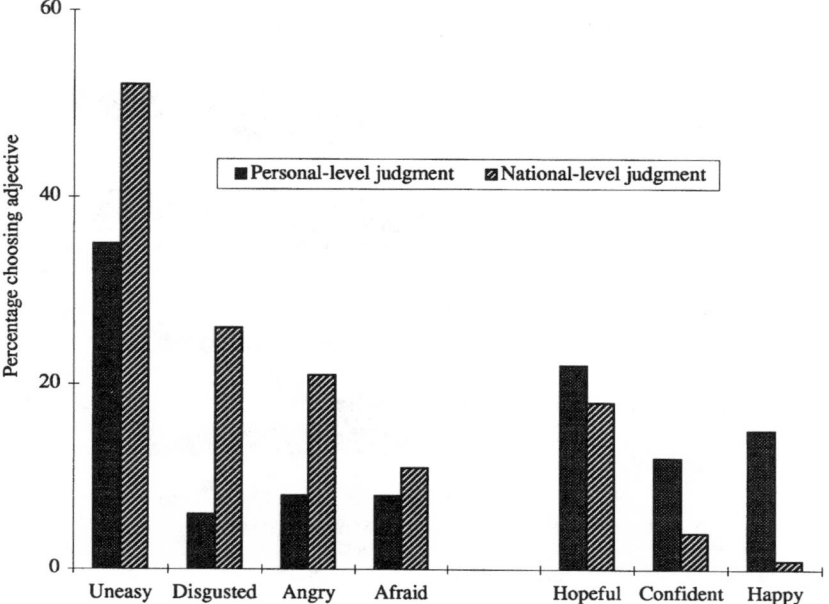

Figure 4.3. Personal- and collective-level economic judgments in the United Kingdom.

Source: Social Surveys (Gallup Poll) Ltd., April 15–21, 1993. "Please look at this card and tell me if any of the words on it describes your feelings about the country's general economic situation. If yes, which ones? Please look at this card again and tell me if any of the words on it describe your feelings about the financial condition of your household. If yes, which ones?"

out of the eight available comparisons, personal-level optimism far exceeds optimism about the national condition. In years such as 1990, this gap is absolutely enormous. The one exception to this pattern was in 1982 during President Reagan's first term in office when national optimism actually exceeded personal optimism.

Figure 4.5 shows a similar pattern for retrospective evaluations of personal and national economic conditions. One would think that assessments of the past would be less subject to bias since people are reporting on actual past occurrences rather than imagined future prospects. But here we see basically the same pattern. The one exception was in 1984 when judgments about recent national-level change were significantly more positive than assessments of changes in people's personal financial situations. In 1994, these two measures pulled to within

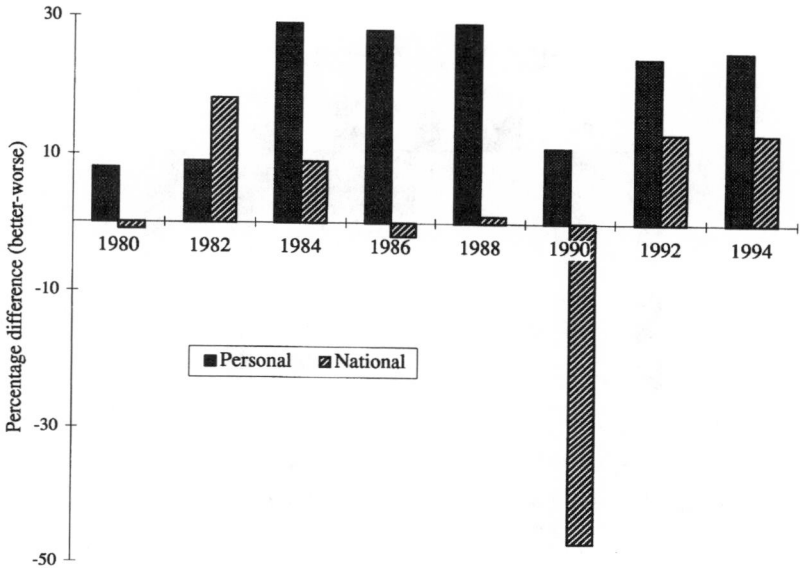

Figure 4.4. Prospective evaluations of economic conditions.
Source: National Election Studies, 1980–94. *Personal*: "Now looking ahead –
do you think that a year from now you [and your family living here] will be
better off financially or worse off, or just about the same as now?" *National*:
"What about the next 12 months? Do you expect the (1986, 1988, 1992:
national) economy to get better, get worse, or stay about the same?"

two margins of error of one another, thus producing no significant difference in either direction.

Finally, Figure 4.6 draws on data from a series of rolling, cross-
sectional surveys done by ABC News and *Money Magazine* to provide
a greater number of over-time comparisons of personal- and national-
level economic assessments. Figure 4.6 summarizes over 400 such comparisons from data collected between 1986 and 1996. At first glance,
what is most striking about this series is that it demonstrates that over
an entire ten-year period, perceptions of collective conditions have consistently and without exception been more negative than people's perceptions of their personal financial conditions. In good economic times
and bad, the gap remains. While the majority of people have consistently
rated national conditions as either "not so good" or "poor," more than
50 percent of the public consistently has rated their personal financial
condition as "good" or "excellent." Not once during this entire ten-year

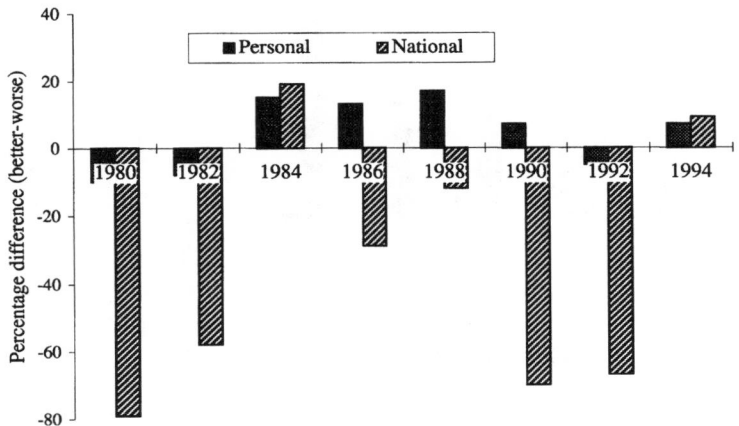

Figure 4.5. Retrospective evaluations of economic conditions.
Source: National Election Studies, 1980–94. *Personal*: "We are interested in how people are getting along financially these days. Would you say that you [and your family living here] are better off or worse off financially than you were a year ago?" *National*: "How about the economy (1990, 1994: in the country as a whole)? Would you say that over the past year the nation's economy has gotten better, stayed the same or gotten worse?"

period were people more pessimistic about their personal situation than about the nation as a whole. Although the two series tend to be highly correlated over time as aggregates ($r = .86$), perceptions of national conditions vary to a far greater extent than personal-level perceptions. The standard deviation surrounding the percentage rating the national economy as "good" or "excellent" is 12 percent. The same figure for the personal series is only 4 percent.

People's perceptions of the impersonal world beyond their immediate life space are clearly subject to greater ups and downs than are perceptions rooted in personal experience. In other words, impersonal perceptions are not only schizophrenic, they are also manic-depressive. Once reported on and relayed to the public, small fluctuations in the collective state of personal conditions can create much grander fluctuations in perceptions of national conditions.

This finding meshes well with the general argument that journalists tend to overinterpret changes in economic conditions such that even small random fluctuations are viewed and written about as meaningful trends. It also jibes with the observation drawn from the Michigan Consumer Surveys that those who report being exposed to economic news

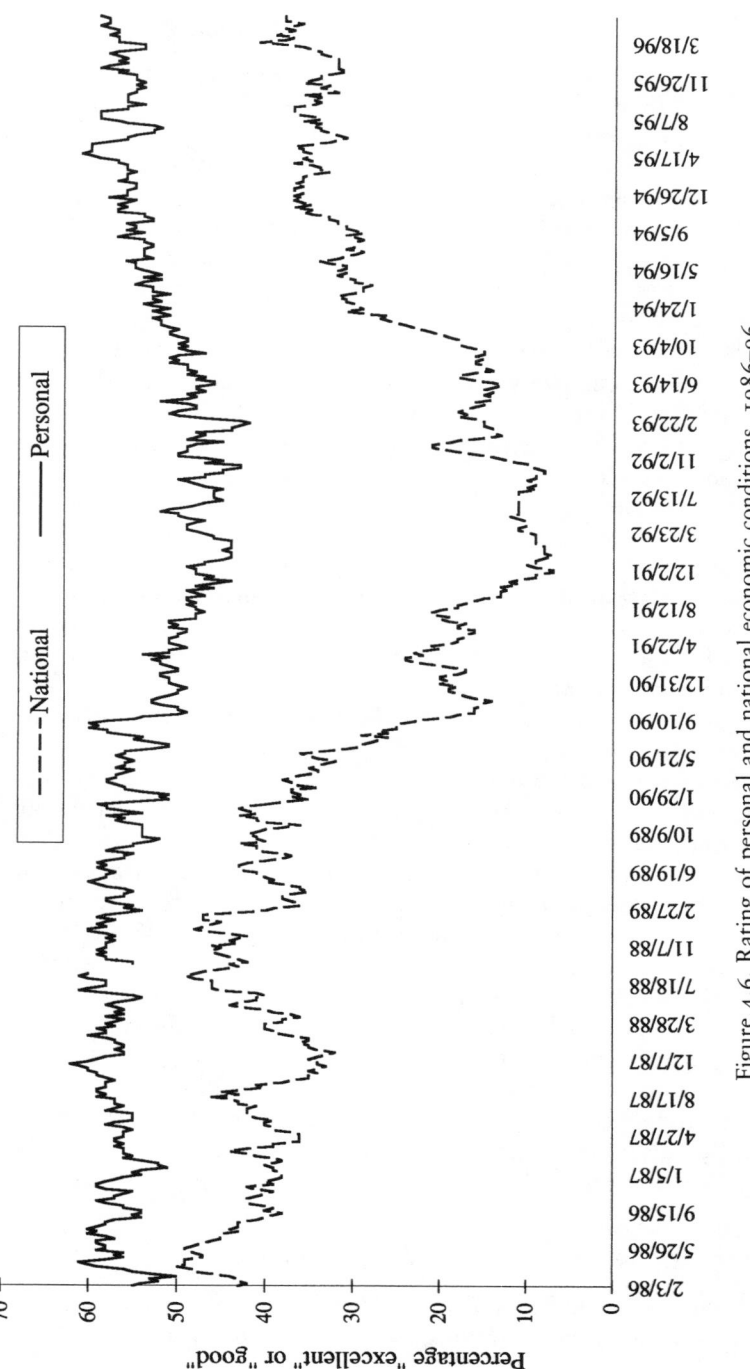

Figure 4.6. Rating of personal and national economic conditions, 1986–96.

Source: Based on weekly data from ABC News/*Money Magazine*, four-week rolling averages. *National:* "Would you describe the state of the nation's economy these days as excellent, good, not so good, or poor?" *Personal:* "Would you describe the state of your own personal finances these days as excellent, good, not so good, or poor?"

experience greater variation in national economic perceptions over time (Haller and Norpoth 1996).

The aggregate pattern of compartmentalization in personal and collective views also is consistent with a great deal of individual-level data drawn from noneconomic issues documenting the relative independence of personal- and societal-level judgments. For example, people's views about their own personal opportunities, status, and achievement are independent of these same judgments about society as a whole (Kluegel and Smith 1978). Along these same lines, women's views about the general existence of discrimination in women's wages are not related to judgments about their own wages (Major 1982). Likewise, estimates of the personal risk of rape have nothing to do with the number of rapes women perceive to be occurring (Gordon et al. 1980). Estimates of personal crime risks more generally also were found to be unrelated to judgments about the frequency or seriousness of crime in several major cities (Tyler 1980), and the same pattern has been replicated for other social problems (Tyler and Cook 1984). Studies of the psychological compartmentalization of personal and collective concerns have more or less independently come to conclusions that jibe nicely with research on the political impact of economic change (Kahneman and Tversky 1982; Borgida and Brekke 1981; Lyon and Slovic 1976; Tyler 1980; Tyler and Lavrakas 1985): Perceptions of mass collectives often do not mirror the aggregate of individual experiences.

This line of reasoning often leads to the conclusion that a personal-experience-based politics would be preferable by far to one depending upon accurate perceptions of collective conditions since personal experiences are anchored in a reality that impersonal perceptions are not. But are personal experiences truly a preferable basis for political accountability? In order to evaluate this question, it is essential to know something about the origins as well as the direction of the gap between personal and impersonal judgments. People clearly tend to be more positive about their personal situations than they are about the state of the collective, at least when that collective is the nation as a whole. It is tempting to jump to the conclusion that doomsayers in the media are simply distorting people's perceptions of the nation they live in. But theoretically this kind of pattern could result from a bias in either collective- *or* personal-level judgments, or some combination thereof.

The Bias Toward Personal Optimism

Although there is an understandable tendency to view personal-level indicators as accurate representations of people's lived experiences (Gavin and Sanders 1996), evidence to date suggests that personal-level assessments also may be biased in a direction that exacerbates the gap between the two. An unrealistically optimistic personal bias has been widely noted in the literature on perceptions of risk, and it is consistent across studies of a large number of potential hazards (Weinstein 1980, 1989). Nor is it limited to potential hazards; people also think that positive events are more likely to happen to them personally, for example, that they are more likely than the average to receive a raise. Just like Garrison Keilor's description of Lake Woebegone, we live in a society where all of our citizens are above average – or at least so our perceptions suggest.

Two general types of explanations have been offered for this phenomenon. Motivational explanations stress the idea that personal pessimism threatens people's feelings of competence and self-worth, so they are compelled to make overly optimistic assessments either to shield themselves from fear or to protect their egos (Weinstein 1989). For example, people generally exaggerate their uniqueness (Funder 1980), and many psychologists argue that this tendency is a quite useful protective response with positive implications for mental health (D. G. Taylor 1982; Alloy and Abramson 1980).

A second theory suggests that personal optimism results from simple cognitive errors. When people think of vaguely defined "others," they tend to think about prototypes of high-risk individuals, which inevitably make the self look better in comparison. This explanation jibes well with the notion of a "representativeness heuristic" (Kahneman and Tversky 1973): When people think about a negative outcome of some kind, they invoke a stereotyped image that, by definition, possesses more risky attributes than they do themselves. This hypothesis has been supported by studies showing that vaguely defined "others" produce greater optimism about self relative to others. When people are forced to think about a specific other, the biased perception disappears (Perloff and Fetzer 1986). Since news values dictate that the kinds of events or risks that are more common and that people might reasonably expect to face receive considerably less coverage than highly unusual events, news coverage may also contribute to overly optimistic personal-level judgments and perceptions of individual risk.

In general, there is less support for motivational explanations for personal-level optimism, that is, the idea that people do not want to see themselves or those close to them as vulnerable to negative outcomes (Perloff and Fetzer 1986). For example, contrary to what this theory would predict, people are no more optimistic about severe hazards than they are about relatively mild ones (Weinstein 1987, 1980). However, personal optimism is strongly correlated with the controllability of the outcome such that the greater the perceived controllability of a negative event, the more overly optimistic people are about avoiding it. This finding suggests that the bias is at least to some extent an ego-defensive reaction (Weinstein 1987). A complete explanation probably requires a combination of ego-defensive motivations and cognitive biases, as when cancer patients make themselves feel better by constructing "hypothetical worse worlds" in their minds in which they are relatively well off (Taylor, Wood, and Lichtman 1983: 31).

Interestingly, the notion of an optimistic personal bias implies a *prospective* focus whereby people anticipate facing fewer risks, experiencing greater job success, and so forth. For events that have not yet occurred, one can perhaps understand how wishful thinking may enter into judgments. But this pattern is apparently not confined to optimism about future events. As shown in Figures 4.1, 4.2, 4.3, 4.5, and 4.6, people also report consistently more favorable personal assessments of *past* experiences.[18]

The size and overall consistency of this ongoing gap make it clear that even in the face of quite different objective circumstances, people tend to believe that their personal worlds are in better shape than the collective in which they share membership. In contrast, pessimistic biases are very rare at the personal level. In other words, prospective optimism and romanticization of the personal past appear to be part of the same overall tendency to view one's immediate life space as more rosy than most.[19] As Tyler and Lavrakas (1985: 145) point out, "Although it might initially seem strange that citizens would separate their personal and social judgments, in fact this separation illustrates the interplay of two basic psychological motivations that guide the formation of personal beliefs: the desire to have correct beliefs about the world and the desire to preserve personally comforting illusions about oneself and the environment." Whatever the underlying causes, this pattern is exceedingly common. Unfortunately, its consequences for American political behavior are less well understood.

18 Of course, assessing the accuracy of perceptions based on these measures is not as straightforward as it might seem since official statistics are by no means a "pure distillation of reality" (Harrison 1985: 43).

19 Some types of questions incorporate more subjective content than others. Measures asking for retrospective unemployment experiences, for example, accurately reflect unemployment statistics to a greater extent than general assessments of change in personal financial conditions. Interestingly, although one might expect more subjective measures to predict subjective political attitudes better, even comprehensive batteries of questions tapping both personal experiences and personal assessments of economic conditions suggest that they have little political impact (Kinder, Adams, and Gronke 1989).

Implications of Bias in Personal and Impersonal Judgments

What kind of conclusions should be drawn about the consequences of this collective split personality that afflicts citizens' perceptions? First and foremost, this pattern suggests that if people did anchor their political attitudes and behaviors in personal experiences, the outcome might not be at all desirable democratically. Living in a perpetual state of "I'm doing better than we are" is a perfect formula for a quiescent public that willingly surrenders the reins of political authority to its leaders. After all, if each individually feels his or her family is doing well relative to others, one has little reason to complain, and the optimistic personal bias could conceivably buoy public attitudes to some extent even in the worst of times. Although personal experiences may be less manipulable sources of information than collective-level perceptions, the biased tendency toward personal optimism might enhance incumbent advantage to an even greater extent than it currently does and insulate officials from electoral accountability. A model of mass political behavior drawing strictly on personal-level assessments rather than national ones would promote the status quo and detract from accountability.

This depiction of mass contentment obviously does not ring true. The American public is hardly complacent and well satisfied with its politicians and their policies. In fact, the enmity directed toward politicians in the United States is partly a function of the fact that political views are derived from perceptions of collective reality that are not buoyed by the excessive optimism that personal judgments are. To paraphrase George Gerbner (1976), it is a mean and scary world out there. But in reality this social fact is not as bad as it seems because none of us live "out there." Instead we live in local and personal worlds that are not continuous in our minds with the larger impersonal one. Thus, we can think crime is on the rise yet not necessarily experience greater personal-level fears. At the polling place, however, we may in fact behave quite differently because of these impersonal perceptions. Yet another, broader consequence that logically flows from this state of affairs is the sense that the larger world in which national politics transpires is quite distant from one's own life and experiences. This sense of distance inevitably contributes to the sense that politics is a "spectator sport."

The media's role in producing unduly negative evaluations of conditions in the nation as a whole has yet to be thoroughly established, but evidence clearly stacks up in favor of this hypothesis. Although studies have not consistently been supportive of the idea that media put more emphasis on negative than positive news of various kinds, there are few advocates championing the idea that media foster a positivity bias with respect to their coverage of social issues. When issue coverage is skewed, then, it tends to be skewed in the direction of greater negativity.

The bias toward personal optimism also sheds new light on concerns surrounding the potential consequences of media negativity. Rather than serving as a doomsayer that distorts perceptions in an unhealthy fashion, media may serve as a welcome antidote to a public unwilling or unable to see itself as vulnerable to a host of potentially negative outcomes and unlikely to hold government leaders responsible for personal problems in any case. In this analysis, a wary media protects the public from its perceived invulnerability through greater emphasis on negative outcomes, both past and future. This counterbalancing could lead to political action that ultimately protects individuals from having to experience some of these very outcomes personally.

Even to the extent that this ideal outcome might transpire, it should be clear that neither a model based on personal perceptions nor one based wholly on perceptions of entities as large as the nation as a whole ensures accountability. The ultimate verdict, of course, depends upon the net balance that results from the extent of positive and negative biases in personal and collective judgments.

OTHER AVENUES TO ACCOUNTABILITY?

In the face of evidence that personal judgments typically have little political impact and of analyses suggesting that neither judgments at the national- or personal-level can be counted on for accuracy, one logical possibility is that intermediate groups may provide the important missing link. The groups with which people identify – the middle class, Hispanics, or poor people, for example – may combine the direct, more easily verified sources of information that characterize personal experiences, with the political relevance of collective-level perceptions. Moreover, perceptions of group well-being constitute a distinct level of judgment relative to national and personal assessments (Conover 1985; Kinder, Adams, and Gronke 1989). The combination of personal salience, easy accessibility, and political relevance makes groups a "natural frame of reference for ordinary Americans attempting to understand the complex world of politics" (Kinder, Adams, and Gronke 1989: 493). For example, in the context of economic accountability, groups may serve as essential mediating entities, making it possible for people to politicize the economic interests of those like them or close to them without necessarily politicizing personal experience (Hensler and Speer 1979). In other words, groups may function as proxies for self-interest (Campbell et al. 1960) and thus provide a normatively desirable basis for promoting political accountability.

Politicization of Personal and Collective Experience

Two previous studies have addressed this possibility. In local and national samples (Conover 1985; Kinder, Adams, and Gronke 1989) respondents were asked to identify a group they felt closest to, and then asked a series of questions about the economic well-being of this group. These questions resulted in a pattern very similar to comparisons of personal- and national-level judgments: In both studies and across multiple measures within each study, perceptions of group economic well-being were systematically less positive than assessments of personal well-being. With respect to their influence on political judgments, Conover (1985) found that group-level evaluations did make an independent contribution to performance evaluations, but at the national level, Kinder and colleagues (1989) found no indication that support for Reagan depended upon group economic well-being.

Both of these studies were based on the premise that group influence should flow primarily through the mechanism of group identification; in other words, the reason group-level judgments influence political attitudes is that they reflect another form of self-interest. Since both of these studies were limited to assessments of only one group per person, they could not compare the influence of judgments about groups with which people did and did not identify. In other words, identification was assumed to be the mechanism, though not directly tested.

In contrast to this interpretation, analyses of a survey including economic perceptions of multiple groups suggest that even the independent contribution of group-level measures is primarily of a sociotropic nature (see Mutz and Mondak 1997). The data Jeff Mondak and I used for our study were drawn from the 1984 South Bend study, a three-wave panel survey including around 1,500 respondents. Despite its local sample, the South Bend study included several desirable features for our purposes, the most salient of which was a battery of items tapping a great diversity of economic perceptions for specific groups in addition to the usual national- and personal-level assessments. Specifically, questions included items asking about perceptions of economic change among women, blacks, Hispanics, poor people, working men and women, the middle class and the well-to-do. Further, it included items tapping subjective and objective membership in many of these groups, as well as questions asking respondents how close they felt to each group.

As in the two previous studies, we found group-based judgments to be distinct from personal and national ones (see Mutz and Mondak 1997 for details). In addition, people had little difficulty providing assessments of how the various groups had fared economically, even when the groups were not ones to which they felt close or belonged themselves. Evidence of the distinctiveness of these judgments is illustrated in Table 4.3. A comparison of two logistic regression models predicting presidential vote

Table 4.3. *Sociotropic, pocketbook, and group-level economic perceptions as determinants of the presidential vote*

	Model I		Model II	
	Coefficient	Standard error	Coefficient	Standard error
Constant	0.47*	0.23	1.13**	0.35
Control variables				
Democrat	−1.82***	0.19	−2.10***	0.24
Republican	2.75***	0.41	2.51***	0.50
Liberal	−0.70**	0.24	−0.60*	0.29
Conservative	0.84***	0.21	0.62*	0.25
Education	−0.03	0.05	−0.01	0.06
Sex	−0.27	0.18	−0.33	0.22
Race	−1.79	0.71	−1.50*	0.72
Economic perception variables				
Family	0.70***	0.15	0.66***	0.19
Nation	0.99***	0.14	0.76***	0.17
Women			0.10	0.22
Blacks			0.43*	0.18
Hispanics			−0.16	0.20
Poor people			0.67***	0.19
Working men and working women			0.06	0.22
Middle class			0.28	0.21
Well-to-do			−0.58*	0.24
(n)	(1,101)		(848)	
Starting log likelihood	−751.04		−581.40	
Ending log likelihood	−381.87		−274.42	
Model chi-square	738.35		613.95	
Proportional reduction in error	.61		.67	

Note: Dependent variable is the presidential vote (1 = Reagan, 0 = Mondale)
*$p < .05$ **$p < .01$ ***$p < .001$.
Source: 1984 South Bend Study

with and without the seven group-based judgments shows (1) that their inclusion does little to reduce the impact of the personal and national variables and (2) that several group-level interests do, indeed, have a significant impact on political views. In particular, perceptions concerning the well-being of three groups – blacks, the poor, and the well-to-do – appear to affect the presidential vote. Moreover, the coefficients for these variables rival in size those for the nation.[20]

Overall, this pattern would seem to lend support to the notion of group-based accountability. But one telltale anomaly to note in Table 4.3 is the sign of the coefficient corresponding to perceptions of the well-to-do. While the conventional wisdom regarding economic voting is that incumbents benefit when the economy does well, the coefficient for the well-to-do is large, statistically significant, and *negative*. Presidents are supposed to be rewarded for economic gains; however, when voters look to particular groups within society, economic success for some of those groups may fuel criticism of the incumbent, not praise. Beyond this peculiarity, these findings leave another important question unanswered. Theories of group influence typically do not predict an across-the-board effect from evaluations of various groups; instead they suggest that only people who are members of, or who feel close to, particular groups should be using them as a basis for political evaluations. In short, the appropriate theoretical interpretation of Table 4.3 is less than clear cut.

We next estimated a series of models to test the assumptions of specific mechanisms of group influence. First, in Table 4.4, we used both objective and subjective indicators of group membership in interaction with evaluations of how these groups were perceived to have fared economically to see whether people were using the standards specifically of groups to which they belonged in order to evaluate presidential candidates. A glance at the interaction coefficients in Table 4.4 suggests that mere membership in a group is not enough to trigger people's use of these standards. Although people who are members of a group could draw on personal experiences as well as personal interactions with other members of their groups to form reliable estimates of group well-being that should help them hold leaders accountable, we found no evidence of group-level accountability. Surprisingly, none of the interactions even approached statistical significance. Blacks were no more likely to hold presidents accountable for perceptions of economic change among blacks than were whites. Likewise, those who saw themselves as middle class or working class were no more likely to vote on the basis of how those groups had fared economically.

Perhaps what is important is not so much membership as the psycho-

---

20 Unlike most previous studies, we found evidence of significant retrospective voting based on personal assessments as well as the usual sociotropic effects. This is consistent with Lau, Sears, and Jessor (1990), who concluded that 1984 was truly "an exceptional case" in the extent to which people politicized their personal financial situations. The uniqueness of 1984 is also consistent with Figure 4.5, where it stands out as the one and only year in which personal and national assessments were quite similar.

Table 4.4. *Effects of objective and subjective group membership*

	Model I (objective)		Model II (subjective)	
	Coefficient	Standard error	Coefficient	Standard error
Constant	0.92**	0.35	0.66*	0.31
Economic perception variables				
Family	0.58**	0.18	0.62***	0.16
Nation	0.77***	0.16	0.80***	0.15
Women	0.05	0.27	−0.06	0.26
Blacks	0.24	0.17	0.41**	0.15
Poor people	0.68***	0.19	—	
Working men and working women	—		0.15	0.21
Middle class	0.28	0.31	0.26	0.23
Well-to-do	−0.40	0.25		
Group membership variables				
Sex (1 = female)	−0.41	0.27	−0.28	0.25
Race (1 = black)	−1.55*	0.74	−1.81*	0.76
Lower income	−0.32	0.36	—	
Upper income	−0.19	0.51	—	
Self-placement, working class	—		−0.52#	0.28
Self-placement, middle class	—		−0.52*	0.25
Interactions (economic perception × group membership)				
Women × sex	−0.07	0.37	−0.04	0.34
Blacks × race	0.44	0.91	0.31	0.90
Poor × lower income	−0.54	0.45	—	
Middle class × middle income	0.25	0.36	—	
Well-to-do × upper income	−0.32	0.59	—	
Working men and working women × self-placement, working class			0.29	0.35
Middle class × self-placement, middle class	—		0.44	0.31
(n)	(952)		(1,055)	
Starting log likelihood	−653.03		−720.14	
Ending log likelihood	−311.73		−349.77	
Model chi-square	682.62		740.72	
Proportional reduction in error	.68		.67	
Addition to chi-square	2.87		2.42	

logical closeness emphasized by group identification. The South Bend survey included measures of the extent to which people felt close to five of the groups for which they were asked to estimate economic change. In Table 4.5, we interact closeness with economic perceptions to test the hypothesis that those who feel close to a group vote partly on the basis of how they perceive that group to have fared economically. Again the results were quite surprising: None of the interactions reached statistical significance. We also estimated models that reflected Conover's (1985) admonition that both actual group membership and psychological affiliation may be necessary conditions for the effects of group identification. However, even these three-way interactions generated no evidence of a group identification effect.

One final way that people might be hypothesized to use the highly accessible information on their own group's well-being in evaluating political leaders is by using that information as a basis for evaluating whether they themselves are being treated fairly by the current leadership. To test the hypothesis that groups function as units of comparison that help people judge their own relative standing, we followed Taylor's (1973) procedure, defining Degree of Disparity between self and group as the absolute value of the difference between the personal and the group economic perception variables.[21] Next, two dummy variables indicated whether the personal family measure performed the same, better, or worse relative to the group. Relative Prosperity was coded 1 if the family was seen as economically outperforming the group and 0 if otherwise; Relative Deprivation was coded 1 if the family was seen as performing less well than the group, and 0 if otherwise. Of course, these three variables were defined separately for each of the seven groups.

We estimated seven models to test the relative deprivation hypothesis, one per group. Each model included all variables in Table 4.3, Model II, plus the three variables needed to contrast group- and personal-level perceptions. The hypothesis in this case predicts positive coefficients for

21 Thus this variable ranged from 0 (when personal and group were perceived to have fared the same as one another) to 2 (when either the personal or group improved while the other worsened).

Notes to Table 4.4

Note: The dependent variable is the presidential vote (1 = Reagan, 0 = Mondale). Models also include several control variables: Democrat, Republican, liberal, conservative, and education (see Table 4.3). Addition to chi-square indicates the gain in model chi-square for the full interaction models versus models that include all main effects reported here, but no interaction terms.
$*p < .05$ $**p < .01$ $***p < .001$ $\#p < .10$.
Source: 1984 South Bend Study.

Table 4.5. *Effects of group identification*

	Coefficient	Standard error
Constant	1.29**	0.41
Economic perception variables		
Family	0.70***	0.19
Nation	0.83***	0.17
Blacks	0.41*	0.20
Hispanics	−0.14	0.21
Poor people	0.94***	0.26
Working men and working women	0.29	0.39
Middle class	0.59	0.41
Group closeness (GC) variables		
GC-Blacks	−0.18	0.14
GC-Hispanics	0.30*	0.14
GC-Poor people	−0.03	0.13
GC-Working people	−0.07	0.17
GC-Middle class	−0.29	0.18
Interactions (economic perception × group closeness)		
Blacks × GC-Blacks	0.04	0.15
Hispanics × GC-Hispanics	−0.09	0.17
Poor people × GC-Poor people	−0.16	0.17
Working men and working women × GC-Working people	−0.19	0.23
Middle class × GC-Middle class	−0.18	0.24
(n)	(846)	
Starting log likelihood	−579.23	
Ending log likelihood	−271.33	
Model chi-square	615.80	
Proportional reduction in error	.70	
Addition to chi-square	3.96	

Note: The dependent variable is the presidential vote (1 = Reagan, 0 = Mondale). Models also include several control variables: Democrat, Republican, liberal, conservative, and education. Addition to chi-square indicates the gain in model chi-square for the full interaction models versus models that include all main effects reported here, but no interaction terms.
*$p < .05$ **$p < .01$ ***$p < .001$.
Source: 1984 South Bend Study.

Relative Prosperity and negative coefficients for Relative Deprivation. In other words, respondents should be more likely to vote to retain the incumbent if their families fared well relative to the group and less likely if their families fared poorly.

In Table 4.6, only the estimate for blacks followed the hypothesized pattern. However, the coefficient for Relative Prosperity for blacks was negligible, and the coefficient for Relative Deprivation was only marginally significant. The model also failed to bring an acceptable gain in performance versus Table 4.3's Model II. Although we cannot rule out the possibility that people use groups as units for social comparison, perceptions regarding the seven groups we examined provided no evidence of comparative economic judgments.

Since none of these theoretical explanations produced much empirical support, we tested one additional possibility, the idea that groups were used not so much as the basis for a judgment about how well one's own personal interests were being served, but as a basis for assessments of global economic equality, or what we have termed "sociotropic fairness." In Table 4.7, we began in Model I with the four economic class groups and also retained the economic perception variable for blacks since it produced significant effects in each of the previous models. In Model II, we added a variable to tap levels of perceived inequality among economic groups. This variable was constructed by taking the standard deviation for the four class group perceptions for each respondent. Thus individuals who perceived great variation in how the different economic groups fared received a high score, whereas respondents who perceived the groups to be faring identically received zeros.

As the chi-square statistics at the bottom of Model I and Model II reveal, performance improved significantly with the addition of the perceived inequality variable. Also, all of the main effects for the class group perceptions were no longer significant. Once variance among these perceptions was controlled for, the direction of individual perception no longer mattered. Our very first model suggested that voters punished the incumbent merely because the economic standing of the well-to-do improved. In contrast, results in Table 4.7 indicate that voters do not punish the incumbent any time the rich are perceived to have gotten richer, but instead only if the rich got richer while the other groups in society stayed the same or even lost ground.

Overall, these results suggest that it is not the direction of change that individuals perceive in any given economic group that matters most; instead, the central issue is whether the groups are perceived to have fared the same, or with some benefitting or suffering more than others. At least for group-based perceptions, sociotropic fairness outweighs even sociotropic well-being as a determinant of the presidential vote. In

Table 4.6. *Effects of perceived relative deprivation*

	Women	Blacks	Hispanics	Poor people	Working men and working women	Middle class	Well-to-do
Family	0.88	0.16	0.47	0.84	0.77	1.44**	0.94**
	(0.58)	(0.37)	(0.42)	(0.54)	(0.51)	(0.55)	(0.32)
Group	-0.09	0.99*	0.05	0.52	-0.09	-0.50	-0.80*
	(0.58)	(0.41)	(0.44)	(0.56)	(0.54)	(0.57)	(0.38)
Degree of disparity	0.36	0.15	0.16	-0.25	0.21	-0.18	0.40
	(0.56)	(0.36)	(0.40)	(0.53)	(0.50)	(0.54)	(0.31)
Relative prosperity	-0.65	0.14	-0.07	0.19	-0.83	-1.29	
	(1.17)	(0.67)	(0.65)	(0.51)	(0.91)	(0.86)	
Relative deprivation	-0.17	-1.28	-0.58	0.60	-0.46	0.49	0.01
	(0.62)	(0.67)	(0.76)	(1.17)	(0.75)	(0.90)	(.52)
Number of cases	848	848	848	848	848	848	848
Starting log likelihood	-581.40	-581.40	-581.40	-581.40	-581.40	-581.40	-581.40
Ending log likelihood	-274.21	-271.64	-274.02	-274.21	-272.61	-269.58	-273.31
Model chi-square	614.36	619.52	614.76	614.38	617.57	623.64	616.17
Proportional reduction in error	.68	.68	.67	.69	.70	.69	.69

Note: The dependent variable is the presidential vote (1 = Reagan, 0 = Mondale). Each column presents results of a separate logistic regression model. In addition to the relative prosperity and relative deprivation variables, all models include the same set of control and economic perception variables: Democrat, Republican, liberal, conservative, education, sex, race, and economic perceptions regarding the family, nation, women, blacks, Hispanics, poor people, working men and working women, the middle class, and the well-to-do. Standard errors are in parentheses.

*$p < .05$ **$p < .01$.

Source: 1984 South Bend Study

Table 4.7. *Effects of perceived group-level inequality*

	Model I	Model II
Constant	0.95**	1.39**
	(0.30)	(0.35)
Economic perception variables		
Family	0.63***	0.64***
	(0.17)	(0.17)
Nation	0.78***	0.76***
	(0.15)	(0.16)
Blacks	0.28	0.28
	(0.15)	(0.15)
Poor people	0.63***	0.18
	(0.17)	(0.23)
Working men and	0.08	0.14
working women	(0.18)	(0.19)
Middle class	0.36	0.30
	(0.19)	(0.19)
Well-to-do	−0.48*	−0.09
	(0.22)	(0.26)
Perceived inequality		−1.43**
		(0.50)
(n)	(1,026)	(1,026)
Starting log likelihood	−702.39	−702.39
Ending log likelihood	−331.46	−327.31
Model chi-square	741.87	750.16
Proportional reduction in		
error	.69	.70

Note: The dependent variable is the presidential vote (1 = Reagan, 0 = Mondale). Models also include several control variables: Democrat, Republican, liberal, conservative, education, sex, and race. Standard errors are in parentheses. $*p < .05$ $**p < .01$ $***p < .001$.
Source: 1984 South Bend Study

Model II, the −1.43 coefficient for Perceived Inequality produces a rather impressive thirty-one-point swing in the estimated likelihood of voting for Reagan under the baseline conditions (education = 2, all other variables = 0). Further, this strong effect does not come at the expense of the remaining economic perception variables. The measures for family, nation, and blacks again produce significant coefficients, indicating that the electoral significance of perceived inequality is largely independent of effects associated with perceptions of well-being.

Although Table 4.7 finally provides some positive evidence concerning why and how group-level economic interests enter into voting decisions, this mechanism was not at all what was anticipated. Instead of finding that groups provide an essential means of filling in the accountability gap between personal economic experiences that have little political impact and perceptions of national conditions that cannot easily guarantee accountability, the findings suggested that even group-level effects were based on people's perceptions of things well beyond their immediate life space. Rather than being tied to groups of which individuals were members or groups they felt close to, these effects were based on their perceptions of how a range of groups were faring relative to one another – a range of groups broad enough that few individuals will have significant amounts of direct experience with each.

Most models of group influence hypothesize a connection between the individual and the group, via either subjective or objective membership or perceived attachment (Conover 1985). This perspective emphasizes the role of self-interest within the voting calculus; groups matter either because group-based perceptions constitute a hidden form of pocketbook voting, or because identification produces a symbolic interest in the group's well-being. Instead, our findings indicated that the influence of group-based perceptions reflected not self-interest so much as another form of sociotropic judgment. Respondents were substantially more likely to judge the president favorably if they felt that class groups had experienced similar rather than dissimilar changes in economic performance. Moreover, this measure of perceived equality contained information relevant to the vote that was independent of the information contained within the broader national-level sociotropic measure.[22, 23]

22 It is, of course, important to remember that our data are limited in both time and place. As with analyses of any given election year, there may be limitations on the generalizability of these findings. In particular, 1984 could have been an aberrant year with respect to the role played by perceptions of fairness. Clearly, inequality was a concern during the 1984 elections, but these perceptions were not specific to 1984 (see Mutz and Mondak 1997 for full discussion).

23 Is it possible that people's perceptions of the extent to which groups have fared equally well stem instead from simple partisan rationalization? In other words, does the Perceived Inequality variable merely capture ideology, such that with a Republican incumbent, liberals see economic development as unfair, conservatives see them as fair, and vice versa? Our evidence suggests this is not the case. First, Model I controlled for ideology, yet the addition of Perceived Inequality in Model II still substantially improved model performance. Second, the coefficients for the ideology variables did not decline in magnitude with the addition of Perceived Inequality in Model II. Third, and most important, Perceived Inequality was essentially uncorrelated with both ideology and our other control variables.

To summarize, group-level effects do exist, but they do not provide an alternative means of ensuring accountability that circumvents high information or interpretation costs. Instead, these effects point further to the importance of media portrayals; in this case, portrayals of how various groups in society are faring. Long ago, George Herbert Mead (1934) observed that special problems arise in increasingly industrialized societies when people use as standards groups in which they are not members, groups in which they have never participated, or even groups that do not exist. When evaluating a broad range of groups, some of the groups will inevitably be beyond individuals' range of personal experiences and associations. Thus, mediated information once again must be depended upon to convey accurate representations of the state of collectives, in this case somewhat smaller, but still relatively impersonal, ones.

Media portrayals of group conflict play an important role in stimulating social identification processes (Price 1989). But there is no guarantee that perceptions of groups are necessarily any more accurate or devoid of biases than are personal or national ones. In fact, some limited evidence suggests that there may be a trade-off such that when judgments are made closer to home – where one would expect greater reliance on personal experience, more readily verifiable information, and less influence from mediated portrayals – they become increasingly subject to the same positivity bias that plagues personal-level judgments. Thus, the advantages of low information costs at the local level are offset by the biases inherent in personal- and local-level judgments.

Evaluations of government and political issues at the local level seem to support this idea. For example, people's ratings of local government tend to be systematically more positive than those of state government, which tend to be more positive than attitudes directed toward the federal government (Conlan 1993). Likewise, the drop in confidence from the early seventies to the early nineties was greatest for the federal government (32%), smaller for state government (16%), and least of all for local government (4%). Illustrating a similar pattern, Figure 4.7 shows that while majorities of Americans perceive crime, unemployment, poverty, violence, drug abuse, racism, and declining moral standards to be large-scale societal problems, very few perceive them to be serious problems in their own local areas.[24] If these issues are as problematic as people claim at the national level, someone must be experiencing them in their local community. As Figure 4.7 suggests, their perceptions sug-

24 This pattern may have been exacerbated in this survey by the choice of broader, vaguer wording for assessments of "society." As suggested by research on biased optimism, prompting thoughts of a more vaguely defined "other" may facilitate even greater contrast between self and other judgments.

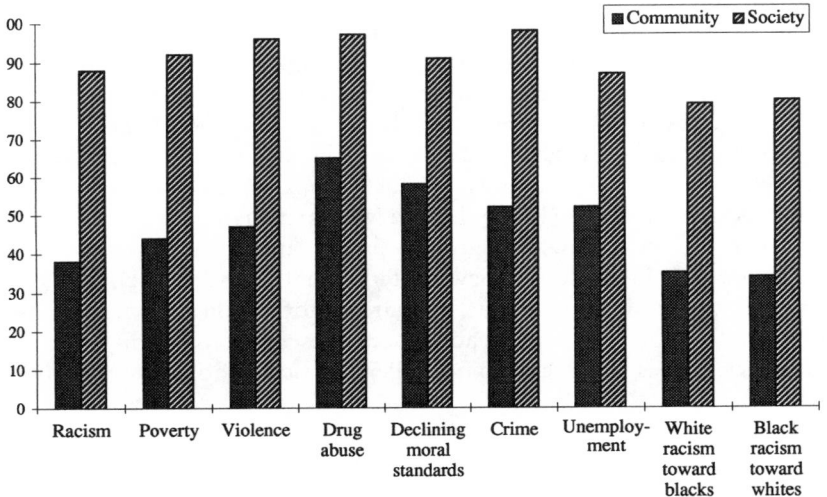

Figure 4.7. Perceived severity of community and societal problems.
Source: *Washington Post* national survey of 1,016 adults, June 28, 1996–July
2, 1996. *Community*: "What about in the community where you live? How big
a problem is . . . in your community? Is it a big problem, somewhat of a problem, a small problem, or not a problem at all?" *Society*: "How big a problem
are each of the following issues in our society today? How big a problem is . . .
in our society today? Is it a big problem, somewhat of a problem, a small problem, or not a problem at all?"

gest otherwise. The truth about this wide range of social problems may
lie somewhere in between people's rosy perceptions of their immediate
lives and local communities and their apocalyptic judgments about the
state of larger, more impersonal collectives.

Despite many attempts to find alternate routes to political accountability, the American public still relies primarily on its perceptions of large-
scale collectives that exist beyond the realm of personal experiences and
contacts. Since these collectives are well beyond the reach of any given
individual's personal life experiences or interpersonal contacts, media
inevitably play an important role in helping form these impressions.
Thus, accountability will depend crucially on the quality as well as the
quantity of media coverage addressing the state of these collectives. Despite the general tendency to impugn a model of democratic accountability based on mediated perceptions as necessarily inferior to one based
on personal experience, when used exclusively either model could result
in punishing leaders for declines that have no basis in collective individ-

ual realities or in rewarding leaders for favorable, but biased, perceptions of one's personal state of affairs.

At the same time, as the general model outlined in Chapter 3 reminds us, collective-level perceptions are not themselves wholly independent of the influence of personal experiences. In the chapter that follows, I examine two prevalent, yet contradictory, theories concerning media's influence on the extent to which people hold political leaders accountable for the effects their policies have on citizens' lives.

5

Connecting the Personal and the Political
MEDIA AS FACILITATOR OR INHIBITOR?

The role assigned to mass media in the theoretical model discussed thus far has been fairly straightforward: Media help determine the perceptions of collective experience that are, in turn, quite important to political judgments. Figure 5.1 expands on the model originally proposed in the top panel of Figure 3.1 by incorporating the sociotropic pattern discussed at length in Chapter 4. Since media may impart information that is at odds with people's day-to-day experiences and personal contacts, it has the capacity to cultivate gaps between people's personal-level and collective-level perceptions. In a sense, then, media have the capacity to alienate people's political judgments from their immediate lives and experiences and to distance them from a politics rooted in everyday life. Without media, their perceptions of mass collectives would, of necessity, be based on generalizations from their own lives and experiences. When attitudes are based instead on media-influenced perceptions of collective experience, accountability may well suffer.

Although these implications can logically be drawn from this model, it is important to recognize that this is not the only conclusion consistent with this model. In fact, based on this very same theoretical model, one could also argue precisely the opposite: that by conveying information about others with similar experiences, mass media encourage the politicization of personal life experiences, and encourage greater accountability.

In this chapter I present the major arguments and evidence behind these two seemingly contradictory theoretical perspectives that have been advanced in this area of research. I then attempt to resolve the inconsistent evidence and expectations using two original studies designed specifically to address this question. If one takes into account the *context* that is assumed under each of these theories and *where* in the process personal experiences are assumed to be politicized, then the apparent contradictions quickly disappear. Ultimately, these questions are impor-

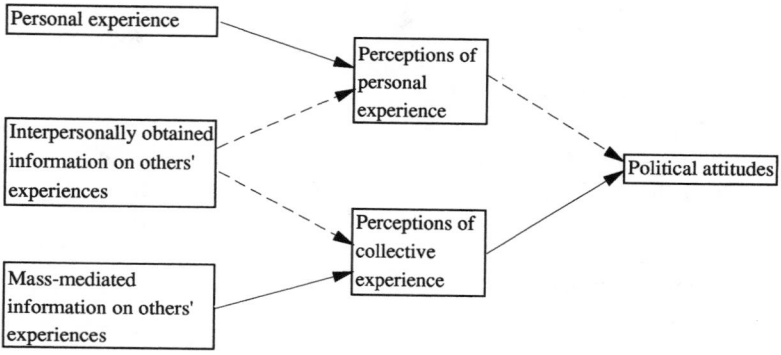

Figure 5.1. General model of influences on and consequences of personal- and collective-level judgments.

tant because of their bearing on questions of political accountability and media's role in this process.

MASS MEDIA AS FACILITATOR

As Tocqueville observed, one compelling reason to expect greater politicization of personal experience among well-informed citizens is that high levels of exposure to news media may promote associations among those with similar interests and experiences:

The effect of a newspaper is . . . to furnish a means for executing in common the designs which they may have singly conceived. . . . It frequently happens . . . in democratic countries that a great number of men who wish or who want to combine cannot accomplish it because, as they are very insignificant and lost amidst the crowd, they cannot see, and know not where to find, one another. A newspaper then takes up the notion or the feeling which had occurred simultaneously, but singly, to each of them. All are then immediately guided towards this beacon, and these wandering minds, which had long sought each other in darkness, at length meet and unite (Tocqueville 1835: 203).

Lane (1962) referred to this process as one of "contextualizing" individual events and experiences. By weaving discrete events into a continuing story, media may enable people to see their problems and concerns as part of a broader social pattern (Lang and Lang 1981).

According to this line of thought, mass media contribute to the politicization of personal experience by exposing people to the similar experiences of others. It is through media coverage that the unemployed worker learns she is one of many thousands nationwide and that the crime victim learns his robbery was not an isolated incident, but rather part of a pattern of increasing drug-related crimes. There are, of course, other ways these individuals might learn about people who share their experiences: The crime victim might talk to neighbors who have been similarly victimized, and the unemployed worker might notice long lines at the local unemployment office.

Nonetheless, media coverage is likely to play an especially important role in encouraging political accountability for personal problems, particularly at the national level. By transcending large distances, media can aggregate incidents and define problems as national in scope. Particularly for low-frequency problems, learning about others' experiences through interpersonal exchanges or personal observation of one's immediate environment cannot provide the breadth of experience necessary to establish that a problem is not personal, or even local, but national in scope.

By devoting a great deal of coverage to an issue in a public forum, mass media also serve to legitimize it as a collective, social-level problem, something for which national leadership can fairly be held accountable.[1] Media's role in promoting problems to the status of social and political issues is well documented (McLeod, Becker, and Byrnes 1974; MacKuen 1981). It also may help to legitimize political blame by encouraging external over internal attributions of responsibility (Weiner et al. 1972), thus increasing the extent to which political actors are deemed responsible for personal problems.[2]

For example, the pattern of self-interested policy attitudes now observed among smokers and nonsmokers appears to be time bound; Green and Gerken (1990) suggest that the shift in the attitudes of nonsmokers toward more self-interested policy views is due to the fact that their claims have gained social legitimacy in recent years. Nonsmokers do not necessarily dislike smoke any more than before, but smoking is now an established *social* problem, enabling self-interest to be more easily channeled toward policy attitudes. By the same token, mothers who have lost children to automobile fatalities have long been against drunk driving, but until the issue became highly publicized through the efforts

1 This is not to suggest that people always hold national leaders responsible for national problems, local leaders for local problems, and so forth, but previous research does suggest that the president is more likely to be held accountable for problems that are perceived as national in scope, regardless of which unit of government actually bears the onus of responsibility.

2 Although evidence on the impact of consensus information is mixed, one domain in which it is clearly influential is in attributions for success or failure with respect to abilities (see Nisbett and Ross 1980). To the extent that the ability to get and hold a job is an ability, one would expect information about others to affect attributions of responsibility for unemployment as well. Some evidence also suggests that the effects of consensus information may be brought about as easily by mediated representations of others as by live ones (O'Connor 1972) and that the effect works best when it is in the form of large numbers of others (Bandura and Menlove 1968).

of Mothers Against Drunk Driving, their personal experiences were not highly politicized (Reinarman 1988). By compiling people's experiences and presenting them in an abstract, aggregated form, mass media may aid people in interpreting individual experiences as parts of broader social trends.

Despite the intuitive logic of this theory, empirical studies addressing the hypothesis that mass media consumption or closely related concepts such as political interest or involvement facilitate the political impact of personal experience have not been successful in uncovering this anticipated pattern.[3] In general, this research question has been a minor issue in studies focusing primarily on other topics. For example, the literature on television and priming has amply demonstrated that exposure to issue-specific television news influences the extent to which the president's handling of that issue affects overall assessments of presidential performance (Iyengar and Kinder 1987). In priming studies, however, the politicization of the issue and its connection to presidential performance is made *for* respondents by asking directly about evaluations of the president's handling of the particular issue. Whether respondents would attribute responsibility to the president on their own is unclear. Thus, the issue of whether news coverage primes personal- or collective-level referents is not specifically addressed by the priming literature. Personal experiences have been found to heighten closely related media effects such as agenda setting for some issues and to weaken it for others (Iyengar and Kinder 1987). The inverse inquiry, whether mass media strengthen or weaken the impact of personal experiences, remains an open question.

MASS MEDIA AS INHIBITOR

The notion that self-interested political attitudes should emanate primarily from those least exposed to mediated information stems from information-processing theories suggesting that, in the absence of alternative sources of information, people will "default" to personal experiences as a source of information on which to base their evaluations of policies and politicians (Weatherford 1983; Mutz 1992b). In the realm of economic judgments, for example, the tendency to default is encouraged by the high information costs associated with being aware of relevant macroeconomic information. Access to this kind of information requires habitual mass media use. In the absence of mass-

---

3 For example, Sears and colleagues (1980) found a general pattern consistent with this prediction, but it did not reach conventional levels of statistical significance (see also Sears et al. 1983).

mediated information about broader social conditions, people must rely on less representative, but highly accessible, personal experiences or interpersonal sources, and these judgments will necessarily reflect more parochial concerns.

To date, there is some indirect, but generally supportive, evidence of the "default source" theory in the realm of economic judgments. Weatherford (1983), for example, compared people who relied heavily on newspapers for political information with those who did not and found that personal experiences weighed more heavily in voting considerations among the information-poor subgroup, while the information-rich relied on perceptions of collective economic conditions. In other words, those without extensive access to mass-mediated information defaulted to their personal experiences when forming collective-level judgments. These findings mesh well with the suggestion that mass media use contributes to a subjective sense of economic knowledge (Adoni and Cohen 1978); heavy media users in Weatherford's study relied on their subjective perceptions whether they were correct or not, while low media users relied on a more readily available information source – their own personal experiences.

Unfortunately, Weatherford was comparing perceptions of prospective collective business conditions with retrospective personal unemployment experiences. These measures made it difficult to obtain clean comparisons since the questions included variations in both content and time frame, as well as personal versus collective emphasis. Other findings have loosely paralleled his results: Conover and colleagues (1986) found that those with inaccurate information about unemployment and inflation relied on personal experiences to form national-level economic perceptions, while respondents with accurate unemployment and inflation knowledge did not. In the absence of mass-mediated information, personal and collective concerns became less distinct, and people defaulted to personal experiences as the basis of their perceptions of social change. Overall, this evidence suggests that information weakens the impact of personal experiences on political evaluations, but again indirectly by means of the well-established link between collective retrospective evaluations and political attitudes (Cohen and Uhlaner 1991; cf. Funk and Garcia 1995).

RESOLVING CONTRADICTORY EXPECTATIONS

In order to resolve these seemingly contradictory expectations, it is important to specify the precise conditions under which each of these theories makes theoretical sense. The left-hand side of the model presented in Figure 5.1 sets forth specific hypotheses about information processing and how different sources of information will be integrated to form the personal and collective judgments in the center of the model. In contrast, the hypotheses suggested by the right-hand side of the model result from the kinds of attributions of responsibility that people make for personal and social problems. Media may serve as both inhibitor and facilitator of the effects of personal experiences by affecting these two processes differently.

At root, the default source theory is concerned with media's role in affecting processes on the left-hand side of this model. The theory makes little sense except in the context of evaluating the extent to which personal experiences should enter into judgments about the state of the collective. When it comes to evaluating presidential performance directly, there are many alternatives that people might use to evaluate the president even in the absence of any information about the state of the national economy. They could evaluate performance based on aspects of the president's character, judgments from other issue areas, or any of a limitless number of alternative dimensions that would create little need for "defaulting" to personal economic experiences. In contrast, when it comes to forming an evaluation of the state of the collective on a particular dimension such as economic well-being, those without relevant macroeconomic information from media should logically default to experiences from their everyday lives. Personal experiences or contacts and mediated information exhaust the realm of potential sources on which to form their impressions.

In contrast, the Tocqueville hypothesis, suggesting that media will *facilitate* the politicization of personal experiences, pertains to the right-hand side of the model in Figure 5.1, that is, the extent to which personal experiences or concerns are tied directly to political judgments. The logic underlying this theory depends upon the tone as well as the amount of coverage to which people are exposed. Media coverage that alerts people to the fact that their experiences are widely shared should encourage them to attribute responsibility to governmental actors. On the other hand, there would be little reason to expect media coverage conveying the impression that people's personal experiences were out of the ordinary to facilitate the connection of the personal and political. Just as silent majorities may be kept silent by a lack of information about like-minded others, news suggesting that one's personal problems are entirely atypical would not promote attributions of responsibility to political leaders. Instead, such coverage should lead people to attribute responsibility to internal or idiosyncratic causes.

Ultimately, then, the contradictory expectations of the Tocqueville and the default source hypotheses do not necessitate a theoretical or empirical showdown. The default source theory applies to the extent to which personal experiences will enter into collective-level judgments, in other words, to the *indirect* politicization of personal experience that occurs via their effects on judgments about the collective by way of influencing subjective assessments of their own personal experiences. On the other hand, the idea that media serve as facilitators of personal-experience-based political attitudes makes sense when one considers the extent to which people *directly* link their personal problems to political actors. This process of attribution should be aided exclusively by coverage suggesting that one's problem or good fortune is widely shared and thus a bona fide social condition, not just an individual one. By enabling people to make this connection, media may encourage the politicization of personal experience just as Tocqueville envisioned it.

For example, when mass media portray national economic conditions as in decline and many individuals also see their personal financial circumstances as in decline, exposure to this coverage should contribute to a greater sense that one's problems are shared by others and thus not entirely attributable to one's personal effort or the lack thereof. Likewise, if most people perceive their personal situations to have improved and national conditions are also perceived to be improving, then recognition of this similarity may trigger the connection of the personal and political and thus encourage rewarding political leaders.

On the other hand, if the tone of media coverage is strikingly different from what most people feel they are experiencing personally, then media exposure may suggest that their own experiences are atypical and that their problems are unique and theirs alone. This perspective would make them highly unlikely to hold government and politicians accountable. If personal economic circumstances are declining while the nation is perceived to be improving or, as is more commonly the case, the nation is perceived to be declining while one's own finances are seen in a more optimistic light, then media exposure would be unlikely to contribute to politicizing personal experiences. To summarize, it is impersonal perceptions that matter most to political attitudes, and it is only when media coverage of the impersonal world coincides with personal experience that these experiences appear to take on additional political significance.

DESIGN OF THE STUDIES

In the remainder of this chapter, I draw on two surveys to examine the politicization of personal unemployment experience at two different points in time. Although the two studies were not identical in all ways, they were designed specifically to address the issues posed by the seemingly contradictory expectations of these two hypotheses. Toward this end, they involved the same issue, the same survey questions, and the same general design, but the studies occurred in two quite different information contexts. The goal was to test hypotheses about when media will serve the facilitative function Tocqueville described and when media will discourage the politicization of personal experience by distancing people's perceptions of personal and collective well-being.

The first survey was conducted in the fall of 1987 at the end of Reagan's second term in office. It consisted of a two-wave sample involving approximately 600 respondents (see Mutz 1992b for details).[4] The second study was conducted a year later in the fall of 1988 at the end of Bush's first year in office, and it included approximately 1,200 respondents interviewed over a five-month period (see Mutz 1994b for details).[5] In both cases, professionally trained, paid interviewers asked respondents a set of parallel questions concerning personal- and collective-level unemployment judgments, as well as questions about news media exposure.[6]

Both studies also employed identical presidential performance evaluations as the political evaluation of interest. This question served as the dependent variable in analyses addressing the hypothesis that mass media should strengthen the direct impact of personal concerns on political preferences. In the first study, additional items tapped state-level unemployment perceptions and assessments of gubernatorial performance.

In evaluating findings it is important to note that these questions did not address presidential performance specific to the handling of unemployment or any issue in particular. This fact is important in several respects. First, it means that the strength of the expected relationships between issue judgments and performance evaluations should be less than for issue-specific performance evaluations. Moreover, the goal of these analyses was not so much to maximize the amount of variance explained, as to evaluate the relative importance of parallel personal- and collective-level judgments under varying contingencies.

Second, it also means that the relationships that do exist will reflect the extent to which the president was, in fact, being held responsible for that particular issue, incorporating both whether people attributed responsibility for the problem to the president in the first place and

4 Data came from two surveys in which interviewers contacted a random sample of 300 respondents in the state of Indiana using random digit-dialing. This resulted in two successive cross-sectional samples spaced at six-month intervals, in June and December 1987.
5 See Chapter 4, footnote 8, for sampling details.
6 Nonresponse does not appear to be correlated with unemployment experience, despite the tendency for telephone surveys to underrepresent the lower end of the socioeconomic spectrum (Schlozman and Verba 1979). Responses to the survey were representative of the extent of unemployment during this time period, and of that found in other non-telephone surveys.

whether citizens felt he was handling the problem well. These relationships are more appropriate for a test of the importance of mass media since quantitative and qualitative characteristics of coverage can play a role in making an issue a factor in presidential evaluations to begin with; to assume the importance of the issue to presidential evaluations as a constant would miss some of mass media's potential impact.[7]

The dependent variable used to examine whether, in the absence of media, people will default to personal-level information to form collective-level judgments was an item tapping retrospective assessments of unemployment at the collective level.[8] With the exception of demographics, party variables, and dummy variables representing personal experiences, all indicators were coded so that the theoretically expected relationships were positive ones.

The Influence of Context

Beyond providing opportunities for replication, the use of studies from two different points in time also provided a strategic advantage in examining the effects of tone of media coverage and the dominant direction of perceptions of collective experience. Differences in the tone of media coverage of unemployment during these two periods were reflected in the predominant perceptions of unemployment held at the time. Data for the first study were collected in 1987 when, despite the fact that the unemployment rate had been steadily dropping for over a year, 34 percent of respondents perceived unemployment to be worse since the previous year, and only 19 percent thought it had gotten better. In contrast, when the second study was done in the fall of 1988, over 40 percent perceived unemployment to have gotten better over the past year, and only 26 percent perceived it to be worse.[9]

Since levels of personal-level concern tended to be optimistic overall during both time periods, this created convenient variation in context across the two studies. One study was done when collective-level perceptions were pessimistic on the whole, and the other when the national employment situation was perceived to be on the upswing. Thus, people

---

7 The one exception to this organizational scheme is a variable indicating the amount of information regarding unemployment the respondent has received interpersonally. This measure does not fall clearly in either camp, but rather represents a level of judgment between these two poles.

8 Conover and colleagues (1987) found that retrospective assessments of economic conditions did not have much influence on economic forecasts, thus suggesting the causal ordering of variables used in the analysis of indirect effects.

9 Based on NES 1988, postelection survey: "Would you say that over the past year, the level of unemployment in the country has gotten better, stayed about the same, or gotten worse?"

encountered contrasting personal- and national-level perceptions in the first study, and consonant, coinciding perceptions during the second.

Measuring Personal Experience

There are obviously many other forms of personal economic experience that may enter more readily into political judgments, but unemployment is well suited to these purposes since the goal was not to explore all of the economic bases of presidential approval, but rather to examine the politicization of parallel personal and collective judgments surrounding a single, well-defined issue. In one sense, unemployment is ideal because it represents a narrowly defined form of personal experience that is nonetheless potentially politically potent.[10] Objective personal unemployment experience also has the advantage of being relatively easy to tap in self-report survey questions. Unlike measures of more subjective phenomena, unemployment experience can be assessed in a manner that is relatively free of simultaneity problems. For example, personal assessments of such things as whether one's family finances have improved or declined may be influenced by anxieties about social-level conditions or assessments of current political leaders (Lau, Sears, and Jessor 1990). However, whether a person in one's family has lost a job or been unable to find employment at some point during the past year is a fairly straightforward question that leaves little room for subjectivity.

At the same time, concrete personal experiences are not the only kind of personal judgments that may be relevant. In particular, increasing personal concern of the kind usually tapped by prospective economic measures may have political consequences as well. But measures of personal *concern* are quite different from measures of personal experience; personal experience is neither a necessary, nor a sufficient condition for personal concern. Instead, it is a subjective perception of one's personal experiences and thus corresponds to the upper box in the center of Figure 5.1.[11] Although measures of subjective personal concern should be more subject to endogeneity problems, asking about presidential approval without reference to unemployment and including controls for partisanship in all analyses greatly reduces this problem.

To circumvent the limitations of either subjective or objective personal assessments, these two studies incorporated both objective measures of past unemployment experience (which tapped levels consistent with ag-

10 Nonetheless, among economic experiences, previous studies suggest that it is particularly *unlikely* to be politicized (Schlozman and Verba 1979).
11 In addition, information about collective conditions could, under some conditions, influence levels of personal concern but, as demonstrated in Chapter 3, the reverse relationship is the more likely one.

gregate unemployment rates at the time) and subjective measures of personal unemployment concern (defined as increasing worries about the self or someone in one's family surrounding finding or losing a job). Incorporating both measures is particularly important because unemployment, like many other economic problems, is more likely to affect certain segments of the population than others. If only actual personal experiences are tapped, the politicization of personal experience can be confounded with characteristics that make certain segments of the population more likely to be affected. Even in times of high unemployment, this issue affects only a relatively small percentage of the population directly. Incorporating both kinds of measures broadens the range of people whose political attitudes could be influenced by personal-level judgments surrounding this issue. Since those exposed to greater amounts of news coverage also will tend to be better-educated people who are less susceptible to layoffs, the extent to which they politicize personal judgments will probably be based on personal concern about unemployment rather than on personal experience. The less educated, on the other hand, will have many more such experiences to politicize, thus creating more potential for increased politicization of personal experiences.

The inclusion of parallel personal and national measures tapping unemployment also made it possible to confirm at the individual level that the context was truly different in the 1987 and 1988 studies. Not only was the aggregate direction of personal and national unemployment perceptions switched, but the distance between personal and national perceptions was significantly greater for individuals interviewed in 1987. By 1988, this gap had narrowed significantly.

The Unique Contribution of Media

In addition to measuring personal experience in multiple ways, these studies also devoted particular attention to the measurement of exposure to mediated information. Assessing people's exposure to news coverage of a specific kind is inevitably difficult outside of experimental settings. Self-report questions on general exposure are notoriously unreliable measures of the reception of mediated messages (Price and Zaller 1993). When survey questions are asked about the reception of specific kinds of content – unemployment news, for example – severe simultaneity problems can result. Those concerned about unemployment, for example, are far more likely to recall and report such exposure.

Thus a central problem in evaluating empirical evidence bearing on media's impact is confusion surrounding what precisely is meant by closely related terms such as "knowledge," "mass media," or "information" and, particularly, how these terms have been operationalized. For example, in his study, Weatherford (1983) defined high and low information as the extent to which citizens habitually relied on printed mass media for information about political issues and campaigns. For Conover and colleagues (1986, 1987), emphasis was on the extent to which citizens extracted correct information from mass media, such as knowledge of the unemployment or inflation rates.

Differing conceptual and operational definitions often make it unclear whether researchers are referring to differences in, say, education, socio-economic status, or political interest, or to actual exposure to media coverage of the issue at hand. These often-confounded influences are important to differentiate because they are tied to different underlying theoretical explanations. Weatherford (1983), for example, attributes the greater politicization among those ranking low in the use of print media to a combination of the default source hypothesis and the fact that macroeconomic downturns affect those of lower socioeconomic status earlier and more severely than others. In other words, low print media usage and low socioeconomic status are likely to characterize the same people, and these people are more likely to politicize their personal economic misfortunes, in part because they have more such experiences to politicize.

In these two studies, I focused on the unique contribution of mass media, beyond what one might predict based on differences in general political knowledge, interest, or education. This focus meant that the studies had to include measures of, and variance in, the actual media content consumed by individual respondents. Ideally, coverage assessments would be based on truly exogenous measures of media content, not ones based strictly on respondent self-reports or on patterns of general exposure that remain confounded with other factors.

Toward this end, I made use of over-time change in the extent of news coverage of unemployment. Since differences between respondents interviewed at times of high and low unemployment coverage cannot be attributed to self-selection or to individual differences, these findings are more directly attributable to media coverage. In the first study, variance in coverage came from the serendipitous occurrence of "Black Monday" in between the first and second waves of data collection. Although the stock market crash did not directly pertain to the issue of unemployment, as a news event it spawned a tremendous amount of general economic coverage that included stories on unemployment. As might be expected, the tone of economic coverage during this period was particularly negative.

The first study also utilized a statewide, rather than a national, sample in order to facilitate a large-scale content analysis of coverage in each individual respondent's newspaper.[12] Although subnational samples can pose potential generalizability problems for some types of studies, when the purpose is to look at variation in people's information environments, the advantages outweigh the problems. Most studies involving national samples have used aggregated media content measures over time from a single, metropolitan source such as the *New York Times*, network newscasts, or news magazines (MacKuen and Coombs 1981; Behr and Iyengar 1985). Unfortunately, aggregation risks the same ecological fallacy that slowed understanding of economic influences on voting. Alternatively, researchers have limited the number of news sources by sampling from a small number of cities or by utilizing only the major newspaper in each in order to make individualized content measures practical (McCombs and Shaw 1972; Weaver et al. 1981; Dalton, Beck, and Huckfeldt 1996). This approach is understandable from a practical standpoint, but has the unintended consequence of limiting the amount of variance in news content since major urban newspapers will tend to have more similar news agendas and emphases.

In the second study involving a national sample, I utilized a computer-assisted content analysis of Associated Press wire service coverage to assess the amount of coverage unemployment received during the five-month period of the rolling, cross-sectional study. To ensure that indicators reflected at least briefly sustained periods of high and low coverage, coverage scores for each day were based on a ten-day weighted average where coverage was assigned a half-life of one day. By matching coverage indicators across the full period of the study with respondents' date of interview, characteristics of the then-current media environment were ascertained. Splitting coverage scores at the median, respondents were designated as having been interviewed during periods of heavy or

12 Newspapers are arguably the main source of people's perceptions of economic change, thus they were the best source for content analysis. Although in response to survey questions more people will typically cite television as their "most important" source of information on what is going on in the world, numerous studies have shown that this is strictly people's *perception* of where they get most of their information. Although there is a lot of news on television, people apparently process and recall very little of it (Robinson and Levy 1992). The smaller news hole of television news apparently combines with its transient presence in front of often-distracted viewers to limit its capacity to pass on information to its viewers. This same pattern of findings has been confirmed in Great Britain (Gunter 1987), and appears to hold even for the expanded array of news program now available to cable subscribers (Robinson and Levy 1996). Despite generally large television audiences, print media are more effective at conveying information to the mass public. Despite declining newspaper readership, the number of people watching a television newscast on a typical day is less than the number who read a newspaper. Since these figures include local and national news broadcasts, an even smaller number are exposed to news about national conditions.

light unemployment coverage.[13] While crude in its ability to identify specific individuals heavily exposed to unemployment news, this design had the crucial advantage of ruling out potential simultaneity problems common to self-reported measures of issue exposure. Calling patterns for the rolling, cross-sectional sample ensured that date of interview was a random event so that groups interviewed during periods of high and low unemployment coverage were otherwise comparable.[14]

In addition to assessing variance in exposure to unemployment coverage, both studies also asked questions tapping the respondents' current knowledge of unemployment. These measures were used to distinguish those who felt they had some knowledge of unemployment conditions from those who did not.[15]

TESTING THE TOCQUEVILLE HYPOTHESIS: MEDIA AS FACILITATOR

The ideal place to look for evidence that media facilitate the politicization of personal concern is in the 1988 study, since it meets all of the necessary conditions for Tocqueville's hypothesis. Both personal and collective perceptions tended to be optimistic on the whole during this period, so for the most part, media were conveying a picture of the world that was consistent with people's own perspectives.[16]

To establish whether the impact of personal variables on presidential approval varied across patterns of news media use, I first calculated the results for a restricted model in which the impact of all variables was constrained to be the same across different media exposure groups. This model was then compared to an unrestricted model in which separate slope and intercept coefficients were possible for different categories of news media use (see Wright 1976 for details).[17] Since measures of media

---

13 By combining measures of individual media exposure with measures of media coverage, I come closer to gauging individual exposure to unemployment news than with either measure individually. Moreover, the similarity of coverage agendas across national media suggests that those with a pattern of heavy news media exposure during a period of heavy unemployment coverage are most likely to have been exposed to this news, and thus most likely to be affected.

14 This was further confirmed by comparing the two groups using the five demographic variables of age, sex, race, education, and family income.

15 Although these same measures could be used either to assess the accuracy of unemployment knowledge or for purposes of identifying those with a subjective sense of unemployment knowledge, analyses indicated that findings produced identical patterns either way.

16 It is noted that this is *not* the same prediction as an interaction between personal and national referents as has on occasion been tested (e.g., Kinder 1981).

17 Non-scalar types were recoded to the scalar pattern closest to their pattern; that is, the one requiring the fewest changes to "match" the scalar pattern. This re-

use in this study were only weakly correlated with one another as is usually the case, it made little sense to combine them into a single additive scale.[18] But most respondents fell within one of four Guttman scalar types: Either they were (1) low in use of all three news media, including television, newspapers, and news magazines; (2) watched television only; (3) watched television and read a newspaper regularly; or (4) used all three news media regularly. Few people exhibited patterns outside of this structure, those who read news magazines also tended to read newspapers and watch television news, those who read newspapers only also watched television, and so on and so forth. These data easily surpassed conventional criteria for a successful Guttman scale with a coefficient of reproducibility of .94.[19]

As illustrated in Table 5.1, the importance of subjectively assessed personal concern about unemployment steadily increased across media exposure groups (from $b = .04$ in the No Media group to $b = .20$ in the All Media group), but this pattern did not represent a statistically significant interaction across groups, nor were any of the individual coefficients significant. The impact of personal experience decreased steadily across each of the media exposure groups, but it also remained consistently insignificant within each pattern of news media use. Overall, the contribution of collective judgments appeared to increase with greater amounts of news exposure, particularly for retrospective and

sulted in a normally distributed scale with the largest concentration of people in patterns 2 and 3.

18 A common problem in measuring media use stems from the fact that these behaviors are often not strongly correlated across media. Thus, a comparison of people high and low in print exposure inevitably includes some who are low on print use but high on other media, or vice versa. Given the strong similarities between national media agendas, this strategy makes it difficult to isolate those most likely to have been exposed to news that was prevalent across media. The raw media measures in this study are positively correlated ($r = .12$), but not to an extent that would justify combining them into a single index indicating high versus low media exposure. The usual approach to this problem is to let indicators for each medium stand alone. However, Campbell et al. (1966) noted that individual differences in media use approximate a Guttman scale, suggesting that, despite weak correlations, underlying media use patterns reflect a unidimensional concept, moving from television to newspapers to news magazine to form a scale of progressively higher levels of media use.

19 The coefficient of scalability was .74, with 83% classified correctly. High and low levels were assigned using the median so as to balance the sample size in the two groups for each medium (Mutz 1994 for details). It should be noted that there is potential for the politicization of personal unemployment experience in all four media groups. Overall, 20% of the sample reported some unemployment experience, but the variation across media groups was not as pronounced as anticipated, personal experiences were reported by 24% of the "no media" group compared to 15% of the "all media" group and 20% of each of the other two groups.

Table 5.1. *Personal and collective unemployment judgments as predictors of presidential approval by patterns of news media use (1988 study)*

	Restricted model	Unrestricted model			
		No media	Television only	Newspaper and television	All media
Sex	-.16 (.08)	.12 (.28)	-.29 (.14)*	-.24 (.14)	.19 (.22)
Race	-.23 (.11)*	-1.34 (.41)**	-.13 (.17)	-.11 (.18)	-.25 (.32)
Education	-.12 (.04)**	-.21 (.13)	-.10 (.06)	-.11 (.06)	-.06 (.10)
Age	-.00 (.00)	-.02 (.01)*	.00 (.00)	-.01 (.00)*	.00 (.01)
Income	.04 (.02)	.10 (.10)	.07 (.04)	-.00 (.04)	.04 (.06)
Democrat	-.63 (.10)***	-.30 (.34)	-.67 (.17)***	-.68 (.17)***	-.59 (.26)*
Republican	.71 (.10)***	.66 (.37)	.51 (.17)**	.78 (.16)***	.93 (.25)***
Personal judgments					
Personal concern	.09 (.04)*	.04 (.14)	.10 (.07)	.10 (.08)	.20 (.12)
Personal experience	.12 (.11)	.29 (.39)	.22 (.18)	.03 (.18)	-.25 (.32)
Collective judgments					
Retrospective	.15 (.04)***	-.01 (.14)	.14 (.07)*	.18 (.06)**	.24 (.11)*
Interpersonal	.10 (.04)*	-.15 (.24)	.11 (.07)	.19 (.07)**	.08 (.10)
Prospective	.18 (.06)**	.18 (.21)	.13 (.10)	.14 (.10)	.37 (.16)*
Media groups					
No media	.11 (.18)				
Television only	.35 (.13)**				
Newspaper/television	.23 (.12)				
Constant	2.38 (.44)***	3.97 (1.89)*	1.63 (1.47)	1.80 (1.45)	.98 (1.29)
Total R²	.31		.34		
(n)	(992)	(150)	(358)	(335)	(149)

Note: Entries are unstandardized regression coefficients with standard errors in parentheses. A comparison of the restricted and unrestricted models suggested no significant difference in the proportion of explained variance (F = 1.09, p > .05; see Wright 1976 for details on these calculations).

* p < .05   ** p < .01   *** p < .001.

prospective unemployment judgments. The coefficient corresponding to retrospective assessment of national conditions went from b = −.01 in the No Media group to a significant b = .24 in the All Media group; likewise, the coefficient for prospective national unemployment was an insignificant .18 among the No Media group, and a highly significant .37 among the All Media group. Despite these general patterns, an omnibus comparison of the restricted and unrestricted models suggested that the difference between the predictive power of the restricted and unrestricted models was negligible (F = 1.09, $p > .05$).

Indicators of media use alone failed to uncover evidence of Tocqueville's hypothesis. However, it is heavy media consumption, in combination with heavy unemployment coverage by the news media, that should produce greater accountability for personal-level judgments. Thus, my next step was to utilize the measures of media content to identify those interviewed during high and low periods of unemployment coverage.

Not surprisingly, levels of media use did not affect the politicization of personal unemployment concern during periods of light media coverage of unemployment. But, as illustrated in Table 5.2, during periods of relatively heavy media coverage of unemployment, high media users were more likely to politicize their personal concerns than were low users. Table 5.2 compares the effects of personal-level unemployment judgments by patterns of news media exposure. In order to retain a sufficient number of cases in each coverage/exposure subgroup, the four patterns of news media use were collapsed into two groups representing high and low patterns of exposure. The significant interaction between personal concern and media exposure demonstrates that exposure increases the importance of personal-level concerns specifically when the potential effects of media are greatest – during periods of heavy unemployment coverage.

For personal experiences, the coefficients are the opposite of the expected direction, though not significantly different from one another.[20] But the apportioning of influence demonstrates how findings bearing on this hypothesis may differ considerably based on the type of personal-level variables examined. Heavy media users have fewer experiences with unemployment to politicize, but their personal concern is far more politically potent, particularly since they are also the type of people most likely to vote and to be politically active.

Thus far, findings have demonstrated that during periods of heavy unemployment coverage, certain types of people are more likely than

---

20 In a pooled model including an interaction between media exposure and personal experience, the difference was not significant.

Connecting the Personal and the Political

Table 5.2. *The politicization of personal unemployment considerations during heavy media coverage (1988 study)*

	Low news media exposure[a]	High news media exposure[a]
Personal-level judgments		
Personal concern about unemployment	.06 (.09)	.31 (.09)**
Personal experience with unemployment	.39 (.20)	−.23 (.23)
Collective-level judgments		
Prospective perceptions of national unemployment	.10 (.08)	.22 (.12)
Retrospective perceptions of national unemployment	.10 (.08)	.22 (.08)**
Interpersonal information about unemployment	.21 (.10)*	.08 (.09)
Constant	.78 (.86)	2.63 (.90)**
Total R^2	.32	.30
(n)	(252)	(277)

Note: Entries are unstandardized OLS regression coefficients with standard errors in parentheses. The dependent variable is the five-point presidential job approval scale. The interaction between media exposure and personal concern is significant (b = 44, $p < .001$), as are the main effects of media exposure (b = 1.35, $p < .001$). N = 529. Demographic and party identification variables were also included in the equations that produced these coefficients.
[a]Low news media exposure is defined as those in the no media and television-only groups. High exposure consists of those in the newspaper and all media groups.
*$p < .05$ **$p < .01$.

others to politicize their personal concerns, but since this comparison was between heavy and light media users, it is difficult to discern whether exposure to news media or some other attribute closely associated with it is driving this phenomenon. Control variables are useful for making a stronger case, but they can only rule out a small number of plausible rival hypotheses. What, then, are the effects of increased levels of media coverage – an influence clearly independent of individual differences?

As Figure 5.2 illustrates, consistent with the results in Table 5.2, heavy coverage of unemployment does increase the importance of personal judgments, but this effect manifests itself differently among those high

163

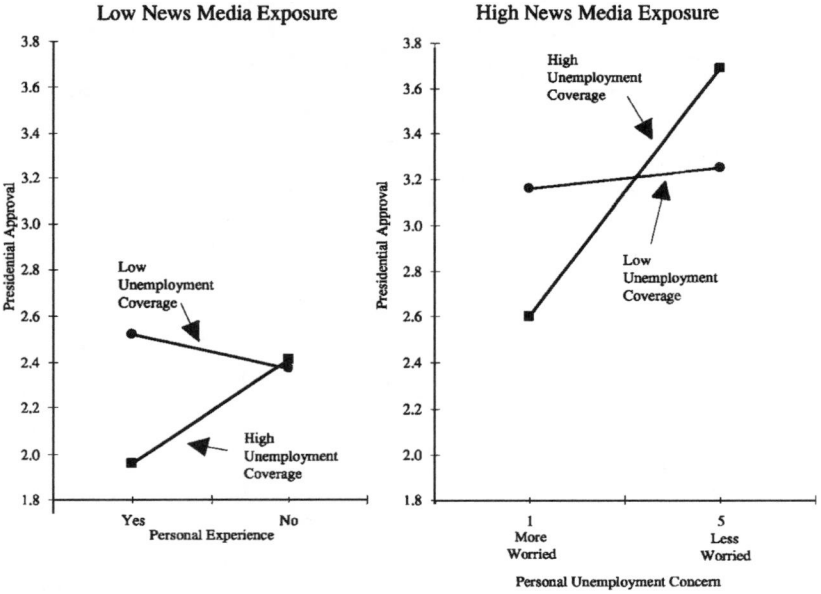

Figure 5.2. Effects of media coverage on the politicization of personal unemployment considerations.

and low in news media exposure. Separate regressions among these two groups produced significant interactions between personal experience and extent of coverage among those who consume little news, and between personal concern and extent of coverage among those who are heavy news consumers. Figure 5.2 illustrates these two interactions. For those with low media exposure, greater coverage corresponds to greater politicization of personal experiences. In other words, when coverage levels are sufficiently high, the news reaches even those low in overall exposure and aids them in politicizing personal experiences. The additional contribution of personal experiences for those interviewed during periods of high coverage produces a large and significant interaction coefficient (b = .60 (.26), $p <$ .05). As shown in the right panel of Figure 5.2, among heavy users, greater coverage corresponds instead to the politicization of subjectively assessed personal concern about unemployment (interaction b = .24 (.12), $p <$ .05).

The significant interactions with coverage levels demonstrate that personal-level judgments play a more powerful role in influencing po-

Connecting the Personal and the Political

litical preferences when media coverage is heavy. Furthermore, the *type* of personal judgments that are politicized makes a great deal of sense given the known demographic correlates of media use. Among the television-dependent and nonmedia groups – people who by virtue of their socioeconomic position are also more vulnerable to economic downturns – actual experiences with unemployment are politicized. Among the two print-intensive media groups, it is subjective personal concern rather than actual experience that becomes politicized during periods of heavy coverage.

In evaluating the impact of media on presidential performance, it should also be noted in Figure 5.2 and Table 5.2 that media use and media coverage both have significant direct effects on presidential performance, in addition to their significant interactions. In both cases, these effects are negative. For example, among generally low media users, being interviewed during a period of high unemployment coverage lowered respondents' approval of Reagan by 1.16, despite the fact that national unemployment remained low throughout this period. In analyses involving levels of news media use, the overall pattern is driven to a large extent by the Television Only group whose enthusiasm for Ronald Reagan surpassed all others. This finding jibes well with the popular, but typically undocumented, claims about Reagan's ability to produce pleasing television images that encouraged a "teflon-like" nonaccountability (cf. Weisman 1984; King and Schudson 1995). It is also consistent with Hetherington's (1996) finding that media use produced greater negativity.

The pattern of results in this study produced clear evidence of Tocqueville's hypothesis when tested specifically under the conditions that should facilitate this finding: similar perceptions at personal and social levels of judgment. But a negative case is equally instructive: What happens during periods of heavy coverage that are characterized by a disjuncture between perceptions of the personal and the collective?

Table 5.3 replicates the key findings from the analysis in Table 5.2, substituting data drawn from the 1987 study when personal and collective perceptions diverged. This analysis used the exact same battery of demographic and party variables, along with measures of personal experience and concern. As shown in Table 5.3, during periods of heavy unemployment coverage that encouraged greater compartmentalization of personal and collective perceptions, the pattern was reversed. Those *high* in media use were, if anything, *less* likely to politicize their personal concerns. They were instead likely to rely on perceptions of national well-being.

In total, this evidence suggests that while Tocqueville's hypothesis has merit, the conditions under which it should apply are fairly specific: The "pictures in our heads" pertaining to the nation as a whole must be

Table 5.3. *The politicization of personal unemployment considerations during heavy media coverage (1987 study)*

	Low news media exposure[a]	High news media exposure[a]
Personal-level judgments		
Personal concern		
about unemployment	50* (.21)	−.05 (.28)
Collective-level judgments		
Retrospective perceptions		
of national unemployment	.34 (.26)	.63* (.27)
Total R²	.33	.43
(n)	(198)	(132)

Note: Entries are unstandardized OLS regression coefficients with standard errors in parentheses. The dependent variable is the five-point presidential job approval scale. Demographic and party identification variables were also included in the equations that produced these coefficients.
[a]High news media exposure was defined as those who read a newspaper seven days a week, around 44% of the sample. Low news media exposure is defined as those who were occasional or nonreaders of newspapers.
*p < .05   **p < .01   ***p < .001.

similar to the perceptions of our immediate lives. When media contribute instead to a disjuncture or compartmentalization of personal and collective judgments, one should not expect greater politicization among those heavily exposed.[21] In fact, under these conditions, the logical outcome should be precisely the opposite: Media coverage suggesting that people's personal concerns are atypical and idiosyncratic should discourage them from holding national leaders accountable.

TESTING THE DEFAULT SOURCE HYPOTHESIS:
MEDIA AS INHIBITOR

The idea that media inhibit the politicization of personal experience pertains most directly to the indirect effects of personal considerations, that is, to the influence that personal concerns have via their influence on

21 These patterns also mesh well with Lau and colleagues' (1990) observation that the 1984 election year was a notable exception in terms of the level of politicization of personal concern that occurred. As Figure 4.5 illustrated, 1984 was also exceptional in that perceptions of personal and national well-being were contrary to the usual pattern of personal optimism and societal pessimism.

perceptions of collective concerns. To examine this hypothesis, I regressed perceptions of national unemployment conditions on independent variables, including indicators of unemployment knowledge and an interaction between knowledge and personal experience. For this hypothesis, the key distinction rests on the extent to which people manage to extract useful information on national conditions from other sources. In order to test the hypothesis that personal-level variables will matter more for the less informed who are forced to default to more easily available sources, a knowledge dummy variable was coded so that the interaction represented the additional effects of personal experience among the uninformed.

Table 5.4 illustrates the results of this analysis using the 1987 sample. While personal unemployment experience alone has no significant effects on perceptions of national unemployment, among the unknowledgeable, personal experience does matter. Those without relevant macroeconomic information default to personal experiences as one source of relevant information about national conditions. It is still not the *only* source of information; people also rely on their interpersonal sources of information, for example. Nonetheless, this pattern does suggest that in the absence of substantial outside information, the model described in Figure 5.1 collapses on itself such that the collective becomes more of an extension of the personal and parochial.

Did these same findings replicate in the 1988 sample? Table 5.5 shows the results of this analysis using the larger, national survey sample. If anything, the pattern was even stronger in 1988. Again, as predicted, personal experiences had no significant effects in the sample as a whole, but specifically among the less knowledgeable, having a personal experience with unemployment lowered evaluations of national unemployment conditions by almost half a point. As shown in Table 5.5, even when one subtracts the main effect (b = .16), this still leaves a net impact of −.29.

Those with low unemployment knowledge were more favorable in their assessments of unemployment regardless of personal unemployment experience. But those who had had no personal experience with unemployment were even more positive in their assessments. As predicted, people with high levels of knowledge did not use their personal experiences in forming evaluations of national conditions. Those without knowledge of the current employment situation relied instead on their own personal unemployment experience.

In evaluating current conditions, both groups relied on their personal concerns about unemployment and their interpersonally obtained information about others' employment problems: The less knowledgeable were no more likely to "default" to these types of measures than were the more knowledgeable. And finally, partisan rationalization also played a

Table 5.4. *Effects of personal- and collective-level unemployment perceptions on assessments of national unemployment conditions (1987 study)*

	National unemployment	
Personal experience with unemployment	.12	(.16)
Personal concern about unemployment	.14	(.06)*
Interpersonal information about unemployment	−.14	(.06)*
Knowledge × personal experience	−.20	(.09)*
Knowledge of employment trends	−.02	(.01)*
Local unemployment rate	.06	(.04)
Party identification		
Republican	.29	(.14)*
Democrat	−.19	(.13)
Demographic controls		
Age	−.02	(.04)
Gender	−.20	(.11)
Race	.03	(.25)
Income	.01	(.05)
Education	.05	(.05)
R^2	.23	
(n)	(300)	

Note: The dependent variable in this equation is a five-point scale representing retrospective perceptions of national unemployment. The knowledge dummy variable is coded 1 for low knowledge and 0 for high knowledge so that the interaction represents the additional effects of personal experience among the less knowledgeable. *$p < .05$.

role in that Democrats were systematically more pessimistic about national unemployment conditions during this Republican presidency.

It is worth noting that in both the 1987 and 1988 samples, the main effect of knowledge was to make people more pessimistic in their assessments of national unemployment conditions. This finding parallels the media exposure coefficients that were also significant and negative. Since income and education are controlled, this cannot simply be an effect of general knowledge or socioeconomic standing. Moreover, unemployment was not particularly high at the time, thus making this finding even more curious. The recurrent finding that the highly knowledgeable and/or those heavily exposed to political news tend to give more negative evaluations

Connecting the Personal and the Political

Table 5.5. *Effects of personal- and collective-level unemployment perceptions on assessments of national unemployment conditions (1988 study)*

	Perception	
Personal experience with unemployment	.16	(.17)
Personal concern about unemployment	.19	(.03)***
Prospective perceptions of national unemployment	.18	(.05)***
Interpersonal information about unemployment	−.14	(.03)***
Unemployment knowledge	−1.01	(.36)**
Knowledge × personal experience	−.45	(.19)*
Party identification		
Republican	.08	(.08)
Democrat	−.24	(.08)**
Demographic controls		
Age	−.00	(.00)
Gender	−.21	(.07)**
Race	−.14	(.09)
Income	.08	(.02)***
Education	−.00	(.03)
R^2	.20	
(n)	(1,062)	

Note: The dependent variable in this equation is a five-point scale representing retrospective perceptions of national unemployment. The knowledge dummy variable is coded 1 for low knowledge and 0 for high knowledge so that the interaction represents the additional effects of personal experience among the less knowledgeable.
*$p < .05$ **$p < .01$ ***$p < .001$.

may instead reflect the fact that political "sophistication" in the contemporary United States goes along with a substantial dose of cynicism – at least at the level of mouthing the old catch phrases. In other words, those exposed to media on a regular basis adopt the savvy, in-the-know perspective of contemporary journalism, which emphasizes the untold story behind the story – usually one that suggests greater negativity.

The Role of Television: Consequences of Qualitative Differences in Coverage

These results lend support to the general theoretical framework outlined thus far. But they also seem to contradict one well-known contention concerning media use and political accountability. This argument, force-fully advanced by Iyengar (1991) in *Is Anyone Responsible*, is that television – uniquely among the dominant sources of political information – insulates political leaders from accountability. In a nutshell, Iyengar suggests that differences in the way television news frames issues have important consequences for the extent to which citizens hold government leaders accountable for personal and national problems. By promoting individualistic over societal or governmental attributions of responsibility, television coverage leads viewers to support the status quo by insulating current leadership from accountability.

Using a series of clever experimental designs in which respondents were exposed to either episodic, event-centered television coverage or thematic portrayals that emphasized societal or collective outcomes, Iyengar found a general pattern wherein episodic portrayals encouraged individualistic attributions of responsibility, while thematic portrayals of the same issue promoted attributions of responsibility to government. Iyengar concluded that television, the ultimate episodic medium, is thus proestablishment and actively, if unintentionally, promotes the status quo. Counter to the general Tocqueville hypothesis then, use of this particular type of medium should *discourage* accountability.

To what extent is evidence conclusive and convincing in this regard? Iyengar's experimental comparisons contrast conditions receiving episodic and thematic coverage, and the results clearly suggest that more thematic issue portrayals will enhance accountability. But the studies do not provide control groups, so they do not tell us how people would react in the absence of exposure to television coverage. In other words, evidence that television suppresses accountability cannot be ascertained from his data. Iyengar's general conclusion that television coverage insulates political leaders from accountability rests on the assumption that those who get their information from television would be more likely to hold leaders accountable if they did not watch television news.

Is television really qualitatively different from other media in this respect? Although it was not designed specifically to address this hypothesis, the 1988 survey was well suited to answer this question due to the inclusion of multiple measures of news media exposure and the scalar patterns of media use.

A glance back at Table 5.1 illuminates two noteworthy findings bearing on the question of television in particular. On the one hand, the first column of Table 5.1 might be construed as supporting this hypothesis. Of the four media use patterns identified, it is the group that *only* watches television that evaluates the president significantly more positively than all others, even after controlling for differences in education, income, and so forth. This coefficient could be construed as indicating a pro-status quo bias.

But, on the other hand, this boost in presidential approval among television watchers is clearly not due to the fact that they are less likely to hold presidents accountable than are those who do not watch television. If one compares the extent to which these four groups hold the president responsible for perceived personal and national problems, there is little evidence that television use in particular suppresses accountability. Greater levels of print use encourage accountability, to be sure, but those who get their news from television appear to be part of a general continuum stretching from those who do not use any of these sources to those who use all of them. Coefficients tying personal concern to presidential approval become progressively stronger as one moves from the No Media to All Media groups. Likewise, personal experience progresses from being incorrectly signed to at least pointing in the general direction of accountability.

The pattern for perceptions of collective-level problems is similar. The Television Only group is more likely than the No Media group to hold the president accountable for perceived changes in national unemployment. Although these coefficients become progressively larger in the multiple media use groups, there is no evidence that television suppresses what otherwise would have been there. Patterns for knowledge of unemployment through personal acquaintances and prospective national evaluations follow similar patterns.

Ultimately then, there is no evidence that television use suppresses accountability, though using alternative sources would appear to encourage higher levels of accountability. This pattern is consistent with logical assumptions about the nature of content across these media as well. Although television news, newspaper news, and news magazine coverage have not been subjected to comparative content analyses evaluating the extent of episodic and thematic emphases, it is easy to see them as forming a continuum moving toward progressively less episodic, more thematic types of coverage. Consistent with this idea, Neuman, Just, and Crigler (1992) found the greatest extent of contextualizing information in news magazines, followed by newspapers and television, respectively.

Television news in particular tends to be dominated by event-oriented coverage since it must respond quickly to the ongoing flow of daily events, with little lead time to provide historical context or background (Iyengar 1990). Television's emphasis on event-centered as opposed to thematic frames is probably due partly to the visual nature of the medium (Postman 1985) and partly to the need to capitalize on television's advantage over other media; that is, its ability to respond quickly in relaying events to the public. In all fairness to television journalists, their medium is probably the least conducive to "contextualizing" as Lane envisioned it.

Daily newspapers insist upon timeliness as well, but their deadlines allow some opportunity for putting events in context. More importantly, the news hole of the average newspaper allows far more information to be conveyed than does a half-hour news broadcast. A script from an average network news broadcast takes up only one-third to one-half of the space on the front page of the *New York Times*. And while space certainly does not guarantee that a story will include contextualizing information, the opportunity to do so is much greater than in television news, and a great many newspapers capitalize on this as a strength in competing for television audiences. Moreover, as demonstrated in Chapter 2, in the last twenty years in particular, the shift in newspaper reporting style has been away from reporting single events and toward creating news roundups and analyses that treat individual events as examples of larger problems.

And even more so than newspapers, news magazines have made a virtue of the generally long lead time given to their reporters: "They [magazine journalists] learned to stand off from the flow of discrete items filling daily newspapers, to look for longer trends. . . . Something in the very format of such papers suggests that knowledge merely agglutinates – that you stick discrete new items onto an unchanged body of past knowledge" (Wills 1983: xvii). News magazines explicitly aim to summarize and connect otherwise disparate news events. Thus, the more of these sources people are exposed to, the more they are also exposed to thematic issue information – the very kind that would encourage greater accountability.

Ultimately, then, the case for television as a suppressor of accountability must rest on the argument that were it not for television, people in the Television Only group would be reading newspapers and/or news magazines regularly. This argument is not an easy one to make. The persistence of the underlying Guttman pattern in media use habits is one reason why. Table 5.6 shows the distribution of the national sample across all of these patterns. Just as Campbell and colleagues (1966) noted over thirty years ago, magazines tend to be the "hardest" medium and spoken media the "easiest" in terms of levels of effort required. If a person uses only one medium, it is quite likely to be television; those who read newspapers are also very likely to watch television news; those who read news magazines are very likely to both read newspapers and watch television news. Both the concentration of frequencies in scalar

Connecting the Personal and the Political

Table 5.6. *Guttman scale of news media use items*

News magazine	Newspaper	Television	Frequency	Type
0	0	0	101	Scalar
0	0	1	361	Scalar
0	1	0	73	Non-scalar
0	1	1	336	Scalar
1	0	0	15	Non-scalar
1	0	1	92	Non-scalar
1	1	0	22	Non-scalar
1	1	1	150	Scalar

Note: 1 denotes high level of media use corresponding to this medium, while 0 represents low use. Five percent of the sample had at least one missing value and thus could not be classified. High and low levels were assigned for each medium as follows: newspaper exposure: 7 days a week (high), 1–6 days (low); news magazines: read regularly (high) or not (low); television news: little or no attention (low), some or a lot of attention (high).

patterns and the demographic correlates of the scale suggest that patterns of media use are based on varying levels of effort.[22]

Would the Television Only group be reading newspapers in television's absence? Given the greater amount of time and effort this would involve, it seems highly unlikely. Moreover, television news viewing and newspaper reading are independent of one another rather than negatively correlated as one might expect if television viewing were displacing newspaper reading (Greenberg and Kumata 1968). Although newspaper reading is displaced by time spent on job-connected activities and child rearing, there is little evidence that television news viewing displaces newspaper reading (Samuelson, Carter, and Ruggels 1963; cf. McCombs 1972). Despite common assertions to this effect, over-time data and early studies of the introduction of television in the United States are similarly unsupportive of this conclusion. Instead, television's displacement effects appear to have been on radio and motion pictures, activities that serve a similar entertainment function (Walker 1950; *Editor and Publisher* 1949a, 1949b).

Instead, it seems far more likely that in the absence of television the Television Only people would fall into the group that is low in use of all kinds of news media, in other words, those even less likely to hold

---

22 Not surprisingly, this scale is correlated with levels of political interest, ranging from a 2.4 on a four-point scale for the No Media group to 3.8 for the All Media group.

government leaders accountable. Ultimately, of course, this is a historical question, and despite the tendency to blame television for all that ails contemporary newspapers, there is little consensus on this view and even less empirical evidence (Schudson 1992; Converse 1962). Viewing television as a medium that extends some information and some capacity to hold government accountable to those who otherwise would have no information and no such capacity obviously casts it in a much more positive light. While the verdict is still out on this matter, evidence to date lends no direct support to the idea that television suppresses accountability among its viewers unless we can safely assume that these same people would otherwise be reading newspapers or newsmagazines.

This chapter has attempted to resolve two seemingly contradictory theories regarding media's role in promoting or obstructing democratic accountability: one suggesting that media facilitate the connection of personal experience and political attitudes (Sears, Steck, and Garhart 1983; Sears, Lau, Tyler, and Allen 1980), and the other predicting precisely the opposite (Weatherford 1983; Conover, Feldman, and Knight 1986; Cohen and Uhlaner 1991). Upon closer examination, it becomes clear that these hypotheses and evidence generally pertain to different parts of this overall process. In addition, the theories make sense only when one makes specific assumptions about the match between personal-level assessments and the mediated presentations of national economic well-being that inform people's collective-level evaluations.

The results from the studies in this chapter extend support both to Tocqueville's assertion about media's capacity to help people politicize their experiences by exposing them to like-minded others, and to the use of personal experience as a "default" source of information on national conditions in the absence of information about the state of the collective. Moreover, they point to some of the consequences that the compartmentalization of personal and collective perceptions may have for political preferences. In one sense, national mass media, by virtue of their very existence, contribute to depoliticizing personal experience. In the days when virtually all information was local in origin, people had no choice but to rely on highly personal and parochial information in forming the perceptions on which their national political attitudes were based. The role contemporary media play in this process depends on characteristics of the current perceptual context.

To the extent that news both on television and in newspapers is shifting toward more thematic coverage of issues consistent with the new long journalism thesis, its capacity to construct perceptions of the collective environment has increased, and thus its capacity to facilitate accountability in the way Tocqueville proposed also has increased. But this assertion hinges on the accuracy of media portrayals of collective experience and on the extent to which people perceive similarities between their own experiences and problems and the collective ones portrayed in national media coverage. To the extent that media coverage increasingly comes to represent a world "out there" with little connection to people's day-to-day lives, it may discourage one of the key processes it is supposed to facilitate in democratic systems – the ability of citizens to hold government leaders accountable for the effects of their policies.

PART III

EFFECTS OF PERCEPTIONS
OF MASS OPINION

6

When Does Success Succeed?

A REVIEW OF THE EVIDENCE

"Nothing succeeds like success,"[1] a well-known French proverb advises. In American politics, "success" is often defined by the accumulation of mass popular support.[2] And the belief that perceptions of popular support will spawn even greater support has become an important tenet of conventional political wisdom.

The goal of Part III is to examine theory and evidence pertaining to the influence of perceptions of collective opinion on political attitudes and behaviors. Toward this end, Chapter 6 reviews the extent and limitations of evidence regarding this general hypothesis. Since evidence appears in studies of a wide variety of political phenomena and under quite different labels, making sense of this literature is not as simple as it might first appear. Likewise, the methodological pluralism used in addressing these questions strengthens the generalizations that can be drawn, while simultaneously limiting opportunities for replication. Chapter 7 takes up the task of proposing a plausible theoretical framework for understanding the mechanisms by which perceptions of collective opinion translate to alterations in individual opinions or behaviors. Chapter 8 then tests these propositions using a series of experiments embedded within representative national surveys.

The intuitive sensibility of the idea that people care what others think has fueled tremendous public handwringing as well as academic concern. So strong are beliefs about the power of perceived public opinion both in the United States and abroad that numerous restrictions have been imposed on the distribution of information about collective others'

---

1 "*Rien ne réussit comme le succes,*" was first attributed to Alexandre Dumas the Elder in *Ange Pitou* (1854), vol. 1.
2 There are some notable exceptions. For example, when an issue is to be decided by the courts, mass opinion may support a viewpoint that is not ultimately the winning one. Likewise, in the case of war, mass public support cannot ensure victory.

views. For example, in countries including France, Spain, Portugal, Brazil, and Venezuela, there is a moratorium on the publication of poll results immediately preceding elections (Rohme 1985). In countries such as Korea, it is simply illegal to publish poll results on political topics. In the United States, where the First Amendment poses what is probably an insurmountable hurdle to the many advocates of restriction, several unsuccessful attempts at restricting exit polls have been launched (Milavsky et al. 1985). Free speech considerations notwithstanding, most Americans perceive public opinion polls to be harmful to the political process (Lavrakas, Holley, and Miller 1991) and think it would be a good idea to restrict the publication of information of this kind.

Likewise, the history of public opinion research demonstrates a persistent concern with effects on political attitudes and behaviors that result from perceptions of mass opinion. Interest sometimes emanates from an applied policy concern. For example, should we have uniform poll closing times across the United States? (Milavsky, Swift, Roper, Salant, et al. 1985). Others are interested in what the long-term consequences of knowledge of mass opinion will be for American society and politics. Geer (1991), for example, argues that information provided by public opinion polls should make partisan realignments a thing of the past. Still others are interested in these questions for purposes of informing political strategy: How much money should be spent campaigning early in Iowa and New Hampshire? Belief in the power of early victories in presidential primaries has led to "front-loading" of state primaries and calls for restructuring the entire nomination process. As Traugott (1992) has noted, objections to the dissemination of information about mass opinion are generally based on normative principles rather than empirical evidence of negative effects.

The notion of impersonal influence clearly suggests that people's perceptions of others' attitudes, beliefs, or behaviors have consequences for their political attitudes and behaviors. But how much real evidence is there for this effect? Despite persistent interest, empirical evidence has never kept pace with the emergence of new concerns fed by the development of mass feedback mechanisms, technological advances in communications, and the sheer prevalence of polling, to name only a few common sources of apprehension.

Today, several areas of research are, at root, concerned with these same phenomena. For example, studies of momentum in presidential primaries and investigations of the consequences of publicized poll results both focus on the effects that knowledge of mass preferences may have on subsequent political behavior. And although they have generated distinctly different research literatures, the "spiral of silence" theory and the "third-person effect" also pertain to the consequences of knowledge of others' views. Moreover, research on the effects of exit polls and the early reporting of election returns also stems from the belief that perceptions of others' opinions will alter subsequent political attitudes or behaviors.

Despite marked similarities among different types of effects, the extent of evidence and scholarly consensus vary tremendously by political context. For example, when conclusions are drawn about the effects of early election calls, the consensus is that evidence from relatively few elections corroborates these concerns. With respect to publicized preelection polls, movement both toward and away from majority opinions has been documented. On the other hand, in presidential primaries it is widely accepted that the dynamics of public opinion are important to a successful candidacy; attracting support early in the primary is believed to facilitate still greater support in subsequent primaries. While there are exceptions to these generalizations in each area of research, the central tendencies are nonetheless quite different.

Weighing evidence in each of these contexts is made doubly difficult by the variety of research methods used to address these questions, and their corresponding strengths and weaknesses. Since the same research problems plague interpretations of these studies across political contexts, I begin with a discussion of methodological difficulties and then briefly review empirical evidence from a large number of studies bearing on the same underlying premise – the idea that perceptions of mass support will generate even greater support.

METHODOLOGICAL ISSUES

The foremost problem facing studies of the effects of perceived opinion is establishing the direction of causality. Evidence of a correlation between individual political attitudes and perceived popular support for those same positions is irrefutable and ubiquitous, but the direction of causality is usually ambiguous. This ambiguity is exacerbated by the fact that, as described in Chapter 3, the false consensus/projection effect provides as compelling a reason to expect people's own opinions to influence their perceptions of others' views as vice versa. Projection effects do not rule out the possibility that perceptions of others' opinions can influence political preferences; they simply make it all the more important and difficult to document the direction of the causal sequence. Even when temporal precedence can be established, an apparent cause-and-effect relationship might still be spurious. For example, if a candidate's promotion of a new program leads to both greater perceived and actual public support for the program, this relationship may falsely be interpreted as an effect of perceptions of mass opinion.

A long time ago, Campbell (1951) advocated experimental or field experimental designs to disentangle these processes. While his suggestion has been heeded to some extent, experiments have brought their own difficulties. The political contexts in which these phenomena occur rarely lend themselves to field experiments, and many experimental studies have sacrificed generalizability by relying on college student subjects. Although student samples are a useful population for studying psychological processes, levels of student political interest and involvement make them problematic for studies of political attitudes.

The inconsistencies in evidence of impersonal influence on political opinions make it more useful to consider general tendencies in findings across multiple studies rather than considering each individual study on its own merits. In this brief review, I necessarily blur some important distinctions in both independent and dependent variables. For example, in some areas of research the dependent variable is vote choice; in others, issue opinions; and in still others, the public expression of an issue or candidate opinion. Likewise, there are minor differences in the hypothesized causal agent. The independent variable is sometimes conceptualized as the expectation of success for an issue or candidate, in other cases the perceived state of, or trend in, mass opinion is assumed to be the driving force.

I review each of the major theoretical paradigms in which this hypothesis has been examined, loosely ordering them according to the extent of supportive empirical evidence pertaining to the effects of perceptions of mass opinion, ascending from least to most supportive. Of course, the absence of evidence for many of these theories is not necessarily evidence of their absence. The core theoretical premise that they share makes them difficult to examine, even using the most rigorous designs. Nonetheless, even among the published studies – those most likely to show significant findings – researchers' generally high expectations have not been met.

I begin with research addressing the spiral of silence and the third-person effect. These sections are followed by reviews of the effects of early election returns and the influence of publicized preelection polls and preelection perceptions of candidate popularity. I conclude this section with evidence bearing on the impact of momentum in presidential primaries. Finally, I consider some unique categories of political judgments in areas where the law dictates consideration of the views of impersonal others.

THE SPIRAL OF SILENCE

According to the spiral of silence theory, one behavior that results from perceptions of mass opinion is the public expression of people's views, or the lack thereof (Noelle-Neumann 1974). In simplest terms, the spiral of silence hypothesizes that people use media coverage to assess the climate of opinion surrounding an issue, and when they perceive themselves to be in the minority, they will refrain from public expressions of opinion. Others who are also scanning the environment for signs of support will find fewer people supportive of their common viewpoint, thus producing a spiral that silences one side of public debate.

This theory has generated a great deal of often ambiguous empirical evidence. A partial explanation for these inconsistencies is that many "tests" have examined different parts of this multifaceted theory. One could independently examine at least a half dozen different empirical propositions comprising the theory, as outlined by Glynn and McLeod (1985). For purposes of this review, the proposition of interest is exclusively whether perceptions of public support for an issue, party, or candidate alter public expressions of opinion toward that entity.

But even within this narrowly defined realm, evidence of support for the spiral of silence is weak and confounded at best. For example, although Noelle-Neumann (1974, 1977) demonstrates a significant relationship between people's own opinions and their perceptions of others' views, cross-sectional data make it impossible to establish the order of the causal sequence. Additional evidence offered in support of her hypothesis is based on observations indicating that expectations of election outcomes predicted actual election outcomes better than preelection opinion polls (Noelle-Neumann 1985). From this pattern, Noelle-Neumann inferred that inflated expectations about public support for one party influenced vote choice. Since voting is essentially a private act, these examples are actually quite difficult to attribute to the spiraling process and fear of social isolation described in her theory (Salmon and Kline 1985). Additional tests have involved experimental manipulations embedded in surveys in which people were asked how willing they would be to express their views publicly in a direct, face-to-face situation such as in a shared train compartment with someone of different or like-minded views. Although these studies have produced some evidence pertaining to people's willingness to express views publicly, their findings are more applicable to face-to-face contexts than to the situations where perceptions of mass opinion influence individual political opinions or behaviors (Kennamer 1990).

In a replication of Noelle-Neumann's work, Glynn and McLeod (1982) found little support for the idea that perceptions of a hostile majority will silence those with minority views. Salmon and Neuwirth (1990) found that people who perceived themselves to be in the majority nationwide were more willing to express opinions than were those who perceived their positions to be in the minority, but these findings did not hold for all types of opinion expression, nor for perceptions of local community opinion. In a study utilizing questions attached to American newspaper surveys asking respondents if they would be willing to speak "on the record" to a reporter writing a news story, Katz and Baldassare (1992) found that those holding minority views were no less willing to be interviewed than those holding majority views. Unfortunately, findings from all of these studies were limited by the constraints of cross-sectional data; even in the case of positive findings, it was difficult to rule out plausible rival interpretations.

Based on overtime, aggregate comparisons, some British election data appear to be compatible with this hypothesis: Public predictions about the outcome of an election that is still months away generally have been correct, thus suggesting that perceptions of public opinion predict actual opinions (Webb and Wybrow 1986). However, the rationale for the spiral's effects on private behaviors remains unclear since people could easily maintain private viewpoints that were inconsistent with their publicly expressed views. Moreover, when these same data were examined at the individual level, results were less convincing. For example, although the correlation between expectations one month and voting intention in the following month was strong, it was lower than either the serial correlation of voting intentions, the correlation between intention and expectation during the same month, and the correlation between voting and expectation the following month (Webb and Wybrow 1986: 278). At the individual level, then, evidence did not support the idea that perceptions of the opinion climate were an important influence on subsequent opinions. Moreover, the kind of "last minute swings" that prompted Noelle-Neumann's formulation of this theory in the first place have not behaved consistently in the fashion that the theory would predict (cf. Merten 1985, Noelle-Neumann 1980).

Glynn and McLeod (1984) found that those who perceived their positions to be gaining support at a given point in time were more likely to discuss an issue than those who perceived their positions as losing support. Moreover, respondents from their panel study of the 1980 presidential election demonstrated that the amount of perceived support for Carter in October predicted 4 percent of the variance in vote preferences for Carter in November. This same pattern did not hold for support for Reagan or Anderson. Overall, variables tapping the perceived climate of opinion or trends in opinion change accounted for very little of the overtime variance in vote choice.

Although his study was not framed explicitly as a test of the spiral of silence, Gibson (1992) also tested the assumption that people are fearful of expressing views they assume to be unpopular. He hypothesized that limited exposure to diverse political views contributes to a culture of intolerance that inhibits people's political freedoms, particularly those involving political expression. In examining the larger environment that may contribute to individuals' reticence to speak out, his hypotheses extended only as far as tolerance within the local community, and here he found a statistically significant negative relationship between tolerance within the community and reluctance to discuss political views. Gibson (1992: 339) parallels the assertions of the spiral of silence in arguing that "People learn from the political culture that intolerance is widespread, that it is acceptable, and that there are tangible risks to asserting views that the intolerant culture finds objectionable." He argues that as a result of perceiving intolerance on the part of others, people will be reluctant to express views that they think are unpopular in their local communities.

It is difficult to safely extend findings based on the local community to more impersonal macro-environments. However, Huckfeldt and colleagues (Huckfeldt et al. 1995a; Huckfeldt and Sprague 1995) argue that people's larger opinion environment will alter their expectations regarding the opinions that will be held by interpersonal contacts. In other words, people will be more likely to think their political discussants are of the opinion that dominates the larger environment. The larger environment in these studies was the neighborhood and the county rather than the more distant kinds of collectives that are generally reported on by mass media. And unlike most spiral of silence research, they were studying the effects of the *actual* distribution of opinion in these collectives rather than people's perceptions of them. Nonetheless, the implication they draw is similar; people's face-to-face interactions may be altered by the larger environment – perhaps by making minorities less willing to express their views, though this outcome was not explicitly tested.[3]

Although the underlying premise of the spiral of silence is certainly compelling, the evidence of its actual impact thus far is not. In a recent meta-analysis of studies using survey data to examine the relationship between people's perceptions of support for their positions and their willingness to express their opinions, the researchers observed a very small but statistically significant correlation (mean = .05), but concluded

---

3 As noted in Chapter 1, footnote 9, in order to differentiate impersonal forms of social influence from personal influence, I have excluded from the definition of impersonal influence situations in which one individual influences another by virtue of a personal relationship and the desire to avoid social disapproval. Thus, if a person refrains from expressing a viewpoint in front of another person because that person fears the other person will think ill of him or her, the mechanism is one of personal influence. See Chapter 7 on the parallels between normative and informational mechanisms, and personal and impersonal social influence.

that overall "the literature provides little support for this notion" (Glynn, Hayes, and Shanahan 1997: 461). They recommended more experimental studies and more studies using measures of actual willingness to speak out rather than people's hypothetical willingness to do so. Such efforts may eventually bear fruit; however, to date, the most methodologically rigorous research designs generally have not supported the theory (Salmon and Kline 1985).

THE THIRD-PERSON EFFECT

As discussed in Chapter 2, the most thoroughly researched component of the third-person effect is the tendency for people to perceive greater media influence on others than on themselves. This tendency is a robust finding that has been well documented across a variety of different areas (Cohen et al. 1988; Tiedge et al. 1991; Vallone, Ross, and Lepper 1985).

When it comes to the consequences of these perceptions for political attitudes and behaviors, the evidence is far weaker. Many of these studies imply, but do not document, consequences of changed perceptions of others' opinions. For example, Cohen and his colleagues (1988) suggest that people's tendency to overestimate the effects of defamatory news stories on public opinion has important implications for the judgments that libel jurors make about damage to reputation, but they do not document these consequences in terms of specific judgments or awards. In a quasi-experimental study of the television miniseries "Amerika," LaSorsa (1989) found that those who perceived themselves as knowledgeable overestimated the extent of opinion change that resulted from viewing this program. He suggests quite logically that this phenomenon may help explain the calls for censorship of this and other media programs, but again brings no direct evidence to bear.

Those studies that explicitly seek to link changed perceptions of others' views to behavioral or attitudinal changes have met with less success. For example, Rucinski and Salmon (1990) found that perceptions of the influence of political ads on others' voting decisions did not predict support for an independent commission to monitor media content. Gunther (1991) also attempted to connect people's estimates of effects on others to subsequent actions or attitudes, but he found no relationship between people's estimates of the extent of attitude change resulting from a defamatory newspaper article and the amount of money in damages respondents judged to be an appropriate penalty. In another study, support for pornography restrictions was found to correlate significantly with the third-person perceptual bias (Gunther 1995). Overall, though, there is little evidence linking third-person perceptions to important political outcomes among the mass public (Perloff 1993).

When Does Success Succeed? A Review of the Evidence

EXIT POLLS AND EARLY ELECTION RETURNS

The preponderance of evidence on the impact of election day knowledge of the campaign outcome suggests that this information has weak to null effects (Marsh 1984; Meier and Saunders 1949; Sudman 1986). This conclusion applies to early calls based on exit poll results as well as those based on actual vote counts that reach West Coast voters before their polling places are closed. Fuchs (1966) and Mendelsohn (1966) concluded that this information comes too late to influence most vote decisions. In a study of the 1964 election, Lang and Lang (1968) found some evidence of decreased eagerness to vote among those who heard about Johnson's victory and were surprised by it, but they also concluded that these effects were very limited, in this case because most people expected Johnson to win long before election day. Wolfinger and Linquiti (1981) found a very small, but significant, difference between late turnout in the West as compared with the rest of the country in the 1972 elections, but not in 1974. They attributed this difference to early calls of the 1972 election, though other explanations are equally plausible (for a discussion, see Tannenbaum 1983).

This issue was raised again after the 1980 election when Reagan's defeat of Carter was announced before polls closed in the West. In the end, studies of this particular election further confirmed that knowledge of election day results did not produce a bandwagon effect, but there was evidence that it depressed turnout in the West and thus may have had an important impact on the outcome of state and local races (Delli Carpini 1984; Sudman 1986).

PUBLICATION OF PREELECTION POLLS

The political effects of perceptions of mass opinion are perhaps most confusing when evaluating the effects of publicized poll results, effects commonly referred to as "bandwagon" or "underdog" effects. Some of the confusion stems from the multiple methodological approaches to this research question, with studies ranging from casual observation to complex experimental and quasi-experimental designs.[4]

But the findings themselves do not make the task any easier. In an early review of this phenomenon, Klapper (1964) concluded that there

---

4 For example, some research compares opinion poll results with actual election results, the idea being that if preelection polls underestimate the winning margin, they must have produced additional support for the winning viewpoint, whereas polls that overestimate actual support lend support to the underdog hypothesis. This method suggests that there has been an underdog effect in several British elections (*Economist* 1974; Marsh 1984b).

was insubstantial evidence of either movement toward or away from majority views. Some contemporary analysts share this view of the more recent accumulation of evidence. In the 1988 Canadian election, Johnston et al. (1992) found that published polls drove public expectations, but found relatively weak evidence for any impact of expectations on vote preferences. In an analysis of eight presidential elections, Granberg and Brent (1983) found minor evidence of bandwagon effects in two of them.[5] In the election context in particular, the consensus typically has been that such effects are either nonexistent or so small as to be politically inconsequential (Atkin 1969; Fleitas 1971; Roshwalb and Resnicoff 1971).

At the same time, other studies have documented movement in the direction of the perceived majority views. As early as 1941, Allard produced shifts toward perceived national opinion in an experimental study. Using exit poll data from three British general elections, McAllister and Studlar (1991) also found evidence of a bandwagon effect in all three cases. In a study utilizing a panel design, Skalaban (1988) documented a small bandwagon effect among voters with weakly held opinions, even after controlling for projection effects. Moreover, in an experimental study embedded within a survey, Marsh (1984) found significant movement in the direction of what respondents were told was the current trend in abortion views.

Some additional studies have used college student subjects who were systematically exposed to information about the opinions of other college students (Ceci and Kain 1982; Kaplowitz et al. 1983). It is difficult to extend findings from studies such as these to the real-world context of public opinion polls; representations of group opinion may trigger group identification in these experiments, whereas this is unlikely to happen with the presentation of highly diffuse and undifferentiated representations of mass opinion. Representations of collective opinion as they are usually conveyed in mass media infrequently address the opinions of specific groups beyond the usual cross-tabulation of opinions by political parties, gender, and race. This problem, combined with the notoriously low level of student political interest, makes the results of these studies more problematic.

With these caveats in mind, studies of student opinion provide some additional evidence of movement toward portrayals of group opinion, even in the absence of group interaction. For example, in a very early study, Wheeler and Jordan (1929) exposed students to the distribution of opinions of other students and induced movement in the direction of group

---

5 These instances were specifically among those who intended to vote for Nixon in 1960 and among those who lacked a preference in the 1976 election.

opinion. In a similar study, Kaplowitz and colleagues (1983) found movement toward student opinion poll results for low-commitment issues. Price (1989) also found that student opinions polarized in the direction of news portrayals of group opinion.

To add to the general confusion, as many studies have demonstrated underdog effects away from majority views as have demonstrated movement in the direction of majority opinion (Gaskill 1974; LaPonce 1966). West (1991), for example, found that exposure to poll results had a negligible impact on choice of presidential candidate, but a significant negative impact on preferences in a statewide referendum on abortion. Fleitas (1971: 436) found that while quantitative poll results alone failed to produce significant effects, these results in combination with a description of the election as a "contest between an advantaged front-runner and a disadvantaged underdog" produced substantial movement in the direction of the underdog. This finding jibes nicely with West's (1991) explanation of how presidential candidate Gary Hart was able to attract support away from Mondale by means of an underdog effect; Mondale led Hart in all of the prenomination polls, but Hart was able to capitalize on the impression that Mondale was "advantaged" by the support of Democratic power brokers.

Still other studies find simultaneous evidence of opinion shifts both toward and away from majority views. In a quasi-experimental study of student attitudes toward the North American Free Trade Agreement, Cloutier, Nadeau, and Guay (1989) found evidence of both bandwagon and underdog effects, although the net influence was in the direction of the majority (see also Navazio 1977). Using experimental cues embedded in a national survey, Lavrakas, Holley, and Miller (1991) also found evidence of both bandwagon and underdog patterns, depending on respondents' levels of education. In all of these studies, simultaneous movement in two directions produced small net effects (Ceci and Kain 1982; Cantril 1980; Marsh 1984a).

Some accounts of the effects of polling stress the inadequacy of all short-term research designs for tapping what may be slow, cumulative, or indirect effects (Beniger 1976; Shapiro et al. 1991). Most of these designs are ill suited to capture what may be the most powerful, yet indirect, effects of polls; for example, poll results may influence fund-raising capabilities, volunteer recruitment, free media attention, and other campaign resources, any of which may, in turn, influence a candidate's prospects for office (Henshel and Johnston 1987).

In the United States, general presidential elections involving two major party candidates have been deemed an unlikely venue for impersonal influence, particularly because of the higher salience of candidates and the availability of party cues. Nonetheless, in British general elections,

Nadeau, Niemi, and Amato (1994) found that expectations based on candidate popularity significantly influenced voter preferences. In the 1970 British general election, Cain found that individuals were more likely to vote for their second-preference candidate when they perceived that their first choice had little chance of winning. In contrast, Johnston and colleagues (1992) found virtually no evidence of effects from perceived popularity in a Canadian election.

Finally, although the focus with respect to preelection polls has been primarily on changes in candidate or issue preference, a few studies have addressed the effects of polls on turnout. DeBock (1972) used poll results to manipulate the expected margins of victory in the 1972 presidential race. Based on reactions from a sample of undergraduates, he concluded that when a race is one-sided, the trailing candidate's supporters may become less intense in their preferences and less motivated to turn out. Consistent with this study, self-reported explanations for nonvoting in the 1988 presidential election suggested that around 20 percent of registered nonvoters may have refrained from voting because they thought Bush's victory was a foregone conclusion (Lavrakas, Holley, and Miller 1991).

Overall, the literature on preelection polls has produced more convincing findings than in previously discussed contexts where impersonal influence may occur. A good number of methodologically rigorous studies have been able to demonstrate the potential for movement both toward and away from perceived mass opinion. This pattern suggests that still other significant findings may have been buried in data pooled across subgroups that responded differently to this type of information.

MOMENTUM IN PRESIDENTIAL PRIMARIES

Changes in the structure of the presidential nomination system have produced a new arena for potential influence due to perceptions of others' views. As direct primaries have proliferated, the sequence of state contests has exacerbated the emphasis on campaign dynamics. Media coverage of the results of these primaries and caucuses – in addition to the usual polls and predictions – has contributed to widespread public awareness of mass opinion and current candidate standings. Dynamic processes are an important aspect of all campaigns (Aldrich 1980), but they are more observable and certainly more widely studied in the context of primary campaigns. According to conventional political wisdom, momentum benefited Carter in 1976, Anderson in 1980, and Hart in 1984.

In the late seventies the idea that a candidate must make a strong early showing was accepted as gospel. Marshall (1983), for example, claimed that a negative early media verdict "will cripple, if not destroy, a candidate." However, as more evidence accumulated with subsequent primaries, there has been greater recognition that the dynamics of primaries provide mixed support for the idea that candidacies in decline tend toward further decline, while candidacies with increasing support tend toward even greater support (Bartels 1988; Brady and Johnston 1987; Sigelman 1989). By 1988, Shafer noted that writing in this area reflected the "fundamental and apparently reliable unpredictability of nomination politics." "The institutionalization of unanticipated consequences" was its defining characteristic (Shafer 1988: 995–6).

In presidential primaries, studies of momentum generally center on the impact of expectations of a candidate's chances of victory on vote choice. Using survey-based data, people are asked to rate each candidate's chances of winning the party nomination, and this measure is then related to items involving candidate liking and vote choice.[6] As in other studies, the projection of expectations onto preferred candidates also occurs in the context of primaries. In general, people are more likely to bend their expectations to coincide with their preferences than vice versa (Granberg and Brent 1983). For example, in a study utilizing two-stage least squares to disentangle potential reciprocal influences, Brady and Johnston (1987) found evidence of projection, but no evidence that viability influenced choice. In Patterson's (1980) panel study of voters in the 1976 election, he found that in the Democratic presidential primary, expectations led to more favorable attitudes toward the candidate in the subsequent interview; for Republicans, the pattern instead suggested a projection effect.

Despite these many qualifications and refinements of the original hypothesis, the general consensus is that people's perceptions of the popularity of candidates and their likelihood of winning often translate to votes (Bartels 1988; Abramowitz 1987; Abramson et al. 1992). But the experiences of recent history have done much to temper the strength of early beliefs in the absolute power of momentum.

STATUTORY CONSIDERATION OF OTHERS' VIEWS

In some cases, political decisions are affected by perceived opinion because people are explicitly instructed to take this kind of information into account. In particular, as part of a legal decision-making process, people are sometimes asked to consider others' views. In such cases per-

---

6 Although momentum and viability are similar, some researchers have differentiated them by suggesting that viability refers to the effects of long-term, relatively stable forces influencing a candidate's chances of election, whereas momentum is something that can change quickly from week to week (Haynes and Gurian 1992).

ceived opinion is not simply a subtle influence on the attitudes of individuals; it is an institutionalized part of legal proceedings.

Legal judgments incorporate others' views in a variety of areas, the most obvious of which is obscenity laws. Elements of the "Miller test" for the obscenity of sexual explicit material clearly incorporate a need for knowing others' views (*Miller v California* 1973). This three-part test for what constitutes obscenity specifies that the "average person" applying "contemporary community standards" should find that the work appeals to the prurient interest. In addition, a work's "patent offensiveness" is also supposed to be judged with reference to contemporary community standards. And finally, the third standard – whether the work "lacks serious literary, artistic, political or scientific value" – is to be judged with reference to the "reasonable person." For each prong of this test, then, judges or, more often, jury members are asked to rely not on their personal judgments, but instead on their perceptions of others' views.

In one decision, it was determined that the phrase "contemporary community standard" included the nation as a whole (*Jacobellis v Ohio* 1964). But the Miller court later deemed this a misinterpretation, stating that, "Nothing in the First Amendment requires that a jury must consider hypothetical and unascertainable 'national standards' when attempting to determine whether certain materials are obscene" (*Miller v California* 1973, quote at 31). Instead, it was left to the individual states to determine the scope of the relevant community, whether it be a statewide standard, some smaller unit, or an unspecified "community."

In similar fashion, juries in defamation trials are asked to determine whether the opinions of substantial numbers of "right thinking" people have been affected by information carried by the mass media (Sack 1980: 49; Loring 1986). Here, jurors' perceptions of others' views play a pivotal role in influencing the size of awards that are deemed suitable compensation for the amount of reputational harm that has occurred (Cohen at al. 1988). Not surprisingly, expert testimony in obscenity cases as well as in libel trials has sometimes included results from public opinion polls in an attempt to influence jury assessments of the views of impersonal others. Consistent with the third-person effect, studies of the accuracy of such perceptions suggest a common tendency for people to overestimate both the extent to which others' views have been influenced (in the case of reputational harm) (Cohen et al. 1988) and the extent of community intolerance of sexually explicit materials (in the case of obscenity) (Linz et al. 1991).

Standards for judging sexual harassment in the workplace incorporate a similarly problematic need for assessing the state of others' opinions. Quid pro quo harassment, where employment benefits are exchanged for sexual favors of some kind, is fairly unambiguous, but a second category of impermissible behaviors – those that "create an offensive or hostile working environment" – are far more elusive (*Meritor Savings Bank v Vinson* 1986; Equal Employment Opportunity Commission 1990). Public opinion regarding harassment standards is now an integral part of the process whereby courts render judgments as to whether an individual's claim of hostile working environment is valid. In the absence of precise guidelines for defining hostile work environment harassment, the courts have imposed a standard of "reasonableness," that is, whether the hostile environment claim was one with which a "reasonable" person would concur.

Some recent court decisions (*Ellison v Brady* 1991; *Robinson v Jacksonville Shipyards* 1988) have altered this language and adopted instead the "reasonable woman" standard, which is "an attempt to determine a representative woman's interpretation of sexual behaviors as the standard by which courts can decide whether a sexual harassment claim is frivolous or trivial" (Thacker and Gohmann 1993: 462). In other words, was the behavior something that a reasonable woman would find harassing?

In all three of these situations – obscenity, libel, and sexual harassment – people are asked to make judgments about the views of impersonal others. The law presumes that people have the ability to assess the views of an average person, a reasonable person and/or the consensus among large numbers of diffuse others with whom they may have no direct contact or experience on these matters. In some cases, juries may be instructed to consider communities that are small enough that people may have some amount of direct contact with members, but typically this is not the case. Moreover, most people's personal contacts constitute a biased sample of even their immediate communities. Thus, accuracy remains a problem even in situations where it is considered desirable to take perceptions of others' views into account.

Legal judgments may seem pretty far afield from the more traditional kinds of political decisions in which impersonal influence processes have been studied. Nonetheless, they make two related points. First, they illuminate the extent to which consideration of others' views may be considered a *worthy* component of political decisions, not simply an unintended and undesirable by-product of things such as a sequential nomination system or the irresponsible way the press covers election results. Perceptions of collective opinion are assumed to have some value in these legal decision-making processes such that society actively encourages people to consider their impressions of others' views. Second, these examples illuminate the relationship between perceptions of collective opinion and societal norms. References to collective others' views in formal regulations are simply attempts to codify the use of societal norms into legal standards. A frequently disputed issue in an era when communication easily crosses community, national, and international borders, is which norm within which community or society should be relevant? In other words, how big is the relevant collective?

The U.S. Supreme Court's recent ruling on the Communications Decency Act has brought precisely this issue to the forefront (*Reno v American Civil Liberties Union* 1997). Part of the reason it ruled against the Communications Decency Act and its effort to eliminate obscenity on the Internet was that the "community standard" in this case was unconstitutionally vague. When a medium freely crosses both national and international borders, how does one define the norms for that community?

CONTINGENT CONDITIONS FOR INFLUENCE

What is perhaps most interesting about research on the effects of perceived opinion is the persistent attention this topic has received despite a lack of encouraging findings. From the 1920s to the present, social scientists have been continuously churning out results that seldom have met generally high lay expectations. Despite the general lack of return on research investments in this topic, there has been some accumulation of knowledge across political contexts. In light of the inconsistencies in method, context, and even dependent variables, it may seem pointless to draw generalizations from such a mixed bag of findings. However, since these regularities have emerged in spite of these inconsistencies, they are all the more noteworthy.

First, the magnitude of people's reactions to portrayals of mass opinion are typically more modest than anticipated. When shifts in the direction of perceived majority views do occur, it is generally under conditions of low information and a weak commitment to one's initial position. The absence of other cues – such as political parties – also encourages people to turn to mass opinion for guidance. For example, effects from poll-based information appear to be more likely in low-information political settings with limited alternative cues (West 1991). In addition, bandwagon reactions to poll findings appear more frequently when people are weakly committed to their preferences.

Although many studies have documented the importance of expectations in influencing primary vote choice (Abramson et al. 1992; Bartels 1988), inconsistencies in these findings have led researchers to propose similar contingencies. Some suggest that influence may only occur for previously unknown candidates (Norrander 1991; Geer 1989; Patterson 1980). Moreover, as is the case with preelection polling effects, momentum appears to be a more potent force when information levels are lowest and uncertainty is highest, that is, early in the primary season (Bartels 1988).

Studies of the effects of perceived opinion include some apparent contradictions as to whether influence is greatest early or late in a campaign, but often they are referring to different components of the influence process and, possibly, different mechanisms of influence as well. On the one hand, the better educated, more attentive and politically informed are more likely to be exposed to and aware of information about mass opinion. Thus survey-based studies tend to show greater effects among the politically involved and somewhat informed. Once exposed, it is the least well-informed and least politically committed who are likely to be influenced (Zaller 1992). Thus experimental studies that equalize exposure across people tend to show that the less politically involved are more influenced.

This dual relationship in which those most aware are least likely to be influenced, combined with the tendency to perceive others as supportive of one's own views, may well be the reason for the persistently modest evidence of effects. In situations where portrayals of mass opinion saturate information channels – such as the case of presidential primaries – these barriers may be overcome, whereas in other situations they are not.

In addition to movement in the perceived direction of dominant views, evidence of underdog effects is now so extensive that they are no longer regarded as flukes. Although underdog effects are seldom predicted, they appear with great regularity in attempts to document bandwagon phenomena. Underdog patterns are most likely when people are strongly committed to their views, particularly if the other side is perceived as unfairly advantaged (Fleitas 1971).

Despite similar patterns of contingent relationships, studies across these various contexts have assumed fundamentally different underlying mechanisms of influence. For example, examinations of the spiral of silence assume that "fear of social isolation" is the motivating force behind people's reluctance to express opinions they perceive to be unpopular (Noelle-Neumann 1984). Such views are then said to be internalized to the extent that they affect even private behaviors such as voting. Marsh (1984a) also points to the power of social approval and punishment as an explanation for the effects of poll results on public opinion. Studies of the impact of the third-person effect seldom posit a specific explanation, though the desire to protect others from potentially harmful or misleading media effects is usually the assumed motivation behind a change in policy attitudes.

Studies of the impact of exit poll results and early election returns tend more toward an expected utility approach. In other words, people who learn that elections are already decided by the time they vote decide quite rationally that it is not worth the effort of voting. In the case of those who still make it to the polls, their votes may be influenced by the knowledge that it is a waste to cast a vote for a sure-loser in a three-way race. Likewise, in a multicandidate primary, one throws away his or her potential to influence the outcome by supporting a candidate who has no hope of winning the primary and/or the general election. Still other explanations touted in the context of general elections and the influence of preelection polls center on the idea that "voters respond to the implicit bonus of being on the winning side (Nadeau, Niemi, and Amato 1994: 378).

Concern surrounding the influence of perceived public opinion on individual political attitudes and behaviors has generated a large body of research. Although these studies are seldom considered as a single literature, experimental and nonexperimental findings across a wide variety of contexts have produced fairly consistent evidence as to who is most likely to be influenced under what kinds of conditions. The most striking general characteristic of this evidence is the extent to which it suggests a much more modest impact than what has been assumed in popular claims about the detrimental impact of knowledge of collective others' views.

Aside from inflated expectations, two additional factors may contribute to this discrepancy. Since these effects are usually contingent upon factors such as levels of information, their evidence easily may be overlooked in studies that look exclusively for across-the-board aggregate impact. In addition, the now well-documented tendency for opinions to shift away from majority views in some contexts may help to mask effects since a significant impact in two different directions will show that no aggregate impact has occurred.

Despite the similarities among the theories and types of effects discussed in this chapter, they have not been united by a single theoretical framework, nor has there been much attention to the process underlying the effects proposed within each of these individual areas of research. In Chapter 7, I attempt to address the issue not only of whether people are influenced and in what direction, but why. In other words, what are the underlying mechanisms or processes of influence that account for the effects of perceived opinion on political attitudes and behaviors? Although the issue of process can be separated from simply identifying contingent conditions, understanding the mechanism by which influence occurs inevitably serves to advance knowledge of when it should occur. Even more importantly, it adds a valuable perspective to our understanding of the desirability of impersonal influence that flows from perceptions of collective opinion.

7

The Social Psychology of Impersonal
Influence from Collective Opinion

In studying effects that flow from perceptions of mass opinion, the often inconsistent evidence is rendered even less interpretable by the lack of a theoretical framework suggesting who should be most susceptible, when, and under what conditions. The blunt prediction of social determinism sheds little light on the subtleties of social influence and corresponds poorly with available evidence. Most research has focused on establishing whether such an effect exists without articulating or examining the process by which it occurs. In a research area rife with inconsistent findings, it is particularly important for research to focus on process. Studies establishing a mechanism of influence will promote an understanding not only of why an effect occurs, but also when and why it does not according to some underlying model. In this manner, seemingly inconsistent evidence can hopefully be rendered interpretable, and reliable predictions can be made.

In this chapter, I analyze the most promising psychological theories for understanding these phenomena. A major reason for the lack of any cumulative understanding of impersonal influence has been the shortage of social-psychological theories explaining or predicting such effects. Moreover, the search for relevant theories has transpired amidst tremendous cultural concern focused on certain kinds of social influence at the expense of others.

THE EMPHASIS ON CONFORMITY

Researchers looking for theoretical guidance as to why people are influenced by perceptions of mass opinion quite naturally have turned to the literature on conformity. Unfortunately, the most widely cited mechanisms of conformity do not adapt well to impersonal contexts. This mismatch has, in turn, hampered the development of theoretical models accounting for impersonal social influence.

To understand the context in which these explanations developed, I begin by examining early twentieth-century apprehensions about the extent of conformity in the United States. Next I examine the landmark social-psychological studies of conformity and their implications for impersonal influence. To what extent should these findings and the concerns they raised be extended to apprehensions about conformity in impersonal contexts? Finally, to remedy the lack of theoretical models appropriate to impersonal contexts, in the last section of the chapter I describe a set of social-psychological mechanisms better suited to account for impersonal influence. These models are then empirically evaluated in the following chapter.

A Nation of Sheep?

Twentieth-century social and political commentary has demonstrated a persistent concern with conformity in the United States. In a review of social criticism at midcentury, Winston White (1961) found that the most consistent theme was the fear of, and attack upon, conformity (see also Lane and Sears 1964). David Riesman's theory that the American character had shifted from conscience as a source of guidance in the nineteenth century to peer groups as a source of guidance in the twentieth century further fanned the flames of anxiety over conformity: "The type of 19th-century citizen, whom we have characterized – a type we call 'inner directed' – becomes increasingly rare under the pressures of our era" (Riesman and Glazer 1954: 495).

There were, however, a few dissenters. Daniel Bell (1960 p. 34) in particular railed against the idea that American culture imposed excessive pressures toward conformity. Bell acknowledged the tendencies in American culture signified by terms such as the "organization man" and "Babbitt," but argued that "in historical perspective there is probably less conformity to an overall mode of conduct today [the 1950s] that at any time within the last half-century of America." Nonetheless, the prevailing conventional wisdom was that Americans were essentially a nation of sheep, characterized by "thoughtlessness and unreasonableness": "The model was an individual deprived of autonomy, one whose actions stemmed not from an inner direction but from external influences forcing themselves upon him and taking control away from him. . . . In fact, it was the intent of the suggestion movement to describe social behavior as 'irrational' in its roots and branches, as synonymous with manipulation" (Asch 1952: 400–1).

The mechanism underlying this excessive conformity was thought to be normative social influence, that is, the desire to be personally rewarded for conforming behavior and to avoid social punishment by con-

The Social Psychology of Impersonal Influence

forming to others' expectations. This was accomplished by "paying close attention to the signals from others" (Riesman, Glazer, and Denney 1950: 22). Americans were characterized by an "anxious inferiority, fearful of censure and desperately eager to please" (Bell 1960: 13). Moreover, "other-directeds" were said to "take for granted that their own goals and their desire for approval from others, far from conflicting with one another, tend to fit together": "While all people want and need to be liked by some of the people some of the time, it is only the modern other-directed types who make this their chief source of direction and chief area of sensitivity" (Riesman, Glazer, and Denney 1950: 38). This type of conformity was said to go beyond the external trappings of "keeping up with the Joneses" and extended to people's innermost attitudes and beliefs about the world.

In one respect, the amount of concern surrounding conformity is quite ironic; the same society that rushed to adopt mass society theory and its atomized individuals as an appropriate metaphor for the undesirable consequences of industrialization, and that romanticized the notion of traditional communities with close-knit relationships ensuring strong social norms, also indicted conformity as one of the great threats to modern society. Although mass society theory was declared "the most influential social theory in the Western world" apart from Marxism (Bell 1960: 24), in the ongoing struggle to balance the interests of individualism and conformity, the bulk of vigilance during this century seems to have been directed toward excessive conformity.

In a sense, impersonal influence represents another wave in this progression of concern, from peer groups as sources of guidance to impersonal others. Riesman and colleagues (Riesman, Glazer, and Denney 1950: 22) included the possibility of impersonal others in their original definition of "other-directedness" when they noted in passing that "What is common to all other-directeds is that their contemporaries are the source of direction for the individual – either those known to him, or those with whom he is indirectly acquainted, through friends and through the mass media." But his main focus was on face-to-face primary groups that had the capacity to reward or punish people for their behavior.

Social Psychological Demonstrations of Conformity

What kind of social psychological evidence was brought to bear on claims about excessive conformity? The most well-known demonstration of conformity in social psychology was contained in the experiments of Solomon Asch, a set of small group studies of the effects of a unanimous majority on individual judgment. These are easily among the most frequently cited studies in social psychology, and they are typically referred to as stunning demonstrations of the tremendous powers of conformity. A short recapitulation of the specifics of these studies is helpful to understanding their prodigious impact. Briefly, these laboratory experiments involved groups of seven to nine people who were asked to match the length of a given line – the standard – with one of three other lines. Two of the lines clearly differed from the test line and one was exactly the same length. Confederates issued their opinions publicly before it was the subject's turn to offer a judgment. Six to eight confederate subjects were instructed to give the same wrong answer on twelve of eighteen repeated trials.

To summarize the results of these experiments, approximately two-thirds of the test subjects' responses were correct and one-third conformed to the majority judgment. About one-quarter of all of the subjects were consistently independent; another one-quarter gave majority-determined estimates from eight to twelve times. In short, while there was evidence of conformity, the subjects also exhibited a great deal of independence; in fact, this was the modal response.

Indeed, Asch counted himself among the group who "doubted that it [conformity] dominated social life" to the extent widely thought (Friend, Rafferty, and Bramel 1990: 30) and intended his experiments as evidence to this effect.[1] Asch questioned the dominant theoretical interpretations of conformity in social science and contended that people were not as passive, malleable, or submissive as research supposedly confirmed: "Current thinking has stressed the power of social conditions to induce psychological changes arbitrarily. It has taken slavish submission to group forces as the general fact and has neglected or implicitly denied the capacities of men for independence" (Asch 1952: 451).

Nevertheless, Asch's experiments were widely interpreted as substantiating the very idea he thought he had refuted, that people were essentially weak in the face of social pressure. An analysis of social psychology textbooks published between 1953 and 1984 has shown that interpretations of Asch's findings have increasingly emphasized conformity and downplayed the independence displayed by his subjects, mainly by mentioning the frequency of errors but not correct responses (Friend, Rafferty, and Bramel 1990). Textbook treatments do this by mentioning findings such as the fact that 75 percent conformed at least once or that the majority conformed at one time or another, rather than the fact that

---

1 "The undeniable power of social conditions has received a particular interpretation in the earlier decades of this century in the US that became a basis for questioning the powers of independence. Here was an error in thinking. . . . My claim was that at a minimum the forces toward independence were no less strong than the forces toward conformity" (Asch 1989).

95 percent of subjects were independent at least once, or that in two-thirds of the trials, no conformity was evident. Moscovici's description of conformity in the *Handbook of Social Psychology* epitomizes this treatment of Asch's findings:

> Even in the face of obvious but conflicting correct response, Asch found that these individuals were more inclined to believe what others said than the evidence of their visual perception. . . . It serves . . . as one of the most dramatic illustrations of conformity, of blindly going along with the group, even when the individual realizes that by doing so he turns his back on reality and truth (Moscovici 1985: 348–9).

Baseline or Ceiling?

Why have so many interpreted Asch's studies as dramatic evidence of the triumph of conformity over reason? The most likely explanation for this interpretation is a misreading of the forces at work in Asch's experimental paradigm. From a social comparison perspective, the Asch setting seemed an unpromising situation for demonstrating conformity effects. The group members were not well acquainted with one another or highly cohesive, and the task was not ambiguous or subjective since it involved judging the length of a simple line. There also was no threat of social retaliation or promise of reward from the other participants in the future. Under any of these additional circumstances, researchers generally predict that the amount of conformity will increase. This was a common assumption among Asch's contemporaries: "If even moderate rates of conformity could be obtained in the Asch situation, then much greater conformity could be obtained in more conducive settings" (Ross, Bierbrauer, and Hoffman 1976: 148).

How generalizable are Asch's results to real-world settings and political attitudes in particular? Should his findings be regarded as a baseline or a ceiling level for conformity? Outside the confines of a laboratory one is seldom faced with a situation meeting the requirements of the Asch paradigm; it is not often that one's ability to judge concrete aspects of the environment is challenged, particularly by a unanimous majority. In the American political environment, one can nearly always find one or two like-minded others, regardless of how radical one's views may be. In the Asch paradigm, even one lone dissenter dramatically reduced the rate of conformity from yielding to the majority on 32 percent of the total estimates, to 5 to 10 percent of the same estimates, depending on the size of the majority (Asch 1951). Interestingly, a unanimous majority of three people was far more effective in bringing about conformity than a majority of eight with one lone dissenter; minimal support from others apparently diminishes the need to conform in the small group context. Subsequent replications demonstrated that when that one fellow dissenter was a friend (as is likely to be the case in real-world contexts), the pressures toward conformity disappeared altogether (Pollis and Cammaller 1968).

More importantly, a novel feature of the Asch situation created a unique "attribution crisis" for the subjects in his experiments (Ross et al., 1976). In most everyday situations, a person who disagrees with others finds ways to live with this conflict by postulating attributions for others' differing behavior. One can attribute contrary judgments either to some potential payoff that others would receive for expressing this judgment ("It would increase John's taxes if Clinton were elected, so of course, he's voting for Bush") or to differences in personal priorities between group members and one's self ("She supports Bush because she is more concerned with foreign policy than domestic issues"). This reduces the pressure to conform by illuminating logical reasons for discrepant judgments short of perceptual incompetence.

But none of these attribution options was available in the Asch situation. Unlike common, everyday social influence settings, the Asch paradigm constructed a highly unusual setting in which the dissenter could not develop an adequate explanation for why his or her judgment was different from others' or to what factor others might attribute this difference in judgment. With a task as unambiguous as comparing line lengths, the risks involved in dissenting from the group increased by virtue of the more severe attributions that would have had to be made by others to account for the difference. To what else short of blindness or insanity could one attribute this difference of opinion? The intense reactions and severe stress experienced by Asch's subjects is quite understandable from this perspective.

The dramatic reception of Asch's findings was not justified. Conformity effects would not necessarily be magnified in the population at large, nor would they be easily generalized outside of this unique laboratory context. The difficulty experienced by his subjects in finding reasonable grounds for differences in perception undoubtedly enhanced the power of the manipulation. In contrast to viewing Asch's studies as a baseline conformity effect, they should be approached as a ceiling, below which real-world conformity rates would be expected to fall (Ross, Bierbrauer, and Hoffman 1976).

While it is true that in real-world settings people experience social pressures from others with whom they have ongoing relationships and that this should logically increase their susceptibility to social influence, it is also true that due to a combination of structural factors and personal motivations, people tend to interact more with similar and like-minded others (Freedman and Sears 1965; Huckfeldt and Sprague 1995).

The Social Psychology of Impersonal Influence

These factors limit the extent to which people are exposed to others with contrary views. Although people are exposed to *some* dissimilar views, contemporary work on the power of personal influence in real-world political settings largely confirms Asch's suspicions that far from being victims of their social environments, even within face-to-face relationships people do not automatically adopt the political views of their close friends and acquaintances (Huckfeldt and Sprague 1995).

The earlier, but far less dramatic, experiments of Muzafer Sherif were probably far more telling for purposes of understanding social influences on political attitudes. In Sherif's experiments – unlike Asch's – the stimuli were ambiguous, as are most decisions regarding the best position on a policy issue or the best candidate for a given office. Sherif's subjects experienced the autokinetic effect – where a single, stationary light in a completely dark room appears to move – and were asked to estimate the distance that the light had moved over a number of trials. Since their own eyes told them very little and since there were no other visible objects to give them perspective on the distance of movement, they had little reason to feel certain of their own personal judgments the way that Asch's subjects had. Although the complete lack of alternative cues on which to base judgments is not common in the political arena,[2] the ambiguity of the stimulus meant that there were many potential explanations to which subjects could attribute their own and others' differing judgments. Moreover, rather than having a single individual face a unanimous majority, Sherif's experimental setting allowed a group of subjects to interact repeatedly over several days and sessions, with each mutually influencing the other over time.

Like Asch, Sherif found that once established, group norms had a substantial influence on individual judgments: "Once such frames of reference are established and incorporated in the individual, they enter as important factors to determine or modify his reactions to situations that he will face later" (Sherif 1936: 227). In addition, he found that it made a huge difference in the extent of convergence toward group norms whether the individual had formed an opinion independently before being exposed to the group. If a subject initially engaged in the task alone, convergence was far less.

One reason Sherif's results were not as dramatic as Asch's was that he did not set up the study as a dichotomous, forced choice situation in which subjects had to choose between their own eyes and others' judgments. Instead, they could formulate judgments that incorporated both their own and others' views and more or less split the difference. This

---

2 The extent of the autokinetic effect gave people no external sources of guidance beyond the judgments of other people engaged in the same task.

assimilation of others' views into one's own, without total surrender is a less striking result, but probably more analogous to how social influence operates in everyday political contexts.

Generalizing to Impersonal Influence

Despite the obvious difficulties involved in generalizing either Asch's or Sherif's studies to real-world contexts, unsubstantiated notions of a "conforming society" reflect the enduring impact of interpretations of this early social-psychological research. This persistent notion of group tyranny has seeped into the kinds of predictions researchers have made about the effects of representations of mass opinion as well.

If conformity is a less powerful force in interpersonal relations than social critics and academics have often thought, what does this suggest about the power of impersonal relations? As discussed in Chapter 6, there is no evidence of overwhelming social determinism at this level of influence either. But this should not necessarily be construed as evidence that impersonal social influence is of negligible importance. What has hindered a better understanding of the impersonal influence process is reliance on the same social-psychological mechanism most widely used to explain interpersonal influence – conformity rooted in the desire for social approval.

When studies of majority influence have found evidence that people's opinions can be shifted upon learning of the opinions held by others (e.g. Hovland and Pritzker 1957; White 1975), the mechanism generally claimed to bring about such influence is "the implicit assumption that behaving like others will elicit approval, whereas dissimilar behavior will bring negative consequences" (Cialdini and Petty 1981). Although a link was forged early on between small group studies of social influence and the potential effects of representations of mass opinion,[3] many of the key factors influencing the extent of conformity in laboratory contexts are missing from real-world public opinion contexts. Given that conformity is not overwhelming even in small group contexts, why should this kind of influence be sustained with the vast and undifferentiated reference public suggested by mass media reports and the results of opinion polls? After all, the collective in this case is not particularly likable, tight-knit, or interdependent, all conditions found to heighten the extent of conformity in laboratory situations. Moreover, when people are anon-

---

3 For example, in her study of the effects of poll results in Britain, Marsh (1984a) considers movement toward majority opinion to be synonymous with "conformity effects." Noelle-Neumann (1974) also uses Asch's conformity paradigm as the theoretical basis of the spiral of silence theory, a theory that explicitly depends on normative social influence, that is, a fear of social isolation.

The Social Psychology of Impersonal Influence

ymous and cannot be personally identified with their judgments, the tendency to conform to others' views is considerably attenuated (Deutsch and Gerard 1955; Crutchfield 1955). Impersonal others are not, by definition, physically present, nor do they have the power to reward or punish in the traditional sense. Thus, people's motivation for responding to representations of impersonal others is unlikely to stem from a desire to avoid ridicule or to ingratiate themselves.[4] To summarize, studies of normative social influence provide limited guidance in understanding shifts that result from representations of the opinions of psychologically distant and anonymous others.

When psychologists consider the social pressure inherent in any given situation, they are generally referring to face-to-face interactions that occur within specific physical locations. If we abandon the notion that social situations are only encounters that occur in face-to-face times and places and replace it with a more inclusive notion defined by people's access to information about others' behavior (Meyrowitz 1985), then the distinction between mass-mediated and face-to-face social environments is largely arbitrary for purposes of studying social influence. However, the distinction between personal and impersonal influence is obviously not entirely arbitrary for purposes of theories of social influence. In personal, face-to-face settings, the observer and the observed can continuously monitor one another; thus there is a tremendous potential for normative social influence. On the other hand, when a person witnesses others' behaviors or opinions through mass media, the people being observed have no capacity to reward or punish the observer for conforming to their norms. As a result, impersonal influence calls for a different kind of social influence paradigm, one that stresses influences on privately held attitudes and behaviors as well as public ones, and one that directs attention away from normative forms of social influence.

Mechanisms of Impersonal Social Influence

Despite seeming agreement as to the merit of the hypotheses underlying studies of impersonal social influence, researchers understand very little about the psychological origins of advantages that accrue to issue positions or candidates who are perceived as having mass public support. Without understanding the mechanism of influence, it is difficult to identify the political contexts or conditions under which it is most likely to occur.

4 The exception to this would be if impersonal information caused one to infer that one's friends and associates held a particular view (Huckfeldt et al. 1995a), and then the perceived *friends'* opinions could bring about normative social influence.

Effects of Perceptions of Mass Opinion

Identifying the mechanisms of influence is also important for understanding the implications of these phenomena. There is a strong derogatory tone in most research on the influence of perceptions of mass opinion. Responding to perceptions of mass opinion is usually implied to be to the detriment of democracy; it is equated with sheeplike behavior and blindly following a crowd. For example, the spiral of silence is considered a mechanism for perpetuating false consciousness (Noelle-Neumann 1974), and poll results are considered "nonsubstantive information . . . [that] would undermine the character of the American electoral system" (West 1991: 152). And while momentum need not be "irrational herd following" (Achen 1989: 212), many observers are "convinced that it occurs and that it is mostly harmful" (Brady and Johnston 1987: 129). As Bartels (1987: 19) suggests, "Once the bandwagon begins to roll, people are supposed to be swept away by the excitement, the new face, the surprising victories, the television interviews, the magazine covers, all more or less in disregard of their own political instincts."

The extent to which this type of influence is truly harmful or irrational depends on the psychological processes underlying the decision making process. For this reason, I turn next to evaluating several different types of potential explanations that have been offered for the impact of perceptions of mass opinion on political attitudes.

Strategic Influence

One of the most widely researched and well-documented mechanisms of impersonal influence involves "strategic" or "tactical" voting, that is, when voters in a race involving three or more candidates shift toward one perceived to have greater support because they do not want to waste their votes on a candidate without a chance of winning. In a presidential primary, they also may strategically use mass support to consider whether the candidate is likely to win in the fall election (Abramowitz 1989; Johnston and Pattie, 1990). The assumption underlying this explanation is that people are rational actors attempting to maximize expected utilities.[5] The effects of early election calls also have been pre-

---

5 Strategic considerations are often used as explanations for choice shifts in contests with three or more candidates, but models also have been formulated for bandwagon phenomena associated with the publication of poll results when there are only two positions or candidates. The underlying idea in these models is that an uncommitted voter should be drawn to support one of two voting blocs if the increment of power he or she would add is larger than the power he or she could have by remaining uncommitted; voters gain additional utility simply by voting for the winning candidate (see, e.g., Brams and Riker 1972; Straffin, 1977; Zech 1975). Subsequent work has generated "bandwagon curves" predicting when

dicted on the basis of a utility-maximizing perspective; turnout should decline as a function of the declining utility of voting once a race has been called. By the same token, when close races produce high turnout, it is usually attributed to the increased probability that one's vote would make a difference.

A major problem with these interpretations is that there is an infinitesimally small chance that one's vote would swing an election to begin with – regardless of whether the race was close or lopsided, or one's candidate was leading or trailing. A strategic voter would have to assume that others would also behave strategically. Nonetheless, the important contribution of these models has been to illuminate scenarios in which citizens respond to information about others' opinions in highly rational ways. Strategic voting, for example, is obviously a well-thought-out response to a complex voting situation. Based on these examples, it is clear that responding to perceptions of mass opinion need not be indicative of irrational or mindless political behavior; instead it is evidence of highly sophisticated political thought (see Popkin 1991).

Evidence of strategic voting is incontrovertible, but it explains a very small proportion of impersonal influence since it occurs only under certain conditions, particularly multiple-choice settings, and only among certain, highly thoughtful people such as political elites (Stone and Abramowitz 1983). Abramson and colleagues (1992) demonstrate that it accounts for only around 10 percent of shifts even among highly politically involved presidential primary voters, thus alternative explanations must account for the bulk of these phenomena.

The strategic mechanism is also problematic for purposes of explaining attitude change. Strategic influence suggests that perceptions of mass opinion may affect behaviors, but not attitudes. Strategic voters, for example, maintain their original preference for the candidate they like most; they simply vote for a less well liked, but more viable, candidate. In order to account for the preponderance of impersonal influence and to extend this theory to changes in opinion as well as behavior, it is necessary to cast a wider net in the search for potential mechanisms.

The Bandwagon Motivation: Going with a Winner

The notion underlying the traditional "bandwagon" idea is that affiliating with the winning team or candidate is intrinsically gratifying. Bartels (1988) cites this as one possible mechanism underlying momentum, and most studies of the influence of preelection polls make reference to

bandwagon effects should occur (e.g., Straffin 1977) as well as the conditions that should produce underdog patterns (e.g., Gartner 1976).

this explanation. Unfortunately, the nature of these psychological rewards has never been dealt with in any depth in political or other settings. Most empirical evidence of this mechanism has been based on a subtractive logic rather than on documentation of the actual gratifications sought or received. For example, Bartels (1988) attributes any direct impact of expectations of victory on choice (after controlling for effects mediated by more favorable candidate evaluations) to the desire to "go with a winner." Likewise, Abramowitz (1989) assumes that any impact of viability that is not strategic is due to the traditional bandwagon mechanism.

While such evidence is suggestive, it is indirect at best and ignores a range of alternative mechanisms. Moreover, the logic may be difficult to extend to situations in which issue opinions rather than candidate preferences are affected. The bandwagon idea made a great deal of sense in an era with large amounts of political patronage. Under these circumstances, vocal candidate supporters and volunteers could potentially expect tangible rewards for supporting a winning candidate. However, by and large, contemporary candidate supporters must be satisfied with gratifications of a purely psychological nature.

Are the gratifications of indirect affiliation enough to alter people's preferences? To date, the only empirical evidence bearing on this mechanism of influence comes from three field studies of college students' attitudes toward winning football teams. What Cialdini and colleagues (1976: 366) have dubbed the tendency to "bask in reflected glory" suggests that people "feel that they can share in the glory of a successful other with whom they are in some way associated" even when they have played no role in bringing about the other's success. In three field experiments, they found that students were more likely to declare their school affiliation publicly (by wearing clothing bearing the school insignia) when their team was successful than when it was not.

On the surface, this evidence seems potentially transferable to political bandwagon phenomenon; however, the type of gratification that people derive from vicarious affiliation limits this mechanism's applicability. Cialdini and colleagues (1976: 384) suggest that this mechanism works only within the rather restrictive set of situations where people express their views in a *public* context and in front of an audience that is homogeneous and like-minded in views. In other words, the increase in public claims of affiliation was not a function of increased positivity toward the university as a result of team success. Instead, "people make known their noninstrumental connections with positive sources because they understand that observers to these connections tend to evaluate connected objects similarly." On a college campus, the students could assume that those they encountered in face-to-face settings shared their support for the school's team, and thus the positive feelings people held toward the school team would rub off on them.

In politics, one can rarely be certain that everyone within view or within earshot supports the same issue or candidate, except in highly controlled circumstances. More importantly, as I have circumscribed the term, impersonal influence does not require people to be in face-to-face contact, let alone a homogeneously supportive social environment. For these reasons, the desire to bask in reflected glory cannot fully account for many empirical examples of influence due to perceptions of mass opinion. What followers of the bandwagon apparently get from it is an enhanced public image in the eyes of others who will be led to think better of them because of their publicly declared affiliation.[6] If basking in reflected glory is, in fact, the mechanism underlying political band-wagons, it suggests that they should be limited exclusively to publicly expressed behaviors and that they should not influence private political behaviors such as voting, for which image enhancement cannot serve as a powerful motivation toward opinion change.

Neither the desire to go with a winner, nor strategic considerations, nor normative conformity can account for many empirical examples of influence due to perceptions of mass opinion. For this reason, I turn next to three possible explanations that share the potential to account for influence on both public and private political attitudes, in heterogeneous as well as homogeneous social contexts.

The Consensus Heuristic

During the Republican battle over its party platform in 1992, supporters of abortion rights carried placards with the slogan "Republicans for Choice: 68 Percent of Our Party Can't Be Wrong" (Pear 1992). In making this appeal, Republican pro-choice advocates were drawing on a time-honored tradition in American culture. From the original 1931 slogan, "Fifty Million Frenchmen Can't Be Wrong,"[7] to the 1960 record album entitled "Fifty Million Elvis Fans Can't Be Wrong," to its more recent incarnation as "Twenty-five thousand solid New Hampshirites (probably) can't be too far wrong" (Bartels 1988: 110), the notion that

---

6 Cialdini's experiments showed that this effect was most pronounced when a person's public prestige was in jeopardy or when one's bond to a successful source was not shared by the audience. An explanation based on simple heightened attraction to a winning team should not produce these findings.
7 This slogan was first attributed to Texas Guinan, whose dance troupe was very popular with American soldiers during World War I. When she and her troupe were refused entry to France in 1931, she adopted the advertising slogan "Too Hot for Paris! Fifty Million Frenchmen Can't Be Wrong!" (*New York World Telegram*, March 21, 1931).

even faceless numbers should be a compelling source of guidance has been with us for a long time.

Social scientists also have theorized for some time about forms of social pressure that do not require the presence of observers. For example, Festinger's social comparison theory argued that people were dependent on the beliefs of others not so much because they feared that others would disapprove of them or like them less, but rather because of their desire to determine the "correct" choice (Festinger 1950, 1954). Likewise, in forming a distinction between normative and informational social influence, Deutsch and Gerard (1955: 635) described the latter as a socialized tendency to regard others' views as valid information about reality. In other words, the most popular viewpoint is also thought to be the best, most correct, or desirable choice; "winners" are implicitly assumed to be good. And, as suggested by the cartoon in Figure 7.1, people are assumed to be relieved to find themselves well within the "norms" of mass behavior and opinion.

In *Propaganda Technique in the World War*, Lasswell (1927: 102) referred to this socialized tendency to associate winning with what is good or right as a "primitive habit of thought": "The illusion of victory must be nourished because of the close connection between the strong and the good. If we win, God is on our side. If we lose, God may have been on the other side." Contemporary terminology for this idea is that people make use of a *consensus heuristic*; in other words, information about consensus views triggers a socialized tendency for people to associate the popular with the good or intelligent choice (Axsom, Yates, and Chaiken 1987; Chaiken 1987). Information indicating a consensus surrounding a candidate or issue may serve as a simple schema indicating that a viewpoint is valid. When media emphasize who or which side of an issue or controversy is ahead or behind, they may inadvertently cue the consensus heuristic, thus altering attitudes toward a candidate or issue.

Despite widespread belief in the rhetorical value of consensus, empirical evidence documenting a consensus heuristic is sparse to date. Nisbett and Ross (1980: 130) cite it as the "most thoroughly researched example of an underutilized schema." They cite two potential reasons for limited evidence of its impact: First, the consensus manipulations used in most research may be too pallid and dull to produce effects; second, perhaps it requires too many inferential steps for people to make use of this kind of information.[8]

---

8 Whatever the reasons, people do appear to utilize consensus information in making attributions about abilities. For example, if people are told that a person succeeded at a task when many others failed, they tend to infer that the person is particularly able. If they are told that a person failed, but so did most others, they will attribute the failure to the difficulty of the task. In this case, the power

Figure 7.1. News media as an important source of information used for social comparison. Reprinted by permission, The New York Times Company, Copyright 1994.

For whatever reasons, few laboratory studies have been able to document the consensus heuristic. In one exception, Axsom, Yates, and Chaiken (1987) found experimental evidence consistent with a consensus heuristic in that opinions shifted in the direction of audience support cues specifically for respondents in a low-issue-involvement condition who also were low in need for cognition. In other words, people unlikely to engage in the systematic processing of issue arguments relied on others' reactions as a cue for purposes of forming opinions.

Everyday experience outside of politics tends to validate the notion

of consensus stems from a contrast between an individual's behavior and the behavior of most others. If winning elections and garnering popular support can be considered an ability, we can generalize this finding to potential reasoning in political contexts with large fields of candidates. When a candidate attracts a lot of support in a primary where others flounder, voters may attribute this success to the superior abilities of the candidate.

that taking cues from others' opinions can be quite rational as a decision making strategy when one wishes to avoid exerting much mental effort. Indeed, in many areas of life it serves people very well; if most people in a city think that a restaurant serves lousy food, it probably does. In the realm of political decisions, the consensus heuristic is obviously far more controversial from a normative perspective. Nonetheless, for better or worse, heuristics seem perfectly suited to decision making in the political arena since heuristics are used when information and involvement levels are low; surely we have come to the right place for a theory explaining how consensus information influences political views. Despite the obvious theoretical potential, the role of the consensus heuristic in the formation of political views has yet to be convincingly documented.

The Cognitive Response Mechanism

Yet another reason people may respond to information about the opinions of distant, impersonal others is because of the thoughts that people generate in response to learning what others think (Petty and Cacioppo 1981, 1986). What is referred to as persuasive-argumentation, or cognitive response theory suggests that one reason attitudes may shift when people learn of others' views is because knowing the opinions of others induces people to think of arguments that might explain those others' positions. By rehearsing these arguments, people engage in a process of self-persuasion whereby their own attitudes move in the direction of the arguments that have been primed by others' views, arguments that would not otherwise have come to mind.

In the case of a presidential primary, for example, when people hear that more and more people are rushing to support a particular candidate, they may mentally rehearse the possible reasons that people might have that would lead them to support such a candidate. If a person is not strongly committed to a particular view, the thoughts that then pass through the individual's mind are most likely to be supportive of the candidate. By means of the positive thoughts generated by information about mass candidate support, information about mass opinion influences the development of the person's own viewpoint; arguments in favor of the candidate are now more salient and well rehearsed in the person's mind than those in opposition.

Evidence for this theory comes primarily from experimental studies in which people were randomly exposed or not exposed to information about the positions of others and then either distracted from generating thoughts in response to these cues or allowed to cognitively elaborate. Results suggested that only when respondents both knew about and thought about others' positions did the manipulations have any effect.

Furthermore, the more arguments that came to mind explaining why others might have taken the positions they did, the more likely the individual was to revise his or her attitude accordingly (Burnstein and Sentis 1981; Burnstein, Vinokur, and Trope 1973).

Not surprisingly, those firmly committed to their views are unlikely to be swayed toward the majority opinion. The tendency to discount disagreeable consensus information has been demonstrated by Kassin (1979a), who showed that when consensus information challenges a person's own views, the person will tend to assume that this information is from a smaller, less reliable sample of others. Likewise, Wells and Harvey (1978) found that when consensus information differed from respondents' own views, they readily assumed a bias in the sample. In the political arena, Americans express a great deal of ongoing skepticism about poll-based information, and this skepticism is probably greatest when it brings unwelcome news. These discounting strategies help highly committed citizens resist influence from representations of mass opinion by rejecting the validity of the information itself. However, this is not the only possible outcome for highly committed citizens; some forms of counterargument may facilitate shifts in the direction of intensifying their original viewpoints, an effect that is more difficult to observe because citizens are often presented with dichotomous political choices.

Boomerangs and Underdogs Although public opinion shifts in the direction of majority opinion have tended to receive the most popular attention and policy concern, no theory accounting for the psychological underpinnings of impersonal influence would be complete without some means of explaining the many studies documenting shifts toward minority positions. This persistent and puzzling finding has cropped up repeatedly in studies of issue as well as candidate attitudes (Cloutier, Nadeau, and Guay 1989; Lavrakas, Holley, and Miller 1991).

The consensus heuristic cannot easily account for "boomerang" or "underdog" effects since it suggests a stable, socialized tendency to associate consensus strictly with desirable choices. Fortunately, the attitude shifts suggested by the cognitive response model are not unidirectional; this model predicts movement either toward or away from others' opinions, based on the extent to which consensus cues induce people to generate thoughts consistent or inconsistent with others' views. When exposed to the contradictory opinions of others, a person strongly committed to his or her viewpoint would be most likely to generate counterarguments defending his or her initial position. By rehearsing these arguments, the individual's own opinion polarizes, intensifying in the direction of the original viewpoint and away from the opinions of others (Petty and Cacioppo 1979b, 1981). In other words, in the process of resisting influence, those most heavily involved may be influenced in the opposite direction. These predictions jibe well with evidence suggesting that underdog effects occur primarily when people are strongly committed to their views (Kaplowitz et al. 1983; Geer 1989; Patterson 1980).

The predictions of cognitive response theory mesh well with earlier findings suggesting that poll results evoke opinion change only when provided along with substantive information about candidates. The influence of representations of mass opinion can be altered dramatically by information that leads people to make unflattering attributions for the popularity of an issue or candidate. For example, Fleitas (1971: 436) found that poll results combined with a negative explanation of the front-runner's popularity produced significant influence in the direction of the underdog. West (1991) similarly suggested that Gary Hart made use of the underdog effect by coupling Mondale's mass popularity with a readily available negative rationalization. In other words, if the thoughts that are rehearsed in response to consensus cues suggest explanations that reflect unfavorably on a candidate, then underdog effects are most likely.

The cognitive response interpretation also provides a potential explanation for the consistently inconsistent findings in research on momentum in presidential primaries. Information regarding majority views could result in movement in the direction of majority or minority opinion, depending upon the intensity of people's views on a given issue or candidate, and on the availability, direction, and persuasiveness of the pool of arguments speaking to each alternative (Burnstein and Sentis 1981). If there are no convincing arguments or counterarguments that can be brought to mind in response to a consensus cue, its impact should be minimal. In short, this model does not suggest that attitude change should result from exposure to consensus views in all situations. The amount of change that results from cognitive elaboration depends upon characteristics of both individuals and the political environment. In the aggregate, these effects may sometimes cancel one another out so as to create the impression of no aggregate influence at all (Marsh 1984a; Henshel and Johnston 1987).

There is plenty of evidence from laboratory studies demonstrating that cognitive responses mediate persuasion, but studies of cognitive response theory have not specifically addressed the capacity of mass opinion cues to bring about attitude change by stimulating cognitive elaboration and a reassessment of one's own views. As with the consensus heuristic, it has yet to be demonstrated as relevant to the influence of collective opinion on political attitudes. Is the process by which a mass collective influences individual opinion different from when a single, highly credible source does the same?

One study suggests that it is. In a laboratory experiment, Harkins and Petty (1981) manipulated both the number of arguments presented in favor of instituting comprehensive university exams and the number of sources presenting those arguments. They found an enhanced persuasion effect when multiple sources presented multiple arguments; this could not be accounted for by the combined influence of these two independent factors. In other words, the opinions of others were particularly effective in inducing attitude change when they were accompanied by specific rationales. Harkins and Petty (1981) concluded that the combination of multiple sources and arguments led to greater processing of the arguments provided; in their experiment, subjects in the multiple-source, multiple-argument condition generated more favorable thoughts about the issue than subjects did in any other condition, and this in turn enhanced attitude change among this group.[9] Although the multiple sources used in their study were not on the same scale as mass opinion, their findings still suggest that numbers matter at least in part because of their influence on the cognitive response process.

INTEGRATING MULTIPLE THEORIES

Reflecting on these potential explanations makes it clear that they are not mutually exclusive options. More likely than not, impersonal influence results from a combination of different kinds of social influence

9 Beyond the mechanisms already mentioned, there are a few additional possibilities. What has been referred to as "familiarity", (Geer 1989; Norrander 1991) "contagion" (Bartels 1988) or suggestibility proposes that people are not consciously considering factors such as viability or electability; instead, impersonal influence occurs because the increased media attention received by primary winners increases voter familiarity with those candidates. Patterson (1980: 116), for example, offers this interpretation as an explanation for Carter's increased popularity following his early successes in the 1976 presidential primaries. Bartels (1988) suggests that contagion is simply a function of the number of times a candidate is mentioned by the media. On the other hand, more media attention most often leads to more critical attention as well, which is unlikely to buoy a candidate's standing (Hagen 1996).

While there is some precedent for the idea that mere exposure can create positive feelings (Zajonc 1968) and that mere suggestion can influence behavior (e.g., Phillips 1980), these studies do not typically posit a precise mechanism explaining why such effects occur. For example, evidence that publicized suicides lead to more subsequent suicides could be a function of something similar to a cognitive response mechanism. Publication causes people to rehearse ideas mentally that would not otherwise come to mind, thus increasing the probability that they will consider suicide themselves.

Despite uncertainty as to the precise mechanism, suggestion is clearly portrayed as least desirable from the perspective of rational political decision making. As Bartels (1988: 111) notes, in this view momentum "looks less like a political process than like a communicable disease."

mechanisms, all operating at more or less the same time in different contexts or among different subgroups. Toward a general theoretical framework, I have distilled the three most promising possibilities that incorporate private as well as public attitude change and that do not require face-to-face, interpersonal interaction.

First, there is clear evidence that strategic considerations influence political behavior in some circumstances and that strategic influence can produce movement both toward and away from collective opinion. However, it is equally clear that the people whose behaviors are most likely to be influenced by strategic considerations are an elite, highly politically involved segment of the citizenry. If this were the only mechanism at work and the very highly politically involved were the only people influenced, then impersonal influence would not amount to a lot. It would influence the behaviors, but not the opinions, of a relatively small segment of the public.

At the other end of the spectrum, the highly unknowledgeable seem likely to use the opinions of others as cues indicating the "correct" or more knowledgeable choice. In other words, they are likely to rely on consensus information as a heuristic cue under conditions of low knowledge and high uncertainty.

Still others may be influenced by representations of mass opinion because this information prompts them to think about the reasons that may have led all those other people to hold that particular view. The segment of the population likely to be most susceptible to this mechanism is the group in the middle with respect to political knowledge and involvement. These people will possess the minimal levels of information necessary to rehearse cognitive responses, yet they will not be so involved as to be precommitted to particular views.

This general framework suggests that although the potential for impersonal influence is not limited to one particular sector of the population, the mechanism driving it is likely to be different for citizens with differing levels of information and involvement in political decision making. I turn next to the task of providing empirical evidence that perceptions of mass opinion do, indeed, play an important role in altering political attitudes and behaviors and that these theories provide tenable explanations for the process underlying impersonal influence.

In the remainder of Part III, I synthesize results from seven different studies involving the influence of representations of mass opinion on political attitudes or behaviors. In each of these studies, perceptions of others' views had a significant impact on political attitudes toward political issues or candidates. I analyze the three different mechanisms outlined in this chapter by utilizing three populations that differ a great deal in terms of people's level of political involvement: a highly involved group comprised of potential donors to presidential primary candidates; a moderately involved group that might vote in presidential primaries, yet cares relatively little about the outcome; and the least involved population and setting – the mass public when confronted with the task of making judgments about an unfamiliar political candidate.

In 1961, Kelman attempted to organize the major theories of social influence into three broad categories. First, there were theories emphasizing normative conformity, or what he called compliance gaining. This mechanism was said to be operating "when an individual accepts influence from another person or group because he or she hopes to achieve a favorable reaction from the other." A second mechanism of social influence involved identification, that is, "when an individual adopts behavior derived from another person or group because this behavior is associated with a satisfying self-defining relationship to this person or group." And the third mechanism, which he dubbed "internalization," was what occurred "when an individual accepts influence because the induced behavior is congruent with his value system" (Kelman 1961: 63–5). In other words, the content of the behavior was intrinsically rewarding, and the person or group influenced the individual by giving him or her some persuasive grounds for changing his or her mind.

Notably, the kind of social influence processes I have termed "impersonal influence" do not fit comfortably in any of these three categories. They do not require positive or negative identification with the collective, nor do they provide a surveillance mechanism for enforcing compliance with the collective's opinion. At the same time, this influence is also not directly a function of compelling arguments that the mass collective puts forth for its positions.

Yet another category is needed in order to explain situations in which perceptions of mass collectives have the power to influence individual opinions and behaviors. Although theories applicable to impersonal contexts have been around for some time in the laboratories of social psychologists, they have yet to be applied to social influences on political attitudes in the same way as have group identification, persuasion via argumentation, and normative social influence. Chapter 8 evaluates these theories in political settings and thus provides a unique opportunity to test the general social-psychological mechanisms as well as their specific applicability to political contexts.

8

The Role of Collective Opinion in Individual Judgment

PROCESSES AND EFFECTS

The general framework described in Chapter 7 suggests that all people may be susceptible to impersonal influence, but for fundamentally different reasons and through different underlying processes. More specifically, the very highly involved are likely to consider others' views for strategic reasons. When the moderately involved respond to perceptions of others' opinions, it is because of the strength and valence of arguments that cues about mass opinion bring to mind. And finally, for the least politically involved, information about mass opinion serves as a heuristic indicating the "correct" or most valid political choice. Following this organizational scheme, this chapter is divided into three major sections. The first two sections provide empirical evidence on the least documented mechanisms of impersonal influence on individual judgments, the cognitive response mechanism and the consensus heuristic. In the third section, I add yet another example to the burgeoning literature on contexts in which strategic uses are made of information about mass opinion. Since the strategic mechanism is strictly an explanation for behavior rather than attitude change, the last study involves an analysis of real-world political behaviors rather than measures of attitudes toward candidates or issues.

To avoid the methodological difficulties characterizing so many previous studies of the influence of perceived opinion on individual judgment, the studies addressing effects on political opinions utilized hybrid survey-experimental designs that capitalized on the control afforded by random assignment and the generalizability offered by random national survey samples. Although the studies differed in small details, the general approach involved the insertion of public opinion cues simulating news about a candidate's or issue's popularity into a survey to manipulate perceptions of mass support. Shortly thereafter, respondents' attitudes were assessed, as were variables involving manipulation checks. In all cases, each respondent was randomly assigned to only one condition using computer-assisted telephone interviewing, and each received only one experimental cue.

Although the experimental designs made it easy to establish causal direction and to eliminate potentially spurious findings, by themselves they lent no insight into the psychological processes underlying attitude change. Toward this end, most of these survey-experiments also incorporated a "thought-listing" question, similar to items used in traditional psychology experiments (e.g., Brock 1967; Greenwald 1968). These items occurred directly after the candidate or issue opinion question and asked respondents to tell the interviewer the kinds of thoughts they were having while answering the previous opinion item. The answers to these open-ended questions were recorded verbatim. They were later "unitized" (Meichenbaum, Henshaw, and Himel 1980) into individual thoughts or units of cognitive response and coded as to the type and direction of argument or idea that was given.

Measures of cognitive elaboration made it possible to answer two kinds of questions necessary for identifying these underlying mechanisms. First, does information about mass opinion influence the number or kinds of arguments that pass through respondents' minds? According to the cognitive response interpretation, news about mass opinion primes respondents to think about reasons for supporting and/or opposing various positions. If this is the case, respondents in control conditions should have fewer such thoughts in mind. The second question these measures help answer is whether the rehearsal of thoughts – those either consistent or inconsistent with the mass opinion cues – is a necessary condition for news about collective opinion to influence individual attitudes. Cognitive response theory suggests that opinion shifts should occur only when respondents have issue- or candidate-relevant thoughts that are mentally rehearsed in response to cues about mass opinion. On the other hand, if a consensus heuristic is at work, respondents who have relatively few thoughts in mind to rehearse should be more likely to change views.

THE COGNITIVE RESPONSE MECHANISM AMONG THE MODERATELY INVOLVED: THE DEMOCRATIC PRIMARY EXPERIMENT

Using an experimental design embedded in a national survey conducted during the 1992 Democratic presidential primaries,[1] I examined cogni-

1 The sampling procedure for this rolling cross-sectional survey insured that each day's interviews could be aggregated with those from other days to produce probability samples for arbitrary contiguous blocks of time. Data collection began in December 1991 and continued through June 1992. The end date for data collec-

tive response theory as an explanation for the effects of mass opinion on the attitudes of moderately involved voters. The experimental cues involved several of the candidates in the 1992 Democratic presidential nomination campaign.[2] To enhance the credibility of these cues, claims about current candidate popularity were made on the basis of what were said to be findings from multiple recent polls.[3]

Self-identified Democrats were randomly assigned to one of nine conditions created by a three-by-three design.[4] One three-level factor manipulated the direction of the cue indicating the amount of support for the candidate.[5] In the positive support condition, cues suggested that recent polls showed that a large number of Democrats supported the candidate as the presidential nominee of the Democratic party. In the

tion varied slightly across conditions depending on when the candidate dropped out of the race.

2 The exact wording of cues was as follows: "As you may have heard, some recent polls show that a (large number of/ very few) Democrats support (candidate name) for the presidential nominee of the Democratic party." Ethical considerations dictated that the information used to cue respondents be information that was actually available in the political environment at the time of the study. This was substantiated through a Nexis computer search of newspapers and other periodicals. In the context of state primaries and caucuses conducted in multiple stages, each by somewhat different rules and each with varying approaches to the selection of delegates, determining which candidate is truly ahead in the nation at any given point in time is fraught with difficulties. The cues used in this experiment involved information that a respondent easily could have come across in the course of perusing the news media during this campaign, even though the cues clearly contradicted one another. In other words, media coverage did not suggest a consensus on who was in the lead.

3 I attribute no special status to poll-based horse race information; voters' impressions could just as well be altered by journalistic interpretations of specific primary outcomes or pure speculation. However, given the proliferation of primary polls during this time period and their disparate findings, poll results served as a credible means by which to convey these impressions. To date, findings are inconsistent as to whether greater impact should flow from perceptions of the state of mass opinion or the direction of opinion change (cf. Kaplowitz et al. 1983; West 1991; McAllister and Studlar 1991; Marsh 1984b), thus these manipulations referred to the extent of candidate support at a given point in time.

4 In addition to the usual problems inherent in self-reports on the likelihood of voting, screening for probable primary voters in a national sample is made extremely difficult by the fact that not all states have direct primaries and that each operates using slightly different rules for eligibility (see Nelson 1993). For purposes of this study, these complications were resolved by including all Democratic party identifiers as potential primary voters.

5 Although these data were collected beginning very early in the primary season, one would expect some support cues to be more credible than others. In order to assess the plausibility of the cues, respondents in the no-cue conditions were asked later in the survey who they thought was leading the Democratic primary race. All three of the candidates featured in this study received mentions in double-digit percentages, thus indicating that no clear consensus existed that would have robbed some cues of all plausibility.

The Role of Collective Opinion in Individual Judgment

negative support condition, polls were said to show that "very few" Democrats supported the candidate. Immediately following this statement, the respondent was asked which of the potential presidential nominees the respondent liked best.[6] In a third, control condition, no cues were given and respondents proceeded directly to this question. A second experimental factor manipulated the candidate to which cues about mass opinion referred. Three candidates – Clinton, Brown, and Harkin – were included in the study. And finally, because levels of political involvement have important implications for persuasibility, an additional question in the survey tapped attitude centrality.[7] As expected given the partisan nature of the sample, the distribution of responses to this question was heavily skewed toward respondents who considered the choice of a primary candidate a "very important" decision to them, with 43 percent of respondents choosing this option. In contrast, only 3 percent considered it "not at all important." Fully 83 percent of the sample was concentrated in the "important" or "very important" categories. This pattern confirmed the idea that even the relatively less involved potential primary voters are at least moderately politically involved.

For purposes of making a meaningful distinction in levels of involvement, yet maintaining an adequate number of people in each cell in analyses involving interactions with other variables, the measure of attitude centrality was dichotomized into two groups: those who thought the decision very important (the highly involved), and those who did not find it very important, that is, all remaining respondents, the overwhelming majority of whom still saw it as an important decision (the moderately involved).

Effects on Cognitive Elaboration

The cognitive response mechanism suggests that information about others' views first triggers the rehearsal of thoughts relating to a candidate's or issue's popularity; these thoughts then facilitate shifts in opinion. Using the cognitive elaboration measures as dependent variables,[8] I ex-

6 "How about you? Which of the candidates now in the running for the Democratic presidential nomination do you like best? Doug Wilder, Paul Tsongas, Bill Clinton, Bob Kerrey, Tom Harkin, or Jerry Brown? The order of candidate names was randomized, but the number of candidates in the list had to be altered as candidates dropped out of the race (see Mutz 1997 for details).
7 "Would you say your decision about which candidate to support is very important, important, not very important, or not at all important to you?"
8 "As you were thinking about your choice of candidate, what kinds of thoughts occurred to you?" Responses were unitized and then further coded into (1) ideas or arguments supportive of the candidate corresponding to the subject's experimental condition or opposed to his opponents; and (2) ideas or arguments op-

amined the first component of this process. Results indicated that the *direction* of positive or negative opinion cues did not influence the overall balance of positive versus negative thoughts that were rehearsed. Instead, people were as likely to rehearse counterarguments to the opinion cues they were given as they were cue-consistent thoughts.

However, the *extent* of cognitive elaboration was in the hypothesized direction with respect to the experimental conditions. Only 73 percent of those assigned to a control condition produced candidate-relevant thoughts, while 84 percent and 89 percent of those in the positive and negative cue conditions did so, respectively. Candidate support cues appear to have prompted people to respond cognitively by thinking about the reasons others might have for supporting or opposing a given candidate. Although those reasons were not always supportive of the position endorsed by mass opinion, information about candidate support stimulated greater cognitive elaboration of all kinds. Logistic regression confirmed the significance of this pattern (see Mutz [1997] for full table of results) and also illuminated the importance of respondents' level of involvement in this decision. Attitude centrality had significant independent effects in the direction one would anticipate; those who deemed this decision more important generated a greater number of cognitive responses overall.[9] However, the relationship between support cues and

posed to the candidate corresponding to the subject's experimental condition or clearly supportive of one of his opponents. Thoughts and arguments completely irrelevant to the choice of a primary candidate were disregarded (e.g., "I have been to Nebraska").

For example, for a person in the positive, negative, or control Clinton conditions, any rehearsal of thoughts that were either pro-Clinton or against one of his opponents would be considered candidate supportive ("He [Clinton] has his finger on the pulse of the middle and working classes; I think I could trust him more than like Jerry Brown; If he [Clinton] was a regular person these scandals would have never come up"). Likewise, for these same groups, any anti-Clinton comments or thoughts clearly favoring another candidate would be considered anti-Clinton ("He's [Clinton] not progressive enough; Brown would be more of a forward moving president; Haven't seen anyone throw any dirt on the man [Kerrey]").

Thought-listing questions that are issue-specific (as is this one) produce an experimental demand for respondents to give more responses relevant to the issue; on the other hand, when asked to list thoughts more generally, more thoughts are generated, but a large proportion of the thoughts will tend to be unrelated to the issue (Cacioppo and Petty 1981). The choice of approach generally depends on the aim of the research; in this case, it was important to obtain as many candidate-relevant thoughts as possible.

9 Since the distribution of the number of cognitive responses per person was highly skewed, for purposes of testing the hypothesis that candidate support cues will prompt greater cognitive elaboration, measures were dichotomized into respondents who did or did not generate cognitive responses relevant to a candidate or

amount of elaboration was driven primarily by respondents for whom this decision was not as central. The significant interaction indicated that those who considered this decision relatively unimportant were induced toward greater elaboration by the cues. Candidate support cues also made a statistically significant impact on the extent of cognitive elaboration in the sample as a whole if one excluded the interaction, but the inclusion of the centrality variable and its interaction made it clear that this effect was driven primarily by those lower in attitude centrality.

Figure 8.1 illustrates the extent of cognitive elaboration by experimental conditions and levels of attitude centrality.[10] For high-centrality respondents, there were negligible differences among positive cue, negative cue, and control conditions. However, for those who viewed this decision as less important, the extent of elaboration was significantly greater among those who received candidate support cues. In other words, among those unlikely to expend a great deal of thought on this decision to begin with, information on candidate support triggered greater cognitive elaboration.

Effects on Opinions Toward Candidates

The second component of cognitive response theory suggests that support cues trigger attitude change by stimulating reflection on positive or negative thoughts about the candidates. This hypothesis was tested using an analysis of variance incorporating the two experimental factors, a three-level thought-listing variable representing the balance of candidate-supportive or candidate-opposed thoughts, and attitude centrality.[11] A cognitive response explanation for attitude change predicts an interaction between the support cue and the presence of candidate-supportive or candidate-opposed thoughts, candidate support cues should shift pref-

the choice of a presidential nominee. For purposes of examining the effects of elaboration on candidate preferences, the direction of elaboration also was taken into account. Measures of the number of candidate-supportive minus candidate-opposed thoughts were trichotomized so that those with negative scores were assigned a -1, those with positive scores $+1$, and those who did not elaborate at all received a o. This strategy allowed categorization on the basis of the extent to which a person predominantly rehearsed arguments supporting the candidate, opposing the candidate, or failed to elaborate at all, an important distinction for purposes of predicting attitude change.

10 In Figure 8.1 and in subsequent figures, numbers in parentheses indicate the sample size for respondents falling into each experimental condition broken down in the figure.

11 Intercoder agreement as to whether the balance of cognitive responses was positive, negative, or neutral was .95.

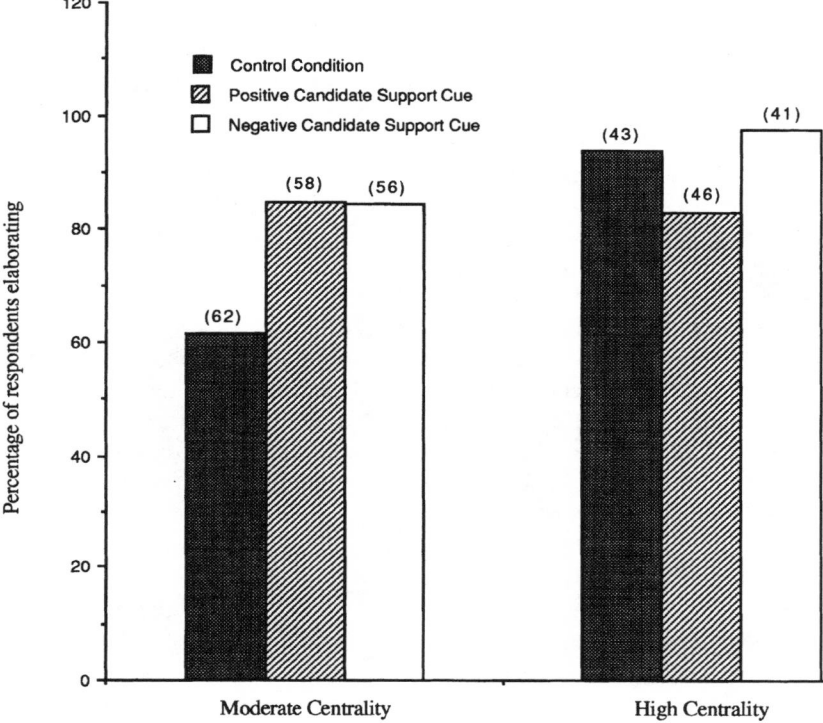

Figure 8.1. Extent of cognitive elaboration by experimental conditions and attitude centrality (Democratic Primary Experiment).

erences in the direction of the cues only if they are successful in eliciting the rehearsal of persuasive arguments. This process should be particularly likely among those for whom the choice of a candidate is less important. If the cues elicit primarily counter-arguments, they should induce shifts in a direction opposite that of the cue and produce an underdog-type pattern.

Results of this analysis suggested that support cues had no direct effects on candidate preference (Mutz 1997 for statistical details).[12] The main effect of candidate condition simply confirmed that there were dif-

12 A common dependent variable was constructed across the three candidate conditions by assigning each respondent a score based on the extent to which their candidate preference corresponded to the candidate for their experimental condition. For example, respondents in any of the three "Clinton" conditions received a 1 if they chose Clinton as their preferred candidate and a 0 if they chose some other candidate.

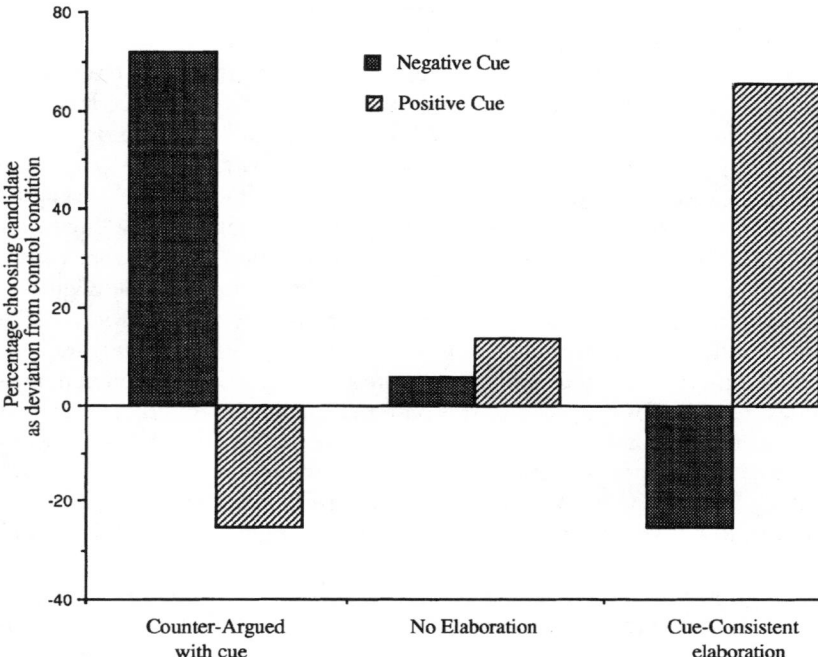

Figure 8.2. Effects of cognitive elaboration on reactions to candidate support cues (Democratic Primary Experiment).

ferential levels of support for the three candidates included in the study. It is also not surprising, or particularly important, that cognitive elaboration was significantly related to choice of candidate; after all, respondents generated these thoughts directly after being asked about their choice of candidate, and it is only natural that they should rationalize and generate thoughts consistent with their preferences.

However, as predicted, even *after* one takes into account the direct effects of cognitive elaboration and the other experimental factors, the interaction between support cues and cognitive elaboration was a significant predictor of candidate preferences. The significant three-way interaction between support cues, cognitive elaboration, and attitude centrality suggested that this same two-way interaction was particularly pronounced among those with only moderate attitude centrality. Together, these two findings lend greater credence to a cognitive response interpretation.

Figure 8.2 illustrates the major findings from this study. Means from each experimental condition are expressed as deviations from corre-

sponding control group means.[13] On the right side of the figure, candidate preferences are in the direction of the cues received: Positive support
cues make it more likely that respondents will express a preference for
the candidate in the cue, while negative support cues produce less support for the candidate named. But this pattern holds only among those
who generated thoughts consistent with the support cues they received.
Among those who counterargued and rehearsed thoughts contrary to
the sentiment described in the cue, candidate preferences were quite logically in the direction of the counterarguments and opposite that of the
cue received. More important for purposes of confirming the cognitive
response model, when no elaboration occurred, respondents' views were
not significantly different from those of control group respondents.

The pattern of findings in Figure 8.2 would not be surprising in and of itself were it not for the fact that this pattern remained even *after* controlling
for the inevitable rationalization of preferences that occurs when people express candidate preferences (that is, the large main effect of cognitive elaboration). And as with the effects of support cues on the extent of cognitive
elaboration, a significant three-way interaction indicated that this overall
pattern was driven primarily by those moderate in attitude centrality.

Could a consensus heuristic account for these effects equally well? The
model underlying the consensus heuristic suggests that people are socialized to use information about consensus views to make decisions
under conditions of high uncertainty and little information. These cues
are quick, efficient mechanisms that do not require additional cognitive
processing to take place (Chaiken 1987). In other words, a heuristic is
something people turn to in the absence of other reasons to support or
oppose a candidate. On the other hand, cognitive response theory suggests that for impersonal influence to occur, additional processing must
transpire; the consensus cues must trigger thinking about reasons to support or oppose the candidate that, in turn, alter the person's attitude.

The results of this experiment suggest that at least among primary
voters, impersonal influence occurs only if cognitive processing takes
place. The lack of deviation from control means in the "No Elaboration"
groups suggests that those most in need of a shortcut did not fall back
on consensus information. Based on the logic of the consensus heuristic,
one might also predict an interaction between support cues and attitude
centrality, such that the cues had a direct impact among those lower in
attitude centrality. This interaction did approach statistical significance,
but the direction of findings was suggestive of a pattern precisely the
opposite of what a consensus heuristic predicts. Although a consensus

13 Mean candidate preference scores for the three control groups were Clinton
(.0145), Brown (.4386), and Harkin (.3043).

heuristic may well be important in contexts involving very low levels of involvement, the weight of evidence in this study suggested that primary voters are too far along the high end of the political awareness spectrum to rely on a decision-making shortcut of this kind.

One alternative interpretation of these effects could be based on group identification. To the extent that Democrats respond to news of other Democrats' opinions simply because they positively identify with the group label, momentum needs no further explanation. If identification with the Democratic group label helps drive this phenomena, one would expect the cues to have greater influence among those who more strongly identify. This was not the case (see Mutz 1997). In short, there was no evidence that group identification produced these effects.

THE CONSENSUS HEURISTIC AMONG THE
UNINVOLVED: THE UNKNOWN
CANDIDATE EXPERIMENT

Thus far, the elusiveness of the consensus heuristic is consistent with previous research that has typically failed to support it. On the other hand, it seems at face value to be a compelling means by which people may make decisions under conditions of low involvement. In a purposeful effort to produce an experimental context conducive to the heuristic value of consensus information, I devised an extremely low involvement situation in which a random national sample of survey respondents was asked to evaluate an unknown potential congressional candidate who was said to be "considering running for Congress next year in a state near yours."[14] Short vignettes described each candidate in this three-by-five design, and all information in the vignettes remained consistent except for experimental manipulations of one candidate issue position and the amount of public support ascribed to the candidate. A three-level factor manipulated whether respondents were told that the candidate was popular or unpopular among his constituents, or they were given no popularity information at all.

In addition to manipulating consensus information, one issue position was attributed to each candidate. These issue positions were pretested to identify strong and weak, positive and negative positions,[15] producing

14 This explanation was followed by a practice vignette that was identical for all respondents.
15 Based on a pretest, two issues were selected. One issue, economic aid to Russia, was of very low salience to the public and thus likely to produce only weak reasons to support or oppose the candidate. For the strong positive and negative issue argument, the candidate was described as either supporting or opposing anticrime legislation. National surveys at the time suggested a consensus behind

five levels of this factor when including a control condition. The purpose of this manipulation was to give respondents a small amount of positive or negative information about the candidate that could potentially be rehearsed via a cognitive response mechanism. The cognitive response hypothesis suggests that consensus support combined with substantive information should enhance effects on candidate ratings beyond any independent impact of these two factors. Including some issue information also helped make the experiment more realistic and less transparent by insuring that candidate popularity was not the only piece of information respondents were given. Furthermore, it allowed a comparison of the relative impact of consensus information and issue agreement for issues that elicit both high and low levels of commitment from the public (crime and aid to Russia, respectively).

Respondents first assessed one identically described candidate to familiarize themselves with the general idea, and were then asked about the experimental candidate.[16] The additional information about the candidate that was consistently given to all respondents was purposefully very minimal:

The next candidate is a 35 year old man with two children who has lived in his community for many years. During this time he has worked for a variety of local businesses. He is known to be (a strong supporter of/strongly opposed to anticrime legislation/increasing U.S. economic aid to Russia) and plans to be active in this area of legislation in Washington. He is also (very popular and has lots of support/not very popular and has little support/no information) among the people in his congressional district.

After rating this candidate,[17] respondents answered a thought-listing question[18] that was later coded according to the same procedure as in the previous experiment. They also were asked for their own opinions on the issues used in the vignettes.[19] Despite pretesting, all people could

    both of these issues, with an overwhelming majority opposed to economic aid to Russia and in favor of anticrime legislation.

16 "We are interested in your thoughts about some people who are considering running for Congress next year in a state near yours. I'll read you a description of a person and ask you to rate that person on a thermometer that runs from 0 to 100 degrees. Ratings between 50 and 100 degrees mean that you feel favorable and warm. Ratings between 0 and 50 mean that you don't feel too favorable and are cool toward that candidate. You may use any number from 0 to 100 to tell me how favorable or unfavorable your feelings are."

17 "On a 0 to 100 scale, how would you rate this candidate?" Since the distribution of responses was very uneven due to respondents' tendency to pick multiples of ten and five, the scores were collapsed into a ten-point scale ranging from 0 (less than 9) to 10 (100).

18 "As you were thinking about this candidate, what kinds of things came to mind?"

19 Based on their experimental condition, respondents were either asked about aid to Russia or anticrime legislation: "Do you favor or oppose increasing U.S. eco-

not be expected to consider the issue positions equally strong positives or negatives, thus the interaction of respondents' own opinions with the positions espoused by the candidate more precisely captured the impact of issue agreement.

Effects on Cognitive Elaboration

In this very minimal information context with a representative national sample of the public, the direction of positive or negative opinion cues did influence the overall balance of positive versus negative thoughts that were rehearsed. In an analysis using the number of positive minus negative thoughts as the dependent variable, the main effect of public support was large and significant ($F = 16.55$, $p < .001$).

Figure 8.3 illustrates the effects of consensus cues on cognitive elaboration. When respondents did not receive consensus cues, the balance of positive minus negative thoughts hovered around zero. In fact, respondents in the control condition rehearsed few thoughts of any kind.[20] When candidates were described as having popular support, the balance was slightly positive. For candidates receiving negative support cues, the balance was greatly tilted in the direction of more negative thoughts. This pattern remained true even though the tally of positive and negative thoughts did not include the open-ended references to candidate popularity that were simply parroted back to the interviewers.

In the Democratic primary experiment, people had sufficiently high levels of information about the candidates that they counterargued extensively with consensus cues; the cues prompted greater cognitive elaboration, but not in any particular direction. In this extremely low information context in which respondents had little additional information about the candidates, consensus cues influenced the *direction* as well as the extent of cognitive elaboration. With no preconceptions or preexisting information to go on, the kinds of thoughts people rehearsed were significantly influenced by how popular the candidate was described to be.

nomic aid to Russia? Is that strongly (favor/oppose) or only somewhat (favor/oppose)?" "Do you favor or oppose anticrime legislation? Is that strongly (favor/oppose) or only somewhat (favor/oppose)?" These items were asked at least five minutes after the experimental section, and there was no evidence that the candidate descriptions altered attitudes toward the issues. Control respondents were split between the two issues to provide manipulation checks.

20 A small number of respondents (n = 31) generated an equal number of positive and negative thoughts and thus also fell into the 0 category. These respondents were included in the analyses shown in Figure 8.3, but omitting them did not change the findings.

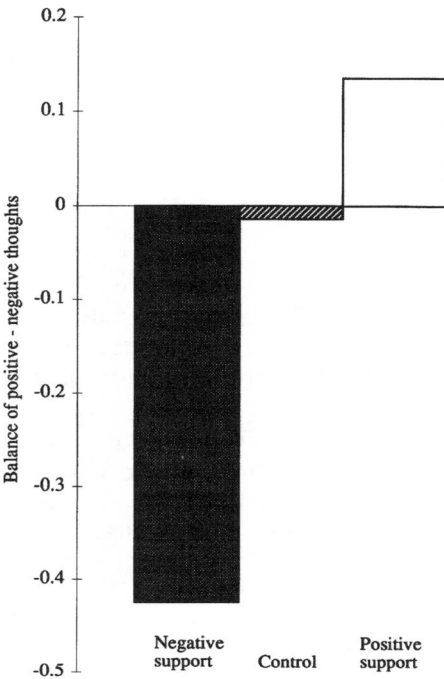

Figure 8.3. Effects of public support on balance of cognitive elaboration (Unknown Candidate Experiment).

Effects on Opinions Toward Candidates

But did these thoughts mediate the effects of consensus cues? Using an analysis of variance with candidate rating as the dependent variable, and controlling for all of the same factors as in the previous experiment, levels of public support produced a large significant effect on candidate ratings ($F = 34.38$, $p < .001$).[21] The unknown candidate apparently succeeded in creating a scenario low enough in information and involvement that the consensus heuristic played an important role in shaping attitudes toward the candidates. As shown in Figure 8.4, in the conditions in which the candidate was described as popular among his con-

21 The analysis of variance included the main effects of public support for the candidate, issue position espoused by the candidate, respondents' own issue positions, and cognitive elaboration, plus the interactions among these variables with demographic and party identification variables serving as covariates.

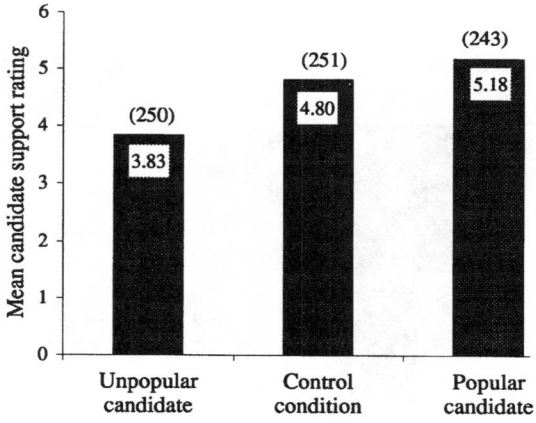

Figure 8.4. Mean candidate ratings by public support cues (Unknown Candidate Experiment).

stituents, he was rated more positively by respondents than in the control condition, and when described as generally unpopular, he was rated significantly less positively than in the control condition. When levels of information were extremely minimal, it appears that respondents did, in fact, utilize consensus information as a heuristic in helping them form candidate judgments. This effect held up even after taking into account respondents' issue proximity to the candidate. More importantly, the impact of public support held up after taking into account thought rehearsal, thus suggesting that in this case the impact of consensus cues was not mediated by the rehearsal of consistent or inconsistent thoughts as it would be if the cognitive response mechanism accounted for these shifts. Figure 8.4 also shows a much stronger impact from negative than positive cues.

Results confirmed in two ways that this was indeed a minimal information situation in which to ask people for political judgments. First, a full 30 percent of the respondents refused to rate the candidate at all and thus were discarded from the sample. Second, even among those who did evaluate the candidate, in response to the open-ended thought-listing item, 115 of them spontaneously mentioned that they felt they really needed more information in order to evaluate him.

Despite low information levels, the analyses also revealed a marginally significant interaction between public support and cognitive elaboration ($p = .068$), suggesting that there may be more to this story that is worthy of attention. As illustrated in Figure 8.5, regardless of

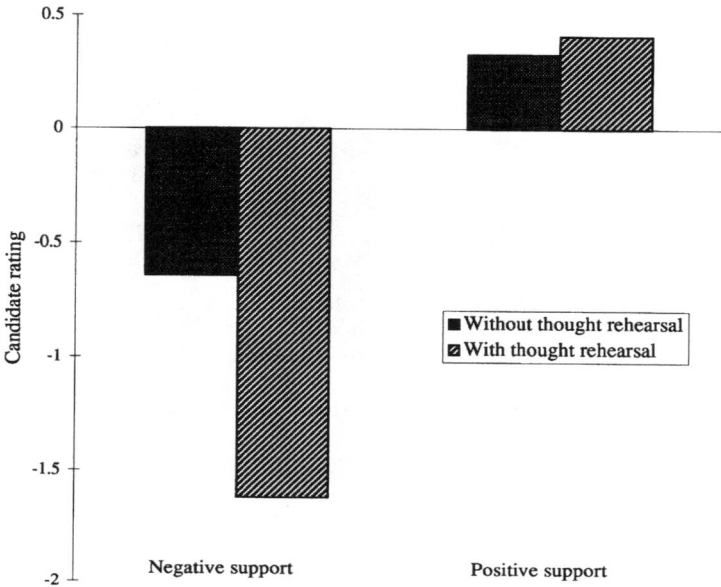

Figure 8.5. Effects of public support cues by cognitive elaboration (Unknown Candidate Experiment).

whether thoughts were rehearsed, those receiving positive support cues tended to shift their views in a positive direction, and those who received negative support cues shifted them in a negative direction. But the interaction between cognitive elaboration and public support cues is driven by the same pattern as in the previous experiment: Among those who rehearsed some thoughts in response to the thought-listing question, the effectiveness of the cues was enhanced. Among those with no thoughts in mind, the effects were reduced. In particular, the negative support cues created far more negative attitudes when they were accompanied by cognitive elaboration. As in the previous experiment, this interaction was still large after controlling for the direct impacts of cognitive elaboration and public support cues. This evidence suggests that the cognitive response mechanism may account for some of the impact of consensus cues in this experiment as well. Despite the artificially low levels of information about the candidate, the experiment still generated some evidence of a cognitive response mechanism. Thus, even in circumstances constructed to favor use of consensus cues as heuristics, cognitive responses may still partially mediate the effects of consensus information.

Qualitative Evidence

The idea that consensus cues stimulate greater thought on the part of respondents is directly validated only by the quantitative analyses. Nonetheless, the content of open-ended comments in the thought-listing questions lent further support to both the consensus heuristic and the cognitive response mechanism.

Not surprisingly, the cognitive responses that people rehearsed primarily consisted of playing back information in the vignette. But the consensus cues often colored interpretations of whether given characteristics were positives or negatives. For example, the candidate's age prompted some to say he would have fresh ideas and "we need some young people in there," and others to say that he was too young for the job. The fact that he had worked "at a variety of local businesses" prompted some to note that experience in the real world of business was helpful for politicians, while others wondered why he could not hold down a job.

In addition, some respondents reiterated the logic of the consensus heuristic virtually verbatim in response to the thought-listing question ("As you were thinking about this candidate, what kinds of things came to mind?"):

How the people respond to him, how they felt about him. If they liked him there had to be a reason.

As suggested by Figure 8.5, the negative support cues were particularly likely to elicit use of the consensus heuristic. Having popular support may not guarantee that one is necessarily good, but not having popular support *must* mean the person has a problem:

Something must be wrong with him because he's not well perceived in his community, so I'd have to check into it.

No one likes him, that primarily. There's gotta be a reason why no one likes him.

Why he isn't popular if he's been living in that town for so long?

He sounded all right 'til you said nobody liked him. There must be a reason.

I didn't even know what he believed, so I went by the fact of his unpopularity, though I didn't know why, so I had to use that as a reference.

I didn't like the fact that nobody could stand him. Obviously he's done things to others that aren't so great.

Still other respondents attempted to link the level of public support the candidate received with some particular explanation, just as the cognitive response mechanism predicts. In some cases it was inferred to be a result of the candidate's policy positions:

The last comment that he wasn't very popular in his community. He's against crime but he doesn't really take the right approach to it. I was mostly for him before you said he wasn't very popular. I got the feeling he wasn't popular because of a bad thing.

Nobody liked him or supported him meaning that . . . he probably doesn't support the people's issues.

This is someone who is disliked by people in his area, so this might be someone who might wish to be more liberal toward criminals.

Still others linked this information to personal characteristics of the candidate that could be relevant to his ability in office:

The fact that he's not popular. I'm hesitant – does he have a problem getting along with people? You have to wonder what's the root of the problem.

He has business experience. Must be an honest person because he was well liked.

Not being very popular with peers was a negative. No political background. He does not seem to serve his peers, so I don't know about his leadership abilities.

He is unliked in his own community, and he is not a people person and I question his people skills, his interaction.

In a few cases, levels of popularity were explained away by the cognitive responses that were generated, just as the counterargument hypothesis suggests:

A hard working business person. The fact that he wasn't popular didn't matter because a lot of time money is what makes you popular. That's what I was thinking.

When you are very good in business, then people don't like you. You have to be a bit conniving when you're in business. It's a case of people being envious and since he is 35 years old and so successful, maybe people perceive him as a very self-centered type of person.

What came through most clearly when respondents wondered aloud was that, at the very least, information about candidate popularity prompted them to think about potential explanations for the candidate's popularity or lack thereof. When told that the candidate currently lacked popular support, this information prompted even those who received otherwise very favorable information to reconsider their views:

I really wasn't thinking. He seemed rather young to . . . well, I guess I was concerned about why he wasn't popular. He sounds like a hard working person.

Uh I guess I wonder why. There are other issues, but if he is not popular I wonder why.

He's young and inexperienced and not liked by his peers for some reason. Why people are unhappy with him.

Why nobody liked him. Does he have a big nose? What? I need more information.

I wish I knew why he wasn't popular. [He] just sounded like he was a strong politician.

Although the consensus heuristic and cognitive response interpretation have traditionally been pitted against one another as explanations for choice shifts (Axsom, Yates, and Chaiken 1987), the open-ended responses illuminate just how fine the line is between these two processes. A person employing the consensus heuristic reasons, "If he is popular, he must be a good/smart/desirable candidate," or conversely, "If he is not popular, there must be something wrong with him." The person who is influenced via the cognitive response mechanism wonders, "Why is he so popular?" and then seizes upon the most satisfactory explanations: "It must be because he is a capable leader" (cue-consistent) or "It must be because he has sold out to big money and runs a lot of negative ads" (counterarguing). Although one process obviously involves more substantive thinking than the other, it is difficult to evaluate where heuristic processing leaves off and cognitive response begins. According to the consensus heuristic, people simply infer that there must be a good reason for the person's popularity; the cognitive response mechanism suggests that they seize upon one or more explanations, the strength of which mediates the overall impact of consensus information.

In quantitative analyses, however, the two processes look quite different. The cognitive response mechanism requires that people have some preexisting information to rehearse, whereas the consensus heuristic is conceptualized as a default mechanism to be used strictly in the absence of other information. Moreover, the cognitive response mechanism can result in movement toward as well as away from consensus cues, while the consensus heuristic generally cannot. In the Unknown Candidate Experiment, if one eliminates from the measures of cognitive elaboration those responses based on information that was given to respondents and that they simply mimicked back (i.e., candidate issue positions, employment, and personal history), evidence of the cognitive response mechanism disappears entirely. Without some minimal information about the candidate's employment, personal history, and (in some cases) issue stands, there was not enough information to produce shifts in ratings.

THE LOCAL MAYORAL EXPERIMENT: THE CONSENSUS HEURISTIC IN A REAL WORLD CONTEXT

Given the paucity of findings corroborating shifts in candidate support as a result of strictly heuristic processing, it is worth considering whether the situation created in this experiment – respondents with virtually no previous knowledge or impressions about a candidate, and little stake in the outcome – is so far removed from reality as to be irrelevant to real world political candidates. On the one hand, results from the Unknown Candidate Experiment along with those of previous studies suggest that the conditions facilitating a direct positive impact of consensus information such as that suggested by the consensus heuristic are relatively rare in American politics. On the other hand, such conditions probably do exist from time to time in the real world, particularly in low-profile races among relative unknowns. Paradoxically, low-profile races seldom generate polls or extensive horse race coverage, thus the potential for consensus cues to reach the public is limited. Moreover, such topics make for highly inefficient studies since a large proportion of respondents will simply provide unusable "don't know" answers when asked to make judgments with so little information, just as in the Unknown Candidate Experiment.

Nevertheless, one field experiment involving real candidates in a non-partisan mayoral race confirmed this potential, at least among a population with low levels of political interest. In an effort to increase the external validity of these findings, an adaptation of a pretest/post-test design was used to examine the effects of bogus poll results on candidate preference. A large class of undergraduate students at the University of Wisconsin-Madison was randomly assigned to one of three experimental conditions during the week preceding the local election. Several weeks prior to this time, the students had been asked by their instructor to indicate their preferences in the upcoming mayoral race while completing a paper-and-pencil questionnaire addressing unrelated topics. These data were used to construct a baseline measure of vote intention.[22]

The week preceding the election, these same students were contacted by telephone from the University of Wisconsin Survey Center ". . . as part of a survey of city residents to find out their attitudes toward the upcoming mayor's race." Those who agreed to participate were then read one of three randomly assigned cues indicating that one candidate or the other now had a commanding lead, or that the two were neck and neck according to "the results of several independent polls." The cue was then followed by a series of questions similar to the pretest questions (Mutz 1992a for details).

As Table 8.1 demonstrates, the pretest results quite logically showed no pattern with respect to candidate preferences by experimental condition, while the post-test data showed a clear pattern corresponding to the cues received by respondents. Although this aggregate evidence does not confirm the process of change at an individual level, it does suggest a pattern of majority influence, even using crude measures of shifts in preferences from one candidate to another. The percentage support for candidate Sensenbrenner increased 14 percent due to the cue suggesting

22 The pretest item read as follows: "Which candidate do you think you will vote for in the Madison mayor's race? Joe Sensenbrenner, Paul Soglin, Not sure/Undecided. How strongly do you feel about your candidate? Do you feel very favorable, favorable, only mildly favorable, or are you not sure or undecided?"

Table 8.1. *Candidate preference by condition*
(Local Mayoral Experiment)

	Public opinion cue (Pre/post cues)		
Candidate preference	Sensenbrenner	Soglin	Tie
Sensenbrenner	40%/54%	29%/23%	40%/43%
Soglin	31/17	23/51	34/37
Undecided	29/29	49/26	26/20
(n)	(35)	(35)	(35)

Note: Entries represent column percentages before and after public opinion cues were administered. Sample comprised of 105 undergraduate students.

he was supported by a majority, and support for candidate Soglin increased 28 percent following the cue giving him the lead. In the condition where candidates were said to be tied, each experienced only a 3 percent pretest/post-test increase. The magnitude of these findings easily exceeded standards for statistical, as well as real-world significance.

By taking advantage of the full nine-point candidate favorability scale, it was possible to look for more subtle changes in the intensity of support for candidates. The full experiment was analyzed as a repeated measures analysis of variance with one three-level between-subjects factor (public opinion cues) and one two-level within-subjects factor (pretest/post-test). As anticipated, these analyses indicated a significant between-condition effect based on the cue received by the respondent ($p < .05$).

Although these findings lend greater external validity to the potential for impersonal influence, it is important to note that this context remains somewhat unusual. As a nonpartisan race, it lacked one of the most common sources of guidance in vote decisions. Moreover, the notoriously low level of college students' interest in politics may limit its generalizability to other contexts (Walker and Heyns 1967; Crutchfield 1955; Allen 1965). Nonetheless, movement was clearly and significantly in the direction of majority opinion, just as a consensus heuristic would suggest.

EFFECTS ON ISSUE OPINIONS

Thus far the studies I have presented have focused on how impersonal influence can affect attitudes toward candidates. Should these same processes be assumed to apply equally well to issue attitudes? Here, again, the evidence with respect to processes of influence has been quite minimal, but it suggests potential for movement both toward and away from majority views. To address these questions, two survey-experiments involving a total of six separate issues were used to expose a random national sample of respondents to systematically different information about mass opinion toward controversial issues.

Issue Experiment No. 1

The first study involved three experimental factors forming a three-by-two-by-three, between-group design. One factor manipulated respondents' levels of commitment to their opinions by using three issues that varied greatly in terms of the general amount of commitment people had to their issue stands.[23] Based on pretests, three issues were chosen to represent high, medium, and low levels of issue commitment. These issues were the death penalty, whether election ballots should be printed in more than one language, and the elimination of the electoral college, respectively.[24]

The second, two-level factor consisted of "pro" or "con" cues for each issue.[25] A third factor indicated the type of motivation emphasized in the cue. Since respondents to this national poll could not be thoroughly debriefed over the telephone, the cues did not overtly misrepresent distributions of opinion concerning these issues. The cues were used, however, to appeal to various underlying motivations to shift attitudes toward majority opinion (Bartels 1988). To approximate the motivation to conform to majority opinion in order to be correct, "smart" cues emphasized that many expert sources endorsed a particular position.[26] "Win" cues, on the other hand, emphasized that one particular side of the issue debate would be the inevitable victor and thus capitalized on respondents' desire to be on the winning side. Finally, "trend" cues portrayed the current trend in a particular direction, without commenting

23 Although this kind of factor has gone by a variety of names including immediacy, familiarity, issue importance, and involvement, here it is referred to as "commitment" to designate the extent to which respondents are expected to have highly committed, preformed opinions before encountering the experimental manipulations.

24 Manipulation checks on levels of commitment to these opinions confirmed that in the absence of experimental cues, the three issues represent a range of precommitment to issue positions ranging from the death penalty (8.19) to multilingual ballots (7.59) to the electoral college (6.76).

25 In the "pro" death penalty condition, for example, respondents received cues indicating that many people were in favor of the death penalty before giving interviewers their own opinions.

26 A pretest using college seniors suggested that the sources chosen for each of the issues were highly credible for each respective issue.

specifically on the sagacity of a particular position or the likely winning side.

Following the cue, all respondents were asked for their own opinions on the issue and how committed they were to their positions.[27] Although in principle, the three types of cues each represent a distinct underlying motivation, manipulating one aspect of perceptions may inadvertently influence perceptions of another characteristic of the same issue. For example, suggesting that one issue position is the likely winner may make people think that the current trend also is in that direction. Or, from information that the trend is moving in a particular direction, people may infer that this is also the smarter position to hold. To control for potential confounding of motivations, each respondent also received two follow-up questions dealing with the two types of cues that were not received. If a person received a trend cue, for example, the person also was asked follow-up questions dealing with whether or not he/she felt his/her position was the "smart" position to take, that is, the position that would be endorsed by experts, and whether he/she felt this position would ultimately win the public debate. The follow-up questions served two purposes. First, they controlled for the likely effects that the cues would have on other than the intended manipulated motivations.[28] As covariates, they also served to increase the efficiency of the model by incorporating non-experimental influences that result from projection and related phenomena.

The results of this experiment suggested that the type of consensus cue made no difference in the persuasiveness of the cues. But the pattern of effects that resulted from the direction of cues was strongly dependent upon the level of precommitment to issue positions. Figure 8.6 illustrates these results. In the case of attitudes concerning the electoral college, the low-commitment issue, respondents receiving the pro-elimination cue were consistently more positive toward this position than those receiving the anti-elimination cue. This remained true within each cue type as well as in the overall pattern.

This pattern was reversed with the high-commitment issue, the death penalty. Here, by contrast, the means suggest greater opposition when exposed to the pro-death penalty cue, indicating a backlash in opposition to the direction suggested by the consensus cue. As with the low-commitment issue, this pattern was consistent within all three cue types as well. For the third, moderate-commitment issue, results within cue

27 For exact question wording, see Mutz (1992a).
28 In the real world, of course, it is likely that the influence of majority opinion may be brought about by combinations of these motivations and inferences that naturally occur together. For experimental purposes, however, efforts have been made to separate the types of motivation.

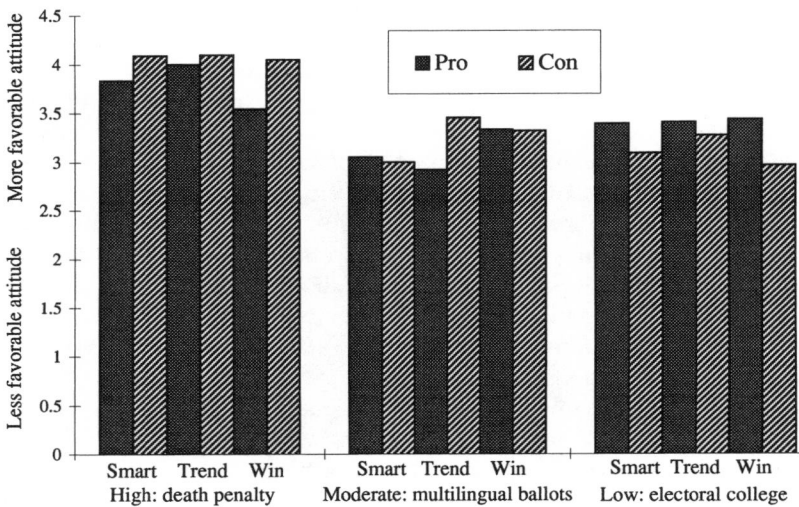

Figure 8.6. Issue attitudes by experimental condition (Issue Experiment No. 1).

types suggested a mixture of these two patterns with negligible differences in two cases.

The statistical significance of these results was tested using analysis of variance including each of the three experimental factors and three covariates.[29] The results of this analysis confirmed the general pattern observed in Figure 8.6. In addition to differences in opinion accounted for by issue, there was a significant interaction between issue and the direction of the cue. The trend covariate also accounted for a tremendous amount of variance in attitudes toward the issues. The nature of the cue, however, mattered little. Subjects responded to smart, trend and win cues in a similar fashion (see Mutz 1992a for statistical details).

Figure 8.7 summarizes the key results by plotting the means for pro and con conditions for each issue, collapsing across the three types of cues. Issues are spaced along the horizontal axis to reflect the level of precommitment to issue opinions in control conditions. The directional cues clearly made a difference in responses to both the high- and low-commitment issues. Respondents receiving cues for low-commitment issues were moved in the direction of that cue. Respondents in the high-commitment issue condition, on the other hand, did not feel compelled

29 These tests were accomplished using several analyses of variance for each issue, with perceptions of the smart, trendy, and winning positions serving as the dependent variables, and type of cue and direction of cue serving as the independent variables.

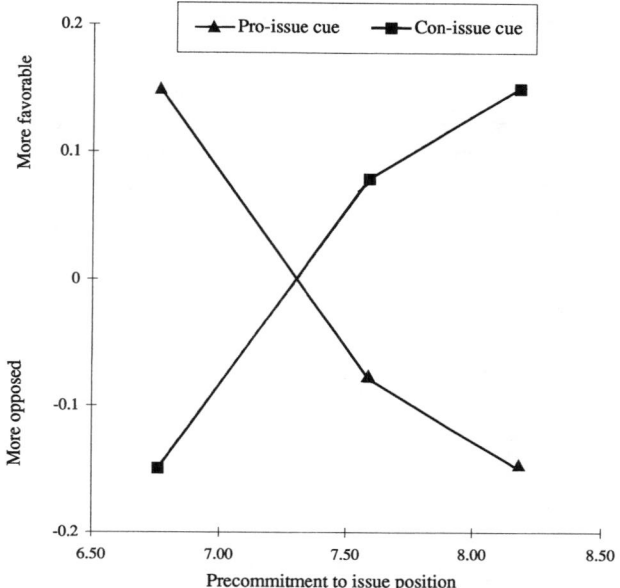

Figure 8.7. Issue opinions by consensus cue and precommitment (Issue Experiment No. 1).

to follow the suggested opinion; in fact, their opinions shifted away from the direction of the cue received, indicating not only a resistance to majority influence, but possibly also the rehearsal of counterattitudinal thoughts.[30]

This experiment generated interesting preliminary evidence that issues, like candidates, are subject to influence from consensus cues, but the design of the study lacked the information necessary to examine the processes underlying this phenomenon. Without control conditions or thought-listing measures, for example, it was impossible to see if addi-

30 Using these same data, it was also possible to test for indirect effects of opinion cue types. For example, if the opinion "trend" cue also influenced perceptions of the wisdom of that position, one would expect to find differences by experimental condition in the extent to which that position was perceived to be the "smart" one to take. Using the questions asked directly after each opinion was elicited, it was possible to test for potential transference of this kind. Results suggested little crossover among the various cues (Mutz 1992a for a summary). It is particularly important to note that contrary to expectations based on the consensus heuristic, neither the "trend" cues, nor the "win" cues elicited perceptions of that issue position as one more likely to be endorsed by experts. In short, public opinion cues that did not explicitly address the issue of expert opinion were not interpreted as indicative of the wise or "smart" choice to make.

tional cognitive responses were prompted by the consensus cues or to what extent respondents shifted views away from previously held positions.

The cognitive response mechanism provides the best single theory to account for the overall pattern of results with movement both toward and away from consensus positions, but it is probably not safe simply to assume that movement in both directions is accounted for by the same process. In fact, it is quite likely that multiple mechanisms of influence are operating simultaneously, perhaps some more effective in one direction than another. A subsequent issue experiment was designed to address these questions.

Issue Experiment No. 2

A second issue experiment included both control conditions and thought-listing measures, in addition to issues ranging across levels of commitment. The design of the study was a three-by-two-by-two, between-subjects experiment. One three-level factor randomly assigned respondents to one of three different issue controversies. These issues included (1) whether girls should be allowed to join the Boy Scouts, (2) whether federal laws should require affirmative action programs for women and minorities provided there are no rigid quotas, and (3) whether there should be a constitutional amendment making it a punishable offense to burn the American flag.[31] As before, the policy issues were chosen to represent a range of levels of issue commitment based on a pretest using a national sample. A second factor manipulated people's awareness of collective opinion. Respondents were assigned to groups that received either no cue or a consensus cue corresponding to current majority opinion for the relevant issue.[32]

The rapid-fire nature of a succession of survey interview questions is clearly not naturally conducive to cognitive elaboration. In most real world contexts, such snap decisions are not necessary. In order to avoid stacking the experimental deck in favor of exclusively heuristic process-

31 Exact wording of favor/oppose cues was as follows: "Recent evidence indicates that most citizens (favor/oppose) (allowing girls to join Boy Scout and Cub Scout troops/federal laws requiring affirmative action programs for women and minorities provided there are no rigid quotas/a constitutional amendment that would make it a punishable offense to burn the American flag)."

32 In the case of girls joining the Boy Scouts, the majority of Americans in the pretest as well as in the control condition in the experiment were opposed to allowing girls to join the Boy Scouts. The majority was in favor of affirmative action without quotas for women and minorities, and in favor of a constitutional amendment that would make it illegal to burn flags.

ing, an additional manipulation randomly assigned respondents to one of two conditions in which they were either given no instructions prior to receiving an issue question or were instructed to "feel free to take a moment or two to think about it before answering." The purpose of this manipulation was to induce systematically greater thinking on the part of some respondents before answering the question. Analysis of the thought-listing questions confirmed that respondents did, in fact, engage in greater elaboration when encouraged to do so.

After the experimental manipulations, respondents were asked for their own issue preferences.[33] This item was immediately followed by a question asking for the level of commitment to their issue preference.[34] Pretest evidence on levels of commitment to these issue positions was corroborated by this manipulation check. In both instances, the flag-burning issue elicited the highest levels of commitment, the Boy Scout issue elicited moderate levels of commitment, and the affirmative action issue had the lowest levels of commitment of the three.[35] As in the candidate experiments, immediately after eliciting the issue position, respondents were asked open-ended thought-listing questions.[36]

One additional item was included in the study because of its connection to the kind of information processing respondents tend to engage in. The individual trait known as "Need for Cognition" refers to a personal tendency to invest greater thought and mental energy in tasks (Cacioppo and Petty 1982). Four questions that had already been evaluated extensively by others for reliability and validity were adapted from a larger battery of items designed to efficiently measure need for cognition (Cacioppo, Petty, and Kao 1984).[37]

33 "How about you? Do you favor or oppose (allowing girls to join Boy Scout and Cub Scout troops/federal laws requiring affirmative action programs for women and minorities provided there are no rigid quotas/a constitutional amendment that would make it a punishable offense to burn the American flag)? Would you say you strongly (favor/oppose) this or only somewhat (favor/oppose) it?" Responses were coded on a four-point scale from strongly oppose (1) to strongly favor (4).

34 "When you say you (favor/oppose) (randomly selected issue), how committed are you to your stand? On a 1 to 10 scale in which 10 means completely committed and 1 means not at all committed, how committed would you say you are?"

35 Differences in issue commitment were statistically significant ($F_{(2,911)} = 21.01$, $p < .001$).

36 "As you were thinking about whether – , what kinds of thoughts occurred to you?"

37 These items were as follows: "Please tell me how well each of the following statements describes you: (a) I really enjoy a task that involves coming up with new solutions to problems. Would you say this statement describes you very well, somewhat, not very well, or not at all well? (b) I only think as hard as I have to. (Scale repeated as needed.) (c) It's enough for me that something gets the job

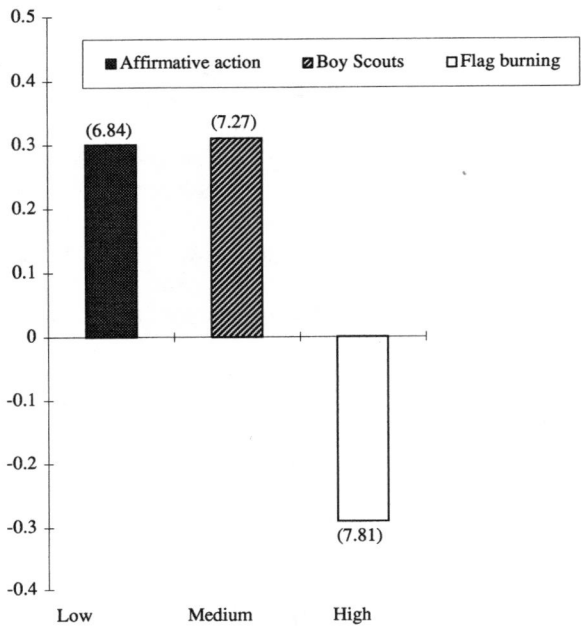

Figure 8.8. Opinion change by precommitment to issue position (Issue Experiment No. 2).

In Figure 8.8, the means for each experimental condition are shown as deviations from corresponding control group means. The results are very similar to those in Issue Experiment No. 1 and the Democratic Primary Experiment. For the two issues that were lower in levels of precommitment, girls in the Boy Scouts and affirmative action, differences between the control means and the means for those receiving public support cues indicated shifts in the direction of the majority cues. These shifts represented 11 to 12 percent increases in favorability toward the majority position. For the flag-burning amendment, the high-commitment issue, respondents shifted in the direction opposite the majority cue. The magnitude of change was roughly the same as for the shifts toward majority views. As expected, this pattern produced no significant main effects, but it created a significant interaction between Issue and public support (F = 5.58, p < .01).

Since there are good theoretical reasons to expect that different mechanisms may be operating in shifts toward and away from majority positions, I analyzed flag burning separately from the other two issues. Both need for cognition and cognitive elaboration were included in the analyses in order to help identify whether the changes were rooted in heuristic or systematic processing.

Table 8.2 summarizes findings about the process underlying movement toward consensus. The strong main effect of public support initially looks suggestive of a consensus heuristic. However, the significant interaction between public support and cognitive elaboration tells a different story. As illustrated in Figure 8.9, the movement toward public support was concentrated within the group of respondents who were, in fact, rehearsing issue-relevant thoughts. Low-elaboration respondents, by contrast, showed no movement in the direction of majority cues. This pattern is precisely the opposite of what heuristic models suggest. Heuristics are employed precisely because people lack other issue-relevant information.

Table 8.3 and Figure 8.10 tell a similar story for movement away from consensus. The group of respondents whose views shifted away from majority opinion were those high in need for cognition, that is, those most prone to systematic, rather than heuristic, processing. Among respondents low in need for cognition, the majority cues produced a negligible impact. Among those high in need for cognition, the support cues produced movement away from majority opinion. As might be expected, those high in need for cognition also rehearsed more issue-relevant thoughts.

To summarize, this series of experiments suggests that the influence conveyed by perceptions of mass opinion is a complex reaction contingent upon characteristics of the individual as well as the information flow surrounding a candidate or issue. The same processes appear to apply to issues as well as to candidates, and they also appear to replicate nicely outside the laboratory in real world political contexts. Purely heuristic responses to information about mass opinion are likely only when information levels are extremely low. In many political contexts, responses to information about mass opinion will be contingent upon the kinds of cognitive responses that people generate upon hearing about others' views (see Appendix: Methodology for a discussion of the validity of the thought-listing measure). The types of cognitive responses generated will be influenced by people's level of commitment to their initial attitudes toward a candidate or issue, and the availability of positive and negative arguments in their information environment.

Table 8.2. *Movement toward consensus: Effects of public support,*
cognitive elaboration, and need for cognition on issue attitudes
(Issue Experiment No. 2)

	Sum of squares	(df)	F-value
Covariates			
Education	1.19	(1)	1.26
Age	.62	(1)	.66
Race	.81	(1)	.86
Republican	.54	(1)	.57
Democrat	.20	(1)	.21
Main effects			
Public support	8.24	(1)	8.77***
Pause	.01	(1)	.01
Issue	.10	(1)	.10
Cognitive elaboration	.06	(1)	.07
Need for cognition	.00	(1)	.00
Interactions			
Public support by pause	.02	(1)	.01
Public support by issue	.19	(1)	.40
Public support by cognitive elaboration	3.90	(1)	4.04*
Public support by need for cognition	.13	(1)	.28
Pause by issue	.28	(1)	.45
Pause by cognitive elaboration	.66	(1)	.94
Pause by need for cognition	1.56	(1)	1.89
Issue by cognitive elaboration	3.92	(1)	4.95*
Issue by need for cognition	.81	(1)	.55
Elaboration by need for cognition	2.83	(1)	3.52

Note: Subsample n = 389. Dependent variable is issue opinion on a four-point
scale where high is more favorable.
$^*p < .05$ $^{***}p < .001$

STRATEGIC BEHAVIOR AMONG THE HIGHLY INVOLVED: CAMPAIGN CONTRIBUTORS IN PRESIDENTIAL PRIMARIES

One remaining mechanism by which perceptions of others' views may
translate to meaningful political outcomes is through the strategic use of
information about mass opinion. Unlike the other two explanations offered in this chapter, the strategic mechanism already has accumulated
considerable support in political contexts, and, in this sense, requires

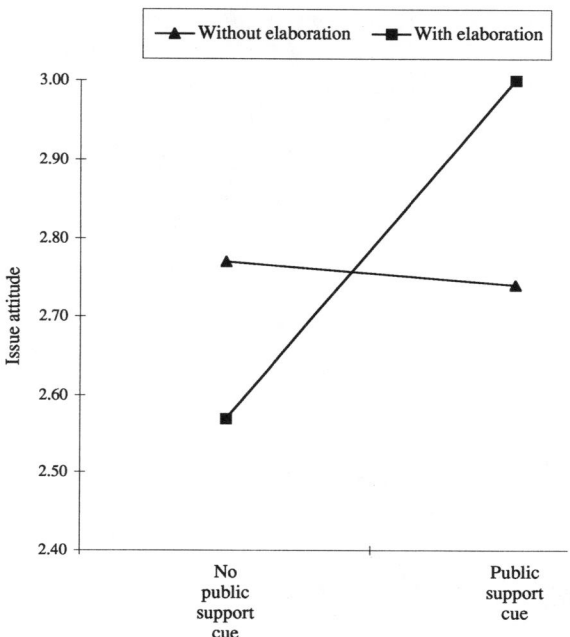

Figure 8.9. Movement toward consensus: Effects of consensus cues by cognitive elaboration (Issue Experiment No. 2).

little independent confirmation. Nonetheless, I strengthen the overall case for impersonal influence by presenting one additional example of the strategic use of information about mass opinion. Beyond adding to existing evidence, this example highlights two additional points concerning strategic responses to mass opinion. First, it shows why strategic responses to information about increasing mass support need not necessarily result in further *increases* in support. In some cases, the rational reaction for campaign contributors is to donate in response to perceptions of *dwindling* public support. This finding is of interest in expanding the kinds of predictions that should be made regarding strategic forms of impersonal influence, but more importantly it underscores the consequences of theorizing specific mechanisms of influence from perceptions of mass opinion.

In addition to calling attention to less obvious forms of strategic behavior, this study also reinforces a point originally made by Bartels (1988) and others about how the strategic explanation for reactions to mass opinion differs from other mechanisms. Unlike the other possible mechanisms of influence, strategic reactions apply strictly to political *be-*

Table 8.3. *Movement away from consensus: Effects of public support, cognitive elaboration, and need for cognition on issue attitudes (Issue Experiment No. 2)*

	Sum of squares	(df)	F-value
Covariates			
Education	10.14	(1)	7.28***
Age	.66	(1)	.47
Race	4.59	(1)	3.30
Republican	.18	(1)	.13
Democrat	.51	(1)	.37
Main effects			
Public support	4.96	(1)	3.56
Pause	1.50	(1)	1.08
Cognitive elaboration	.13	(1)	.10
Need for cognition	3.65	(1)	2.62
Interactions			
Public support by pause	.18	(1)	.13
Public support by cognitive elaboration	.91	(1)	.65
Public support by need for cognition	8.69	(1)	6.24*
Pause by cognitive elaboration	.41	(1)	.29
Pause by need for cognition	.53	(1)	.38
Elaboration by need for cognition	.52	(1)	.38

Note: Subsample n = 199. Dependent variable is issue opinion on a four-point scale where high is more favorable.
*p < .05 ***p < .001

haviors, and not to opinions. In fact, citizens are said to respond strategically only when the behaviors are not consistent with their opinions. The classic example is when a voter votes for someone other than his or her most well liked candidate because the other candidate has a more solid chance of winning than the citizen's personal favorite. This study is particularly well suited to examine a mechanism that influences political behaviors because it utilizes as dependent variables measures of actual political contributions rather than survey-based attitudes or intentions.

Observers of American electoral behavior have long assumed that potential contributors are influenced by their perceptions of collective others' views (Overacker 1932). Contributors surely want to avoid wasting their money on a candidate without a chance of winning, just as strategic voters want to avoid wasting their votes on noncontenders. Strategic considerations might be expected in even greater magnitude in campaign con-

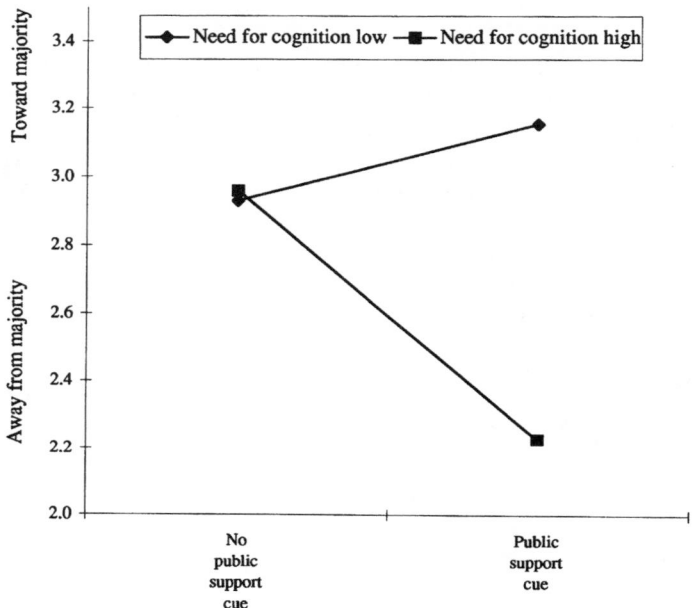

Figure 8.10. Movement away from consensus: Effects of consensus cues by need for cognition (Issue Experiment No. 2).

tributing than in voting. Simply by virtue of their extraordinarily high levels of political interest and knowledge, potential contributors should be more likely to engage in strategic thinking. Potential contributors also may be more strategic when they consider the possibility of throwing money – as opposed to single votes – away on a candidate who has little chance of success. By the same token, contributors donating to candidates to whom they know many others are also donating may strategically enhance the return on their investment (Jacobson and Kernell 1983).

Interestingly, one finds precisely the opposite strategic assumption in the literature on direct mail fundraising. Here the operating principle is that contributors are motivated by perceptions of *decreasing* mass support for their position. As Kayden (1985: 95) notes: "The small donor derives satisfaction – a moral uplift – from contributing to a campaign. The issues that provide satisfaction are apt to be issues in which the donor is in the minority. After all, if one is in the majority, why worry?" Many direct mail appeals include frequent references to the almost certain demise of a campaign unless the recipient donates immediately. Outside the context of direct mail fundraising, it is also common for candidates to vie for the "underdog" role for similar reasons (Adams

1983). The perception that a campaign is embattled and needs immediate help may be an effective fundraising tactic, particularly in determining the timing of donations. In the face of an imminent threat, loyal
supporters of a candidate may be prompted to give money by news that
their candidate is threatened or losing ground.[38] Thus, the strategic
mechanism is also a compelling reason to withhold money in response
to news of mass popularity; if one's chosen candidate is already doing
well, what need is there to send additional money?

The fact that both types of strategic reactions make a great deal of sense
reiterates the importance of positing specific mechansims to account for
patterns of impersonal influence. When both kinds of processes may be
transpiring, one or both of these strategic reactions may be masked in casual observation unguided by specific theoretical predictions.

Loyalty-based contributing in the face of threat and hesitancy-based
contributing in the face of uncertainty represent two distinctly different
predictions as to the pattern of contributing that should transpire in
response to perceptions of candidate support. Loyalty-based contributing should be more likely among candidates whose supporters are
strongly committed to their candidacy and whose candidacy represents
an ideological position that is distinct from that of other candidates in
the party. The weaker the strength of a constituency's support for a
particular candidate and the less distinguishable that candidate is from
other alternatives, the more likely contributors will be influenced by
hesitancy-based strategic considerations; if two or more candidates appear roughly equally attractive, then viability should play a positive role
in increasing the frequency of donations.

The 1988 presidential primary and preprimary period provided an
excellent setting in which to examine the effects of changing perceptions
of public support on strategic contributor behavior. Since neither of
these races was between two well-defined major contenders, the extent
of horse race emphasis was tremendous. The type of primary activist
who intends to vote for a given candidate, but who will not donate
money until he or she is convinced that the candidate has a solid chance
of winning, will probably find other candidates well within the realm of
acceptability as well. This type of contributor is unlikely to be an ardent
or impassioned supporter of a chosen candidate. In 1988, whose sup-

---

38 Although information about candidates in a large pre-nomination field tends to
be low, potential contributors – particularly at the primary stage – are likely to
be among the most actively involved and well informed (Brown, Hedges, and
Powell 1980). These characteristics make loyalty-based contributing all the more
plausible; when highly committed voters are faced with information indicating a
majority or trend away from their viewpoint, they may rally behind their candidate (see, e.g., Fleitas 1971; Ceci and Kain 1982; Price 1989).

porters were only weakly committed and likely to be hesitant to give monetary support without perceptions of increasing viability? In contrast, whose supporters were likely to be spurred into action by news of an embattled candidacy?

Of course, all campaign constituencies include some of each kind of supporter; constituencies for a given candidate are never all of one cloth. Nonetheless, some candidates' constituencies were more likely than others to fill one or the other of these two profiles. As I have shown elsewhere (Mutz 1995a), on the Democratic side, Jesse Jackson had an intensely loyal following and Gore's supporters also were surprisingly strongly committed to his candidacy. Of the four major candidates, Jackson and Gore also were the most ideologically distinct. Gephardt and Dukakis were perceived by their supporters to be less ideologically distinct and had less intense support among their respective backers as well. Thus, the constituencies supporting candidates Dukakis and Gephardt were assumed to be more prone to exhibiting signs of hesitancy-based strategic contributing, and Jackson and Gore's supporters were assumed to be more likely to exhibit signs of loyalty-based contributing, particularly in Jackson's case.

In this study, I focused specifically on the effect that perceived support for candidates had on decisions to contribute that were *not* a result of changes in the size of a candidate's constituency. "Strategic contributing" refers to situations in which perceptions of public support alter the flow of contributions directly, not by changing people's attitudes toward candidates, nor by changing their preferred candidate. Instead, media coverage of the horse race simply alters people's perceptions of an already-liked candidate's chances of victory and thus facilitates strategic contributions.

In order to eliminate nonstrategic reasons that changes in perceptions of public support might lead to changes in the flow of donations received by a campaign, I included a variety of control variables in the models used to test these hypotheses (see Mutz 1995a, 1995b for statistical details).

The dependent variables used in this study were constructed from information on contributions to primary candidates available from the Federal Election Commission for a forty-two-week period from July 1, 1987, through the date in 1988 when the candidate was no longer in the race. These data were aggregated by week to form measures of the number of donations from private individuals each candidate received each week. Since the "exhibition" season is a crucial time during which candidates must scramble to raise seed money if the campaign is to continue (Orren 1985), it was important to begin the time series well before the primary season itself. Moreover, horse race coverage is probably most influential in shaping public perceptions of support for candidates when there are no actual primaries to guide perceptions.

Perceptions of public support for candidates were tapped by assessing

Table 8.4. *Predictors of donations to campaigns with weak constituency support*

	Coefficient	T-ratio
Gephardt campaign		
Intercept	46.15	.64
Gephardt horse race spin	98.23	2.73**
Gephardt voter support	41.20	3.00***
Primary outcomes	96.26	1.81
Amount of media coverage	−1.16	1.72
Size of war chest	9.10	1.54
All-candidate trend	.43	2.03*
Total R²		.64
Dukakis campaign		
Intercept	156.94	.94
Dukakis horse race spin	121.66	1.81
Dukakis voter support	58.51	3.16***
Primary outcomes	−40.42	.18
Amount of media coverage	−1.93	1.40
Size of war chest	8.81	2.90***
All-candidate trend	2.36	8.73***
Total R²		.76

Note: Coefficients are iterated Yule-Walker estimates. Dependent variable is the number of donations to a candidate-authorized campaign committee. Gephardt n = 39 weeks; Dukakis n = 42 weeks. R² represents the measure of fit of the structural part of the model after transforming for the autocorrelation.
*p < .05 **p < .01 ***p < .001

the spin on horse race coverage pertaining to each candidate's chances. A computer-aided content analysis assessed the spin regarding whether the candidate was portrayed as winning or losing, gaining or losing ground according to each paragraph. To create a composite measure indicating the amount of positive spin relative to negative spin for each candidate, I constructed a weekly ratio of the number of positive to negative spin news stories.

As indicated in Table 8.4, the dynamics of donations to the Gephardt and Dukakis campaigns were similar in many respects. For example,

The Role of Collective Opinion in Individual Judgment

both were able to boost the number of donations their campaigns received by bringing more voters into the fold. Most importantly, the horse race spin presented in coverage of their campaigns had similar significant effects, although the coefficient was marginally significant in Dukakis's case ($p < .10$). For Dukakis, the size of the coefficient suggests that in a week of media coverage with twice as much positive as negative spin, the Dukakis campaign could expect roughly 120 more donations relative to what would be expected with coverage balancing positive and negative spin. For Gephardt, the coefficient for media spin was clearly significant, but slightly smaller, suggesting around one hundred additional donations. In general then, the Democratic campaigns with weak constituency support demonstrated the predicted pattern of response to perceived candidate viability: Supporters hedged their bets when the campaigns did not appear to be faring well and donated more often when the candidate's popularity was perceived to be on the upswing.

For purposes of illustration, Figure 8.11 shows the simple bivariate relationships between media spin and the number of donations to the Gephardt and Dukakis campaigns. The three peaks in contributions to Gephardt are each preceded by peaks in media spin.[39] The two major peaks in donations to Dukakis – in September 1987 and late February 1988 – are also preceded roughly a month before by the two most pronounced peaks in media spin.[40] Even some of the more minor peaks in

---

39 The positive spin forming a minor peak in late August corresponds closely to the timing of a straw poll announced August 30 showing Gephardt running first in Iowa. This is followed by a similar peak in donations at approximately a month's lag. The second and largest peak in horse race spin is followed by a modest surge in contributions, again at approximately a month's lag from peak to peak and valley to valley. The sharp dip in horse race spin in November closely corresponds to the release of a *Des Moines Register* poll showing Gephardt losing ground to the other candidates in Iowa. The third peak in positive media spin occurred in January and was almost as high as the earlier peak. It also was followed roughly a month later by several consecutive weeks in which Gephardt attracted well over 250 donations.

40 In August 1987, optimism abounded, but a series of mishaps in September apparently brought down the positive media spin surrounding his campaign. The effects of declining spin in September are visible in the drop-off in donations in October. Dukakis media spin bounced back in October and November as he won the New Hampshire caucuses, came in second in a series of CBS/*New York Times* polls, and first in a New Hampshire poll. The campaign remained buoyed through December as he accumulated endorsements from many mayors and city council members, and was dubbed one of the top six governors and "the leader of the innovation pack" by *U.S. News and World Report*. The highest peak in Dukakis media spin was in January 1988. During this month, a poll of New Hampshire Democrats conducted by Gallup for the *Boston Globe* showed him retaining his wide lead; moreover, a *Des Moines Register* poll later in the month showed Dukakis in a three-way tie among Iowa caucus participants. This peak in positive spin dropped off and then leveled out at the beginning of February, when Dukakis

253

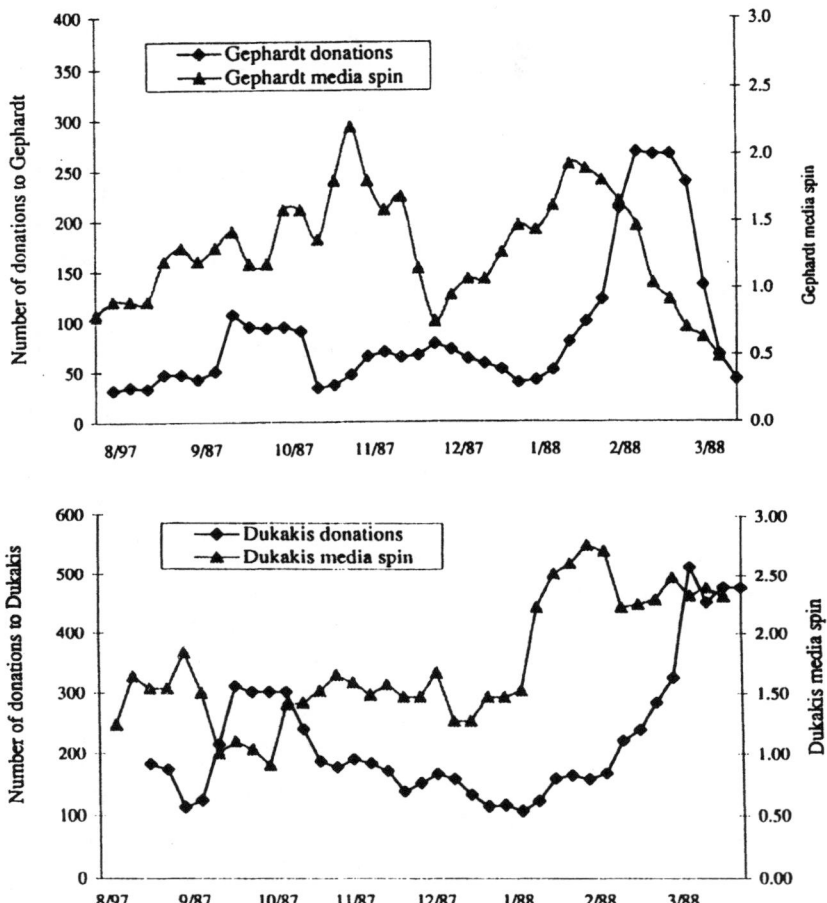

Figure 8.11. Relationship between favorability of media spin and number of donations to Democratic candidates with weak constituent support.

Dukakis spin are mirrored by small increases in donations from October through January.

As Table 8.5 demonstrates, donations to the Jackson and Gore campaigns followed a far different pattern.[41] As hypothesized, horse race

came in third in the Iowa caucuses, just as the peak in donations in late February dropped off and leveled out in early March. Time lines for major campaign events for the candidates were obtained from "CBS News Campaign '88 Primaries and Caucuses, Book 2," which covers the entire time period included in this study.

41 The overall fit for the Jackson equation is not nearly as good as for the other candidates. The weakness of this model may result from several causes. Research

The Role of Collective Opinion in Individual Judgment

Table 8.5. *Predictors of donations to campaigns
with strong constituency support*

	Coefficient	T-ratio
Gore campaign		
Intercept	−46.93	.97
Gore horse race spin	−28.28	2.85**
Gore voter support	13.07	1.61
Primary outcomes	−88.61	2.92**
Amount of media coverage	1.00	2.27*
Size of war chest	6.41	1.75*
All-candidate trend	.18	1.44
Total R^2		.67
Jackson campaign		
Intercept	68.70	2.13*
Jackson horse race spin	−19.99	2.54**
Jackson voter support	3.22	1.56
Primary outcomes	76.02	3.20***
Amount of media coverage	−.41	2.33*
Size of war chest	8.49	1.60
All-candidate trend	.03	1.08
Total R^2		.48

Note: Coefficients are iterated Yule-Walker estimates. Dependent variable is the number of donations to a candidate-authorized campaign committee. Gore n = 42 weeks; Jackson n = 42 weeks. R^2 represents the measure of fit of the structural part of the model after transforming for the autocorrelation.
*p < .05 **p < .01 ***p < .001

spin was a significant negative predictor of donations for both candidates. However, the size of the coefficients indicates that these negative effects were of a much smaller magnitude than the positive effects observed for Dukakis and Gephardt. Jackson and Gore gained only around

on the 1984 primaries has suggested that the media treated Jackson's candidacy fundamentally differently from other candidates (Broh 1987), and the same may well have occurred in 1988. The weakness of the Jackson model might also result from the fact that many of Jackson's supporters were outside of the Democratic party's traditional financial base and thus may have been motivated by different considerations. A still more likely explanation is that the Federal Election Com-

twenty or thirty additional donations from having their campaigns portrayed as threatened or losing ground, while Gephardt and Dukakis
gained nearly a hundred or more donations in response to equivalent
shifts in horse race spin. Although there is some evidence corroborating
the idea that strongly supportive constituencies rally behind their candidates in times of need, the strength of this strategic pattern pales in
comparison with that of candidates with weak constituency support.[42]

Although this pattern of findings makes some sense based on the profile of loyalty-based and hesitancy-based strategic contributors, it is difficult to have much confidence in it given the small number of candidates
whose contributions I examined. Ultimately, my confidence was greatly
enhanced by the very similar pattern I found among Republican primary
contenders.

As a standing vice-president, Bush was the clear front-runner in the
Republican nomination race. Based on the rationale underlying strategic
contributing, his supporters should be least likely to be influenced by
perceptions of others' views. Dole and Kemp were less well known also-

mission (FEC) data are a less accurate reflection of the total number of donations
Jackson received than they are for other candidates. Jackson's campaign probably
attracted a greater number of smaller donors that the FEC records do not take
into account. Unfortunately, there are no reliable sources of information on contributions under two hundred dollars, nor is it possible to ascertain precisely what
percentage of the total number of contributions fell under this limit for each
candidate.

42 Several plausible rival interpretations of the relationships between media spin and
contributions depicted in Table 8.5 can be ruled out and thus increase confidence
in the loyalty-based interpretation. First, there is no evidence in either case that
positive media spin brings about increased contributions; only if one considered
illogically long lag times such as two to three months would the peaks in media
spin and contributions begin to suggest the pattern that characterizes hesitancy-
based contributing. Second, although the idea that contributions might be driving
media spin is plausible – particularly based on the data from Jackson's campaign
– it seems highly unlikely. Reporters use fund-raising success as a benchmark for
judging candidate popularity, but reliable information on fund-raising progress is
not available to reporters on a continuous, ongoing basis. The FEC has a small
number of filing deadlines spaced many months apart and thus cannot account
for the continuous similarity of the trends. Moreover, candidates' own ongoing
claims about fund-raising successes are treated by reporters with understandable
suspicion and given little news play, precisely because reporters fear being used
by candidates to instigate bandwagon-type phenomena (Arterton 1984).
Nonetheless, I attempted to eliminate this possibility by reexamining these relationships after removing from the sample of horse race coverage all media coverage explicitly dealing with campaign finance. Results were virtually identical to
the original ones. Nor is horse race spin merely a surrogate for the results of the
latest public opinion poll. Removing all poll-based stories from the sample of
coverage did not change the relationships between horse race spin and contributions, but polls may still have indirect effects on the tone of coverage in stories
on other topics.

rans, thus giving their supporters ample reason to be concerned about viability. Pat Robertson's candidacy was altogether different; he was a political outsider but with a ready-made constituency from his work as a well-known televangelist on the Christian Broadcasting Network. Moreover, the religious fervor of his supporters would lead one to predict that they would rally behind their candidate in the face of adversity as Jackson's supporters did. Indeed, polls showed that Robertson supporters were far more strongly committed to their candidate than were supporters of other candidates (Mutz 1995b).

Consistent with the findings for the Democrats, when mass opinion was portrayed as increasingly supportive of Kemp or Dole, more donations flowed into their campaigns shortly thereafter. Even taking into account over-time changes in the size of their constituencies, the total amount of coverage they were receiving, ongoing primary events, the size of their war chests, and the kind of media spin alternative candidates were receiving, the frequency of donations to Kemp and Dole were clearly a function of how the opinions of the mass public were presented in coverage of their campaigns (Mutz 1994b). Dole's contributors and Kemp's contributors were influenced to roughly the same extent as the Democratics by perceptions of mass support for their respective candidates.

Bush's donations represented a predictable departure from the pattern seen with Kemp and Dole. The spin on front-runner Bush's own campaign had no effect on his potential contributors, just as predicted. Interestingly, however, coverage of support for Kemp had a very strong and significant negative effect on support for Bush. The less viable the media portrayed Kemp to be, the more contributions flowed into the Bush campaign. Apparently early Kemp supporters – most likely those in the conservative wing of the Republican party – moved into Bush's camp when the media portrayed Kemp's chances as low and away from the Bush camp when media coverage portrayed him as more viable.

Figure 8.12 illustrates the relationship between Kemp's media spin and donations to Bush over time. The pattern suggested by the multivariate analysis is clear. When Kemp's spin peaks briefly in August, for example, it is followed a few weeks later by a downturn in Bush donations. When Kemp's spin falls in September, it is followed a few weeks later by a tremendous surge in contributions to Bush. Again in early December, when media coverage portrayed Kemp as being at the height of his viability in this campaign, this was followed shortly thereafter by the biggest dip in Bush donations of the entire primary and preprimary season. For a front-runner then, the question in potential donors' minds is not whether the candidate is viable, but rather how viable the likely alternatives are.

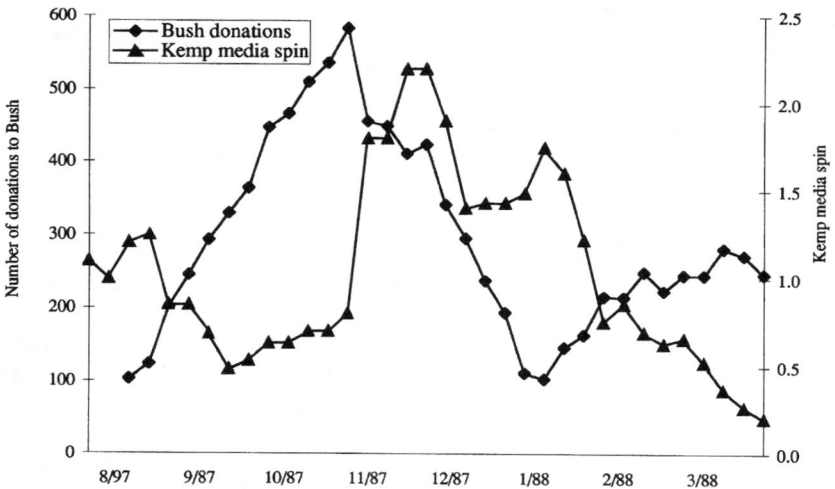

Figure 8.12. Relationship between favorability of Kemp media spin and number of donations to Bush.

As with supporters of Jesse Jackson, portrayals of support for Robertson were related to the flow of donations, but this influence was a negative one, indicating that his strongly committed supporters rallied behind him and increased the number of donations that flowed into the Robertson coffers when he was portrayed as losing ground and then relaxed when he was portrayed as gaining ground.

Overall then, the representations of others' views conveyed by horse race coverage had significant effects on political behavior that were independent of effects these perceptions had on political attitudes. Strategic considerations among highly politically involved primary campaign contributors can provide both positive and negative incentives toward contributing to primary candidates, although for most candidates viability serves as a positive incentive for supporters to donate. Moreover, the benefits of underdog status among candidates with intense support are considerably less than the benefits that less distinctive candidates receive from portrayals of increasing mass support.

IMPLICATIONS FOR ACCOUNTABILITY

In most discussions of impersonal influence, political observers concur that this phenomenon occurs to some extent and that it is a pernicious force, an unhealthy sign of vacuous citizens making political choices on the basis of irrational decision-making processes (Brady and Johnston

1987). The American public basically agrees with this judgment, citing polls and other mass feedback mechanisms as detrimental to the political process (Lavrakas, Holley, and Miller 1991). The studies described in this chapter suggest that this characterization is, at best, greatly over-simplified. The contribution of these models has been to illuminate scenarios in which citizens respond to information about others' opinions in ways that are both potentially beneficial and, at times, potentially detrimental to the democratic process. In order to sort out their varied implications for democratic accountability, I consider each of these mechanisms in turn.

Strategic use of information about others' views is obviously indicative of a highly informed and extremely thoughtful public. These people are unfortunately not numerous. Moreover, despite the obvious rationality of this process from the individual's perspective, it has the potential to harm accountability. For example, if enough people vote strategically and people's perceptions of the most popular candidate are incorrect, then preelection predictions could conceivably alter the outcome of an election. In practice, however, there are few examples of elections where this has actually occurred. Although third-party candidates are hurt to some degree by strategic considerations, this seldom changes the outcome of a race (Abramson et al. 1995). One can only speculate about whether other forms of political behavior, such as campaign contributing, are sufficiently influenced, but the implications of strategic behavior for accountability are constrained by the very small number of people likely to respond to information about mass opinion in this manner.

From the perspective of promoting accountability, evidence of the consensus heuristic illustrates a disturbing mechanism by which impersonal influence affects political attitudes and behaviors. Even in the political realm – the realm of legitimate controversy and dissent – lack of consensus support triggered citizens' concerns about potential candidates. As discussed in Chapter 7, in many areas of life, relying on the collective judgments of others is a sensible way to make decisions in the absence of full information. But in the political realm it will not necessarily result in the same judgment that a well-informed citizen might make. Issues and candidates can amass popular support for both legitimate and extraneous reasons. Moreover, impressions of mass consensus may be inaccurate because of politicians' attempts to distort impressions of their popularity to cultivate additional support. Media coverage that relays these impressions may result in still greater inaccuracy. Ultimately, accountability is ill served by citizens who rely on their impressions of others' views as their sole source of guidance.

Fortunately, the consensus heuristic requires extremely low levels of information in order to be applicable to political candidates and controversies. Although there was no evidence of a consensus heuristic in either of the two issue experiments, an Unknown Issue Experiment, paralleling the extremely low information environment of the Unknown Candidate Experiment, might well have produced similar effects. Nonetheless, the potentially negative implications of the consensus heuristic are limited by the same factors as the strategic use of information about mass opinion. Few political situations involve the extremely low levels of information produced in the Unknown Candidate Experiment, and in the uncommon situation where information on a candidate or issue is this low, the likelihood that such a citizen will be sufficiently involved politically to bother voting or even expressing an issue opinion seems slight. It is worth remembering that even with the demand characteristics of survey interviews, almost a third of the original respondents in this study refused to rate the candidate at all with so little information. The most important exception to this conclusion of limited implications for accountability is probably in contests for lesser offices where even the politically involved may have little information and thus may fall back on heuristic devices in order to choose a candidate. However, when information levels are that low, people are also unlikely to have encountered information about collective others' views, thus further limiting opportunities for heuristic use of collective opinion.

The bulk of impersonal influence from perceptions of mass opinion involves the integration of consensus information with other candidate or issue knowledge. The studies in this chapter demonstrate how people make use of consensus information in ways that are far removed from their sheeplike reputation. The cognitive response mechanism suggests that information about others' views may stimulate greater political thought and reflection along with reconsideration of one's original views. In short, people were prompted to ponder the reasons underlying trends in mass opinion. From the perspective of promoting accountability, the more pondering the better. Reflection on the reasons for differing political views provides not only the opportunity to change one's mind and adopt a normatively better viewpoint, but also a deeper understanding of one's own position. Mentally rehearsing the reasons that people might have for holding differing views could potentially lend greater legitimacy to an undesired political outcome.

A complete normative assessment of attitude change brought about by cognitive elaboration depends in part on the quality of the arguments and counterarguments that people generate. In the Unknown Candidate Experiment, responses were obviously constrained by the quality and amount of information given to respondents in the vignettes. As shown in the right panel of Table 8.6, respondents' thoughts were dominated by the candidate's personal traits (experience, family man, etc.) and re-

Table 8.6. *Types of cognitive responses to*
candidate preference questions

	Democratic Primary Experiment		Unknown Candidate Experiment	
	As % of cognitive responses	As % of respon-dents	As % of cognitive responses	As % of respon-dents
Image/personal traits or qualities	41	44	45	51
Issue positions/policies emphasized	31	39	52	35
Campaign characteristics	9	13	—	—
Viability/electability/strategic	7	10	2	3
Lack of information/familiarity	5	8	7	21
Ideological factors	3	6	—	—
Party characteristics	1	1	—	—
Popularity/public support	—	—	9	24
(n)	(496)	(309)	(1,350)	(869)

flections on the issue positions he advocated. But since respondents were simply handed information about the candidate immediately before asking for their views, this study probably provides unrealistically high estimates of issue-related thought rehearsal.

Since the Democratic Primary Experiment involved real candidates and did not offer respondents any information about them, it provides a more reasonable assessment of the extent to which thought rehearsal involved substantive considerations. In this study thoughts clearly ran the gamut from the heavily issue-centered ("He wants to drop the tax rate; he's concerned about the environment; I agree with his view on government corruption; he wants a socialized medicine policy and corporate funding of the presidential race eliminated") to the highly image-oriented ("I like him better because he has a fight in him; nobody will be able to push him around; I think Brown is a wimp; he reminds me of a little girl") to the somewhat absurd ("Actually, this Clinton, I tell you, I tie him in with the guy who was trying to run from the KKK"). The instability and uncertainty surrounding primary candidates' positions on issues makes it impractical to assess the accuracy of cognitive responses, but again, Table 8.6 provides a general breakdown of the types of thoughts that were generated. References to candidates' personal traits and qualities predominated, with references to issue positions or issue priorities a close second. Interestingly, there were no significant differences by support conditions in the types of responses generated, although some types of considerations were brought up more for some candidates than others. The additional cognitive responses generated in the support cue conditions appear to come roughly equally from all of the various types of possible considerations. In short, both experiments suggest that a good deal of attention was focused on substantive considerations surrounding the candidates. To the extent that these kinds of thoughts mediate the effects of representations of mass opinion, we should all breathe a sigh of relief.

Ultimately, however, the quality of thoughts mediating the effects of consensus information can only be as good as the quality of the information environment surrounding citizens. In the realm of candidate coverage, we know a good deal about the availability of various kinds of information about candidates. In a process that parallels the cognitive response mechanism, journalists – like other members of the public – want to offer explanations for candidate popularity or lack thereof. More often than not, the kinds of explanations they seize upon have to do with campaign strategy and tactics rather than the substance of candidates' campaign (Greenfield 1982; Popkin 1991). Seldom do journalists suggest that a candidate has more support because his or her policies are simply more in tune with potential voters. If Candidate Jones has a substantial lead over Candidate Smith, it must be because Jones's consultants were superior, her ads more negative, or perhaps news coverage was biased in her favor. The explanations offered for mass support may tend to be delegitimizing ones. Of course citizens need not buy into journalistic explanations for levels of mass popularity; they are free to draw on other sources to formulate alternative theories. Still, to the extent that the availability of persuasive arguments is skewed toward some candidates at the expense of others, the benefits of being perceived as having collective opinion on your side may differ from candidate to candidate or issue or issue.[43]

To summarize, impersonal influence appears to involve several simultaneous mechanisms of influence. Among these, the cognitive response mechanism appears to be most widely applicable to political contexts. Strategic behavior is limited to a very small, extremely well informed segment of the public, and purely heuristic processing is limited to people

---

43 Although front-runners consistently receive more coverage, content analyses have been inconsistent with respect to whether this status brings them coverage that is more positive or more negative on balance. In his study of 1984 Democratic primary contenders, Hagen (1996) found that the leaders received more scrutiny and less positive coverage of their policy views and personal qualities.

and contexts at the other end of the information spectrum. Since many people and political contexts are not at either extreme, the cognitive response model provides a promising framework for both explaining and predicting a wide variety of shifts in attitudes toward candidates and issues. Moreover, it fits nicely with both extant laboratory findings and current election data. It suggests that the effects of representations of collective opinion can be predicted based on the extent of involvement and the availability of information favoring or opposing various candidates or viewpoints. Information suggesting that others' views may differ from one's own triggers a reassessment of one's own position that is carried out by sampling political information in one's environment. All three experiments that included measures of cognitive elaboration confirmed that a cognitive response mechanism was at work in facilitating impersonal influence on political attitudes.

These results are also consistent with social psychological studies emphasizing the interdependence of processing modes such as Chaiken's (1987) distinction between heuristic and systematic processing, and Petty and Cacioppo's (1981) similar delineation of central versus peripheral routes to persuasion (Chaiken and Maheswaran 1994). Typically heuristic and systematic processing have been viewed as separate, alternative routes to persuasion. In a given situation, a person was hypothesized to be influenced by either one or the other. However, as demonstrated most clearly in the Unknown Candidate Experiment, heuristic cues can influence systematic processing. The same candidate description with identical information in it was interpreted quite differently by respondents receiving high- and low-popularity cues. From the perspective of political decision making, the systematic route has been routinely applauded, while the use of heuristic processing has cast severe doubts on the quality of citizens' decisions. The interdependence of these two modes suggests that it is not an either–or proposition. Information about the level of public support enjoyed by an issue or candidate is yet another piece of information that must be integrated with what the citizen knows about a given controversy. It is in the routine process of making sense of sometimes consistent, sometimes contradictory information that the citizen's views are influenced.

At its best, democratic decision making involves careful consideration of one's own and others' views – mentally mulling over the information one has accumulated, constructing and reconstructing various lines of argument, and weighing and rehashing arguments pro and con. In contrast, most situations in which impersonal influence occurs have been characterized as representing the polar opposite – contentless, empty-headed responses to sensationalized campaign news that needs to be restricted or outlawed. These studies suggest that impersonal influence processes are not all of one cloth; at the very least, they suggest that those quick to condemn mass feedback mechanisms such as primaries and poll results need to examine more closely the actual mechanisms both facilitating and restraining the effects of perceived opinion on political behavior. More often than not, responses to information about mass opinion may be mediated by the cognitive responses that individuals generate.

Upon reaching this conclusion, a natural question to ask is whether the social influence conveyed by polls and other mass feedback mechanisms is similar to that conveyed by friends and neighbors. Perhaps people respond to information about the views of mass others in much the same way that they respond to information about the views of those in their immediate social environments: "What should a reasonable citizen do when confronted with the fact that some person in his or her immediate social environment holds a divergent preference or opinion? . . . Under these conditions, a reassessment of whether his or her current candidate choice is the correct one would appear to be eminently reasonable and rational" (Huckfeldt and Sprague 1995: 49).

In interpersonal contexts, people do not automatically conform to the beliefs of a friend or acquaintance. Instead, they rationally reassess their own views in light of this new information (Huckfeldt and Sprague 1995). The cognitive response mechanism suggests that this same process can be stimulated by information about the views of mass, impersonal others. To the extent that cognitive response mechanisms account for impersonal influence, fears of massive impact may be unfounded since effects are constrained by the availability and persuasiveness of existing arguments for and against candidates or issue positions. Moreover, voters' age-old fascination with learning about others' views may even serve a valuable purpose by stimulating greater political thought.

PART IV

CONCLUSION

9

Impersonal Influence and the Mass Society Tradition

The term "mass society" has fallen out of usage.[1] Nonetheless, the basic tenets of mass society theory are alive and well as we approach the twenty-first century. For example, the recent work of Robert Putnam (1995) argues that television has caused both a decline in civic involvement and a decrease in the extent to which people trust one another. Although evidence of these claims remains ambiguous to date,[2] both arguments are clearly within the mass society tradition; mass media are conceptualized as displacing close-knit interpersonal networks and thus producing an alienated public. Likewise, concerns surrounding "stunted public discourse" and the need to revitalize public deliberation (e.g., Fishkin 1991, 1995) testify to the perseverance of these same themes in contemporary political theory. Recent books by Lasch (1995) and Elshtain (1995) also posit that conversation is a thing of the past, and that "the death of public discourse" is imminent. Democracy is said to have a future only if "citizens come back out of their bunkers and start talk-

---

1 Neuman (1991) documented the precipitous drop in use of this term in the 1980s and 1990s using the Social Science Citation Index. In this piece, he also traces the history of the influential mass society tradition and outlines several theories for its disappearance.

2 Evidence is inconclusive on several counts. First, the "decline" that Putnam suggests is not a decline in the absolute number of voluntary groups individuals belong to according to the General Social Survey (GSS) data. Instead, it is the absence of the *increase* that one might have expected based on the increased educational levels that have occurred over this historical period. Based on GSS data, the absolute number of groups people belong to has not changed significantly over time. Second, evidence tying television to this trend in either correlational or causal fashion is still lacking (Norris 1996; Ladd 1996). Still other critiques have focused on whether those same measures of voluntary association remain as appropriate today as when originally formulated given changing repertoires for collective action. Although evidence based on measures of interpersonal trust show some evidence of decline (but see Smith 1996 for problems with these comparisons), efforts to causally link such feelings with television usage have not proven successful (Potter 1991).

ing" (Gray 1995: 1). Political observers readily view the past as an era in which the public actively informed itself and talked endlessly about political topics on a day-to-day basis (e.g. Bloom 1987). Likewise, the burgeoning collection of studies of social capital call for reinvigorating face-to-face associations and promoting denser interpersonal networks of mutual trust as the key to democratic success. While these are certainly worthy goals, the general argument being made by advocates of social capital is surprisingly similar to the one advanced by mass society theorists at mid-century.

Mass society theory clearly lives on in spirit if not in name. There are many variations on this theme, but its central tenets have remained consistent: Revolutions in transportation and communication have brought once geographically disparate people into contact with one another, thus forming a new kind of social relationship. The old primary group ties to family and local community have been displaced by supralocal affiliations. Modern life has destroyed important social bonds and produced alienated, atomized individuals who are at the mercy of agents of mass persuasion. Since people no longer have interpersonal relationships to serve as buffers between themselves and the information espoused by the powerful national media, they inevitably fall prey to the false consciousness that it promotes.

Although writers are typically vague about when, precisely, things were so much better, the question remains an important one. The answers are not as clear as the rhetoric might have us believe (see, e.g., Schudson 1992). In the heyday of mass society research, most social scientists ultimately rejected the idea that *gemeinschaft* and *gesellschaft* represented temporally sequential phases in American history. But the central themes of mass society theory – the eclipse of community and rise of impersonal associations – have reemerged nonetheless. Indeed, the widespread popular appeal of theories such as Putnam's testify to just how closely the mass society tenets jibe with people's understanding of contemporary society. The lingering spirit of mass society theory is also evident in widespread nostalgia for a past state of affairs that is generally assumed to have been preferable to the current one. Themes emphasizing community decay and deterioration have little trouble finding sympathetic audiences today. The vogue of inexorable decline that served as the centerpiece of mass society theory now echoes throughout foundation initiatives, popular books and articles, and political commentary, as well as in academe.

It is tempting to interpret the historical transitions described in Chapter 2 and the consequences documented in subsequent chapters within this same mass society framework: Mass media have displaced personal relationships, leaving people susceptible to a new, more powerful and centralized reference group in the form of mediated representations of mass collectives. Distorted perceptions of the state of the collective damage accountability and produce greater susceptibility to domination by a centralized authority. As suggested by the analyses in previous chapters, a close examination of the mechanisms underlying processes of impersonal influence suggests that this interpretation is probably a mistake. While the role of perceptions of mass collectives in forming political attitudes poses some obvious risks, a fuller examination illuminates the extent to which it may serve as a boon to democratic accountability as well.

In this chapter, I use mass society theory as a theoretical framework for explicating what impersonal influence suggests about the nature of social influences on political attitudes and behaviors in twentieth- and perhaps twenty-first-century America.[3] Mass society theory has had no shortage of critics, and this at least partially explains the modified vocabulary that is now used to describe these very same phenomena. Unfortunately, its many shortcomings have largely obscured the extent to which the theory focused attention on important changes in the nature of social influence. What mass society theory got right was that these were tremendous social transformations with significant consequences for social and political behavior. But what it got wrong was equally as important in misdirecting both research attention and public concern. Mass society theory was correct in its identification of some of the potential dangers of these historical trends; however, by focusing on one type of social influence at the expense of others, it directed attention away from the type of social influence most affected by these changes.

After discussing the implications of these historical shifts for different forms of social influence, I attempt to provide a more balanced view of impersonal influence than has previously been offered, one that simultaneously acknowledges the risks, as well as the benefits, that it poses for democratic accountability.

---

3 Characterizing mass society theory is inevitably difficult because there are so many variations of it. Kornhauser (1959: 23) identified aristocratic and democratic critics of mass society who differed on fundamental issues: "One sees mass society as a set of conditions under which elites are exposed to mass pressures. The other conceives of mass society as a set of conditions under which non-elites are exposed to elite pressures. Nevertheless, they share a common image of mass society as the naked society, where the direct exposure of social units to outside forces makes freedom precarious." Regardless of outlook, they also share several central themes, including growing atomization and the loss of community; the rise of centralized, national media; widespread readiness of the mass public to embrace new ideologies in their quest for community; and eventual domination by the pseudocommunity in the form of loyalty to a totalitarian regime.

Conclusion

THE EVOLUTION OF SOCIAL INFLUENCE

Impersonal influence does not portend social determinism either from mass media or from the influence of interpersonal communication. Mass media may alter people's perceptions of others' experiences or viewpoints, but this does not result in citizens who blindly follow mass opinion or whose views of reality are shaped exclusively by what they read in the paper. Instead, as detailed in the empirical studies, both people's personal preferences and experiences *and* their perceptions of the impersonal world enter into the judgments they make; it is not an either–or proposition. Media play a particularly important role in shaping impersonal perceptions, and impersonal perceptions, in turn, play a particularly important role in shaping political judgments. Nonetheless, citizens are not necessarily doomed to excessive conformity or to puppetlike manipulation at the hands of those who control media content. These conclusions are consistent with contemporary research on the influence of interpersonal social relationships on political attitudes (Huckfeldt and Sprague 1995), as well as with what Asch actually found in his original conformity experiments back in the 1950s. The normative social influence conveyed by interpersonal political discussion is obviously important, but the American public also demonstrates a great deal of independence, even in face-to-face settings.

Widespread claims about the collapse of community imply that normative social influence has been on the wane throughout this century. Although social networks have become increasingly independent of geography, American social history suggests that *gesellschaft* has not displaced *gemeinschaft* so much as it has added another dimension of experience on top of it (Bender 1978). In other words, Americans are, and probably always have been, concerned with what their friends, neighbors, and acquaintances think of them, and these relationships continue to influence the formation of their political views. *Gemeinschaft* and *gesellschaft* do not refer to the past and the present so much as to two different kinds of social relations that persist in parallel.

Nonetheless, many accounts of these historical transitions imply that the rise of an industrialized, mass-mediated society has necessarily produced a decrease in the total amount of social influence operating on its citizens. Since the emergence of mass society theory, social theorists have generally assumed a trade-off between population size and the degree of social control (Beniger 1987). Interpersonal communication in small communities supposedly affords a high degree of social control, while mass communication networks linking large populations produce considerably less control (Tönnies 1940; Fromm 1941); in fact, so much less social control is produced that it has been invoked to explain crime rates and a host of other public pathologies. This assumption has been one of the least challenged lynchpins of mass society theory, and it is an assumption that continues to be made today. Despite prevalent criticism of mass society theory on a host of other fronts, its claims about the extent of social influence now have the status of self-evident truths (Beniger 1987). A decline in the frequency of interpersonal contact among alienated, atomized individuals presumably translates into less social influence and social control in contemporary society.

In order to understand why such a claim does not necessarily hold true, it is useful to return to the distinction between different forms of social influence. *Normative* social influence refers to "an influence to conform with the positive expectations of others"; in other words, to take a position that will lead others to have positive feelings toward a person, rather than a position that leads to disapproval or social approbation (Deutsch and Gerard 1955: 629). *Informational* social influence, on the other hand, refers to "an influence to accept information obtained from another as evidence about reality." So even when people have no motivation to be positively regarded by others, they may still be influenced by others' judgments because those judgments are "taken to be a more or less trustworthy source of information about the objective reality with which he and the others are confronted" (Deutsch and Gerard 1955: 635).

Mass communication networks in large-scale societies are not capable of the same degree of normative social influence as interpersonal networks in small communities. Without the social pressure created by face-to-face contact and the knowledge of others as concrete individuals, there can be little or no approval or punishment for holding particular views. In the political context, this is especially noteworthy because people tend to dislike face-to-face political disagreements (MacKuen 1990; Lane 1965). In fact, the most common reason people give for not engaging in political conversation is that such interactions can become unpleasant and disturb personal relationships (Almond and Verba 1963). Normative social influence is clearly alive and well in the realm of face-to-face political discussions.

One might assume that mass media, because of its impersonal nature, would have little bearing one way or the other on explicitly *social* influence processes. Indeed, most conceptualizations of media power focus on its ability to persuade people to hold particular views by virtue of the type or amount of information it provides on matters of public controversy. Likewise, the concern of mass society theorists was that media, in the hands of unscrupulous leadership, could be used to indoctrinate the public through propaganda promoting its positions. This type of mass persuasion has little to do with *social* influence, thus mass media

Conclusion

were seen as having little bearing on issues involving social pressure and social influence processes.

Such a conclusion would be premature, however. Although mass media have a very limited capacity to exert normative social influence on the behaviors or attitudes of individual citizens, the increased complexity of contemporary social problems has combined with the increased availability of information about impersonal others to create a much greater potential for informational forms of social influence to be promulgated by mass media. A fundamental problem with mass society theory was that it depicted mass media and interpersonal communication as opposing forces; it did not take into account the fact that media were, in a sense, a social environment with a unique capacity for social influence outside of the traditional mechanisms of normative conformity.

THE INCREASING IMPORTANCE OF EXPERTISE

When people make judgments about collectives beyond the realm of their own life experiences, they are forced to rely on knowledge obtained from others. The trustworthiness of interpersonal relationships might make friends and acquaintances a likely source to turn to. But a second dimension of credibility – expertise – is equally, if not more, important in judging information about collective opinion and experience: "The mass media, while perhaps remote in comparison with one's usual interpersonal contacts, possess greater expertise on most topics than most individual sources; it is, after all, the business of many media institutions to gather, check out, edit, and present information that people otherwise would not have available (Chaffee and Mutz 1988: 31). And while bias certainly exists in media content, it is far more pronounced in individuals. For example, in a recent replication of the Erie County Study, interpersonal sources were judged overwhelmingly biased as sources of information about a hotly contested race (Finn 1987).

The complexity of the tasks facing citizens who are involved in the political process means that it is increasingly likely that they will rely on media expertise for information serving as the basis of many of their decisions. One might assume that the rising centralization of American government would simplify the life of the citizen decision maker. Most versions of mass society theory suggest precisely this: Either by means of total withdrawal from political involvement, or by enthusiastically embracing an overarching ideological movement, citizens greatly simplify their role in the political process. The prediction of simplification made some sense based on other trends as well: As the number of local governments declined and larger entities took over many of their responsibilities, this might logically have streamlined the process of fig-

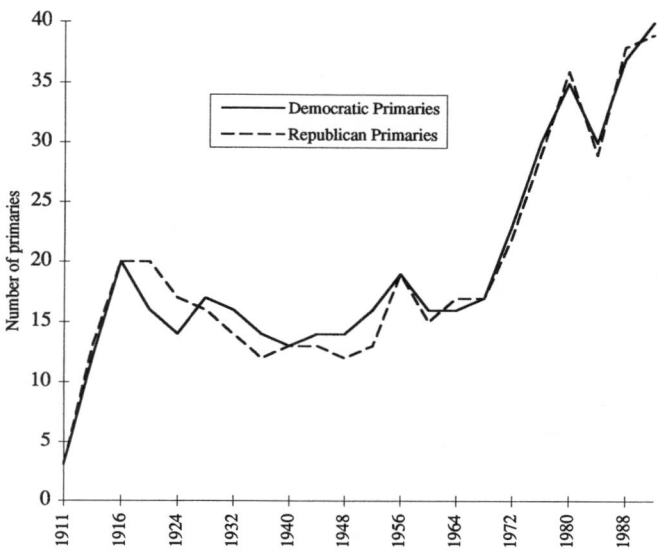

Figure 9.1. Increase in number of direct presidential primaries.
Source: Data are from Jackson and Crotty (1996).

uring out which side of an issue to endorse or whom to support for which office. If power and responsibility are more concentrated at one level of government, then one has fewer levels on which to focus attention in order to decide who is responsible for what.

However, if anything, contemporary voters are asked to make more political decisions than ever before. Changes during two key historical periods account for most of the increased demands on citizens. At the beginning of this century, the Progressive movement successfully championed greater citizen involvement in political decision making at a variety of levels. In addition to extending suffrage, the direct election of senators also was established in 1913. Again in the 1960s and 1970s, reform efforts aimed at increasing direct citizen participation succeeded in expanding citizens' opportunities.

One major reform responsible for extending citizen decision making was the direct primary election. As illustrated in Figure 9.1, many states adopted direct primaries during the Progressive era. Later, in the 1970s, an even steeper increase occurred in the number of direct presidential primaries, as well as the percentage of delegates selected in this manner. The rising importance of direct primaries clearly placed more decisions in the hands of the American voter. This century also has marked a tremendous increase in the number of states allowing citizens to vote on

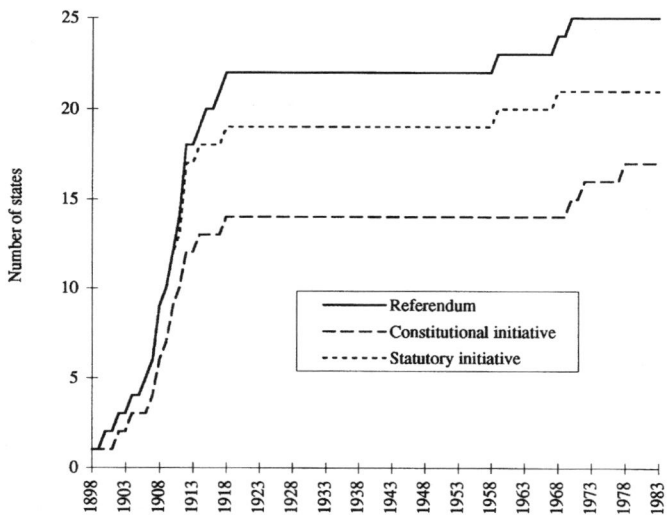

Figure 9.2. Increase in number of states allowing direct legislation. *Source*: Magleby (1984).

referenda and ballot initiatives. Figure 9.2 shows that this pattern roughly corresponds to the one for presidential primaries: There is a sharp increase in the first twenty years of the century and then again in the 1960s and 1970s.

In addition to voting on specific candidates and public policies, today's citizen also has more policy issues on which he or she might potentially form opinions. If one looks simply at those issues that make it as far as being introduced in Congress, it is an overwhelmingly large number, so great that no voter could reasonably be expected to have opinions on all of them, let alone well-informed views. The sheer number of congressional bills considered by each individual Congress now regularly runs over ten thousand, compared with only one or two thousand before the mid-nineteenth century. Given limited public capacity to process information, a smaller proportion of these bills now catches the public eye, and even fewer are familiar in much detail. As the federal government and its programs have increased in size and complexity, social problems and political issues also have become more intricate and perplexing for the electorate. The issues faced by the recent Clinton administration serve as prototypical examples: Health care, the budget deficit, and welfare reform are exceedingly complex issues in which few lay citizens have extensive expertise.

Avenues for direct participation obviously extend greater opportunities for citizen participation, but they also pose informational burdens: More people have more decisions about which to make up their minds. The size of this task is insurmountable for even the most conscientious citizen. For this reason, people desperately need shortcuts to help them make political decisions without optimal levels of information. As they rely less on political parties, something else must help fill this void. The imagined communities of impersonal influence provide some such guidance.

Reliance on others' opinions is one shortcut to opinion formation that is now readily available in most political settings. It is clearly not the only one (see e.g., Sniderman, Brody, and Tetlock 1991), but it is a reasonably sensible one given the impossibility of acquiring and processing huge amounts of information in the course of day-to-day life. People's fundamental lack of information about the world beyond their personal experiences and contacts leads them to rely on media coverage for information about the state of collective affairs because it is likely to be more accurate than personal experience. Likewise, they sometimes rely on others' views in forming political opinions either because they lack adequate information themselves or because others' views cause them to question their own judgment. Since others may know something they do not, it is worth reconsidering. When people rely on what they know of others' experiences, it is a rational strategy for assessing the state of a collective that quite logically seems far beyond the reaches of their own personal experiences.

Erich Fromm, one of the best-known writers in the mass society tradition, provides an example that illuminates just how much we now take for granted the idea that others have information we ourselves lack. He contrasts the efforts of a local fisherman and a city dweller, both asked to predict the next day's weather. When asked to forecast,

[T]he fisherman, with his long experience and concern with this problem of weather, will start thinking. . . . Knowing what the direction of the wind, temperature, humidity and so on mean as a basis for weather forecast, he will weigh the different factors according to their respective significance and come to a more or less definite judgment. He will probably remember the radio forecast and quote it as supporting or contradicting his own opinion. If it is contradictory, he may be particularly careful in weighing the reasons for his opinion; but, and this is the essential point, it is *his* opinion, the result of *his* thinking which he tells us (Fromm 1941: 191).

According to Fromm, the city dweller, on the other hand, believes he knows a great deal about the next day's weather even though he really does not. He thinks for a minute and gives us an opinion that is a simple parroting of the radio forecast. The fisherman, who forms an opinion on the basis of his own immediate verifiable experience, is contrasted in a positive light to the city dweller, who has simply accepted the media version of reality. According to Fromm, the city dweller has fallen prey to "pseudo-thinking," one of the principal perils of mass society.

Fromm's outdated example illuminates the extent to which expertise has come to play an increasingly important role in contemporary affairs, political and otherwise. Few today find it intuitively obvious why the fisherman is claimed to have a better grasp on reality than the city dweller. Professional weather predictors have access to sophisticated equipment that usually gives them more and better information than the casual observations of most individuals, fisher people or not. When one wants to know the next's day's weather, is it more sensible to pay attention to mass media or to stick one's finger in the wind?

Even by the standards of 1941, there are central problems with this analogy that Fromm does not address. First, we are not all fishermen and many, if not most, of us, do not have experience with weather prediction. Even in Fromm's era, many people had little access to weather cues in the course of their day-to-day experience. Thus, relying exclusively on personal experience could make decision making both burdensome and highly inaccurate. Moreover, even those who have had relevant personal experiences may lack the expertise to integrate and interpret that information.

In a recent effort to revive the idea that economic accountability flows through personal experiences rather than mass-mediated ones, one study similarly argues that "The economy is like the weather. To find out how warm it is, how strong the wind is blowing, or whether it is raining, we do not have to turn on our television sets" (Haller and Norpoth 1995: 4). These authors have an excellent point if we are talking about the economy within a small radius of our homes and work places. Signs of local economic distress should certainly be visible. But when judging the state of a collective as large as the nation as a whole, this analogy quickly breaks down. The observations and personal experiences of a person in Ohio tell her little about the economy in California, just as the fisherman in Rhode Island will have few experiences or observations on which to base predictions or even retrospective reports on the weather in Utah.

Technical expertise has become an increasingly important part of understanding many political and social issues. The overwhelming complexity of current political affairs has left people eager for alternative bases for forming political views. To the extent that social influence poses a danger to twentieth- and twenty-first-century America, it is in the form of increased informational social influence and not greater normative social influence. For a public both wary and weary of bias, skeptical of politicians, and overburdened with political decisions, information about the opinions and experiences of others provides valuable cues for purposes of forming political views. Unlike mass society theory, impersonal influence does not require an all-powerful media capable of bending public opinion to its will. That too would be inconsistent with the available evidence. Instead, impersonal influence points to the impact of media that flows from media's capacity to convey information about that state of the larger society or "imagined community" outside the realm of personal experience.

THE DISJUNCTURE BETWEEN PERSONAL AND POLITICAL WORLDS

Although the apocalyptic predictions of mass society theory have not materialized, impersonal influence has not been without its negative consequences. As early as 1927, John Dewey recognized the potential for a large-scale society to render its citizens confused and detached:

The confusion which has resulted from the size and ramifications of social activities has rendered men skeptical of the efficiency of political action. Who is sufficient unto these things? Men feel that they are caught in the sweep of forces too vast to understand or master. Thought is brought to a standstill and action paralyzed. Even the specialist finds it difficult to trace the chain of "cause and effect" (Dewey 1927: 135).

If Dewey found political affairs complicated in the 1920s, one can only imagine how complex and distant the large-scale society of contemporary America would seem. The staggering informational demands of the contemporary democratic system naturally lead to consequences beyond simply an increased role for impersonal social influence.

It is important to underscore the difference between what Dewey described and the kind of alienation characterized in descriptions of mass society. What impersonal influence and the rise of national media systems have *not* necessarily done is to produce a sense of interpersonal estrangement. People do not necessarily feel alienated and atomized from one another as a result of the rise of mass media; in fact, through mass media they now share a great deal with a great number of people even though they may be physically separated by great distances. When people are exposed to information and entertainment that they know others are exposed to as well, they share a common psychological reality that not only facilitates impersonal forms of social influence, but also makes them feel closer to distant others. As Schudson (1995: 25) notes, "That you and I read the same front page or see the same television news as the president of the United States and the chair of IBM is empowering; the impression it promotes of equality and commonality, illusion though it is, sustains a hope of democratic life."

Mass media occasionally make it possible to achieve social integration of the highest order. What Dayan and Katz (1992: 48, 53) refer to as the "high holidays of mass communication" include large-scale media events such as the Super Bowl, the first moon landing, the Olympics, or the Watergate trials. What is important about these occasions is that they draw people together to view historical events in progress, they "reawaken a sense of collectivity" and "connect people not only to one another but to values and beliefs that are central to the society": "These events call a nation together to sit down and be counted. They have caused people to dress up, rather than undress, to view television. They have brought friends and neighbors into the living room to watch together because one wants real people, not just the furniture, to share the experience" (Dayan and Katz 1992: 48).

For a media event to meet all of the specifications for a "high holiday" – enormous audiences that watch events in groups in real time – is relatively rare. But to facilitate impersonal influence, it is not necessary that audiences be physically together or that they all watch the same thing at the same time. What is central for impersonal influence is far easier to come by: not that all people have the same simultaneous perception of the world out there, but rather that they have such perceptions at all and that these perceptions are more than projections of their immediate life space and experiences. For these purposes it matters not whether the event is simulcast or delayed, or whether people gather physically at the time of a broadcast.

Exposure to a common, mediated political culture also gives citizens a common political language with which to discuss political issues. In this respect the changes I have outlined make political communication easier: We all speak roughly the same political language. Arguments about political issues tend to be familiar and well scripted: "A symbolic phrase or two – a reference here or there to the 'welfare mess,' to mention only one example – can call to mind a whole line of argument" (Mutz , Sniderman, and Brody 1996: 5).

Instead of sundering social bonds, these historical changes have added a new kind of social relationship, one in which people are connected to one another in abstract, impersonal ways. If not the totalitarianism predicted by mass society theory, what are the consequences of these changes? The studies in this book suggest that they have led to a compartmentalization or disjuncture between the worlds of politics and personal experience. The primary impact of these trends has been to produce a bifurcation of the private and political worlds that is very difficult for American citizens to overcome (Bender 1978). The public sphere has not disappeared or disintegrated so much as it has moved further away from the day-to-day lives of most Americans. In the political context, in particular, this shift has induced important changes in how people think about politics and in how they connect their personal lives to the political world. Just as Riesman and Glazer (1954: 495) suggested, people in modern society

> can see no relation between their political opinions and the actual course of political life. . . . On the contrary, the obscurity and remoteness of the more decisive national and international political happenings, the general feeling that instead of "we" (the common people), it is some alien "they" (the distant powers) who manage events (among those social groups who assume events to be manageable at all) – these developments have made politics an anxious and frustrating topic.

Mass society theory quite accurately pointed to the implications of the increased distance between the government and the governed: "There are far fewer positions from which the major structural connections between various activities can be perceived, and fewer men can reach these vantage points" (Mannheim 1940: 59). In his classic treatise on the politics of mass society, Kornhauser (1959: 94) described the situation as one in which people cannot understand the workings of the overall system, in part because "increasing distance between centers of decision and daily life make it more difficult for people to grasp the meaning of issues at stake. Faced with the impersonality and incomprehensibility of national relations, . . . the individual may withdraw from participation in the larger society." Impersonality is inevitable when government is remote and large scale. But it is not withdrawal from participation that inevitably results. After all, people were equally, if not more, withdrawn from political life in colonial America compared with today.

Instead, the compartmentalization of the personal and political worlds simply leaves people at a loss as to how to grasp the workings of such a distant, large-scale organization. It leaves them feeling as if they know less because the system now requires that they know more and that this information be of a fundamentally different kind – abstract information beyond the realm of their day-to-day experiences. Paradoxically, efforts to increase public involvement in political decisions may have helped produce a public that feels more removed. Even as the Progressive movement introduced things like the referendum, direct election of senators, and popular primaries and gave women the franchise, "somehow the popular control of government seemed farther away than ever. . . . In economic as well as political life, the public appeared more removed from decision making at exactly that time that, formally, it was more involved" (Schudson 1978: 131).

Proponents of mass society theory were insightful in identifying feelings of alienation as an important consequence of a large-scale industrialized society, but they erred in locating that alienation exclusively at the interpersonal level rather than where it is actually most pronounced – in the feelings people have about the distant, large-scale institutions of

Conclusion

government. The widespread negativity toward government and large-scale institutions more generally (see e.g., Lipset and Schneider 1983) has been widely documented and decried. But these same feelings of distrust are curiously uncorrelated with lower levels of citizen participation (Teixeira 1987; Sniderman 1981). While many factors have no doubt contributed to lower levels of political trust in the United States (e.g., Citrin 1974), few analyses have focused on the most obvious reason: that it may be an inevitable consequence of an extremely large, highly industrialized society (Gorz 1982).

CONFORMITY AND THE COMMUNITARIAN SOLUTION

One commonly offered solution to the problematic psychological disjuncture that large-scale societies erect between people and government is exemplified by communitarian approaches that emphasize renewing local community politics and institutions (Barber 1984; Bellah et al. 1985). If large scale is the problem, then small scale must be the solution. Recently a burgeoning number of advocates have proposed improving links between government and public by advocating a "town meeting" style of democracy. For example, the "National Conversation" sponsored by the National Endowment for the Humanities proposes to reinvigorate public deliberation through a series of face-to-face meetings involving citizens who gather to discuss their concerns and possible solutions to them. Likewise, a project sponsored by The American Civic Forum seeks to "renew citizenship" by "recaptur[ing] the vibrant middle ground of civil society, where citizens can associate voluntarily yet think publicly and are thereby empowered to solve public problems themselves" (American Civic Forum 1994: 1).

While these efforts are certainly admirable, they are, for a variety of reasons, unlikely to provide solutions to the bifurcated perspective on politics experienced by many citizens. For one, as Bender (1978) suggests, they often impute the notion of community into various contexts on the assumption that any locality-based social interaction constitutes community, regardless of the quality of the relationships involved. This practice "markets the illusion of community while evading the realities of modern social life. Among its disadvantages for our common life is its encouragement of an unspecified feeling of loss and emptiness that in turn makes Americans vulnerable to the manipulation of symbols of community – whether in political rhetoric or in advertising copy" (Bender 1978: 144). People obviously do not have "relationships" with mass collectives, and thus there is no pretense of having imagined communities of the mind stand in for real communities. But neither can specially planned meetings transport us back to the small New England town or the Greek polis.

Although communitarian movements can certainly complement politics anchored in large-scale, mediated discourse, they are "fundamentally limited by the mismatch between their local bases and large scale system integration": "It is almost impossible to see the manifold ways in which human actions create large scale markets, for example, and certainly to understand complex economic processes on the basis simply of aggregation upward from those specific relationships of buying, selling, making, using, etc." (Calhoun 1988: 223). In theory, involvement in local politics is supposed to provide the core civic education of democratic citizens. But in practice, attending meetings of the local school board gives one little insight into the extent or complexity of large-scale social problems. Even with increased local involvement, national political institutions will continue to seem remote and unresponsive to individual needs, and most experiences at the local level will not render them comprehensible and approachable. Increased local political involvement is obviously a worthy goal in itself, and it may well increase the efficacy with which people approach local government, but it will not enable them to easily connect their own experiences to the activities of government at the national level. As Calhoun (1988: 223-4) suggests, these large, bewildering institutions "can be grasped well only through statistics, theories, cybernetic concepts and other intellectual tools which are both poorly distributed among the population, and also at odds with the direct understanding which people gain of their immediate surroundings. The lifeworld, by contrast, can be understood intuitively; it is a 'lived reality,' not an abstraction."

Communities represent a level of judgment in between the personal and the national that might logically serve as the essential link promoting accountability between people's everyday lives and experiences and national political institutions. Similarly, they might help to bridge the disjuncture that makes politics and politicians seem alien, remote, and untrustworthy to most members of the public. Unfortunately, national and international affairs cannot be understood by analogy to local community activities, despite contemporary rhetoric to the contrary. As Castells (1983: 331) suggests, "when people find themselves unable to control the world, they simply shrink the world to the size of their community." Appeals to this kind of sentiment are now commonplace. Ross Perot reassuringly promised that running the country and solving its many problems was no different from running a business or, better yet, taking a look under the hood of the car to tune up a carburetor. Similarly, Reagan comforted us by suggesting that the seeming complexity of balancing the federal budget was really as simple as balancing the family checkbook (Calhoun 1988).

Even if it were possible for people to grasp national-level activities from face-to-face involvement in local community politics, these modes of political activity alone would do little to enhance the accountability of national political actors. The decisions affecting citizens are now increasingly made by holders of large capital and national, rather than local, power. Repertoires for collective action have changed to reflect shifts in the concentration of power and capital toward national-level organizations (Tilly 1983: 468). Instead of appealing to local and immediately available power holders, the forms of collective action most often employed today involve activities that lend themselves easily to coordination among many localities. For example, whereas in the past, collective action might involve sacking the private residence of a wrongdoer, today it is more likely to involve action in a visible public place, perhaps with petitions directed at holding a distant national actor responsible. In this sense, even local, face-to-face political activity is now more national in scope. Strikes, demonstrations, and rallies are now deliberately constructed to attract the attention of national leaders, often through media, whereas comparable activities in the previous century were intended to be seen and heard only by those immediately present. Local involvement is ideally supposed to familiarize citizens with the mechanics of government, to "help the ordinary citizen to see how the processes function in limited circumstances" (Laumann 1973: 135). But strategies for collective action have quite logically followed the locus of power, and thus self-consciously local, face-to-face groups provide less effective schooling on influencing national political affairs.

A community-centered model of accountability also holds the potential to systematically disadvantage poorer, less-privileged communities. For those who are well-off, community involvement and local political activism may sometimes provide effective channels of influence and access to political power at higher levels. However, people in poor communities are less likely to have such connections, and as a result, their demands are even less likely to be heard (Bender 1978).

Last, but not least, a major difficulty with the communitarian solution stems from structural changes that have conspired to further limit this approach's capacity to successfully address the problems of accountability and psychological distance. In particular, changes in patterns of community formation have led to increasing sociospatial segmentation by lifestyle choice and socioeconomic position. This "demographic balkanization" (Frey 1995) has limited direct interpersonal relationships increasingly to similar individuals. In communities of this kind, the inherent dangers of the communitarian model are greatly exacerbated. Although mass society theory has contributed to a widespread tendency to romanticize all things small scale and local in orientation, local norms are not necessarily good or tolerant norms. The federal government has been able to accomplish many things – such as changing the treatment of African Americans – precisely by overriding the social norms of many local communities.

The communitarian model limits the potential for rising informational conformity since the politics of what is close to home will be less baffling and more comprehensible than politics of a large-scale nation. Citizens will not be at the mercy of experts, nor are they likely to make extensive use of cues involving mass opinion. But there is a clear trade-off involved between the extent of normative and informational conformity pressures. The homogeneity of local communities undoubtedly contributes to an enhanced potential for normative social influence. As Blau (1974: 623) has noted, "The attenuation of profound social bonds that firmly integrate individuals in their communities is often deplored. But strong in-group bonds restrain individual freedom and mobility, and they sustain rigidity and bigotry. Diverse intergroup relations, though not intimate, broaden horizons and promote tolerance and they are the basis of macro-social integration."

In short, there is no way to turn back the clock. In a large-scale society, the renewal of local community politics will not serve as a substitute for representative political institutions and mediated public discourse at the national level:

Community strength and local involvement, though powerful bases for mobilization, do not constitute adequate bases for democracy. Democracy must depend also on the kind of public life which flourished in cities, not as the direct extension of communal bonds, but as the outgrowth of social practices which continually brought different sorts of people into contact with each other, and which gave them adequate bases for understanding each other and managing boundary crossing relations (Calhoun 1988: 227).

The limitations of communitarian approaches are simply too great to overcome the trends in large-scale societal integration. Community politics is valuable in its own right, but it is quite limited in its ability to address this particular set of problems.

IMPERSONAL POLITICS AND DEMOCRATIC ACCOUNTABILITY

The dramatic historical metaphor outlined by mass society theory continues to color interpretations of situations in which impersonal influence occurs. The prevailing wisdom has been that attention to widespread others' views is antithetical to the democratic spirit; likewise,

Conclusion

reliance on perceptions of collective experience rather than on well-grounded personal or local experience is implicitly assumed to harm the quality of political decisions. All of the attention focusing on how media often do a very poor job of accurately reporting the state of collective affairs has tended to obscure the extent to which impersonal influence processes are absolutely essential to the functioning of a large-scale democracy. In other words, even if it were possible to eliminate all forms of impersonal influence, we would not be well advised to do so. In a large-scale democracy, impersonal influence serves important functions despite its inherent risks. The case for the beneficial impact of impersonal influence is somewhat different for perceptions of collective opinion and perceptions of collective experience, so I address these two issues in turn.

Accountability and the Collective Experiences of Others

People appear to rely heavily on perceptions of collective experience in forming political judgments. Past treatments of this phenomenon have focused on the very real accountability risks such sociotropism poses. Since people's perceptions may not accurately reflect the collective reality, they may not hold political leaders accountable for the effects of their past or future policies. However, the alternative bases of accountability are even more bleak. Because judgments made about one's personal life and experiences tend to be systematically biased, they are not the panacea often hoped for. Encouraging a politics rooted in personal experience may sound appealing, but as documented in Chapter 4, aggregated personal judgments do not ensure accuracy and accountability either. Conceiving of problems in private terms can limit effective public action (Warner 1968). Moreover, judgments at the level of the community incorporate a similar positivity bias and serve as a poor substitute for accurate judgments of the larger collective.

The accountability of leaders of large-scale geographical areas depends crucially on media. But media's role in this process is complex because they can function in two different capacities, each with different consequences for accountability. On the one hand, mass media coverage of social trends can encourage accurate perceptions of social conditions. This is obviously a valuable function for mass media to serve, especially when citizens are relying primarily on social-level perceptions as a basis for political decisions.

On the other hand, as discussed in Chapter 5, mass media may at times serve as an obstacle to the politicization of personal experiences by providing a steady flow of information that establishes in people's minds a social world beyond personal experiences and interpersonal contacts. Widening the gap between personal and social judgments is dysfunctional to the extent that people's social perceptions become independent of their aggregated personal experiences, and democratic accountability breaks down. Those who do not have accurate perceptions of social conditions may punish politicians for problems that have not truly occurred or reward them for improvements that have no basis in collective individual realities.

In combination, these observations point to a decidedly different normative evaluation of the sociotropic basis of political judgments. Perceptions of collective experience may well be a manipulable basis for political judgments, but they are probably the best of the possible alternatives. Interestingly, mass society theory characterized national media systems as the antithesis of democratic accountability: They were essentially handmaidens to the rise of a totalitarian state. In contrast, impersonal influence suggests that a well-developed national media system is an essential component of maintaining democratic accountability in a large-scale society. Without it, people's perceptions of the collective could not realistically be expected to reflect national-level realities, and leaders could not be held adequately accountable. This is not to suggest that media currently provide an accurate ongoing portrait of collective affairs. In fact, the empirical examples detailed throughout the book suggest this is often not the case. Nonetheless, due to a lack of alternative routes to political accountability, mass media provide the greatest potential for making such a system work.

Ultimately, accountability problems arise when media either help to create or fail to dispel situations in which people share erroneous cognitive beliefs about others' opinions or experiences. Social psychologists refer to a situation in which people share false ideas about the state of the social world as a state of "pluralistic ignorance." Pluralistic ignorance is not used to refer to the personal distortions a given individual may make in perceiving others due to individual cognitive bias, but instead suggests that a number of people share the *same* cognitive error in a systematic direction.

Psychologists originally explored this ubiquitous phenomenon by focusing on people's perceptions of other groups (such as church congregations) that they knew from face-to-face interactions. Their underlying concern centered on the extent to which these false beliefs had the power to inspire conformity to their (falsely perceived) expectations of others. But again, the emphasis on normative conformity overshadowed other processes by which a state of pluralistic ignorance about even highly impersonal others might influence individuals' judgments.

Studies of famine prevention efforts provide some particularly striking examples of the consequences of pluralistic ignorance when this notion is expanded to large-scale collectives such as whole nations. The Chinese famine of 1958–61 continued for three years and killed close to 30 million people without any public admission that it was occurring: "Not only was the world ignorant of the terrible state of affairs in China, even the population itself did not know about the extent of the national calamity and the extensive nature of the problems being faced in different parts of the country. . . . Indeed the lack of adversarial journalism and politics hurt even the government, reinforcing the ignorance of local conditions. . . . The pretence that everything was going all right in Chinese agriculture and rural economy to a great extent fooled the national leaders themselves" (Dreze and Sen 1989: 212–13).

Economists Dreze and Sen (1989) argue that many sub-Saharan African countries have experienced similar problems in responding to famine as a result of restrictions on the flow of accurate information. In contrast, African countries with open and largely uncensored presses have been more successful in their famine prevention efforts: "A free press contributes greatly to bringing out the information that can prevent famine such as facts about the early effects of droughts and floods, and about the nature and results of unemployment. . . . The most elementary source of basic information about a threatening famine is the news media, especially when there are incentives, which a democratic system provides, for revealing facts that may be embarrassing to the government, facts that an undemocratic regime would tend to censor" (Sen 1994: 34). Likewise, in post-independence India, the government cannot get away with neglecting prompt and extensive measures at the first signs of a famine: "And these signs are themselves more easily transmitted given India's relatively free media and newspapers, and the active and investigative role that journalists as well as opposition politicians can and do play in this field" (Dreze and Sen 1989: 212).

According to this view, a free press is the best possible insurance against pluralistic ignorance. While formal "early warning" systems based on complex economic predictions have proved to be of limited utility in preventing famines, "warnings of imminent dangers have tended to come from general reports of floods or droughts or economic dislocations and from newspaper coverage of early hardship and visible hunger" (Dreze and Sen 1989: 263). A relatively free press is the best early warning system that a country threatened by famine can possess. In fact, Sen concludes that "No substantial famine has ever occurred in a country with a democratic form of government and a relatively free press" (Sen 1994: 34).

The function of the press in these examples is more than simply disseminating non-parochial information and encouraging accurate perceptions of the state of a large collective. Its power lies partly in the fact that publication means not only that everyone knows, but also everyone knows that everyone knows, about a given state of affairs (Katz 1981). This awareness of widespread simultaneous reception adds significantly to the power of the press. Since the neglect of famine threats results not so much from lack of food or knowledge as from nonresponsive authorities, knowing that everyone else also knows puts pressure on political elites to do something in response. In other words, an elite version of impersonal influence operates wherein political leaders respond to their perceptions or anticipation of public outrage.

Can this same lesson be extended to other countries and issues? Does the press serve as an effective early warning system against potential social and economic disasters that the United States or other countries might face? Ultimately, the problem in extending this conclusion lies in the fact that even in countries with relatively free media like the United States, one cannot count on media to reliably convey impressions about the state of collective experience and opinion. For example, even within the narrow realm of hunger prevention, an adversarial press provides protection against some problems more than others. While India's press serves as an important and effective triggering mechanism to protect against famines, it provides much less protection against endemic undernutrition because "starvation deaths and extreme deprivation are newsworthy in a way the quiet persistence of regular hunger and nonextreme deprivation are not." Endemic hunger is "primarily a statistical picture rather than being immediately palpable and – no less importantly – being 'big news' " (Dreze and Sen 1989: 214).

News values are only one of a sizable list of factors that have the capacity to distort Americans' impressions of the state of their collective. As noted in the Indian example, problems that are widespread and common are, by virtue of those very facts, unlikely to receive tremendous news attention, and thus perceptions of their frequency may be greatly underestimated. In contrast, unusual events may receive disproportionate attention and thus inflate perceptions of the extent of a social problem (cf. Pritchard and Hughes 1997). For example, reporting on news and public affairs programs about a relatively small number of cases of sexual abuse by clergy members succeeded in establishing clergy sexual abuse as a severe problem in the minds of many members of the public (Jenkins 1995). More dramatic and more visual events or problems also tend to receive disproportionate attention because they make interesting narratives and/or pictures.

The bias toward event-centered coverage may shortchange social problems that do not stem from a simple news peg. In this respect, the trend toward "long journalism" documented in Chapter 2 may be quite welcome news. The greater length of articles, the greater emphasis on connecting events to one another, and the general increase in contextualization of events all suggest that contemporary news coverage is de-emphasizing individual events and paying increasing attention to portraying large-scale social phenomena over time. This emphasis on collectives, rather than individuals, and events that are linked to other similar events across times and places means that trends are more newsworthy than they used to be. Thus, news reporting is now capable of turning "mere statistics" into crises worthy of government attention.

Yet another problem stems from the fact that in all of the situations described above, some types of statistics are more likely to reach the press than others. In particular, government and special interest organizations with the resources to spoon-feed numbers to the press on a regular basis will have the upper hand in having their versions of collective reality relayed to citizens. Journalists' reliance on official government sources and their regular use of information drawn from press releases distributed with political motives in mind has been well documented over the years. The increased competition among news organizations only intensifies the commercial pressures that push news organizations in this direction. Moreover, even when reporters are given perfectly accurate information about the state of collective experience or opinion, often they do not have the training necessary to evaluate this information in an informed or critical way, or to sort the wheat from the chaff in terms of the kinds of statistical data they receive.

Distorted statistics are not the exclusive province of government or powerful special interest groups. For example, in recent fund-raising advertisements for a national organization to provide services to the homeless, an organization claimed that there were 27,000 homeless children in Sacramento, CA, when the true number was closer to 500. The inflated statistic was later justified on the grounds that the public's consciousness needed to be raised on this important issue. In other words, a good cause justifies hyperbole and exaggeration (Berger 1996). Similar post hoc claims were made to justify some widely publicized statistics on battered wives. Our national self-perceptions are regularly shaped by coverage of statistics that few reporters or citizens are capable of challenging based on their own knowledge. Statistical agencies enjoy an aura of professionalism in the United States that makes them difficult to challenge. Although that reputation is in some ways deserved, it overlooks the kinds of political judgments that inevitably enter into deciding what to measure and how to measure it (Alonso and Starr 1987).

Even when news coverage accurately portrays the collective experiences of the nation as a whole, errors in the way people process this information can skew the impressions they receive. The substantial literature on erroneous social assessments demonstrates that such perceptions are biased not only by people's own personal views, but also by a range of nonmotivational factors, such as bias in their sample of personal acquaintances, and factors that increase people's ability to recall, visualize, or imagine paradigmatic instances of behavior. As reviewed in previous chapters, these beliefs are often quite resilient to empirical challenges.

When it comes to promoting accountability for the effects that public policies have on collective experience, the negativity of the American press may be the lesser of two evils. In emphasizing bad news over good, it may inadvertently protect against overly optimistic personal and local sentiments by presenting a predominantly negative picture of ongoing affairs that ultimately serves as an early warning system to prevent those catastrophes from being realized. In some cases, that warning is probably unnecessary, but it may nonetheless serve an important preventative purpose. The problem is that it may also divert resources and elite attention from problems that are more deserving. Moreover, if our early warning system is, in effect, trigger-happy, then it may well lose its credibility by crying wolf one too many times. Nonetheless, because it is the *only* readily accessible ongoing source of general information about the state of the nation as a collective, it is not in imminent danger of losing its monopoly on this function.

Relying on the press to convey impressions of collective experience is clearly not an ideal arrangement. Nonetheless, it may be preferable to the personal tendency to see the world through rose-colored glasses. In addition, this path to accountability has the advantage of eliciting elite reaction more easily than a system that requires members of the public to individually or collectively pressure political elites for a response to their personal problems and concerns. The awareness that others are simultaneously aware of a given problem or condition may bring about an elite response without any extensive public reaction (e.g., Cook et al. 1983).[4]

Accountability and the Collective Opinions of Others

As with sociotropic politics, scholars and political observers have tended to look at the extent to which people are influenced by perceptions of others' views as yet another sign of what is wrong with our contemporary political system. Indeed, mechanisms such as the consensus heuristic pose obvious problems for the quality of citizen judgments and accountability of political leaders. To the extent that the trend toward a greater

---

4 Of course, this same preemptive elite reaction in anticipation of a public response could constitute a potential danger to accountability if the public truly does not want any elite action on behalf of a particular problem.

decision-making burden continues, use of the consensus heuristic could threaten the quality of democratic decision making. But evidence to date suggests that the consensus heuristic is limited to situations of *extremely* low information. The increased flow of information reaching today's citizens makes it increasingly unlikely that they will have absolutely no information and no thoughts at all on a given topic. Thus, the potential for empty-headed compliance with majority opinion is limited.

Ultimately, the informational forms of social influence that characterize impersonal influence processes may not be as pernicious to American politics as normative social influence. The logic underlying this conclusion is that while social influence of either variety has the capacity to corrupt individual decision making and constrain individual judgment, the nature of the *processes* underlying informational social influence make them infinitely preferable. Rather than adopting others' views as a means of obtaining social approval, people conforming on an informational basis are doing so for largely rational reasons. The rational bases of the strategic use of others' views are immediately apparent, but the mechanism underlying the bulk of reactions to information about others' opinions – a cognitive response mechanism – involves a process that is even more attractive from the perspective of promoting deliberation and accountability.

The cognitive response mechanism suggests that the influence flowing from perceptions of collective opinion is not automatic, nor is it mindless and empty-headed. Beyond serving as evidence of the absence of an undesirable process, these studies also imply that impersonal influence may serve the interests of accountability in some positive ways. Social interaction, it is generally agreed, occurs primarily among homophilous contacts; in other words, likes talk to likes. The same is true for face-to-face interactions of a political nature. Since people tend to choose likeminded political discussants, these interactions are limited in their ability to expose people to diverse viewpoints. Fortunately, individual selectivity is only half of the equation; the availability of various types of people in their immediate environments also conditions the nature of people's political interactions, thus exposing them to some interpersonal political disagreement (Huckfeldt and Sprague 1995). However, because of the trend toward more homogeneous communities, mass media are increasingly important sources of information about people different from oneself (Calhoun 1988). Although the restricted range of political views that receive mass media coverage has been rightly criticized, these views are, in the end, still likely to be less parochial than most people's interpersonal contacts (Mutz and Martin 1997). As a result of media portrayals of others' views, people are exposed to a broader range of political ideas; they become aware that alternative viewpoints are possible and legitimate and are prompted to reevaluate whether their own views are correct. This opportunity to question and to reevaluate one's position is far from pernicious; in fact, it appears to be what people often do when exposed to discrepant views on the part of friends and acquaintances as well (Huckfeldt and Sprague 1995).

This is not to suggest that interpersonal interactions are, in all important ways, identical to exposure to others' views via mass media. There is obviously greater potential for interaction and discussion in a face-to-face interaction. But there is also a higher probability that an interpersonal discussion partner will be like-minded and thus discourse will consist largely of mutual reinforcement. Sennett (1976: 255) touches on this same general idea in arguing that "The more the myth of empty impersonality, in popular forms, becomes the common sense of society, the more will that populace feel morally justified in destroying the essence of urbanity, which is that men can act together, without compulsion to be the same." In other words, the contemporary search for more community and greater intimacy even in the realm of political discussion is likely to lead to political interactions that do not cross lines of difference.

The importance of exposure to differing viewpoints should not be understated. As Asch (1952: 131–2) describes:

> The other is capable of arousing in me a doubt that would otherwise not occur to me. The clash of views generates events of far-reaching importance. I am induced to take up a particular standpoint, to view my own action as another views it or as the action of another person, and, conversely, to view another's action as my own. Now I have within me two standpoints, my own and that of the other; both are now part of my way of thinking. In this way the limitations of my individual thinking are transcended by including the thoughts of others. I am now open to more alternatives than my own unaided comprehension would make possible.

Although Asch is commenting on interpersonal interactions, his account echoes George Herbert Mead's (1934: 156) far earlier description of the internal conversation that people carry on with the "generalized other":

> And the more abstract that conversation is, the more abstract thinking happens to be, the further removed is the generalized other from any connection with particular individuals. It is especially in abstract thinking, that is to say, that the conversation involved is carried on by the individual with the generalized, rather than with any particular individuals. Thus it is, for example, that abstract concepts are concepts stated in terms of the attitudes of the entire social group or community; they are stated on the basis of the individual's consciousness of the attitudes of the generalized other toward them, as a result of his taking these attitudes of the generalized other and then responding to them.

Despite its potential for coercion, we seldom question the value of interpersonally obtained information about others' views. Since people tend to avoid political discussions that involve conflicts of opinion, there is a certain benevolence to the impersonality of mediated information. Without becoming involved in face-to-face conflict, people can at least engage in an internalized conversation that crosses lines of difference.

One novel program designed to reinvigorate democracy has attempted to overcome the traditional limitations of interpersonal communication by combining its benefits with a diverse and representative national sample. Fishkin's (1991) "deliberative opinion poll" is an interesting effort to synthesize the best of both worlds – face-to-face interaction among heterogeneous people – but it is unfortunately not practical as a permanent solution to the ongoing problem of bridging the personal and the political in a large-scale society.

The general nature of my conclusion may, at first, strike many as implausible. We are accustomed to thinking of face-to-face interactions as infinitely preferable to what media have to offer. Nonetheless, representations of abstract others' views appear to be capable of stimulating greater thought and reflection, just as Mead and Asch described. These representations of others' views need not always be the opinions of mass collectives, but when large numbers of people endorse a particular view, it is more likely to bring about increased reflection and less likely to be attributed to idiosyncratic individual characteristics that demand no additional consideration.

The exemplars for rational-critical discourse and public deliberation are all built on the assumption of small groups gathered in face-to-face settings. But interpersonal communication has not always been regarded as the ideal channel for political communication. In contrast to mass society theorists past and present, the founders of the United States were extremely wary of the power of interpersonal influence and normative social pressures. They counted on the sheer size of the country to limit the impact of interpersonal ties. The principle of "extended sphere" was intended as a safeguard; if elections were held over a large geographic area, they reasoned that it would be difficult for candidates to communicate interpersonally with large numbers of constituents: "In a small district a candidate could gain familiarity with the voters by contacting them directly during the campaign. . . . Even the number of immediate personal acquaintances in a small constituency can be a significant factor. But when the size of the district is increased, 'impersonal' forces play a larger role" (Ceaser 1979: 66–7). The founders saw impersonal forces as preferable to personal ones. Their idea of impersonal influence was the force of a man's reputation, slowly evolved over time. The choice of a large-scale, geographically disparate basis for political decision making was a purposeful one, and they made it fully realizing that it would limit candidates' abilities to personally contact voters and interact with them in face-to-face settings – the very type of communication that is now so wistfully revered. Having made these choices, we are now stuck with some inevitable consequences of large-scale society: These include a distant national government and a system of political accountability that depends heavily on mass media.

When the proponents and agents of the modern idea of the nation put forward the view that life on a bounded, continuous, and common territory, beyond the confines of kinship, caste, and religious belief, united the human beings living within that territory into a single collectivity . . . , they committed themselves, not often wittingly, to the mass society (Shils 1962: 51).

The twentieth century has witnessed a tremendous amount of concern centering on the proverbial "man in the grey flannel suit," the conformist George Babbitt of Sinclair Lewis's novel who, out of an intense concern for the approval of others, completely relinquishes his independence of judgment. But the kind of social influence that now threatens the political decisions of everyday citizens is not normative conformity, if indeed, it ever was. While mass society theory emphasized the extent of conformity to social norms that exists in face-to-face societies (which all societies are to some extent), impersonal influence emphasizes the extent of informational conformity that characterizes societies with well-developed national media systems and large-scale national institutions. Impersonal influence recognizes and takes into account constraints on the independence of individual judgment that emanate from the larger social environment as opposed to individuals' personal networks. The new danger stems not so much from a weakness in character or from an anxiously inferior personality type, as from an inability to keep up with unrealistic information demands. There is simply too big a gap between communal life and the size of the social totality to facilitate the ideal public sphere, at least when conceived strictly in interpersonal terms.

Like most scholars drawn to study the areas I have characterized as involving impersonal influence, my original interest in these topics was spawned by concern with the potential negative consequences these situations posed: If exposure to poll results altered public opinion or if media reports inaccurately characterized economic conditions, surely the interests of democracy were not being served. And if horse race coverage and early primary results altered people's attitudes toward candidates, surely the system should be reformed in order to eliminate the potential for impersonal influence.

Despite this initial orientation, the research process ultimately has led me to a quite different conclusion. Impersonal influence is not simply an unfortunate consequence of a free and sometimes irresponsible press; it is also necessary and important in the positive contributions it makes to a democratic system. Impersonal influence contributes to the potential for democratic decision making in two key ways: by exposing people to a broader variety of viewpoints than they are likely to encounter interpersonally and by exposing them to a greater diversity of experiences than their personal lives and interpersonal contacts make possible.

Attitudes toward impersonal influence usually miss the point by simply casting media as the culprit; if we could simply go back to the good old days, before the so-called collapse of the local community, before the rise of television and a well-developed national media, then all would be better. It is a common, but misguided, idea that we can fix what is wrong either by limiting people's exposure to others' views or by turning back the clock and promoting a more face-to-face, interpersonal politics. Even with all of its shortcomings, the press is more than a necessary evil in a large-scale society. No amount of interpersonal communication can overcome the problems of scale posed by contemporary society. In an effort to avoid potentially dangerous conformity, we have lost sight of how essential impersonal influence processes are to the functioning of a large-scale democracy, especially one where people tend to live and work among homogeneous others. Thus, the macro-level consequences of these micro-level processes are not things to be avoided or prevented or engineered out of the system.

What has worried many within the mass society tradition is that the consensus necessary to produce normative social influence at a local level has simply been superseded by the broader social environment represented in media coverage. Impersonal influence suggests a need to rethink the basic psychological processes underlying social influence in contemporary American politics. Information about others with differing views or experiences forces the citizen to reassess his or her position. In so doing, the person is led down a cognitive path that otherwise would have been left untraveled.

The process by which impersonal others influence individual attitudes is neither as rational as studies of strategic influence might suggest, nor as strictly irrational as most bandwagon research has asserted. Long before mass society theory took hold, Tocqueville (1835) helped to establish tyranny of the majority as a central concern in American political culture:

The nearer men are to a common level of uniformity, the less are they inclined to believe blindly in any man or in any class. But they are readier to trust the mass, and public opinion becomes more and more mistress of the world. . . . So in democracies public opinion has a strange power. . . . It uses no persuasion to forward its beliefs, but by some mighty pressure of the mind of all upon the intelligence of each it imposes its ideas and makes them penetrate men's very souls. The majority in the United States takes over the business of supplying the individual with a quantity of ready-made opinions and so relieves him of the necessity for forming his own. So there are many theories of philosophy, morality, and politics which everyone adopts unexamined on the faith of public opinion.

The good news is that there is little evidence of the kind of tyranny Tocqueville describes. Forcing a person to rethink a position is not the same as forcing a person to change a position; thus the outcome of exposure to others' views is far from predetermined, and the process is far from the thoughtless, empty-headed one typically associated with this type of influence. Just as social influence in face-to-face settings "does not transfer units of influence, nor is the receiver of the new information compelled to change his or her opinion, nor does social influence occur as some form of mysterious social telepathy" (Huckfeldt and Sprague 1995: 49), so too impersonal social influence occurs through less than deterministic, though well-documented, social-psychological mechanisms. More importantly, much of the deliberation that may once have occurred in face-to-face meetings of people with differing views may now occur in an individual's internalized conversation with generalized others. This situation is not ideal, but it may well be preferable to the alternative: that is, that people seldom are confronted with the need to reexamine their views at all.

Appendix: Methodology

Since cognitive responses play such a prominent role in understanding the influence of mass opinion cues in these experiments, it is important to have confidence in these particular measures. The thought-listing questions made the transition from the laboratory to a telephone survey fairly easily. But how confident can one be that the thought-listing measures truly tap the extent of respondents' internal dialogue that occurs before expressing a choice of candidate? Past research on the use of thought-listing questions has examined both reactivity and rationalization as potential problems with measures of this kind. In this study, respondent preferences purposely were assessed *before* eliciting cognitive responses in order to prevent possible reactivity (Cacioppo and Petty 1981). It is still possible, however, that the cognitive responses represent nothing more than post hoc rationalizations of candidate preference; for example, candidate support cues could influence feelings toward a candidate (for reasons unrelated to cognitive response), and these new attitudes could, in turn, influence cognitive responses as respondents attempt to construct a line of reasoning after the fact.

Path analytic studies of cognitive response measures generally have concluded that cognitive responses mediate affective responses rather than the other way around (Cacioppo and Petty 1981). Findings specific to these particular studies also suggest a mediating role for cognitive responses in influencing attitudes; in all of the studies, the interaction between cognitive elaboration and the direction of the experimental cues indicates that the cues were effective *only* when accompanied by thought rehearsal. If rationalization alone were at work, it should be equally likely across all experimental conditions, thus producing strictly main effects of consensus cues.

In evaluating this possibility it also is important to note that in analyses where cognitive response measures are directional (i.e., representing the balance of positive versus negative thoughts), their relationship with issue preferences are strong, just as rationalization would suggest. But the interactions between cognitive elaboration and consensus cues are assessed *after* controlling for the main effects of cognitive elaboration. In other words, people's tendency to rationalize is captured in the main effects. The significant interactions with consensus cues suggest that the elaboration measures tap important aspects of cognitive processing that go well beyond rationalization.

It is also possible that the mass support cues induced greater cognitive elaboration not so much because people were prompted to find a rationale for others' views, but because the cues provided respondents with more time to think during the survey interview. Fortunately, several factors make this highly unlikely. First, cues were delivered before the candidate or issue preference questions, and respondents had no way of gaining time for reflection by anticipating what the following question would be based on the cue alone. Moreover, the mention of a candidate's name or the issue controversy did not occur until shortly before preferences were elicited, so it is unlikely that those in cue conditions had more time to think about their candidates or issues. Because only thoughts relevant to the choice of candidate or issue position were coded, cognitive elaboration in the treatment groups could not be artificially inflated by cognitive elaboration related to thinking about polls in general, for example. Finally, since the candidate and issue preference questions directly followed the support cues, it seems more likely that people who received cues were *distracted* from thinking immediately before the candidate preference question rather than having additional time for thought rehearsal; it is very difficult to listen to a survey interviewer's statements and think simultaneously about a somewhat different question.

One final methodological concern involves the generalizability of these studies. The subject pool and setting make the collection of findings more generalizable than most found in experimental research, but the manipulations occurred directly before opinions were assessed. The immediacy of the cues may have created significant short-term changes that evaporated shortly thereafter. On the other hand, the relatively brief amount of time that respondents had to think about and reassess their views may well have undermined the full extent of their potential effectiveness. In the real world, people can reflect on more than the things that immediately come to mind; they can also further sample their information environments and seek out new explanations for trends in mass opinion (McPhee 1963; Huckfeldt and Sprague 1995).

These quick, one-shot cues also had to compete with an ongoing stream of information about candidates and issues. Nonetheless, information about candidate support had a significant impact on opinions toward candidates and issues. Furthermore, this process occurred partly by means of arguments that voters themselves provided.

References

Abramowitz, A. I. 1987. Candidate Choice Before the Convention. *Political Behavior* 9: 49–61.

——— 1989. Viability, Electability, and Candidate Choice in a Presidential Primary Election: A Test of Competing Models. *Journal of Politics* 51: 977–992.

Abramowitz, A. I., and W. J. Stone. 1984. *Nomination Politics: Party Activists and Presidential Choice.* New York: Praeger.

Abramson, J. B., F. C. Arterton, and G. R Orren. 1988. *The Electronic Commonwealth.* New York: Basic Books.

Abramson, P. R., J. H. Aldrich, P. Paolino, and D. W. Rohde. 1992. "Sophisticated" Voting in the 1988 Presidential Primaries. *American Political Science Review* 86:55–69.

——— 1995. Third-Party and Independent Candidates in American Politics: Wallace, Anderson, and Perot. *Political Science Quarterly* 110: 349–67.

Achen, C. H. 1989. Democracy, Media, and Presidential Primaries. In P. Squire (ed.), *The Iowa Caucuses and the Presidential Nominating Process.* Boulder, CO: Westview Press.

Adams, W. C. (ed.) 1983. *Television Coverage of the 1980 Presidential Campaign.* Norwood, NJ: Ablex.

Adoni, H., and A. A. Cohen. 1978. Television Economic News and the Social Construction of Economic Reality. *Journal of Communication.* 28:61–70.

Adoni, H., A. A. Cohen, and S. Mane. 1983. Social Reality and Television News: Perceptual Dimensions of Social Conflicts in Selected Life Areas. *Journal of Broadcasting.*

Adoni, H., and S. Mane. 1984. Media and the Social Construction of Reality: Toward an Integration of Theory and Research. *Communication Research* 11: 323–40.

Allard, W. 1941. A Test of Propaganda Values in Public Opinion Surveys. *Social Forces* 20: 206–213.

Alloy, L. B., and L. Y. Abramson. 1980. The Cognitive Component of Human Helplessness and Depression: A Critical Analysis. In J. Garber and M. E. P. Seligman (eds.), *Human Helplessness: Theory and Applications.* New York: Academic.

Almond, G. A., and S. Verba. 1963. *The Civic Culture.* Boston: Little, Brown.

Alonso, W., and P. Starr. 1987. *The Politics of Numbers.* New York: Russell Sage Foundation.

References

American Civic Forum. 1994. News release, November 30.

Anderson, B. 1983. *Imagined Communities: Reflections of the Origin and Spread of Nationalism*. London: New Left Books.

Andreassen, P. B. 1987. On the Social Psychology of the Stock Market: Aggregate Attributional Effects and the Regressiveness of Prediction. *Journal of Personality and Social Psychology* 53:490–6.

Ansolabehere, S., and S. Iyengar 1995. *Going Negative*. New York: The Free Press.

Antonovsky, A., and O. Anson. 1976. Factors Related to Preventative Health Behaviors. In J. W. Cullen et al. (eds.), *Cancer: The Behavioral Dimensions*. Washington, DC: National Cancer Institute.

Antunes, G. E., and P. A. Hurley. 1977. The Representation of Criminal Events in Houston's Two Daily Newspapers. *Journalism Quarterly* 54:756–60.

Arena, J. 1995. The Information Society Under Construction: Retail Credit and the Discourse of Technology. Paper Presented to the American Association for Public Opinion Research, May.

Arterton, F. C. 1984. *Media Politics*. Lexington, MA: D. C. Heath.

Asch, S. E. 1951. Effects of Group Pressure upon the Modification and Distortion of Judgments. In H. Guetzkow (ed.), *Groups, Leadership and Men*. Pittsburgh, PA: Carnegie Press.

    1952. *Social Psychology*. New Jersey: Prentice-Hall.

    1989. Personal communication to R. Friend, Y. Rafferty, and D. Bramel. Reported in R. Friend, Y. Rafferty, and D. Bramel. 1990. A Puzzling Misinterpretation of the Asch "Conformity" Study. *European Journal of Social Psychology* 20:29–44.

Asher, H., and M. Barr. 1994. Public Support for Congress and Its Members. In T. E. Mann and N. Ornstein (eds.), *Congress, the Press, and the Public*. Washington, DC: American Enterprise Institute and Brookings.

Atkin, C. K. 1969. The Impact of Political Poll Reports on Candidate and Issue Preferences. *Journalism Quarterly* 46: 515–21.

Attfield, C. L. F., D. Demery, and N. W. Duck. 1991. *Rational Expectations in Macroeconomics: An Introduction to Theory and Evidence*, 2d ed. Oxford: Blackwell Publisher.

Axsom, D., S. M. Yates, and S. Chaiken. 1987. Audience Response as a Heuristic Cue in Persuasion. *Journal of Personality and Social Psychology* 53: 30–40.

Bagdikian, B. H. 1987. *The Media Monopoly*, 2d ed. Boston: Beacon Press.

Ball-Rokeach, S. and M. L. DeFleur. 1976. A Dependency Model of Mass Media Effects. *Communication Research* 3:3–21.

Bandura, A., and F. L. Menlove. 1968. Factors Determining Vicarious Extinction of Avoidance Behavior Through Symbolic Modeling. *Journal of Personality and Social Psychology* 8:99–108.

Barber, B. 1984. *Strong Democracy: Participatory Politics for a New Age*. Berkeley and Los Angeles: University of California Press.

Barnhurst, K. G. 1991. The Great American Newspaper. *The American Scholar* 60: 106–12.

    1994. *Seeing the Newspaper*. New York: St. Martin's.

Barnhurst, K., and D. C. Mutz. 1997. American Journalism and the Decline in Event-Centered Reporting. *Journal of Communication*, 47: 27–53.

Barnhurst, K. G., and J. C. Nerone. 1991. Design Trends in U. S. Front Pages, 1885–1985. *Journalism Quarterly* 68:796–804.

References

Bartels, L. M. 1987. Candidate Choice and the Dynamics of the Presidential Nominating Process. *American Journal of Political Science* 31:1–30

1988. *Presidential Primaries and the Dynamics of Public Choice*. Princeton, NJ: Princeton University Press.

Bauer, R. A., ed. 1966. *Social Indicators*. Cambridge: MIT Press.

Baughman, J. L. 1987. *Henry Luce and the Rise of the American News Media*. Boston: Twayne Publishers.

1992. *The Republic of Mass Culture*. Baltimore: Johns Hopkins University Press.

Becker, L. B., M. E. McCombs, and J. M. McLeod. 1975. The Development of Political Cognitions. In S. H Chaffee (ed.), *Political Communication: Issues and Strategies for Research*. Beverly Hills: Sage.

Behr, R. L., and S. Iyengar. 1985. Television News, Real World Cues, and Changes in the Public Agenda. *Public Opinion Quarterly* 49:38–57.

Bell, D. 1960. *The End of Ideology: On the Exhaustion of Political Ideas in the Fifties*. New York: Free Press.

Bellah, R. N., R. Masden, W. M. Sullivan, A. Swidler, and S. M. Tipton. 1985. *Habits of the Heart: Individualism and Commitment in American Life*. Berkeley and Los Angeles: University of California Press.

Bender, T. 1978. *Community and Social Change in America*. New Brunswick, NJ: Rutgers University Press.

Beniger, J. R. 1976. Winning the Presidential Nomination: National Polls and State Primary Elections, 1936–1972. *Public Opinion Quarterly* 40:22–38.

1987. Personalization of Mass Media and Growth of the Pseudo-Community. *Communication Research* 14: 352–71.

Berelson, B. R., P. F. Lazarsfeld, and W. N. McPhee. 1954. *Voting: A Study of Opinion Formation in a Presidential Campaign*. Chicago, IL: The University of Chicago Press.

Berger, C. R. 1996. Hyperbole, Deceit, and Just Causes. *International Communication Association Newsletter* 24:2–3.

Biderman, A. D., L. A. Johnson, J. McIntyre, and A. W. Weir. 1967. Report on a Pilot Study in the District of Columbia on Victimization and Attitudes Toward Law Enforcement. Washington, DC: U. S. Government Printing Office.

Blau, P. M. 1974. Parameters of Social Structure. *American Sociological Review* 39:615–35.

Blood, D. J., and P. C. B. Phillips. 1995. Recession Headline News, Consumer Sentiment, the State of the Economy and Presidential Popularity: A Time Series Analysis 1989–1993. *International Journal of Public Opinion Research* 7:2–22.

Bloom, A. D. 1987. *The Closing of the American Mind*. New York: Simon & Schuster.

de Bock, H. 1976. Influence of In-State Election Poll Results on Candidate Preference in 1972. *Journalism Quarterly* 53:457–62.

Boorstin, D. J. 1974. *The Americans: The Democratic Experience*. New York: Vintage.

Borgida, E., and N. Brekke. 1981. The Base-Rate Fallacy in Attribution and Prediction. In J. H. Harvey, W. J. Ickes, and R. F. Kidd (eds.), *New Directions in Attribution Research*. Vol. 3. Hillsdale, NJ: Lawrence Erlbaum.

Brady, H. E., and R. Johnston. 1987. What's the Primary Message? Horse Race or Issue Journalism? In G. R. Orren and N. W. Polsby (eds.), *Media and Momentum*. Chatham, NJ: Chatham House.

Brams, S., and W. H. Riker. 1972. Models of Coalition Formation in Voting Bodies. In J. L. Bernd (ed.), *Mathematical Applications in Political Science VI*. Charlottesville: University of Virginia Press.

Brock, T. C. 1967. Communication Discrepancy and Intent to Persuade as Determinants of Counterargument Production. *Journal of Experimental Social Psychology* 3:269–309.

Brody, R. A. 1991. *Assessing the President: The Media, Elite Opinion, and Public Support*. Stanford: Stanford University Press.

Brody, R. A., and B. I. Page. 1975. The Impact of Events on Presidential Popularity: The Johnson and Nixon Administrations. In A. Wildavsky (ed.), *Perspectives on the Presidency*. Boston: Little, Brown.

Broh, C. A. 1983. Presidential Preference Polls and Network News. In W. C. Adams (ed.), *Television Coverage of the 1980 Presidential Election*. Norwood, NJ: Ablex.

1987. *A Horse of a Different Color: Television's Treatment of Jesse Jackson's 1984 Presidential Campaign*. Washington, DC: Joint Center for Political Studies.

Brosius, H., and A. Bathelt. 1994. The Utility of Exemplars in Persuasive Communication. *Communication Research* 21:48–78.

Brown, C. E. 1982. A False Consensus Bias in 1980 Presidential Preferences. *Journal of Social Psychology* 118:137–8.

Brown, C. W., R. B. Hedges, L. W. Powell. 1980. Modes of Elite Political Participation: Contributors to the 1972 Presidential Candidates. *American Journal of Political Science* 24:259–90.

Brown, R. D. 1989. *Knowledge Is Power: The Diffusion of Information in Early America, 1700–1865*. New York: Oxford University Press.

Burnstein, E., A. Vinokur, and Y. Trope. 1973. Interpersonal Comparison Versus Persuasive Argumentation: A More Direct Test of Alternative Explanations for Group-Induced Shifts in Individual Choice. *Journal of Experimental Social Psychology* 9:236–45.

Burnstein, E., and K. Sentis. 1981. Attitude Polarization in Groups. In R. E. Petty, T. M. Ostrom, and T. C. Brock (eds.), *Cognitive Responses in Persuasion*. Hillsdale, NJ: Lawrence Erlbaum.

Cacioppo, J. T., and R. E. Petty. 1981. Social Psychological Procedures for Cognitive Response Assessment: The Thought-Listing Technique. In T. V. Merluzzi, C. R. Glass, and M. Genest (eds.), *Cognitive Assessment*. New York: Guilford.

1982. The Need for Cognition. *Journal of Personality and Social Psychology* 42: 116–131.

Cacioppo, J. T., R. E. Petty, and C. F. Kao. 1984. The Efficient Assessment of Need for Cognition. *Journal of Personality Assessment* 48: 306–7.

Cain, B. E. 1978. Strategic Voting in Britain. *American Journal of Political Science* 22: 639–55.

Calhoun, C. 1988. Populist Politics, Communications Media and Large Scale Societal Integration. *Sociological Theory* 6:219–41.

1991. Indirect Relationships and Imagined Communities: Large-Scale Social Integration and the Transformation of Everyday Life. In P. Bourdieu and J. S. Coleman (eds.), *Social Theory for A Changing Society*. Boulder, CO: Westview.

References

Campbell, A., P. E. Converse, W. E. Miller, and D. E. Stokes. 1960. *The American Voter*. New York: Wiley.

— 1966. *Elections and the Political Order*. New York: Wiley.

Campbell, D. T. 1951. On the Possibility of Experimenting with the Bandwagon Effect. *International Journal of Opinion and Attitude Research* 5: 251–60.

Cantril, A. H. 1980. *Polling on the Issues*. Cabin John, MD: Seven Locks Press.

Cappella, J. N., and K. H. Jamieson. 1994. Broadcast Adwatch Effects: A Field Experiment. *Communication Research* 21:342–65.

Castells, M. 1983. *The City and the Grassroots*. Berkeley and Los Angeles: University of California Press.

Ceaser, J. W. 1979. *Presidential Selection: Theory and Development*. Princeton, NJ: Princeton University Press.

Ceci, S. J., and E. L. Kain. 1982. Jumping on the Bandwagon with the Underdog: The Impact of Attitude Polls on Polling Behavior. *Public Opinion Quarterly* 46:228–42.

Chaffee, S. and Mutz, D. C. 1988. Comparing Mediated and Interpersonal Communication Data. In R. P. Hawkins, J. M. Wiemann and S. Pingree (eds) *Advancing Communication Science: Merging Mass and Interpersonal Processes*. Newbury Park, CA: Sage.

Chaiken, S. 1987. The Heuristic Model of Persuasion. In P. Zanna, J. M. Olson, C. P. Herman (eds.), *Social Influence: The Ontario Symposium*. Vol. 5. Hillsdale, NJ: Lawrence Erlbaum.

Chaiken, S., and D. Maheswaran. 1994. Heuristic Processing Can Bias Systematic Processing: Effects of Source Credibility, Argument Ambiguity, and Task Importance on Attitude Judgment. *Journal of Personality and Social Psychology* 66: 460–73.

Cialdini, R. B., R. J. Borden, A. Thorne, M. R. Walker, S. Freeman, and L. R. Sloan. 1976. Basking in Reflected Glory: Three Football Field Studies. *Journal of Personality and Social Psychology* 34:366–75.

Cialdini, R. B., and R. E. Petty. 1981. Anticipatory Opinion Effects. In R. E Petty, T. M. Ostrom, and T. C. Brock (eds.), *Cognitive Responses in Persuasion*. Hillsdale, NJ: Lawrence Erlbaum.

Citrin, J. 1974. Comment: The Political Relevance of Trust in Government. *American Political Science Review* 68:973–88.

Clarke, P., and F. G. Kline. 1974. Media Effects Reconsidered: Some New Strategies for Communication Research. *Communication Research* 1:224–40.

Clarke, H. D., and M. C. Stewart. 1994. Prospections, Retrospections and Rationality: The "Bankers" Model of Presidental Approval Reconsidered. *American Journal of Political Science* 38:1104–23.

Cloutier, E., R. Nadeau, and J. Guay. 1989. Bandwagoning and Underdoging on North-American Free Trade: A Quasi-Experimental Panel Study of Opinion Movement. *International Journal of Public Opinion Research* 1: 206–20.

Cohen, B. C. 1963. *The Press and Foreign Policy*. Princeton, NJ: Princeton University Press.

Cohen, J., D. C. Mutz, V. Price, and A. Gunther. 1988. Perceived Impact of Defamation: An Experiment on Third-Person Effects. *Public Opinion Quarterly* 52:161–73.

Cohen, L. R., and C. J. Uhlaner. 1991. Participation, Closeness and Economic

References

Voting in the 1960 Presidential Election. Paper Presented at the Annual Meetings of the American Political Science Association, Washington, DC, August.

Cohen, Y. 1986. *Media Diplomacy*. London: Frank Cass.

Coleman, J. S. 1980. The Nature of Society and the Nature of Social Research. In R. F. Rich (ed.), *Knowledge: Creation, Diffusion, Utilization* 1, no. 3: 333–50.

Collins, R. L., S. E. Taylor, J. V. Wood, and S. C. Thompson. 1988. The Vividness Effect: Elusive or Illusory? *Journal of Experimental Social Psychology* 24: 1–18.

Conlan, T. J. 1993. Federal, State, or Local? Trends in the Public's Judgment. *The Public Perspective* (January/February) 5, no 1:3–5.

Conover, P. J. 1985. The Impact of Group Economic Interests on Political Evaluations. *American Politics Quarterly* 13: 139–166.

Conover, P. J., S. Feldman, and K. Knight. 1986. Judging Inflation and Unemployment: The Origins of Retrospective Evaluations. *Journal of Politics* 48: 565–88.

——— 1987. The Personal and Political Underpinnings of Economic Forecasts. *American Journal of Political Science* 31:559–83.

Converse, J. 1987. *Survey Research in the United States: Roots and Emergence, 1890–1960*. Berkeley and Los Angeles: University of California Press.

Converse, P. E. 1962. Information Flow and the Stability of Partisan Attitudes. *Public Opinion Quarterly* 26:578–99.

Cook, F. L., T. Tyler, E. G. Goetz, M. T. Gordon, D. Protess, D. R. Leff, and H. L. Molotch. 1983. Media and Agenda-Setting: Effects on the Public, Interest Group Leaders, Policy Makers, and Policy. *Public Opinion Quarterly* 47:16–35.

Crespi, I. 1980. Polls as Journalism. *Public Opinion Quarterly* 44:462–76.

Crossen, C. 1994. *Tainted Truth: The Manipulation of Fact in America*. New York: Simon & Schuster.

Crutchfield, R. S. 1995. Conformity and Character. *American Psychologist* 10: 191–98.

Czitrom, D. J. 1982. *Media and the American Mind: From Morse to McLuhan*. Chapel Hill: University of North Carolina Press.

Dalton, R. J., P. A. Beck, and R. Huckfeldt. 1996. The Media and Voters: Information Flows in the 1992 Presidential Election. Paper presented at the annual meeting of the American Political Science Association, San Francisco.

Davis, F. J. 1952. Crime News in Colorado Newspapers. *American Journal of Sociology* 57:325–30.

Davison, W. P. 1983. The Third-Person Effect in Communication. *Public Opinion Quarterly* 47:1–15.

Dayan, D., and E. Katz. 1992. *Media Events: The Live Broadcasting of History*. Cambridge: Harvard University Press.

Delia, J. G. 1987. Communication Research: A History. In C. R. Berger and S. H. Chaffee (eds.), *Handbook of Communication Science*. Newbury Park, CA: Sage.

Delli Carpini, M. X. 1984. Scooping the Voters?: The Consequences of the Networks' Early Call of the 1980 Presidential Race. *Journal of Politics* 46:866–85.

References

Deutsch, M., and H. B. Gerard. 1955. A Study of Normative and Informational Social Influences Upon Individual Judgment. *Journal of Abnormal Social Psychology* 51:629–36.

Dewey, J. 1927. *The Public and Its Problems.* New York: Henry Holt & Company.

Doob, A., and G. MacDonald. 1979. Television Viewing and Fear of Victimization: Is the Relationship Causal? *Journal of Personality and Social Psychology* 37:170–9.

Dreze, J., and A. Sen. 1989. *Hunger and Public Action.* New York: Oxford University Press.

Dubow, F., E. McCabe, and G. Kaplan, 1978. Reactions to Crime: A Critical Review of the Literature. Unpublished manuscript, Center for Urban Affairs and Policy Research, Northwestern University.

DuBow, F., and A. Podoloefsky 1982. Citizen Participation in Community Crime Prevention. *Human Organization* 41:307–14.

Dunn, D. 1969. *Public Officials and the Press.* Reading, MA: Addison-Wesley.

Dunwoody, S., and K. Neuwirth. 1991. Coming to Terms with the Impact of Communication on Scientific and Technological Risk Judgments. In L. Wilkins and P. Patterson (eds.), *Science as Symbol.* Boulder, CO: Greenwood.

Durkheim, E. 1898. Representations individuelles et representations collectives. *Reveu de Metaphysique et de Morale.* Vol. 6.

1893. *De la division du travail social: Etude sur l'organisation des societes superieures.* Paris: Alcan.

1903. *L'Annee sociologique.* Vol. 6. Paris: Alcan.

Economist. 1994. Measuring Crime. October 15:21–3.

Economist. 1974. Do Polls Affect Voting? October 12.

Editor and Publisher. 1949a. Newspaper Reading Affected Least by TV, Survey Shows. March 5, 50.

1949b. Effect of TV. May 21, 36.

Ellison v Brady. (54 FEP Cases 1347, 1991, USCA, 9th Circ.)

Elshtain, J. B. 1995. *Democracy on Trial.* New York: Basic.

Equal Employment Opportunity Commission. 1990. Policy on Current Issues of Sexual Harassment. Number N-915. 050. Washington, DC: U. S. Government Printing Office.

Erbring, L., E. N. Goldenberg, and A. H. Miller. 1980. Front Page News and Real World Cues: A New Look at Agenda Setting by the Media. *American Journal of Political Science* 24:16–47.

Eulau, H., and M. S. Lewis-Beck, eds. 1985. *Economic Conditions and Electoral Outcomes: The United States and Western Europe.* New York: Agathon Press.

Fabrigar, L. R., and J. A. Krosnick. 1995. Attitude Importance and the False Consensus Effect. *Personality and Social Psychology Bulletin* 21: 468–79.

Fan, D. P. 1988. *Predictions of Public Opinion from the Mass Media.* Westport, CT: Greenwood.

Feldman, S. 1982. Economic Self-Interest and Political Behavior. *American Journal of Political Science* 26: 446–466.

Feldman, S., and P. Conley. 1991. Explaining Explanations of Changing Economic Conditions. In H. Norpoth, M. S. Lewis-Beck, and J. Lafay (eds.), *Economics and Politics: The Calculus of Support.* Ann Arbor: University of Michigan Press.

References

Fenno, R. F., Jr. 1974. If, as Ralph Nader Says, Congress Is the Broken Branch, How Come We Love Our Congressmen So Much? In Norman Ornstein (ed.), *Congress in Change*. New York: Praeger.

Festinger, L. 1950. Informal Social Communication. *Psychological Review* 57: 271–82.

———. 1954. A Theory of Social Comparison Processes. *Human Relations* 7:117–40.

Fiedler, T. 1987. Dayton Hudson's Pyrrhic Victory. *Corporate Report Minnesota*. November 26, 59–64.

Fields, J. M., and H. Schuman. 1976. Public Beliefs About the Beliefs of the Public. *Public Opinion Quarterly* 40:427–48.

Fine, B. 1941. Propaganda Study Instills Skepticism in 1,000,000 Pupils. *New York Times*, February 21, p. A1.

Finn, S. 1987. Electoral Information Flow and Students' Information Processing: A Computerized Panel Study. In M. McLaughlin (ed.), *Communication Yearbook 10*. Newbury Park, CA: Sage.

Fiorina, M. P. 1981. *Retrospective Voting in American National Elections*. New Haven: Yale Univerity Press.

Fishkin, J. S. 1991. *Democracy and Deliberation: New Directions for Democratic Reform*. New Haven, CT: Yale University Press.

———. 1995. *The Voice of the People: Public Opinion and Democracy*. New Haven, CT: Yale University Press.

Fleitas, D. W. 1971. Bandwagon and Underdog Effects in Minimal Information Elections. *American Political Science Review* 65:434–38.

Freedman, J. L., and D. O. Sears. 1965. Selective Exposure. In L. Berkowitz (ed.), *Advances in Experimental Social Psychology*, Vol. 2. New York: Academic Press.

Frey, W. H. 1995. The New Geography of Population Shifts: Trends Toward Balkanization. In R. Farley (ed.), *State of the Union: America in the 1990s*. Vol. 2. New York: Russell Sage.

Friend, R., Y. Rafferty, and D. Bramel. 1990. A Puzzling Misinterpretation of the Asch Conformity Study. *European Journal of Social Psychology* 20:29–44.

Fromm, E. 1941. *Escape from Freedom*. New York: Farrar and Rinehart.

Fuchs, D. A. 1966. Election Day Radio-Television and Western Voting. *Public Opinion Quarterly* 30:226–37.

Funder, D. C. 1980. On Seeing Ourselves as Others See Us: Self-Other Agreement and Discrepancy in Personality Ratings. *Journal of Personality* 48: 473–93.

Funk, C. L., and P. A. Garcia. 1995. Direct and Indirect Sources of Public Perceptions About the Economy. Paper presented at the the Annual Meeting of the American Association of Public Opinion Research, Ft. Lauderdale, FL, May.

Furstenberg, F. F. 1971. Public Reaction to Crime in the Streets. *American Scholar* 40:601–610.

Gartner, M. 1976. Endogenous Bandwagon and Underdog Effects in a Rational Choice Model. *Public Choice* 25:83–9.

Gaskill, G. 1974. Polls and the Voters. *New Society* 4: 23–24.

Gavin, N. T., and D. Sanders. 1996. Economy, News and Public Opinion: Britain in the Mid-1990s. Paper presented to the Annual Meeting of the American Political Science Association, San Francisco, CA.

Geer, J. G. 1989. *Nominating Presidents*. New York: Greenwood.

References

1991. Critical Realignments and the Public Opinion Poll. *Journal of Politics* 53:434–53.

Gerbner, G., and L. Gross. 1976. Living with Television: The Violence Profile. *Journal of Communication* 26:173–201.

Gerbner, G., L. Gross, M. Jackson-Beeck, S. Jeffries-Fox, and N. Signorielli. 1977. Violence Profile No. 8. *Journal of Communication* 27:171–80.

Gibson, J. L. 1992. The Political Consequences of Intolerance: Cultural Conformity and Political Freedom. *American Political Science Review* 86:338–56.

Gitlin, T. 1990. Blips, Bites and Savvy Talk. *Dissent*. (Winter): 19–27.

Glaberson, W. 1996. Newspaper Owners Do the Shuffle. *New York Times*, Monday, February 19: C1.

Glynn, C. J., A. F. Hayes, and J. Shanahan. 1997. Perceived Support for One's Opinions and Willingness to Speak Out: A Meta-Analysis of Survey Studies on the "Spiral of Silence. " *Public Opinion Quarterly* 61: 452–463.

Glynn, C. J., and J. M. McLeod. 1982. Perceptions of Public Opinion, Communication Processes and Voting Decision. Paper Presented at the International Communication Association Convention, Boston, MA.

1984. Public Opinion Du Jour: An Examination of the Spiral of Silence. *Public Opinion Quarterly* 48:731–40.

1985. Implications of the Spiral of Silence Theory for Communication and Public Opinion Research. In K. Sanders, L. L. Kaid, and D. Nimmo (eds.), *Political Communication Yearbook*. Vol. 1. Carbondale: Southern Illinois University Press.

Goidel, R. K., and R. E. Langley. 1995. Media Coverage of the Economy and Aggregate Economic Evaluations: Uncovering Evidence of Indirect Media Effects. *Political Research Quarterly* 48:313–28.

Goodman, S., and G. H. Kramer. 1975. Comment on Arcelus and Meltzer: The Effect of Aggregate Economic Conditions on Congressional Elections. *American Political Science Review* 69:1,255–65.

Gordon, M. T., and L. Heath. 1981. The News Business, Crime, and Fear. In D. A. Lewis (ed.), *Reactions to Crime*. Beverly Hills: Sage Publications.

Gordon, M. T., S. Riger, R. K. Lebailly, and L. Heath. 1980. Crime, Women and the Quality of Urban Life. *Journal of Women in Culture and Society* 5:144–60.

Gorz, A. 1982. *Farewell to the Working Class*. Boston: South End.

Graber, D. A. 1980a. *Crime News and the Public*. New York: Praeger.

1980b. *Mass Media and American Politics*. 3rd ed. Washington, DC: Congressional Quarterly Press.

1984. *Processing the News*. New York: Longman.

Granberg, D., and E. Brent. 1980. Perceptions of Issue Positions of Presidential Candidates. *American Scientist* 68:617–25.

1983. When Prophecy Bends: The Preference-Expectation Link in U. S. Presidential Elections, 1952–1980. *Journal of Personality and Social Psychology* 45:477–91.

Gray, J., 1995. Does Democracy Have a Future? *New York Times*, January 22, Book Review page 1.

Green, D. P., and E. Gerken. 1989. Self-Interest and Opinion Toward Smoking. *Public Opinion Quarterly* 53:1–16.

Greenberg, B. S., and H. Kumata. 1968. National Sample Predictors of Mass Media Use. *Journalism Quarterly* 45:641–705.

References

Greenfield, J. 1982. *The Real Campaign*. New York: Summit Books.

Greenwald, A. G. 1968. Cognitive Learning, Cognitive Response to Persuasion, and Attitude Change. In A. G. Greenwald, T. C. Brock, and T. M. Ostrom (eds.), *Psychological Foundations of Attitudes*. New York: Academic.

Greve, F. 1995. Pollster May Have Misled GOP on Contract. *Seattle Times*, November 12.

Gunter, B. 1987. *Poor Reception: Misunderstanding and Forgetting Broadcast News*. Hillsdale, NJ: Erlbaum.

Gunther, A. C. 1991. What We Think Others Think: The Role of Cause and Consequence in the Third Person Effect. *Human Communication Research* 18:335–72.

——— 1995. Overrating the X-Rating: The Third Person Perception and Support for Censorship of Pornography. *Journal of Communication* 45:27–38.

——— 1998. Inference: Effects of Mass Media on Perceived Public Opinion. *Communication Research*, in press.

Gusfield, J. R. 1981. *The Culture of Public Problems: Drinking-Driving and the Symbolic Order*. Chicago: The University of Chicago Press.

Habermas, J. 1984. *The Theory of Communicative Action*. Vol. 1, *Reason and Rationalization of Society*. Boston: Beacon.

Hagan, J. 1980. The Legislation of Crime and Delinquency: A Review of Theory, Method, and Research. *Law and Society Review* 14:603–28.

Hagen, M. G. 1996. Press Treatment of Front-Runners. In W. Mayer (ed.), *In Pursuit of the White House: How We Choose Our Presidential Nominees*. Chatham, NJ: Chatham House.

Haller, H. B., and H. Norpoth. 1994. Let the Good Times Roll: The Economic Expectations of U. S. Voters. *American Journal of Political Science* 38:625–50.

——— 1995. News and Opinion: The Economy and the American Voter. Paper presented to the Midwest Political Science Association, Chicago, IL.

——— 1996. Reality Bites: The National Economy and the American Public. Paper presented to the American Political Science Association, San Francisco, CA.

Hallin, D. C. 1984. The Media, the War in Vietnam, and Political Support: A Critique of the Thesis of an Oppositional Media. *Journal of Politics* 46:2–24.

——— 1994. Soundbite News: Television Coverage of Elections, 1968–1988. *We Keep America on Top of the World*. New York: Routledge.

Hansen, R. D., and J. M. Donoghue. 1977. The Power of Consensus: Information Derived From One's Own and Others' Behavior. *Journal of Personality and Social Psychology*. 35:294–302.

Harkins, S. G., and R. E. Petty. 1981. Effects of Source Magnification of Cognitive Effort on Attitudes: An Information Processing View. *Journal of Personality and Social Psychology* 40:401–13.

Harrington, D. E. 1989. Economic News on Television: The Determinants of Coverage. *Public Opinion Quarterly* 53: 17–40.

Harrison, M. 1985. *TV News: Whose Bias?* London: Macmillan Press.

Hart, R. P. 1994. *Seducing America: How Television Charms the Modern Voter*. New York: Oxford University Press.

Hawkins, R. P., and S. Pingree. 1982. Television's Influence on Constructions of Social Reality. In D. Pearl, L. Bouthilet, and J. Lazar (eds.), *Television and Behavior: Ten Years of Scientific Progress and Implications for the Eighties*. Vol. 2. Washington, DC: Government Printing Office.

References

Hawkins, R. P., S. Pingree, and I. Adler. 1987. Searching for Cognitive Process in the Cultivation Effect. *Human Communication Research* 13:553–7.

Hayes, S. P. 1936. The Predictive Ability of Voters. *Journal of Social Psychology* 7:191–3.

Haynes, A. A., and P. H. Gurian. 1992. The Impact of Candidate Spending on Vote Outcomes in Presidential Prenomination Campaigns. Paper presented at the Annual Meeting of the Midwest Political Science Association, Chicago, IL, April.

Hayward, F. M. 1979. Perceptions of Well-Being in Ghana: 1970 and 1975. *African Studies Review*. 23, no. 1:109–25.

Heath, L. 1984. Impact of Newspaper Crime Reports on Fear of Crime: Multimethodological Investigation. *Journal of Personality and Social Psychology* 47:263–76.

Heath, L., and J. Petraitis. 1984. *Television Viewing and Fear of Crime: Where Is a Mean World?* Unpublished manuscript, Loyola University.

Heilbroner, R. 1991. Reflections: Economic Predictions. *The New Yorker*, July 8, 70–7.

Heinz, A. M. 1985. The Political Context for the Changing Content of Criminal Law. In E. S. Fairchild and V. J. Webb (eds.), *The Politics of Crime and Criminal Justice*. Newbury Pk., CA: Sage.

Henshel, R. L., and W. Johnston. 1987. The Emergence of Bandwagon Effects: A Theory. *Sociological Quarterly* 28: 493–511.

Herbst, S. 1993. *Numbered Voices: How Opinion Polling Has Shaped American Politics*. Chicago: University of Chicago Press.

Hess, S. 1988. *The Presidential Campaign*. 3d ed. Washington, DC: Brookings Institute.

Hetherington, M. J. 1996. The Media's Role in Forming Voters' National Economic Evaluations in 1992. *American Journal of Political Science* 40:372–95.

Hirsch, P. M. 1980. The "Scary World" of the Nonviewer and Other Anomalies: A Reanalysis of Gerbner et al.'s Findings on Cultivation Analysis. Pt. 1. *Communication Research* 7: 403–56.

Holbrook, T., and J. C. Garand. 1996. Homo Economicus? Economic Information and Economic Voting. *Political Research Quarterly* 49:351–75.

Holley, J. K. 1991. The Press and Political Polling. In P. J. Lavrakas and J. K. Holley (eds.), *Polling and Presidential Election Coverage*. Newbury Pk., CA: Sage.

Hovland, C. I., and H. A. Pritzker. 1957. Extent of Opinion Change as a Function of Amount of Change Advocated. *Journal of Abnormal and Social Psychology* 54:257–61.

Huckfeldt, R., P. A. Beck, R. J. Dalton, and J. Levine. 1995a. Political Environments, Cohesive Social Groups, and the Communication of Public Opinion. *American Journal of Political Science* 39:1,025–54.

Huckfeldt, R., P. A. Beck, R. J. Dalton, J. Levine, and W. Morgan. 1995b. Ambiguity, Distorted Messages, and Nested Environmental Effects on Political Communication. Unpublished manuscript, Indiana University.

Huckfeldt, R., and J. Sprague. 1995. *Citizens, Politics and Social Communication: Information and Influence in an Election Campaign*. New York: Cambridge University Press.

Hughes, M. 1980. The Fruits of Cultivation Analysis: A Reexamination of Some Effects of Television Watching. *Public Opinion Quarterly*. 44, no. 3:287–301.

References

Iyengar, S. 1990. Framing Responsibility for Political Issues: The Case of Poverty. *Political Behavior* 12:19–40.

———. 1991. *Is Anyone Responsible? How Television Frames Political Issues.* Chicago: University of Chicago Press.

Iyengar, S., and D. R. Kinder. 1987. *News That Matters: Television and American Public Opinion.* Chicago: University of Chicago Press.

Jackson, J. S., III, and W. Crotty. 1996. *The Politics of Presidential Selection.* New York: HarperCollins.

Jacobs, L. R., and R. Y. Shapiro. 1994. Questioning the Conventional Wisdom on Public Opinion Toward Health Reform. *PS: Political Science and Politics* 27:208–14.

Jacobellis v. State of Ohio 1964. (378 U.S. 184).

Jacobson, G. C., and S. Kernell. 1983. *Strategy and Choice in Congressional Elections.* New Haven, CT: Yale University Press.

Jencks, C. 1991. Is Violent Crime Increasing? *The American Prospect* 4:98–109.

Jenkins, P. 1995. Clergy Sexual Abuse: The Symbolic Politics of a Social Problem. In J. Best (ed.), *Images of Issues: Typifying Contemporary Social Problems.* New York: Aldine.

John, R. R. 1995. *Spreading the News: The American Postal System from Franklin to Morse.* Cambridge: Harvard University Press.

Johnston, D. 1983. The Cop Watch. *Columbia Journalism Review* 22:51–4.

Johnston, R. J., A. Blais, H. E. Brady, and J. Crete. 1992. *Letting the People Decide: Dynamics of a Canadian Election.* Stanford, CA: Stanford University Press.

Johnston, R. J., and Pattie, C. J. 1990. Tactical Voting in Great Britain in 1983 and 1987: An Alternative Approach. *British Journal of Political Science* 21: 95–107.

Jones, C. O. 1988. *The Reagan Legacy: Promise and Performance.* Chatham, NJ: Chatham House.

Jones, E. T. 1976. The Press as Metropolitan Monitor. *Public Opinion Quarterly* 40:239–44.

Judd, C. M., and J. T. Johnson. 1981. Attitudes, Polarization and Diagnosticity: Exploring the Effects of Affect. *Journal of Personality and Social Psychology* 41:26–36.

Kahneman, D., P. Slovic, and A. Tversky (eds.). 1982. *Judgment Under Uncertainty: Heuristics and Biases* New York: Cambridge University Press.

Kahneman, D., and A. Tversky. 1973. On the Psychology of Prediction. *Psychological Review* 80:237–51.

———. 1982. Evidential Impact of Base Rates. In D. Kahneman, P. Slovic, and A. Tversky (eds.), *Judgment Under Uncertainty: Heuristics and Biases.* New York: Cambridge University Press.

Kaplowitz, S. A., E. L. Fink, D. D'Alessio, and G. Blake Armstrong. 1983. Anonymity, Strength of Attitude, and the Influence of Public Opinion Polls. *Human Communication Research* 10:5–25.

Kassin, S. 1979a. Base Rates and Prediction: The Role of Sample Size. *Personality and Social Psychology Bulletin* 5: 210–213.

———. 1979b. Consensus Information, Prediction, and Causal Attribution: A Review of the Literature and Issues. *Journal of Personality and Social Psychology* 37:1,966–81.

Katz, E. 1981. Publicity and Pluralistic Ignorance: Notes on "The Spiral of Silence." In H. Baier, H. M. Kepplinger, and K. Reumann (eds.), *Public Opin-*

References

ion and Social Change: For Elisabeth Noelle-Neumann. Wiesbaden: Westdeutscher Verlag.

Katz, C., and M. Baldassare. 1992. Using the "L-Word" in Public: A Test of the Spiral of Silence in Conservative Orange County, California. *Public Opinion Quarterly* 56:232–5.

Katz, E., and P. F. Lazarsfeld. 1955. *Personal Influence.* Glencoe: Free Press.

Kayden, X. 1985. Effects of the Present System of Campaign Financing on Special Interest Groups. In G. Grassmuck (ed.), *Before Nomination: Our Primary Problems.* Washington, DC: American Enterprise Institute.

Keenan, K. 1986. Polls in Network Newscasts in the 1984 Presidential Race. *Journalism Quarterly* 63:616–18.

Kelley, R. 1979. *The Cultural Pattern in American Politics: The First Century.* New York: Knopf.

Kelman, H. C. 1961. Processes of Opinion Change. The *Public Opinion Quarterly* 25, no. 1:57–78.

Kennamer, J. D. 1990. Self-Serving Biases in Perceiving the Opinons of Others. *Communication Research* 17:393–404.

Kerbel, M. R. 1994. Covering the Coverage: The Self-Referential Nature of Television Reporting of the 1992 Presidential Campaign. Paper presented to the Midwest Political Science Association, Chicago, IL, April.

Kernell, S. 1986. *Going Public: New Strategies of Presidential Leadership.* Washington, DC: Congressional Quarterly Press.

Keynes, J. M. 1936. *The General Theory of Employment, Interest and Money.* New York: Harcourt, Brace, Jovanovich.

Kielbowicz, R. B. 1989. *News in the Mail: The Press, Post Office, and Public Information, 1700–1860s.* Westport, CT: Greenwood.

Kiewiet, D. R. 1983. *Macroeconomics and Micropolitics: The electoral effects of economic issues.* Chicago: University of Chicago Press.

Kiewiet, D. R., and D. Rivers. 1985. A Retrospective on Retrospective Voting. In H. Eulau and M. S. Lewis-Beck (eds.), *Economic Conditions and Electoral Outcomes: The United States and Western Europe.* New York: Agathon.

Kinder, D. R. 1981. Presidents, Prosperity, and Public Opinion. *Public Opinion Quarterly* 45:1–21.

1983. Diversity and Complexity in American Public Opinion. In A. W. Finifter (ed.) *Political Science: The State of the Discipline.* Washington, DC: American Political Science Association.

1989. Economics and Politics in the 1984 American Presidential Election. *American Journal of Political Science* 33:491–515.

Kinder, D. R., G. S. Adams, and P. W. Gronke. 1989. Economics and Politics in the 1984 American Presidential Election. *American Journal of Political Science* 33:491–515.

Kinder, D. R., and D. R. Kiewiet. 1979. Economic Discontent and Political Behavior: The Role of Personal Grievances and Collective Economic Judgments in Congressional Voting. *American Journal of Political Science* 23:495–527.

1981. Sociotropic Politics: The American Case. *British Journal of Political Science* 11:129–61.

Kinder, D. R., and W. Mebane. 1983. Politics and Economics in Everyday Life. In K. Monroe (ed.), *The Political Process and Economic Change.* New York: Agathon.

References

Kinder, D. R., S. J. Rosenstone, and J. M. Hansen. 1983. Group Economic Well-Being and Political Choice. Pilot Study Report to the 1984 NES Planning Committee and NES Board.

King, E., and M. Schudson. 1995. The Illusion of Ronald Reagan's Popularity. In M. Schudson, *The Power of News*. Cambridge: Harvard University Press.

Kish, L., and I. Hess. 1959. A Replacement Procedure for Reducing the Bias of Nonresponse. *The American Statistician* 13:17–19.

Klapper, J. T. 1964. *Bandwagon: A Review of the Literature*. Unpublished manuscript, Office of Social Research, Columbia Broadcasting System.

Kluegel, J. R., and E. Smith, 1978. Evaluations of Social Inequality: Attribution, Experience and Symbolic Perceptions. Paper presented at the Annual Meeting of the American Psychological Association.

Kornhauser, W. 1959. *The Politics of Mass Society*. Glencoe, IL: Free Press.

Kramer, G. H. 1983. The Ecological Fallacy Revisited: Aggregate- Versus Individual-Level Findings on Economics and Elections, and Sociotropic Voting. *American Political Science Review* 77:92–111.

Kraus, S. 1996. Winners of the First 1960 Televised Presidential Debate Between Kennedy and Nixon. *Journal of Communication* 46:78–96.

Krosnick, J. A. 1990. Americans' Perceptions of Presidential Candidates: A Test of the Projection Hypothesis. *Journal of Social Issues* 46:159–82.

Krueger, J., and R. W. Clement. 1994. The Truly False Consensus Effect: An Ineradicable and Egocentric Bias in Social Perception. *Journal of Personality and Social Psychology* 67:596–610.

Kundera, M. 1991. *Immortality*. New York: HarperPerennial.

Kunreuther, H. 1978. *Disaster Insurance Protection*. New York: John Wiley.

Ladd, E. C. 1988. Voters and the U. S. Economy: Boom and Gloom. *Christian Science Monitor*, April 12, p. 6.

1996. A Vast Empirical Record Refutes the Idea of Civic Decline. *The Public Perspective* 7, no. 4.

Lane, R. E. 1962. *Political Ideology: Why the American Common Man Believes What He Does*. New York: Free Press.

1965. The Need to Be Liked and the Anxious College Liberal. *The Annals of the American Academy of Political and Social Science* 361:80.

Lane, R. E., and D. O. Sears. 1964. *Public Opinion*. New York: Prentice-Hall.

Lang, G. E., and Lang. K. 1968. *Voting and Nonvoting: Implications of Broadcast Returns Before Polls Are Closed*. London: Blaisdell.

1981. Watergate: An Exploration of the Agenda Building Process. In G. C. Wilhoit and H. DeBock (eds.), *Mass Communication Review Yearbook 2*. Beverly Hills, CA: Sage.

La Ponce, J. A. 1966. An Experimental Method to Measure the Tendency to Equibalance in a Political System. *American Political Science Review* 60: 434–438.

Lasch, C. 1988. A Response to Joel Feinberg. *Tikkun* 3:43.

1995. *The Revolt of the Elites and the Betrayal of Democracy*. New York: Norton.

Lasorsa, D. L. 1989. Real and Perceived Effects of "Amerika. " *Journalism Quarterly* 66:373–8, 529.

1992. How Media Affect Policy-Makers: The Third-Person Effect. In Kennamer, J. D. (ed) *Public Opinion, The Press and Public Policy*. New York: Praeger.

References

Lasswell, H. D. 1927. *Propaganda Technique in the World War*. New York: Alfred Knopf.

Lau, R. R., and D. O. Sears. 1981. Cognitive Links Between Economic Grievances and Political Responses. *Political Behavior* 3:279–302.

Lau, R. R., D. O. Sears, and T. Jessor. 1990. Fact or Artifact Revisited: Survey Instrument Effects and Pocketbook Politics. *Political Behavior* 12:217–42.

Lau, R. R., T. A. Brown, and D. O. Sears. 1978. Self-Interest and Civilians' Attitudes Toward the Vietnam War. *Public Opinion Quarterly* 42:464–83.

Laumann, E. 1973. Bonds of Pluralism: The Forms and Substances of Urban Social Networks. New York: J. Wiley.

Lavrakas, P. J. 1982. Fear of Crime and Behavioral Restrictions in Urban and Suburban Areas. *Population and Environment* 5: 242–264.

Lavrakas, P. J., J. K. Holley, and P. V. Miller. 1991. Public Reactions to Polling News During the 1988 Presidential Election Campaign. In P. J. Lavrakas and J. K. Holley (eds.), *Polling and Presidential Election Coverage*. Newbury Park, CA: Sage.

Lazarsfeld, P. F., B. Berelson, and H. Gaudet. 1944. *The People's Choice*. New York: Duell, Sloan & Pearce.

Levine, A. 1980. *When Dreams and Heroes Died*. San Francisco: Jossey-Bass.

Linz, D., E. Donnerstein, K. C. Land, P. L. McCall, J. Scott, B. J. Shafer, L. J. Klein, and L. Lance. 1991. Estimating Community Standards: The Use of Social Science Evidence in an Obscenity Prosecution. *Public Opinion Quarterly* 55:80–112.

Lipset, S. M., and W. Schneider. 1983. *The Confidence Gap: Business, Labor, and Government in the Public Mind*. New York: Free Press.

Loring, C. 1986. *Book of Approved Jury Instructions, 7. 01 Intentional Torts*. St. Paul, MN: West Publishing Co.

Lyon, D., and P. Slovic. 1976. Dominance of Accuracy Information and Neglect of Base-Rates in Probability Estimation. *Acta Psychologica* 40:287–98.

MacKuen, M. B. 1981. Social Communication and the Mass Policy Agenda. In M. B. MacKuen and S. L. Coombs (eds.), *More Than News: Media Power in Public Affairs*. Beverly Hills, CA: Sage.

1990. Speaking of Politics: Individual Conversational Choice, Public Opinion, and the Prospects for Deliberative Democracy. In J. A. Ferejohn and J. H. Kuklinski (eds.), *Information and Democratic Politics*. Urbana: University of Illinois.

MacKuen, M. B., and S. L. Coombs. 1981. *More Than News: Media Power in Public Affairs*. Beverly Hills, CA: Sage.

MacKuen, M. B., R. S. Erikson, and J. A. Stimson. 1992. Peasants or Bankers? The American Electorate and the U. S. Economy. *American Political Science Review* 86:597–611.

Madow, W. G., H. H. Hyman, and R. J. Jessen. 1961. *Evaluation of Statistical Methods Used in Obtaining Broadcast Ratings*. House Report No. 193, 87th Congress, 1st Session. Washington, DC: U. S. Government Printing Office.

Magleby, D. B. 1984. Direct Legislation: Voting on Ballot Propositions in the United States. Baltimore: Johns Hopkins University Press.

Maier, M. H. 1995. *The Data Game: Controversies in Social Science Statistics*. 2d ed. Armonk, NY: M. E. Sharpe.

Major, B. 1982. Individual Differences in What Is Seen as Fair. Paper presented

References

at the Nags Head Conference on Psychological Aspects of Justice, Kill Devil Hills, NC.

Mannheim, K. 1940. *Man and Society in an Age of Reconstruction.* London: Routledge & Kegan Paul.

Marks, G., and N. Miller. 1987. Ten Years of Research on the False-Consensus Effect: An Empirical and Theoretical Review. *Psychological Bulletin* 102: 72–90.

Markus, G. B. 1988. The Impact of Personal and National Economic Conditions on the Presidential Vote: A Pooled Cross-Sectional Analysis. *American Journal of Political Science* 32:137–54.

Marsh, C. 1984a. Back on the Bandwagon: the Effect of Opinion Polls on Public Opinion. *British Journal of Political Science* 15:51–74.

———. 1984b. Do Polls Affect What People Think? In C. F. Turner and E. Martin (eds.), *Surveying Subjective Phenomenon.* Vol. 2. New York: Sage.

Marshall, T. R. 1983. The News Verdict and Public Opinion During the Primaries. In W. C. Adams (ed.), *Television Coverage of the 1980 Presidential Campaign.* Norwood, NJ: Ablex.

Mazur, A., and G. S. Hall. 1990. Effects of Social Influence and Measured Exposure Level on Response to Radon. *Sociological Inquiry* 60:274–84.

McAllister, I., and D. T. Studlar. 1991. Bandwagon, Underdog, or Projection? Opinion Polls and Electoral Choice in Britain, 1979–1987. *Journal of Politics* 53:720–41.

McCombs, M. E. 1972. Mass Media in the Marketplace. *Journalism Monographs* 24: 1–63.

McCombs, M. E., and D. L. Shaw. 1972. The Agenda-Setting Function of Mass Media. *Public Opinion Quarterly* 36:177–87.

McLeod, J., L. B. Becker, and J. Byrnes. 1974. Another Look at the Agenda-Setting Function of the Press. *Communication Research* 1: 131–166.

McPhee, W. N. 1963. Note on a Campaign Simulator. In W. N. McPhee, Formal Theories of Mass Behavior, pp. 169–83. New York: Free Press.

Mead, G. H. 1934. *Mind, Self and Society from the Standpoint of a Social Behaviorist.* Edited and with an introduction by C. W. Morris. Chicago: University of Chicago Press.

Meehl, P. E. 1977. The Selfish Voter Paradox and the Thrown-Away Vote Argument. *American Political Science Review* 71:11–30.

Meichenbaum, D., D. Henshaw, and N. Himel. 1980. Coping with Stress as a Problem-Solving Process. In H. W. Krohne and L. Laux (eds.), *Achievement Stress and Anxiety.* Washington, DC: Hemisphere.

Meier, N. C., and Saunders, H. W. 1949. *The Polls and Public Opinion.* New York: Henry Holt & Company.

Mendelsohn, H. 1966. Election Day Broadcasts and Terminal Voting Decisions. *Public Opinion Quarterly* 30:212–25.

Mendelsohn, H., G. J. O'Keefe, J. Lin, H. T. Spetnagle, C. Vengler, D. Wilson, M. O. Wirth, and K. Nash. 1981. Public Communications and the Prevention of Crime. Presented at the meeting of the Midwestern Association of Public Opinion Research, Chicago.

Meritor Savings Bank v Vinson. 1986. 106 S. Ct. 2399, 477 U. S. 57, 91 L. Ed. 2d 49.

Merten, K. 1985. Some Silence in the Spiral of Silence. In K. R. Sanders, L. L. Kaid, and D. Nimmo (eds.), *Political Communication Yearbook, 1984.* Carbondale: Southern Illinois University Press.

References

Merton, R. K. 1968. *Social Theory and Social Structure*. New York: Free Press.

Meyrowitz, J. 1985. *No Sense of Place: The Impact of Electronic Media on Social Behavior*. New York: Oxford University Press.

Milavsky, J. R., A. Swift, B. W. Roper, R. Salant, and F. Abrams. 1985. Early Calls on Election Results and Exit Polls: Pros, Cons, and Constitutional Considerations. *Public Opinion Quarterly* 49:1–15.

Miller v California. 1973. (413 U. S. at 24).

Miller, A. H. 1974. Political Issues and Trust in Government: 1964–1970. *American Political Science Review* 68:951–72.

Miller, W. E., and D. Stokes. 1963. Constituency Influence in Congress. *American Political Science Review* 57:45–56.

Mondak, J. J. 1995. *Nothing to Read: Newspapers and Elections in a Social Experiment*. Ann Arbor: University of Michigan Press.

Moscovici, S. 1976. *Social Influence and Social Change*. London: Academic Press.

1981. The Phenomenon of Social Representations. In J. P. Forgas (ed.), *Social Cognition: Perspectives on Everyday Understanding*. London: Academic Press.

1984. On Social Representations. In R. M. Farr and S. Moscovici (eds.), *Social Representations*. New York: Cambridge University Press.

1985. Social Influence and Conformity. In G. Lindzey and E. Aronson (eds.), *Handbook of Social Psychology*. Vol. 2. New York: Random House.

Mullen, B., J. L. Atkins, D. S. Champion, C. Edwards, D. Hardy, J. E. Story, and M. Vanderklok. 1985. The False Consensus Effect: A Meta-Analysis of 115 Hypothesis Tests. *Journal of Experimental Social Psychology* 21:262–83.

Mutz, D. C. 1992a. Impersonal Influence: Effects of Representations of Public Opinion on Political Attitudes. *Political Behavior* 14:89–122.

1992b. Mass Media and the Depoliticization of Personal Experience. *American Journal of Political Science* 36:483–508.

1994. The Political Effects of Perceptions of Mass Opinion. In M. X. Delli Carpini, L. Huddy, and R. Y. Shapiro (eds.), *Research in Micropolitics: New Directions in Political Psychology*, Vol. 4. Greenwich, CT: JAI Press.

1995a. Effects of Horse Race Coverage on Campaign Coffers: Strategic Contributions in the Presidential Primaries. *Journal of Politics*. 57:1015–1042.

1995b. Media, Momentum and Money: Horse Race Coverage in the 1988 Republican Primaries. In M. W. Traugott and P. Lavrakas (eds.), *Polling and Presidential Campaign Coverage*. New York: Guilford.

1997. Mechanisms of Momentum: Does Thinking Make It So? *Journal of Politics* 59:104–25.

Mutz, D. C., and S. Chan. 1995. The Impact of Self-interest on Public Opinion Toward Health Care Reform. Paper presented to the American Association for Public Opinion Research, Ft. Lauderdale, FL, May.

Mutz, D. C., and P. S. Martin. 1997. Communication Across Lines of Difference: Mass Media, Social Context and the Future of the Public Sphere. Paper presented to the American Political Science Association, Washington, DC, September.

Mutz, D. C., and J. J. Mondak. 1997. Dimensions of Sociotropic Behavior: Group-Based Judgments of Fairness and Well-Being. *American Journal of Political Science* 41:284–308.

References

Mutz, D. C., P. M. Sniderman, and R. A. Brody. 1996. Political Persuasion: The Birth of a Field of Study. In D. C. Mutz, P. M. Sniderman, and R. A. Brody (eds.), *Political Persuasion and Attitude Change*. Ann Arbor: University of Michigan Press.

Mutz, D. C., and Soss, J. 1997. Reading Public Opinion: The Influence of New Coverage on Perceptions of Public Sentiment. *Public Opinion Quarterly* 61: 431–451.

Nadeau, R., R. G. Niemi and T. Amato. 1994. Expectations and Preferences in British General Elections. *American Political Science Review* 88:371–83.

Nadeau, R., R. G. Niemi, and D. P. Fan. 1996. Elite Economic Forecasts, Economic News, Mass Economic Expectations, and Presidential Approval. Paper presented at the Annual Meeting of the Midwest Political Science Association, Chicago.

Navazio, R. 1977. An Experimental Approach to Bandwagon Research. *Public Opinion Quarterly* 41:217–25.

Nelson, M. Ed. 1993. *The Elections of 1992*. Washington, DC: Congressional Quarterly Press.

Nerone, J., and K. Barnhurst. 1995. Design Changes in U. S. Newspapers, 1920–1940. *Journal of Communication* 45 (1995): 9–43.

Neuman, W. R. 1991. What Ever Happened to Mass Society Theory? Paper presented at the Annual Meeting of the American Association for Public Opinion Research, Phoenix, AZ, May.

Neuman, W. R., M. R. Just, and A. N. Crigler. 1992. *Common Knowledge: News and the Construction of Political Meaning*. Chicago: University of Chicago Press.

New York World-Telegram. 1931. Fifty Million Frenchmen Can't Be Wrong. March 21.

Nisbett, R. E. and Borgida, E. 1975. Attribution and the Psychology of Prediction. *Journal of Personality and Social Psychology* 32: 932–943.

Nisbett, R., and L. Ross. 1980. *Human Inference: Strategies and Shortcomings of Social Judgment*. New York: Prentice-Hall.

Noelle-Neumann, E. 1974. The Spiral of Silence: A Theory of Public Opinion. *Journal of Communication* 34:43–51.

1977. Turbulences in the Climate of Opinion: Methodological Applications of the Spiral of Silence Theory. *Public Opinion Quarterly* 41:143–58.

1980. Mass Media and Social Change in Developed Societies. In G. C. Wilhoit and H. deBock (eds.), *Mass Communication Review Yearbook*. Beverly Hills, CA: Sage Publications.

1984. *Spiral of Silence*. Chicago: University of Chicago Press.

1985. The Spiral of Silence: A Response. In K. Sanders, L. L. Kaid, and D. Nimmo (eds.), *Political Communication Yearbook, 1984*. Carbondale: Southern Illinios University Press.

Nord, D. P. 1985. The Public Community: The Urbanization of Journalism in Chicago. *Journal of Urban History* 11:411–41.

Norrander, B. 1991. Patterns of Voting in the Super Tuesday Primaries: Momentum and Ideology. Paper presented to the Western Political Science Association, Seattle, WA, March.

Norris, P. 1996. Does Television Erode Social Capital? A Reply to Putnam. *PS: Political Science and Politics* 29:474–80.

O'Connor, R. D. 1972. Relative Efficacy of Modeling, Shaping, and the Com-

References

bined Procedures For Modification of Social Withdrawal. *Journal of Abnormal Psychology* 79:327–34.

Orren, G. R. 1985. The Nomination Process: Vicissitudes of Candidate Selection. In M. Nelson (ed.), *The Elections of 1984*. Washington, DC: Congressional Quarterly Press.

O'Sullivan, J. 1988. Britain: Under the Iron High Heel? *Commentary* 88 (September):52.

Overacker, L. 1932. *Money in Elections*. New York: Macmillan.

Page, B. I., R. Y. Shapiro, and G. R. Dempsey. 1987. What Moves Public Opinion? *American Political Science Review* 81:23–44.

Palmer, P. J. 1987. Community, Conflict, and Ways of Knowing. *Change* 19: 20–5.

Parisot, L. 1988. Attitudes About the Media: A Five Country Comparison. *Public Opinion* (January/February): 18–19, 60.

Park, R. E. 1938. Reflections on Communication and Culture. *The American Journal of Sociology* 44, no. 2:187–205.

Patterson, T. E. 1980. *The Mass Media Election*. New York: Praeger.

1993. *Out of Order*. New York: Knopf.

Patterson, T. E., and R. Davis. 1985. The Media Campaign: Struggle for the Agenda. In M. Nelson (ed.), *The Elections of 1984*. Washington, DC: Congressional Quarterly Press.

Patterson, T. E., and R. D. McClure. 1976. *The Unseeing Eye: The Myth of Television Power in National Elections*. New York: Putnam.

Pear, R. 1992. G. O. P. Faces Fight on Abortion Issue. *New York Times*, May 26.

Pepinsky, H. E., and P. Jesilow. 1984. *Myths That Cause Crime*. 2nd ed. Cabin John, MD: Seven Locks Press.

Perloff, R. M. 1993. Third-Person Effect Research 1983–1992: A Review and Synthesis. *International Journal of Public Opinion Research* 5:167–84.

Perloff, L. S., and B. K. Fetzer. 1986. Self–Other Judgments and Perceived Vulnerability to Victimization. *Journal of Personality and Social Psychology* 50:502–10.

Peters, C. 1980. *How Washington Really Works*. Reading, MA: Addison-Wesley.

Petty, R. E., and J. T. Cacioppo. 1979a. Effects of Forewarning of Persuasive Intent and Involvement on Cognitive Responses and Persuasion. *Personality and Social Psychology Bulletin* 5:173–76.

1979b. Issue Involvement Can Increase or Decrease Persuasion By Enhancing Message-Relevant Cognitive Responses. *Journal of Personality and Social Psychology* 37:1,915–26.

1981. *Attitudes and Persuasion: Classic and Contemporary Approaches*. Dubuque, IA: Wm. C. Brown.

1986. *Communication and Persuasion*. New York: Springer-Verlag.

Phillips, D. P. 1980. Airplane Accidents, Murder, and the Mass Media: Towards a Theory of Limitation and Suggestion. *Social Forces* 58:1,001–24.

Pilisuk, M., and C. Acredolo. 1988. Fear of Technological Hazards: One Concern or Many? *Social Behaviour* 3:17–24.

Pollis, N. P., and A. Cammaller. 1968. Social Conditions and Differential Resistance to Majority Pressure. *Journal of Psychology* 70:69–76.

Popkin, S. L. 1991. *The Reasoning Voter*. Chicago: University of Chicago Press.

319

References

Popkin, S. L., J. W. Gorman, C. Phillips, and J. A. Smith. 1976. Comment: What Have You Done for Me Lately? *American Political Science Review* 70:779–813.

Porter, T. M. 1986. *The Rise of Statistical Thinking 1820–1900.* Princeton, NJ: Princeton University Press.

——— 1994. Probability, Statistics and the Social Sciences. In I. Grattan-Guinness (ed.), *Companion Encyclopedia of the History and Philosophy of the Mathematical Sciences.* Vol. 2. London: Routledge.

Postman, N. 1985. *Amusing Ourselves to Death.* New York: Viking.

Potter, W. J. 1986. Perceived Reality and the Cultivation Hypothesis. *Journal of Broadcasting and Electronic Media* 2:159–74.

——— 1991. The Relationship Between First- and Second-Order Measures of Cultivation. *Human Communication Research* 18:92–113.

Price, V. 1989. Social Identification and Public Opinion: Effects of Communicating Group Conflict. *Public Opinion Quarterly* 53:197–224.

Price, V., and S. Allen. 1990. Opinion Spirals, Silent and Otherwise: Applying Small-Group Research to Public Opinion Phenomena. *Communication Research* 17:369–92.

Price, V., and J. Zaller. 1993. Who Gets the News? Alternative Measures of News Reception and Their Implications for Research. *Public Opinion Quarterly* 57:133–64.

Pritchard, D. 1986. Homicide and Bargained Justice: The Agenda-Setting Effect of Crime News on Prosecutors. *Public Opinion Quarterly* 50:143–59.

——— 1992. The News Media and Public Policy Agendas. In J. D. Kennamer (ed), *Public Opinion, The Press and Public Policy.* New York: Praeger.

Pritchard, D., and D. Berkowitz. 1989. The Influence of the Press and Public Opinion on Political Responses to Crime in Nine American Cities From 1950 to 1980. Paper presented to the Annual Meeting of the International Communication Association, San Francisco, CA.

Pritchard, D., J. P. Dilts, and D. Berkowitz. 1987. Prosecutors' Use of External Agendas in Prosecuting Pornography Cases. *Journalism Quarterly* 64:392–8.

Pritchard, D., and K. D. Hughes. 1997. Patterns of Deviance in Crime News. *Journal of Communication* 47:49–67.

Protess, D. L., F. L. Cook, J. C. Doppelt, J. E. Ettema, M. T. Gordon, D. R. Leff, and P. Miller. 1991. *The Journalism of Outrage: Investigative Reporting and Agenda Building in America.* New York: Guilford.

Public Perspective. 1992. Americans' Verdicts on the Economy in December Continued the Pattern Begun Earlier in the Fall. January/February, 21–5.

——— 1993. I'm Okay, But the Country Isn't, 5.

Putnam, R. D. 1995. Tuning In and Tuning Out: The Strange Disappearance of Social Capital in America. *PS: Political Science and Politics* 28:664–83.

Ratzan, S. C. 1989. The Real Agenda Setters: Pollsters in the 1988 Presidential Campaign. *American Behavioral Scientist* 32:451–63.

Reinarman, C. 1988. The Social Construction of an Alcohol Problem: The Case of Mothers Against Drunk Drivers and Social Control in the 1980s. *Theory and Society* 17:91–119.

Reno v. American Civil Liberties Union. 1997 (117 S. Ct. 2329).

Riesman, D., and N. Glazer. 1954. The Meaning of Public Opinion. In D. Riesman, *Individualism Reconsidered.* New York: Free Press.

References

Riesman, D., N. Glazer, and R. Denney. 1950. *The Lonely Crowd: A Study of the Changing American Character.* New Haven, CT: Yale University Press.

Robertson, L. S. 1975. The Great Seat-Belt Campaign Flop. *Journal of Communication* 26:41–5.

Robinson v Jacksonville Shipyards. 1988 (54 FEP Cases 83, 1988, DC Mfla).

Robinson, J. P., and M. R. Levy. 1996. News Media Use and the Informed Public: A 1990s Update. *Journal of Communication* 46:129–35.

Robinson, M. J., and M. Clancey. 1985. Teflon Politics. In M. J. Robinson and A. Ranney (eds.), *The Mass Media in Campaign '84.* Washington, DC: American Enterprise Institute.

Robinson, M. J., and M. A. Sheehan. 1983. *Over The Wire and on TV.* New York: Russell Sage.

Rohme, N. 1985. A Worldwide Overview of National Restrictions on the Conduct and Release of Public Opinion Polls. *European Research* (January): 30–7.

Rosenstone, S. J. 1983. *Forecasting Presidential Elections.* New Haven, CT: Yale University Press.

Rosenstone, S. J., J. M. Hansen, and D. R. Kinder. 1986. Measuring Change in Personal Economic Well-Being. *Public Opinion Quarterly* 50:176–92.

Roshco, B. 1975. *Newsmaking.* Chicago: University of Chicago Press.

Roshwalb, I., and L. Resnicoff. 1971. The Impact of Endorsements and Published Polls on the 1970 New York Senatorial Election. *Public Opinion Quarterly* 35:410–14.

Ross, L., G. Bierbrauer, and S. Hoffman. 1976. The Role of Attribution Processes in Conformity and Dissent: Revisiting the Asch Situation. *American Psychologist* 31:148–57.

Ross, L., D. Greene, and P. House. 1977. The False Consensus Effect: An Egocentric Bias in Social Perceptions and Attribution Processes. *Journal of Experimental Social Psychology* 13:279–301.

Sack, R. D. 1980. *Libel, Slander, and Related Problems.* New York: Practicing Law Institute.

Salmon, C. T., and F. G. Kline. 1985. The Spiral of Silence Ten Years Later: An Examination and Evaluation. In K. Sanders, L. L. Kaid, and D. Nimmo (eds.), *Political Communication Yearbook.* Vol. 1. Carbondale: Southern Illinois University Press.

Salmon, C. T., and Neuwirth, K. 1990. Perceptions of Opinion Climates and Willingness to Discuss the Issue of Abortion. *Journalism Quarterly* 67:567–77.

Samuelson, M., R. F. Carter, and L. Ruggels. 1963. Education, Available Time, and Use of Mass Media. *Journalism Quarterly* 40: 491–6, 617.

Scheingold, S. A. 1991. *The Politics of Crime: Criminal Process and Cultural Obsession.* Philadelphia: Temple University Press.

Schlozman, K. C. and S. Verba. 1979. *Injury to Insult.* Cambridge: Harvard University Press.

Schudson, M. 1978. *Discovering the News: A Social History of American Newspapers.* New York: Basic.

    1992. Was there Ever a Public Sphere? If So, When? In C. Calhoun (ed.), *Habermas and the Public Sphere.* Cambridge: MIT Press.

    1995. *The Power of News.* Cambridge: Harvard University Press.

References

Sears, D. O., and J. Citrin. 1982. *Tax Revolt: Something for Nothing in California*. Cambridge: Harvard University Press.

Sears, D. O., and C. L. Funk. 1990. Self-Interest in Americans' Political Opinions. In J. J. Mansbridge (ed.), *Beyond Self Interest*. Chicago: University of Chicago Press.

Sears, D. O., C. P. Hensler, and L. K. Speer. 1979. Whites' Opposition to Busing: Self-Interest or Symbolic Politics. *American Political Science Review*: 73: 369–384.

Sears, D. O., and R. R. Lau. 1983. Inducing Apparently Self-Interested Political Preferences. *American Journal of Political Science* 27:223–52.

Sears, D. O., R. R., Lau, T. R. Tyler, and H. M., Allen, Jr. 1980. Self-Interest Versus Symbolic Politics in Policy Attitudes and Presidential Voting. *American Political Science Review* 74: 670–684.

Sears, D. O., L. Steck, R. R. Lau, and M. T. Gahart. 1983. Attitudes of the Post-Vietnam Generation Toward the Draft and American Military Policy. Paper presented at the Annual Meeting of the International Society of Political Psychology, Oxford, England.

Seidman, D., and M. Couzens. 1974. Getting the Crime Rate Down: Political Pressure and Crime Reporting. *Law and Society Review* 8:457–93.

Sen, A. 1994. Freedom and Needs: An Argument for the Primacy of Political Rights. *New Republic*, January 10 and January 17.

Sennett, R. 1976. *The Fall of Public Man*. New York: Alfred A. Knopf.

Shafer, B. E. 1988. Scholarship on Presidential Selection in the United States. *American Political Science Review* 82:955–63.

Shapiro, R. Y., J. T. Young, K. D. Patterson, J. E. Blumenfeld, D. A. Cifu, S. M. Offenhartz, and T. E. Tsekerides. 1991. Media Influences on Support for Presidential Candidates in Primary Elections: Theory, Method, and Evidence. *International Journal of Public Opinion Research* 3:340–65.

Shaw, D. L. 1968. The Nature of Campaign News in the Wisconsin Press 1852–1916. *Journalism Quarterly* 45: 26–9.

Sherif, M. 1936. Group Influences upon the Formation of Norms and Attitudes. In M. Sherif (ed.), *The Psychology of Social Norms*. New York: Harper & Brothers.

Shils, E. A. 1962. The Theory of Mass Society. *Diogenes* 39:45–66.

Shrum, L. J. 1995. Assessing the Social Influence of Television: A Social Cognition Perspective on Cultivation Effects. *Communication Research* 22:402–29.

Shrum, L. J., R. S. Wyer, and T. C. O'Guinn. 1994. *Cognitive Processes Underlying the Effects of Television Consumption*. Unpublished manuscript, Rutgers University, New Brunswick, NJ.

Sigal, L. V. 1973. *Reporters and Officials: The Organization and Politics of Newsmaking*. Lexington, MA: D. C. Heath.

Sigelman, L. 1989. The 1988 Presidential Nomination: Whatever Happened to Momentum? *PS: Political Science and Politics* (March).

Sigelman, L., and D. Bullock. 1991. Candidates, Issues, Horse Races, and Hoopla: Presidential Campaign Coverage, 1888–1988. *American Politics Quarterly* 19:5–32.

Skalaban, A. 1988. Do the Polls Influence Elections? Some 1980 Evidence. *Political Behavior* 10:136–50.

Skogan, W. G., and M. G. Maxfield. 1981. *Coping with Crime: Victimization, Fear, and Reactions to Crime in Three American Cities*. Beverly Hills, CA: Sage.

References

Slovic, P. B. Fischhoff, and S. Lichtenstein. 1987. Behavioral Decision Theory Perspectives on Protective Behavior. In N. D. Weinstein (ed.), *Taking Care: Understanding and Encouraging Self-Protective Behavior*. New York: Cambridge University Press.

Smith, B. L. 1941. Propaganda Analysis and the Science of Democracy. *Public Opinion Quarterly* 5:250–9.

Smith, T. W. 1996. Trends in Misanthropy. Paper presented at the fifty-first Annual Conference of the American Association of Public Opinion Research, Salt Lake City, UT, May.

Sniderman, P. M. 1981. *A Question of Loyalty*. Berkeley and Los Angeles: University of California Press.

Sniderman, P. M., and R. A. Brody. 1977. Coping: The Ethic of Self-Reliance. *American Journal of Political Science* 21:501–21.

Sniderman, P. M., R. A. Brody, and P. E. Tetlock. 1991. *Reasoning and Choice: Explorations in Political Psychology*. New York: Cambridge University Press.

Soss, J., and D. Mutz. 1993. Social Influences on Political Attitudes: The Role of Imagined Communities. Paper presented at the Annual Meetings of the American Political Science Association, Washington, DC, September.

Sproule, J. M. 1989. Progressive Propaganda Critics and the Magic Bullet Myth. *Critical Studies in Mass Communication* 6:225–46.

Stigler, G. J. 1973. General Economic Conditions and the National Elections. *American Economic Review* 63:160–7.

Stockman, D. A. 1981. In J. Kaplan (ed.), *Barlett's Familar Quotations*. 16th ed. Boston: Little, Brown, 1992.

Stone, W. J., and A. I. Abramowitz. 1983. Winning May Not Be Everything, But It's More Than We Thought. *American Political Science Review* 77:945–56.

Stott, W. 1973. *Documentary Expression and Thirties America*. New York: Oxford University Press.

Straffin, P. D. 1977. The Bandwagon Curve. *American Journal of Political Science* 21:695–709.

Sudman, S. 1986. Do Exit Polls Influence Voting Behavior? *Public Opinion Quarterly* 50:331–9.

Tannenbaum, P. H. 1983. *Turned On TV/Turned Off Voters*. Beverly Hills, CA: Sage.

Taylor, D. G. 1982. Pluralistic Ignorance and the Spiral of Silence: A Formal Analysis. *Public Opinion Quarterly* 46:311–55.

Taylor H. F. 1973. Linear Models of Consistency: Some Extensions of Blaylock's Strategy. *American Journal of Sociology*. 78: 1192–1215.

Taylor, S. E. 1982. Adjusting to Threatening Events: A Theory of Cognitive Adaptation. Katz-Newcomb Lecture, University of Michigan, Ann Arbor.

Taylor, S. E., J. V. Wood, and R. R. Lichtman. 1983. It Could Be Worse: Selective Evaluation as a Response to Victimization. *Journal of Social Issues* 39:19–40.

Teixeira, R. A. 1987. *Why Americans Don't Vote: Turnout Decline in the United States, 1960–1984*. New York: Greenwood.

Thacker, R. A., and S. F. Gohmann. 1993. Male/Female Differences in Perceptions and Effects of Hostile Environment Sexual Harrassment: "Reasonable" Assumptions? *Public Personnel Management* 22:461–72.

Tiedge, J. T., A. Silberblatt, M. J. Havice, and R. Rosenfeld. 1991. Discrepancy

References

Between Perceived First-Person and Perceived Third-Person Mass Media Effects. *Journalism Quarterly* 68:141–54.

Tilly, C. 1983. Speaking Your Mind Without Elections, Surveys, or Social Movements. *Public Opinion Quarterly*. 47:461–78.

Tims, A. R., J. R. Freeman, and D. P. Fan. 1989. The Cultivation of Consumer Confidence: A Longitudinal Analysis of News Media Influence on Consumer Sentiment. *Advances in Consumer Research* 16:758–70.

Tipton, L. 1992. Reporting on the Public Mind. In J. D. Kennamer (ed.), *Public Opinion, the Press and Public Policy*. New York: Praeger.

Tocqueville, A. 1835. *Democracy in America*. R. D. Heffner (ed.), 1956. New York: Mentor.

Tönnies, F. 1940. *Fundamental Concepts of Sociology: Gemeinschaft and Gesellschaft*. Trans. C. P. Loomis. New York: American Book.

Traugott, M. W. 1992. The Impact of Media Polls on the Public. In T. E. Mann and G. R. Orren (eds.), *Media Polls in American Politics*. Washington, DC: Brookings Institute.

Traugott, M. W., and R. Rusch. 1989. Understanding the Proliferation of Media Polls in Presidential Campaign Coverage. Paper presented at the Annual Meeting of the Midwest Association for Public Opinion Research, Chicago, November.

Tufte, E. R. 1978. *Political Control of the Economy*. Princeton, NJ: Princeton University Press.

Tversky, A., and D. Kahneman. 1974. Evidential Impact of Base Rates. In D. Kahneman, P. Slovic, and A. Tversky (eds.), *Judgment Under Uncertainty: Heuristics and Biases*. New York: Cambridge University Press.

Tyler, T. R. 1978. Drawing Inferences from Experiences: The Effect of Crime Victimization Experiences Upon Crime-Related Attitudes and Behaviors. Unpublished dissertation, University of California, Los Angeles.

——— 1980. Impact of Directly and Indirectly Experienced Events: The Origin of Crime Related Judgments and Behaviors. *Journal of Personality and Social Psychology* 39:13–28.

——— 1984. Assessing the Risk of Crime Victimization: The Integration of Personal Victimization Experience and Socially Transmitted Information. *Journal of Social Issues* 40:27–38.

Tyler, T. R., and F. L. Cook. 1984. The Mass Media and Judgments of Risk: Distinguishing Impact on Personal and Societal Level Judgments. *Journal of Personality and Social Psychology* 47:693–708.

Tyler, T. R., and P. J. Lavrakas. 1983. Support for Gun Control: The Influence of Personal, Sociotropic, and Ideological Concerns. *Journal of Applied Social Psychology* 13:392–405.

——— 1985. Cognitions Leading to Personal and Political Behaviors: The Case of Crime. In S. Kraus and R. M. Perloff (eds.), *Mass Media and Political Thought*. Beverly Hills: Sage.

Tyler, T. R., and R. Weber. 1982. Support for the Death Penalty: Instrumental Response to Crime or Symbolic Attitude? *Law and Society Review* 17:21–45.

U. S. News and World Report. 1987. Television's Blinding Power. July 27, 18–21.

Udry, R. J., L. T. Clark, C. L. Chase, and M. Levy. 1972. Can Mass Media Advertising Increase Contraceptive Use? *Family Planning Perspectives* 4:37–44.

References

Vallone, R. P., L. Ross, and M. R. Lepper. 1985. The Hostile Media Phenomenon: Biased Perception and Perceptions of Media Bias in Coverage of the Beirut Massacre. *Journal of Personality and Social Psychology* 49: 577–85.

Van der Pligt, J., P. Ester, and van der Linden. 1983. Attitude Extremity, Consensus and Diagnosticity. *European Journal of Social Psychology* 13:437–9.

Van Raaij, W. F. 1990. Economic News, Expectations and Macro-Economic Behaviour. *Journal of Economic Psychology* 10: 473–93.

Walker, E. L., and R. W. Heyns. 1967. *An Anatomy for Conformity*. Pacific Grove, CA: Brooks-Cole.

Walker, J. 1950. Adman Tells Desire for Readership Facts. *Editor and Publisher*. May 27, p 44.

Wallen, R. 1943. Individuals' Estimates of Group Opinion. *Journal of Social Psychology* 17:269–74.

Warner, S. B., Jr. 1968. *The Private City: Philadelphia in Three Periods of Its Growth*. Philadelphia: University of Pennsylvania Press.

Warr, M. 1994. Public Perceptions and Reactions to Violent Offending and Victimization. In A. J. Reiss, Jr., and J. A. Roth (eds.), *Understanding and Preventing Violence*. Vol. 4, *Consequences and Control*. Washington, DC: National Academy Press.

Wattenberg, B. 1984. *The Good News Is the Bad News Is Wrong*. New York: Simon & Schuster.

Weatherford, M. S. 1982. Interpersonal Networks and Political Behavior. *American Journal of Political Science* 26:117–43.

———. 1983a. Economic Voting and the "Symbolic Politics" Argument: A Reinterpretation and Synthesis. *American Political Science Review* 77:158–74.

———. 1983. Evaluating Economic Policy: A Contextual Model of the Opinion Formation Process. *Journal of Politics* 45: 866–888.

Weaver, D. H., D. A. Graber, M. E. McCombs, and C. H. Eyal. 1981. *Media Agenda-Setting in a Presidential Election*. New York: Praeger.

Weaver, D. H., and M. E. McCombs. 1980. Journalism and Social Science: A New Relationship? *Public Opinion Quarterly* 44:477–94.

Webb, N., and R. Wybrow. 1986. The Spiral of Silence: A British Perspective. In I. Crewe and M. Harrop (eds.), *Political Communications: The British General Election Campaign of 1983*. New York: Cambridge University Press.

Weiner, B., I. Frieze, A. Kukla, L. Reed, S. Rest, and R. M. Rosenbaum. 1972. Perceiving the Causes of Success and Failure. In E. E. Jones (ed.), *Attribution: Perceiving the Causes of Behavior*. Morristown, NJ: General Learning Press.

Weinstein, N. D. 1980. Unrealistic Optimism About Future Life Events. *Journal of Personality and Social Psychology* 39:806–20.

———. 1987. Unrealistic Optimism about Susceptibility to Health Problems: Conclusions from a Community-wide Sample. *Journal of Behavioral Medicine* 10: 481.

———. 1989. Optimistic Biases About Personal Risks. *Science* 246:1232–33.

Weisman, S. R. 1984. Can the Magic Prevail? *New York Times Magazine*. April 29.

Wells, G. L., and J. H. Harvey. 1978. Naive Attributors' Attributions and Predictions: What Is Informative and When is an Effect an Effect? *Journal of Personality and Social Psychology* 36:483–90.

References

West, D. M. 1991. Polling Effects in Election Campaigns. *Political Behavior* 13: 151–63.

Wheeler, D., and H. Jordan. 1929. Change of Individual Opinion to Accord with Group Opinion. *Journal of Abnormal and Social Psychology* 24:203–6.

White, G. M. 1975. Contextual Determinants of Opinion Judgments: Field Experimental Probes of Judgmental Relativity Boundary Conditions. *Journal of Personality and Social Psychology* 32:1,047–54.

White, W. 1961. *Beyond Conformity*. New York: Free Press.

Wides, D. H. 1976. Self-Perceived Economic Change and Political Orientations. *American Politics Quarterly* 3:395–411.

Wills, G. 1983. *Lead Time: A Journalist's Education*. New York: Doubleday.

Wolfinger, R., and P. Linquiti. 1981. Network Election Day Predictions and Western Voters. *Public Opinion* 3:56–60.

Wood, G. S. 1991. *The Radicalism of the American Revolution*. New York: Vintage.

Wright, G. C., Jr. 1976. Linear Models for Evaluating Conditional Relationships. *American Journal of Political Science* 20:349–73.

Yankelovich, D. 1991. *Coming to Public Judgment: Making Democracy Work in a Complex World*. Syracuse, NY: Syracuse University Press.

Yinon, Y., A. Mayraz, and S. Fox. 1994. Age and the False-Consensus Effect. *The Journal of Social Psychology* 134:717–25.

Zajonc, R. B. 1968. Attitudinal Effects of Mere Exposure. *Journal of Personality and Social Psychology Monograph* 9:1–28.

Zaller, J. R. 1992. *The Nature and Origins of Mass Opinion*. New York: Cambridge University Press.

——— 1996. The Myth of Massive Media Impact Revived: New Support for a Discredited Idea. In D. C. Mutz, P. M. Sniderman, and R. A. Brody (eds.), *Political Persuasion and Attitude Change*. Ann Arbor: University of Michigan Press.

Zillmann, D., J. W. Perkins, and S. S. Sundar. 1991. *Impression-Formation Effects of Printed News Varying in Descriptive Precisions and Exemplification*. Unpublished manuscript, University of Alabama, Tuscaloosa.

Zucker, H. G. 1978. The Variable Nature of News Media Influence. In B. D. Rubin (ed.), *Communication Yearbook 2*. New Brunswick, NJ: Transaction.

Index

Index

Index

Index

Index

Index

Parisot, L., 55
Park, R. E., 18
partisanship, 34, 59, 62–3, 79–81, 115,
    142, 155, 168, 180, 221
Patterson, T. E., 34, 36–7, 58, 77, 109,
    116–17, 191, 194, 214
Pattie, C. J., 206
Pear, R., 209
Pemantle, W., xx
Pepinsky, H. E., 116
Perkins, J. W., 120
Perloff, L. S., 66, 186
Perloff, R. M., 53, 129
personal influence, 4, 17, 203–4, 216,
    264, 267–8, 270–1, 277, 279, 282,
    284, 290–4
  across lines of difference, 292
  advantage of over media, xvi
  and conformity, 270
  and gemeinschaft, 11
  and large scale society, 294
  and selective exposure, 68
  contrasted with impersonal influence,
    17
  interpersonal communication of
    economic information, 67–8, 78, 93
  measurement of, 93
  Personal Influence (book), xvi–xvii, 4–5
  power of, xvi, 272
  trustworthiness of, xvi, 5, 17, 27, 29
  undesirability for political
    communication, 292
pessimism
  from partisan rationalization, 166
  in collective-level judgments, 121, 123,
    126, 154
  in economic judgments, 111
  in personal-level judgments, 129–30
Peters, C., 52
Petraitis, J., 74
Petty, R. E., 204, 212–13, 215, 221, 243,
    263, 297
Phillips, P. C. B., 99, 113, 117
Pilisuk, M., 74
Pingree, S. , 75
pluralistic ignorance, 285–6
pocketbook, as basis for political
    evaluation, 4, 100–3, 109
polling, 3, 57, 64, 180
  as legal evidence, 192
  as negative influence, xv, 259, 264, 293
  history of, 36–7
  impact of exit polls, 15, 181, 187–8
  impact of preelection polls, 181–3, 187,
    189–90, 206
  media coverage of, 37, 180
  skepticism of, 213

Pollis, N. P., 202
Popkin, S. L., 54, 57, 99, 207, 262
Porter, T. M., 35
postal system, 31
Postman, N., 172
Potter, W. J., 75–6, 79, 267
Powell, L. W., 250
Price, V., 10, 19, 31, 143, 156, 186, 189,
    250
priming, 70, 72, 149
Pritchard, D., 52–3, 287
Pritzker, H. A., 204
Protess, D. L., 52, 81
Public Perspective, 12
Putnam, R. D., 267–8

Ratzan, S. C., 37
Reagan, Ronald, 8, 124, 133, 141, 153,
    165, 184, 187, 281
Reinarman, C., 149
Reno, Janet, 194
Resnicoff, L., 188
Riesman, D., 198–9, 279
Riker, W. H., 206
risk perception, 66–7, 70, 73–5, 118–19,
    128–30
Rivers, D., 13, 100
Robertson, L. S., 73, 257–8
Robinson, M. J., 36, 117
Rohde, D. W., 194, 259
Rohme, N., 180
Roper, B. W., 180
Rosenstone, S. J., 67, 100
Roshco, B., 34
Roshwalb, I., 188
Ross, L., 63, 148, 186, 201–2, 210, 281
Ruggels, L., 173
Rusch, R., 37

Sack, R. D., 192
Salant, R., 180
Salmon, C. T., 183, 186
Samuelson, M., 173
Sanders, K., 113, 129
Saunders, H. W., 187
Scheingold, S. A., 6
Schlozman, K. C., 99, 101, 153, 155
Schneider, W., 280
Schudson, M., 8, 14, 30, 32, 34, 61, 165,
    174, 267–8, 277, 279
Schuman, H., 64
Sears, D. O., 13, 100, 102–3, 132, 135,
    149, 174, 198, 202
Seidman, D., 116
self–interest, 100, 139
Sen, A., 286–7
Sennett, R., 291

Index

DATE DUE

Demco, Inc. 38-293